MW00579870

M

Generals in the Palacio

Generals in the Palacio

The Military in Modern Mexico

RODERIC AI CAMP

New York   Oxford
OXFORD UNIVERSITY PRESS
1992

Oxford University Press

Oxford   New York   Toronto
Delhi Bombay Calcutta Madras Karachi
Kuala Lumpur Singapore Hong Kong Tokyo
Nairobi Dar es Salaam Cape Town
Melbourne   Auckland

and associated companies in
Berlin   Ibadan

Copyright © 1992 by Oxford University Press, Inc.

Published by Oxford University Press, Inc.,
200 Madison Avenue, New York, New York 10016

Library of Congress Cataloging-in-Publication Data
Camp, Roderic Ai.
Generals in the Palacio : the military
in modern Mexico / Roderic Ai Camp.
p. cm. Includes bibliographical references (p.   ).
ISBN 0-19-507300-2
1. Mexico—Armed Forces.   2. Civil-military relations—Mexico.
3. Mexico—Armed Forces—Officers. I. Title.
UA603.C35   1992   306.2'7'0972—dc20   91-28333

1 3 5 7 9 8 6 4 2
Printed in the United States of America
on acid-free paper

To Roger

Acknowledgments

The military in Mexico has intrigued me for many decades, beginning with my contact as a student with General Carlos Berzunza, who first exposed me to Mexico's military culture and nationalism. A decade later, in the mid-1970s, an anecdote from a marine colonel traveling to the Soviet Union again intrigued me with the cross-national implications of military culture. This project is unlike most previous projects; here I can offer few public acknowledgments. I am deeply indebted for their insights to those Mexicans who helped me. U.S. officer observations have also provided invaluable perspectives. I appreciate, too, the trenchant comments and suggestions of Jake Jacobson, Daniel C. Levy, David Ronfeldt, Peter H. Smith, Steven Wager, and Edward J. Williams on various chapters of this book. And I am grateful as well for the help of the Bancroft Library, the Tulane Library, and the Library of Congress in obtaining difficult sources. Part of this research was supported by a Woodrow Wilson Center for International Scholars fellowship.

New Orleans   R.A.C.
September, 1991

Contents

Tables

Exhibits

Generals in the Palacio

1

The Officer Corps:
Theory and Context

Of all the leadership groups and all the institutions exercising political power in Mexico in the past half century, none have been examined as sparsely as the officer corps and the military. The lack of attention paid to the Mexican military is remarkable, considering the theoretical implications it offers as a case study of a Third World society that has successfully limited the military's political involvement, establishing a longer reign of civilian supremacy than any country in Latin America. In the context of the broader, comparative literature on military withdrawal, this neglect is unfortunate, given the appraisal that generally "little has been published on a systematic, comparative basis about the process, or processes, of military disengagement from politics."[1]

Researching the Military in Mexico

Methodologically, the working hypotheses for this study were extracted from the general literature on civil-military relations, and from Third World and Latin America case studies. My preliminary work on the Mexican military in the 1970s and 1980s also generated Mexico-specific hypotheses, which also have been offered previously. Although the historical literature has been useful in producing valuable interpretations, several other sources or approaches have contributed to the overall thrust of this analysis. It is interesting that the literature on Latin America, with the exception of a few classic introductions to civil-military relations, excludes sociological studies of the United States armed forces, probably the best examined in the world. This is an unfortunate oversight, for although societally the United States has very little in common with Mexico or Latin America, remarkable similarities occur between any two military cultures, even in the context of civil-military relations. Empirical examinations of officer values and origins, in particular, are the most complete in the United States literature, and therefore offer revealing comparative perspectives for this work.

Because the Mexican military has erected obstacles to outside examination, the scholar has to resort to different methodological approaches to acquire fresh data. This study focuses on the officer corps, specifically on the rank of

3

general. Generals, especially those in top staff and command positions, exercise decision-making authority over the armed forces. Additionally, as Frank McCann suggests in his own examination of the Brazilian general, an important justification for looking at Mexican generals is that

> officer generations are overlapping time lines that link the army to the past and
> project it into the future. Because generals are on active duty the longest, they
> are the ones who give the institution direction and a sense of historical conti-
> nuity. They set policy in the context of their accumulated experiences and
> intellectual baggage.[2]

Because a shifting pool of generals and national civilian politicians has determined the military's role, as well as the broader context of Mexican civil-military relations, these two groups of leaders are compared and analyzed in some detail. The basis for some of these comparisons is collective biography. Collective biography provides only one element among this book's resources, revealing many interesting characteristics and trends about the Mexican military, making it more clearly understood as an institution and in its relationship to civilian elites. Collective biography also provides some empirical evidence in support of, and for disproving, certain assertions about the Mexican case. Typically, prior analyses of the armed forces have focused on the army alone, but data on top naval and air force officers have made possible some interservice comparisons.

To facilitate increased attention on societal variables in civil-military relations, this book makes use of, for the first time, general surveys of Mexican attitudes toward military intervention in politics. The results of national polls cross-tabulated with numerous variables, both background and attitudinal, offer many significant insights into Mexican society.

Finally, documental evidence on internal military policies, especially in regard to promotion policies, has been located and examined in defense publications, Senate records, and the official army–air force magazine. Individual officer records, studied over time, shed considerable light on presidential policies toward promotion, portending changes in civil-military relations. Similarly, frank political elite attitudes toward the broader relationship have been expressed publicly only since 1946, in the Senate *Memorias*, as a consequence of several controversial promotion recommendations. These discussions reveal not only legislative attitudes toward the executive branch but the political elite's views of the military.

The Focus

The primary focus of this analysis is not on civil-military relations specifically but on shedding some light on the composition, experiences, background, and behavior of the officer corps, particularly its general cohort, in Mexico. The secondary purpose of this analysis is to provide, in some cases for the first time, some fresh empirical data for testing claims and assumptions of others concerning civil-military relations and the role that the officer corps plays. Simultaneously, it is hoped that a more thorough understanding of the officer corps and, more significant, of consequences stemming from officer formation will provide new, if not complete, insights about the Mexican success story of military nonintervention in politics.

If Mexico has been often cited in the literature as a key example of military subordination to civilian rule, why has the Mexican case been so neglected, especially given the abundance of social science analysis of its rather unique political model? Two decades ago, David Ronfeldt could write that the

> contemporary Mexican military may be the most difficult such institution to research in Latin America. Certainly it is the most difficult national institution to research in Mexico. The few studies that have been completed, the statistical data that can be compiled, and the press and biographic material that are available enable the historical analyst to gain only a cursory knowledge of post-1940 processes and seminal events.[3]

One of the most important characteristics about the Mexican military that must be understood from an academic point of view and that is suggestive of an aspect of Mexico's unique civil-military formula is the military's intense desire to remain unexamined, indeed enigmatic. More than any single Latin American military, the Mexican military openly discourages analysts, domestic and foreign, from exploring its institutional behavior in the post-1946 era. Mexican scholars have paid it little attention because of the military's openly antagonistic attitude. Restricted access to historical archives has discouraged, even intimidated, scholars. The few who have tried to penetrate this barrier quickly sensed their isolation. Major domestic political analyses of the Mexican system tend to omit the military altogether. For example, the principal survey on Mexican politics, until that of Miguel Basáñez in the 1980s, is Pablo González Casanova's, the only general Mexican political analysis to have been translated into English. Yet his interpretation, which spends two pages on the military, offers no comments or insights whatsoever into the officer corps as a political actor.[4] U.S. political scientists, protected by geographic distance, have had greater opportunities to produce such an analysis but no better access to relevant materials. In fact, of the political research I personally have carried out in Mexico, this is the only project I have been warned against pursuing.

Military historians have given us much more substance to work with than have political scientists in the Mexican context. Their efforts, although not examining the post-1946 period, provide a basic foundation for carrying out this research agenda. As Edwin Lieuwen, the pioneer in this respect, argued, Mexico's

> experience has shown that, once a major social revolution has taken place, determined executives can launch a comprehensive program to mold the armed forces into a disciplined, professional army that would shun political activities.

The task involved a liberal use of Machiavellian techniques to break the power
of the citizen-officers of the revolution and a well-planned educational program
designed to instill in the new young officers the concept of the "good soldier."[5]

Mexico, therefore, provides a unique example of a military leadership's
transforming itself into a civilian political elite, simultaneously transferring the
basis of power from the army to a civil state. Importantly, the transfer of power
occurred after a revolution, and regardless of how one classifies that particular
revolution, similar upheavals have not occurred elsewhere, providing a unique
historical context from which the Mexican pattern emerges.[6]

Given the uniqueness of the Mexican case, it is fair to argue that the
abundant literature on civil-military relations generally, and Latin American
specifically, has very little to offer. In some respects, that assertion is true,
especially because theorists largely have concerned themselves with authoritarian regimes wherein military-civil power is shared, or with more politically
competitive societies wherein the military cyclically, if temporarily, involves
itself directly in politics, neither of which adequately reflects the Mexican
model. Nevertheless, keeping in mind the many singular features of the Mexican case, which itself suggests several working hypotheses, this literature
provides important theoretical arguments about military withdrawal from and
military subordination to civil authority applicable to Mexico.

Some Working Hypotheses: The Theoretical Context

I concur with recent analysts that no single explanatory theory adequately
interprets the removal of the Mexican military, or any other Third World
military, from direct political participation. I will show that the Mexican
military has remained outside the political arena for reasons that can be found
in other cultures. I will also argue, however, that Mexico provides some
original conditions, uncommon to most other Third World cultures, that
have contributed heavily to the military's subordination to civilian authority.
Among these is Mexico's extreme emphasis on subordination in officer-forma-
tion courses; the military's autonomy from civilian intervention in its *internal*
affairs, notably promotion; and the linkage provided by the military-political
officer in Mexico's recent past.

Nine working hypotheses from which to analyze the Mexican case, some of
which will be examined more thoroughly than others, are offered in the
following pages. The factors most theorists have considered fall into two broad
categories: the imperatives of the military, which stem from its internalized
professionalism, and the imperatives of society, the values or ideology society
conveys about the military's role. The intermixture of these two broad categories is what is likely to determine military intervention.[7]

The most unusual circumstance from the Mexican perspective, a critical
variable in making civilian supremacy possible, is that contemporary Mexico is
the product of a major social upheaval from 1910 through 1920. As I have

argued elsewhere, it might be suggested that the military did not withdraw from politics in the 1930s and 1940s; rather, the postrevolutionary military had never, in the true sense of the word, intervened in political affairs in the first place. In the context of civil-military relations, the Revolution did not produce military intervention as traditionally understood but, rather, the established military, as one of several quasi-state institutions with its own political interests and its political-military representative, Porfirio Díaz, were defeated by a civilian-grown variety of armed force.

When violence became the only means through which this post-1910 generation of civilian leaders could express disagreement with established political authorities, then the means of force developed into essential tools of political life. The institutionalized military, the Federal Army, only briefly sustained its supremacy in the exercise of force, once it came under the direction of a new civilian political leadership in 1912 (against a rebellion by a former revolutionary), and at the head of a military-civilian coup against elected civilian authorities in 1913-1914. Those most politically skilled, however, were not the Federal Army officer corps, nor its civilian political representatives, but leaders extracted from opposing guerrilla forces. After 1920 forces loyal to victorious revolutionaries, that is, having guerrilla roots, put down rebellions by dissident peers vying for political control.[8]

The point of my argument is that an army of *civilian* origin defeated an established army, and that both Mexico's political and military leaderships after 1920 were products of a shared revolutionary experience. This shared experience is the first of several variables that help to explain civil-military relations in Mexico. The fact that Mexico's officer corps and its political leadership originate from a major revolutionary upheaval has several important implications. The first consequence is more exaggerated but offers certain similarities to the large-scale influx of "civilian officers" in the U.S. Army, notably during wartime. In other words, the presence of civilian influence in the officer corps affects "professional" military values, certainly those attitudes involving civil-military relations. As S. E. Finer suggests, the distinction between a revolutionary versus a regular army is extremely important because "such armies tend to incorporate every active element of a nation including many which are usually regarded as the antithesis of the regular soldier, such as the intellectual, the author and the politician."[9] Mexico's experience, of course, easily illustrates this argument. Not only did its most important politicians from 1920 through 1946 share this revolutionary background but so did many other leading figures, such as novelists Mariano Azuela or Martín Luis Guzmán, and muralist David Alfaro Siqueiros. Similar patterns have occurred in other societies characterized by social revolution, such as China, but in many other respects these cases are not comparable. For example, the Chinese borrowed an external ideology, one relying on a philosophy of authoritarian, civil control, institutionalizing civilian dominance through the *presence of political cadres* in the armed forces. Civil, party political socialization became all-encompassing in the Chinese case, as did the overwhelming influence of a single leader.

For Talukder Maniruzzaman, the essential explanatory variable for long-term military disengagement in a Third World culture is social revolution and the rise of a coalition of classes because, he asserts, it is conducive to the dominance of ideology and politics over guns.[10] It is true that social upheaval opens up political debate in a society, but it does not necessarily lead to elimination of any particular political practice, unless a consensus develops to alter traditional political behavior. There is no question, and it has been empirically tested, that militarism as a tradition feeds on itself.[11] This is only logical; political behavior is learned. The more the military has intervened, the more it is likely to intervene at some future point. Unless a consensus emerges among military *and* political leaders to withdraw the use of force as a legitimate political tool, eliminating the officer corps as a skilled political actor, permanent military withdrawal is not likely to occur.

A second working hypothesis is that the Mexican Revolution produced the favorable environment described by Maniruzzaman, and the prevailing leaders, although not without serious, almost successful challenges as a consequence of their revolutionary experience, successfully defended their control. Their very defense of that power led them, in part, to see the necessity of delegitimizing military intervention, to introduce some political and structural means for accomplishing that goal. In short, the Revolution produced a coalition of groups that eventually, if haphazardly, evolved a revolutionary ideology, or at least rhetoric, including the concept of military subordination to a central, established political leadership. I argue that many Mexicans, political leaders included, were favorably inclined toward such an attitude not because of some philosophical or morally superior argument that civilian was preferably to military leadership but because of personal experiences with the tragic consequences of violence, deeply embedded on a generation individually connected to loss of life and destruction of personal property. Thus, Mexican leadership sought a way to reestablish permanent order and peace without further resort to violence. The Revolution was critical to civil-military relations in that it facilitated new leadership choices and, more important, made the desire for peace preeminent.

Interestingly, although major theorists have suggested that societal sources are one of two important categories of significant civil-military variables, at least in terms of military political intervention, the actual examination of societal, as distinct from elite, values concerning military political involvement, in the case of Latin America, is negligible. As a consequence, the relevance of societal values is strongly suspected, but little empirical evidence has been collected. With the assistance of survey research, citizen values concerning military intervention will be explicitly developed in the Mexican case, and, I believe, will be shown to have significant consequences for the present relationship.

For the military to refrain from political intervention, a third condition is necessary. That critical element is what Alfred Stepan identifies as a "political led strategy toward the military."[12] For Stepan, that strategy, to be successful, requires that the chief executive's political powers as a leader be directed toward winning professional, not merely personal, allies within the military establishment. The Revolution produced an unusual blend of military leaders with political skills. As will be demonstrated in the following historical narrative, these postrevolutionary leaders, who were of military extraction, skillfully executed such a philosophy, opening up the officer corps, and subsequently the rank of general, to men who would give their loyalty to the secretary of defense, to the president, and ultimately to the state produced by Mexico's political model.

Moreover, the specific strategy worked out by the political leadership seems to be characterized by two other conditions. Throughout the evolutionary stages, during which the political leadership builds up gradual but firm support for civilian supremacy, it must constantly praise the military. As one major theorist, S. E. Finer, comments in a recent reevaluation of his classic work, *The Man on Horseback*, Mexico, as well as the more tenuous cases of Colombia and Venezuela, suggest the importance of honoring the individual, corporate, and ideological interests of the military.[13] The second condition, based on analyses of the Turkish and Mexican cases, is that the political-military leader must have the skill and the patience to pursue a slow, gradual, and protracted process to disentangle the armed forces from politics.[14]

The revolutionary origins of Mexico's post-1920s army has led observers to believe that the leaders successfully avoided dividing the military and political leadership into two disparate groups, especially in terms of class origin and values. Expressed differently, a fourth variable in the ability of a society to both effect and sustain military nonintervention in politics is the elimination or prevention of a caste mentality on the part of the officer corps. C. Wright Mills first suggested this argument in terms of the social homogeneity of leadership, whether it be economic, intellectual, military, or political. Essentially, he believed that such homogeneity impacted on a convergence of interests and values.[15] Major historical evaluations of the Mexican case have accepted Mills's theory, arguing that the "middle-of-the road governments of the past quarter century have been in tune with the social philosophy of the officer class. This is an added reason why militarism has been no problem in Mexico since 1940."[16] Whether one can ascribe similar values and ideology to a leadership's shared social background is open to debate, class analysis to the contrary. Nevertheless, this book will provide in considerable detail some empirical comparisons of the highest ranks in the officer corps and top civilian politicians, examining the potential consequences of differences in background, and the extent of interlocks between the two groups. The Revolution itself provides the foundation for bridging the two elites, military and political, because both had, or at least it has been assumed that both had, firsthand revolutionary experience. It is convincing that the experience helped create a shared sense of legitimacy essential to the inculcation and acceptance of the doctrine of civilian supremacy.[17]

To a certain extent, the Mexican military, at least since 1946, has created its own version of a caste image, reflected in its aggressive posture against probing examinations of its institutional characteristics and leadership. The posture has led in many respects to social isolation as well, not only from the average Mexican but from other elite groups, including businesspeople, intellectuals, and politicians. Stepan complains that a severe weakness among Latin American civilian cultures is the failure to incorporate military sociology and strategy into education curricula. He argues that people in the areas of communications and politics should be knowledgeable about all aspects of military life because such people are indispensable to military and intelligence oversight, particularly in the legislative body.[18] It would be difficult to fault his logic, but to attempt to carry out oversight in Mexico might, in some respects, destroy rather than strengthen one of the foundations of civilian supremacy. Civilian leadership sets the basic parameters of Mexican military activity, including budget and size; the military decides its own policies without civilian scrutiny. Interestingly, as will be developed later, although civilians have refrained from institutionalizing military studies, the military, at its most advanced level, has recently allowed a highly select group of civilians to study within its ranks.

Revolutionary leadership ties have long since disappeared, requiring other variables to substitute for them. A fifth hypothesis offering insight into the Mexican case is that in pursuit of a political strategy, the political leadership created a government party, an institution providing the basis for an intergenerational pool of leaders. In the eyes of some historians, the strength and persistence of this civil institution has been a critical variable in sustaining civilian supremacy, a thesis accepted and supported in this work.[19] The existence of a strong party and, equally important in my opinion, an executive branch bureaucracy, reflects a larger theoretical argument offered by Samuel Huntington, who believes that the inclination to intervene cannot be discovered within the military but in the presence of strong political institutions.[20] Originally, Huntington asserted that one means of civilian control over the military is maximizing civilian power over governmental institutions, or constitutional restrictions.[21] He suggested that these have limited effectiveness because civilians generally compete for power among themselves. Mexico, however, gradually eliminated civilian competition, confining it to a political leadership associated with the government party, reinforcing political institutions through monopolistic control over the branches of government. Naturally, the recent revival of electoral competition not only has altered political behavior between the state and opposition, especially since 1987, but potentially has implications for civil-military relations in a political model in which previously identifiable and strong open civilian divisions never weakened the civilian component.

Mexico has been fortunate in the past fifty years because military officers in pursuit of political ambitions, either for personal or ideological reasons, have not really had the opportunity to make the distinction, as Finer so insightfully proposes, between loyalty to a government and loyalty to a nation. When such distinctions occur, the officer corps begins "to invent [its] own private notion of the national interest, and from this it is only a skip to the constrained substitution of this view for that of the civilian government."[22] Indeed, Mexican political leadership has engaged in a persistent effort to establish within its own ranks, and among co-opted groups, such as intellectuals, that loyalty to it, even to a given administration, is tantamount to loyalty to the state and to the nation. It has been quick to accuse dissidents of any ideological stripe of treason, as if it alone had a monopoly on political loyalty.

A sixth working hypothesis in the Mexican case is the importance of professionalism. In the literature on civil-military relations and the potential for military intervention and withdrawal, especially in the case of Latin America, probably no single explanatory variable has received more attention than the level of military professionalism. Professionalism, as Huntington defined it, would make the military a tool of the state, keeping it out of politics by granting it a certain amount of independence and autonomy.[23] Protecting the military's autonomy from prying civilian eyes has been carried to an extreme in Mexico, as I suggested above.

The most critical element in the more traditional definition of professionalism—developing an institutional sense of identity and behavior—is the level of discipline conveyed in the officer's socialization process, and to whom subordination is ultimately directed. As I will illustrate later, William S. Ackroyd believes that Mexico has one of the highest levels of military discipline in Latin America or the Third World; I will show that that discipline facilitated the formation of a homogeneous, obedient officer corps, among whose values is an extreme sense of loyalty to superior authority, including that of the president.[24] Ultimately, the quality of professionalism within the officer corps depends largely on the thought and self-perception of the corps.[25] According to historians, the self-perception has included not a desire for political power but for recognition of the vital role of the corps in preserving internal order and defending national sovereignty. The corps also wants its profession to be respected by citizens and politicians.[26] Whatever their perceptions prove to be, long-term disengagement from politics requires officers to have favorable views of their appropriate roles and of civilian politicians' actions.[27]

Professionalism, defined in terms of developing a strong sense of corporate identity, and skills and knowledge about the area of expertise, does not preclude, as has been so clearly demonstrated in Latin America and elsewhere, intervention by the military—in fact, it may encourage intervention. If the military feels more competent than others to judge its internal characteristics, such as size, recruitment, and equipment, the feeling may bring it into competition with civilian authorities. It also may be very reluctant to coerce governmental opponents, believing such coercion to be an infringement of its national loyalty and autonomy.[28]

In earlier arguments about elimination of a caste mentality among the officer corps, the importance of a certain level of autonomy within the military was suggested. In Mexico, the lack of competitive opposition traditionally protected the military from civilian political intervention, as distinct from military involvement in politics. An important hypothesis that the Mexican case appears to illustrate is that civilian leadership has made a special attempt to refrain from interfering in what might be truly deemed "internal" military matters, such as promotion, discipline, and assignments.[29] This seventh working hypothesis posits the view that civilian interference in "internal" military matters prompts military political involvement. This variable can be empirically tested to some degree, and an examination of promotion records affords some important insights into the officer corps and civil-military relations.

Within the general literature, the most unique hypothesis emerging from the Mexican case, even more significant than the initial revolutionary origins of civil-military groups, is the interpretation offered by Colonel Franklin D. Margiotta: the key to nonintervention "is to keep the Army involved in politics. The military may become involved anyway, so individual officers might be encouraged (or at least permitted) to run for political office."[30] This reasoning, first offered in the early 1970s, based in part on president Lázaro Cárdenas's (1934–1940) inclusion of the military in an open, active sector of the government party, to achieve elite unity, implies that military involvement in politics has many positive consequences, including a bridge between political-military leaders, eliminating the ambitions of politically motivated officers, and limiting but maintaining a direct military presence in political leadership. These conditions and their repercussions were extremely important in the transitional stages in the 1930s, 1940s, 1950s, and 1960s but, as I will attempt to prove, dissipated after the 1970s, thus giving them historical validity only as an explanatory variable. This pattern did assist, however, what Claude Welch has aptly described as a transformation of military *participation* in politics to military *influence* in politics.[31]

Finally, a ninth hypothesis—one that might be offered more appropriately as an explanation for the reintroducing of the military into politics rather than sustaining its exclusion from politics—is the importance of the military to national security. Contemporary military power, according to one theorist, is centered largely on the military's ability to establish itself at the apex of the national security structure.[32] In Mexico, the military has always been part of the national security formula, even after civilian dominance was symbolized in the designation of a nonmilitary president in 1946. However, a strong argument can be made that since the 1980s internal security issues in Mexico have multiplied, exacerbated by drugs, and that the military, called on to combat the more overt manifestations, has increased its presence in internal political matters. Its role is likely to contribute to a reformulation of its responsibilities politically and in the decision-making process, which might place at greater risk the solidity of established civil-military relations.

Each of the following chapters will examine one or more of these hypotheses, testing their validity in the Mexican case, and where possible, drawing on comparative data from Latin American and United States case studies. Some, as the analysis will suggest, offer more explanatory power for Mexico than others. Certain hypotheses are extremely useful in understanding the past behavior of the officer corps, and civil-military relations in general, rather than the contemporary scene. For example, the view that the civilian leadership purposely placed the military in national political offices is very useful in understanding the evolution of the relationship in Mexico through the 1970s, but this variable no longer retains such importance. Its disappearance as a notable bridge between civil and military leaders implies potential consequences for the future relationship. Mexico's development into a modified one-party system, led by a pragmatically oriented, cohesive civilian elite, positively influenced the subordination of the military to the state and contributed to the permanence of the relationship. Among other topics, successive chapters explore the historical patterns in civil-military relations, the interlocks between civilian and military elites, the trends within the military leadership since 1946, the values and prestige of the officer corps through civilian and military eyes, the role of education and socialization in the military, and the background of the officer corps and its consequences for civil-military relations. The final chapter provides speculative interpretations of the importance of some of the working hypotheses in understanding Mexico's military, and the possible direction of civil-military relations into the twenty-first century.

Notes

1. Claude E. Welch, Jr., *No Farewell to Arms? Military Disengagement from Politics in Africa and Latin America* (Boulder, Colo.: Westview Press, 1987), 10.

2. Frank D. McCann, "Brazilian Army Officers Biography Project" (Paper presented at the 15th National Latin American Studies Association, Miami, December 1989), 4.

3. David Ronfeldt, "The Mexican Army and Political Order since 1940" (Santa Monica: Rand Corporation, 1973), 7.

4. Pablo González Casanova, *La democracia en México* (Mexico: ERA, 1965), and *Democracy in Mexico* (New York: Oxford University Press, 1970), 36–38. The work by Miguel Basáñez, which has more insights about the military as a political actor, is *La lucha por la hegemonía en México, 1968–1980* (Mexico: Siglo XXI, 1981).

5. Edwin Lieuwen, *Arms and Politics in Latin America* (New York: Council on Foreign Relations, 1960), 121.

6. George Philip, *The Military in South American Politics* (London: Croom-Helm, 1985), 77.

7. Martin Edmonds, *Armed Services and Society* (Leicester, U.K.: Leicester University Press, 1988), 82.

8. Roderic A. Camp, "Civilian Supremacy in Mexico: The Case of a Post-Revolutionary Military," in *Military Intervention and Withdrawal*, ed. Constantine P. Danopoulous (London: Routledge, 1991), 5–6.

9. S. E. Finer, *The Man on Horseback: the Role of the Military in Politics* (Boulder, Colo.: Westview Press, 1988), 180.

10. Talukder Maniruzzaman, *Military Withdrawal from Politics: A Comparative Study* (Cambridge, Mass.: Ballinger, 1987), 212.

11. Robert D. Putnam, "Toward Explaining Military Intervention in Latin American Politics," *World Politics* 20, no. 1 (1967): 106.

12. Alfred Stepan, *Rethinking Military Politics: Brazil and the Southern Cone* (Princeton: Princeton University Press, 1988), 138.

13. Finer, *The Man on Horseback*, 306.

14. Maniruzzaman, *Military Withdrawal from Politics*, 211.

15. C. Wright Mills, *The Power Elite* (New York: Oxford University Press, 1959), 283.

16. Edwin Lieuwen, *Mexican Militarism* (Albuquerque: University of New Mexico Press, 1968), 149.

17. Gordon C. Schloming, "Civil-Military Relations in Mexico, 1910-1940: A Case Study" (Ph.D. diss., Columbia University, 1974), 317–318.

18. Stepan, *Rethinking Military Politics*, 130.

19. Schloming, "Civil-Military Relations in Mexico," 318.

20. Samuel P. Huntington, *Political Order in Changing Societies* (New Haven: Yale University Press, 1968), 198.

21. Samuel P. Huntington, *The Soldier and the State: The Theory and Politics of Civil-Military Relations* (Cambridge: Harvard University Press, 1964), 81–82.

22. Finer, *The Man on Horseback*, 23.

23. Huntington, *The Soldier and the State*, 83–84.

24. William S. Ackroyd, "The Military in Mexican Politics: The Impact of Professionalization, Civilian Behavior, and the Revolution" (Paper presented at the 28th Meeting of the Pacific Coast Council of Latin Americanists, San Diego, October 1982), 13.

25. Frederick M. Nunn, "Oh the Role of the Military in Twentieth-Century Latin America: The Mexican Case," in *The Modern Mexican Military: A Reassessment*, ed. David Ronfeldt (La Jolla: Center for U.S.-Mexican Studies, University of California, San Diego, 1984), 45.

26. Lieuwen, *Mexican Militarism*, 149.

27. Welch, *No Farewell to Arms?*, 20–21.

28. Finer, *The Man on Horseback*, 23.

29. Franklin D. Margiotta, "Civilian Control and the Mexican Military: Changing Patterns of Political Influence," in *Civilian Control of the Military: Theories and Cases from Developing Countries*, ed. Claude E. Welch, Jr. (Albany: State University of New York Press, 1976), 253.

30. Franklin D. Margiotta, "The Mexican Military: A Case Study in Non-intervention" (M.A. thesis, Georgetown University, 1968), 165.

31. Claude E. Welch, Jr., "Civilian Control of the Military: Myth and Reality," in *Civilian Control of the Military, Theory and Cases from Developing Countries*, ed. Welch (Albany: State University of New York Press, 1976), 22.

32. Amos Perlmutter, "The Military and Politics in Modern Times: A Decade Later," *Journal of Strategic Studies* 9 (March 1986): 5.

2

The Historical Context

Mexican historiography offers a rich literature on many aspects of the nine-teenth and twentieth centuries. The military has been well examined as a crucial actor in the revolutionary decade, the 1910s, but its institutional charac-teristics, transition from an established state institution to a popular army or armies, and its emergence anew as a state institution have never been analyzed in any detail, in part because the postrevolutionary army imposed obstacles to civilian interpretations of its image, function, and leadership. Nevertheless, what little literature exists about the Mexican military in other periods is historical in scope, and thus the overall historical picture is clearer than any contemporary understanding of its leadership and behavior since the 1950s.

Rather than merely highlighting the general findings of that literature as a prelude to my analysis of the officer corps in recent years, I would like to identify and suggest the significance of selected presidential policies that con-tributed to the military's withdrawal from the decision-making arena, and its gradual subordination to civilian authority.

The nature of civil-military relations and the evils attributed to direct military participation in politics are generally associated with Porfirio Díaz, who, like many post-1920 presidents, was himself a military officer. There is no question that Díaz and his collaborators destroyed the tenuous civilian control and legitimacy represented by Benito Juárez and his successor, Sebastian Lerdo de Tejada, with the Plan de Tuxtepec rebellion against the government in 1876, which ironically set forth "no reelection" as its motto. Díaz had long harbored political ambitions for the presidency, and actually had competed against Lerdo de Tejada to be president of the supreme court (in effect, to be next in line for the nation's highest office should the president die or resign) but lost in the voting. Díaz resorted to the force of arms, instead of the ballot box, to achieve power.

Díaz contributed to the heritage of Mexican civil-military relations in several ways. He set back the possible evolution of civilian supremacy by at least half a century, although it is doubtful whether any single civilian politi-cian possessed the skills and charisma to lead the polity in 1876 without resorting to violence. When Díaz arrived in the presidency, it was only natural that he brought some comrades in arms into the cabinet, and appointed others to the most important governorships. By incorporating large numbers of battle-hardened officers directly into politics, he legitimized the military's political role, its supremacy over civilian leadership, and, more important, the rule of law. To sustain his political control at a time of dissension, he frequently transferred zone commanders, so they and their civilian counterparts would find it difficult to conspire against him.[1] In doing so, he contributed not only to the gradual strengthening of the presidency and, by definition, the national executive branch but also to the gradual weakening of civilian governors' powers, powers that to this day never have been fully recovered.[2]

These features of the Díaz era are well known and frequently discussed, but what is less understood and important to underline is that Díaz, over time, contributed to the expansion of civilian leadership at the national political level. A careful examination of his presidency reveals a gradual but persistent decline in career military backgrounds among his most influential collaborators. By the early twentieth century, prominent military figures were only a small minority among influential politicians. The evidence suggests that Díaz selected individuals personally loyal to him on the basis of shared career experiences, a criterion not unlike that of later presidents, but politics became essentially a civilian occupation, and civilians ultimately constituted the lion's share of its practitioners. This pattern suggests that historically, in Mexico and elsewhere, the military does not have sufficient human resources to provide continuous political leadership over time, nor do military leaders themselves, even when firmly in control of political institutions, necessarily continue recruiting from military ranks to fill important political offices.[3]

The rapid decline of an overt military presence among Mexico's political leadership does not necessarily signify a decrease in the military's decision-making influence. On the other hand, it does indicate three important characteristics of the civil-military relationship. First, in Mexico and elsewhere, military officers must form an alliance with civilian sympathizers who have the skills and the inclination to be politically active. This was the case, for example, in Chile, Brazil, and Argentina in the 1970s and 1980s. This was no less true in the nineteenth than in the twentieth century. Second, physically removing the military from political office is a first step, however small, in conveying to the population, the political leadership, and the officer corps itself, that the political arena is the purview of civilians, not military men. From a theoretical viewpoint, a declining but persistent military representation in political offices since 1946 has contributed to the growth of civilian supremacy. Third, Díaz created a large core of civilian loyalists to fill his top offices, men who had spent most of their lives in public office. In the context of the nineteenth century, it might be possible to describe this group of Mexicans as harbingers of "professional" politicians; they understood that their successful pursuit of that career depended exclusively on their relationship, direct or indirect, to Porfirio Díaz himself.

Simultaneously, Díaz in his own way, however limited, began to professionalize the officer corps. Many of its top leaders by 1900 were Colegio Militar graduates, and thus developing the beginnings of their own corporate identity. Their acquisition of a separate identity, regardless of whether it included subordination to civilian control, meant that Díaz initiated what others might consider a caste mentality. In contrast, the idea that political and entrepreneurial leadership should be separate was never formalized in the nineteenth century in any way, either in practice or through separate formation.

When the rebellion of 1910 burst out, followed by full-scale violence in 1913, the composition of Mexico's political leadership and the civil-military relationship were altered. Francisco Madero, a civilian revolutionary who briefly replaced the Porfiriato leadership, ultimately contributed to this change. First, he legitimized a civilian presidency, the first since 1876. Second, a central theme of his political platform, presented in his book on the presidential succession of 1910, attacked militarism. Both his leadership and his platform could be cited by later revolutionaries desirous of civilian control over the political system.[4] Some lower-ranking officers, sympathetic to the Revolution, joined forces with one of several popular armies, but those who rose to senior rank after 1920 were exceptional, not typical. By 1920 most senior officers in the Federal Army had retired, died in combat, or been placed on inactive status. Elements of the victorious Constitutional Army replaced the establishment officer corps. Because political leadership from 1920 to 1946, with one exception, was military, the Revolution established the dominance of military leadership, albeit a different type of leadership, with popular roots similar to those of its civilian counterpart.

By reintroducing military officers in large numbers from the president on down to political positions, the postrevolutionary leadership not only established firm control of the decision-making apparatus but once again legitimized for all Mexicans the military's direct role in politics. This postrevolutionary heritage, constructed on the foundation Díaz introduced in his own rise to power, created a barrier to the goal of civilian supremacy later presidents hoped to achieve.

The Revolution also provided an additional critical ingredient to this tried formula: a desire for a lasting peace. Governments after 1920, like governments after 1871, had the advantage of a populace accepting of certain political deficiencies in return for domestic tranquility and stability.[5] The Revolution had claimed the lives of nearly a tenth of all Mexicans, a decimation that rendered the survivors especially sensitive to public discord. It is certain that even through the 1960s civilian governance justified its compromises and relationships, in part, as efforts to avoid violent confrontation.[6]

Postrevolutionary Era of Military Leadership

Immediately upon General Alvaro Obregón's accession to the presidency in 1920, he, like Díaz, began to recruit skilled civilians with college degrees to his cabinet and other important political posts. At the same time he tried further to limit overt military political activity, not necessarily because he believed in civilian supremacy but because the practicalities of remaining in power called for this strategy. According to Lieuwen, Obregón made repeated attempts, mostly futile, to restrict officers to their military function, ordering troop commanders not to talk to opposition politicians. Those who disobeyed were cashiered from the army, their property confiscated.[7] Obregón not only resorted to political blackmail and censorship but applied restraints from a more institutional angle. He improved upon Díaz's tried-and-tested procedure of circulating zone commanders when in early 1923 he expanded the number of zones from twenty to thirty-five. He publicly justified decentralization by saying that because rebels and bandits were under control, large troop concentrations were no longer required. His real reason was to fragment further regional military commands, reducing challenges to the national government.[8]

President Plutarco Elías Calles, (1924–1928), as he did in so many other areas of Mexican political life, made the most important contributions to altering civil-military relations. He used a reconstituted Colegio Militar, beginning in 1924, to produce a generation of professionally trained officers, and instituted important procedural changes facilitating that policy. In 1926 he introduced a promotions law, ending some of the irregularities that had prevailed since 1910, including eliminating "finger generals," individuals promoted at the whim of a superior officer. Advancement in the lower officer ranks was to be based on professional training and competitive examinations.[9] Calles also reinforced Obregón's policies regarding officer behavior, penalizing officers sympathetic to the opposition, using the two service journals, *Revista*

Exhibit 2-1
Officer Rank Structure of the Mexican Armed Forces

Navy	Army	Air Force
Admirals	*Generals*	*Generals*
Admiral	Division General	Division General
Vice Admiral	Brigade General	Wing General
Rear Admiral	Brigadier General	Group General
Captains	*Chiefs (Jefes)*	*Chiefs (Jefes)*
Naval Captain	Colonel	Colonel
Frigate Captain	Lt. Colonel	Lt. Colonel
Corvette Captain	Major	Major
Officers		
Naval Lieutenant	First Captain	First Captain
Frigate Lieutenant	Second Captain	Second Captain
Corvette Lieutenant	Lieutenant	Lieutenant
Coastguardsman	Second Lieutenant	Second Lieutenant

Source: Ley Orgánica de la Armada de México, *Diario Oficial*, January 14, 1985, p. 14.

del Ejército and *La Patria*, to denounce their political ambitions, and cashiering or transferring suspected opposition partisans.[10]

Most important, two months after General Obregón's assassination as president-elect, in September 1928, Calles told assembled leading generals that *no army officer should become either provisional or permanent president* because this not only would give the people an unfavorable impression of the army but also would split the army into rival factions, leading to violence. Instead, he suggested, the army and the Congress would make the final selection, agreeing beforehand on a candidate.[11] At this juncture, they chose Emilio Portes Gil, a lawyer and important political figure from Tamaulipas, as interim president. His successor in 1929, Pascual Ortiz Rubio, although an officer of the rank of general in the latter years of the Revolution, had not been on active duty since 1920, nor was he considered a military leader. Thus, for brief periods, 1928–1929 and 1929–1932, through Calles's influence, himself an important military figure, governing through civilian leadership was reintroduced.

Although many of Mexico's most important generals continued to hold influential political posts during the 1928–1934 period, they did not use their power to enhance unduly the institutional interests of the army. On the contrary, according to Lieuwen, they recognized its contribution as larger than necessary.[12] Also, many prominent military leaders were thinking of their own political and personal interests rather than the military's interests as a corporate body. It was the younger, newly trained officers who for the most part developed a sense of institutional loyalty, in the same way that civilian politicians developed a similar sense of institutional loyalty to party and state. Nevertheless, the political-military officers, of whom Calles, General Lázaro Cárdenas, and lesser military lights were representative, made the switch to civilian supremacy possible by identifying themselves with the new civilian-dominated political leadership, not with their military cronies.

The orientation of Calles, Cárdenas, and others toward the supremacy of civilian leadership by the end of the 1920s distinguishes them from most of their colleagues elsewhere in Latin America.[13] In part, the popular roots of the post-1920s army and the fact that most of these generals did not pass through a socializing process that would have strengthened their institutional identity and loyalty explain the difference. Moreover, the political-military officers in power during the 1920s confronted rebellion in their ranks, not inadequate or distasteful civilian political leaders whom the military, as a group, needed to replace. In the eyes of the military leadership desirous of institutionalizing the armed forces, the problems came not from the civilian sector but from the officer ranks. Thus, a period of a decade or so was needed to permit a shaking out among remaining generals and troop commanders, leaving a smaller, more coherent pool of generals at the top.

During this same period of transition (1929), elements of the military, under General José Escobar, for the last time after 1920 rebelled in large numbers against the central government. As Gordon Schloming notes, the rebellion differed from its more comprehensive predecessors in 1923 and 1927:

It was the first time that a significant number of subunits under regional command preferred loyalty to the national government over a personal loyalty to their rebel generals. Apparently the professionalizing reforms inaugurated by Amaro [the general in charge of military professionalization] had indeed inculcated a national and institutional loyalty in important segments of the junior officer ranks.[14]

Calles laid the groundwork for the beginnings of the transition from a revolutionary to a institutionalized army, and from a military directly involved in politics to one functioning as a separate state actor. After the interim years, during which three men served as president, it was General Cárdenas who solidified what Calles and Amaro had initiated. In the words of the most careful analyst of civil-military relations during late 1930s, "His principal lasting contribution in this respect was *to centralize the civilian pyramid of power by uniting governmental and party authority in the person of the President.*"[15] Cárdenas accomplished this task in several ways.

Cárdenas used professionalization as a key for removing politically active or interested officers. As will be seen from the data presented on generals in later sections, his positive results have been over exaggerated. Instead, he set this pattern in motion. Shortly after taking office, in 1935, he ordered proficiency tests for all infantry officers below the rank of colonel. Those who failed the test were required to take remedial training, the results of which were to be the sole criterion for promotion. According to Donald Harrison, Cárdenas eliminated from the officer corps men who had come up through the revolutionary army by virtue of politics and favoritism.[16] Actually, he eliminated men who without any merit or military skill had risen in the ranks. Many officers with considerable ability had also received promotions on the basis of politics and favoritism; they remained.

Professionalization was integral to Cárdenas's ultimate political goals for the military. For Cárdenas, however, professionalization did not mean developing a separate caste identity, one that would encourage the military to act as an independent arbiter of political affairs. He expressed his views very clearly in addressing the 1935 graduating class at the Colegio Militar, forerunner of the Heroico Colegio Militar:

> We should not think of ourselves as professional soldiers . . . but rather as armed auxiliaries organized from the humble classes. . . . it is the duty of young officers to broaden the collective spirit of the nation and help incorporate the humble into the whole program of the Revolution.[17]

To give future general officers a sense of institutional identity that was nonpolitical, and to retain a shared bond with civilian leaders, Cárdenas used professionalization techniques in several ways. First, he encouraged the promotion of younger, academy-trained officers to positions of strategic command. Such men were not of sufficient rank to be zone or battalion commanders, but he used them to create a buffer zone between the troops and generals of dubious loyalty to the government.[18] Second, he encouraged the recruitment of cadet officers from the popular classes, promoting men from the ranks to cadet status. Third, he lowered maximum-age limits and reduced the maximum career span for an officer below the rank of general, forcing the retirement of some older generals, making room for a younger, postrevolutionary generation.[19] Cárdenas introduced a structural change having the potential for reducing the military's power as well as expanding its range of skills, dividing the Secretariat of War and Navy into two autonomous ministries, the Secretariat of National Defense (army and air force) and the Secretariat of the Navy.[20] Except for splitting the Secretariat of War and Navy, none of his actions toward the military were particularly original; they were variants of actions that Calles had already tried.

Cárdenas's most controversial and important contribution was his conception, theoretically and pragmatically, of the relationship between the military and the new civilian political institution, the National Revolutionary Party (PNR). His attitudes toward professionalism were tied to his views on the military's relationship to the party. Cárdenas believed that military professionalization should occur

> at a rate commensurate with party institutionalization. Such a strategy was essential to civilian control: political passivity or neutrality in the officer corps is a luxury regimes can afford only *after* they have achieved some minimal level of national integration that promotes an underlying value consensus on the fundamental nature of the regime. This integration was effectively achieved through the centralizing and institutionalizing power of the official party, presided over by a civilianized leadership. . . .[21]

In other words, he attempted a balancing act between professionalizing the officer corps and, in a sense, professionalizing the civilian leadership, for which the party served as the umbrella organization, teaching loyalty, discipline, and skills through political experience.

Although the party did become the focus of civilian political loyalty for those hopeful of successful political careers after 1929, Cárdenas could not foresee that the federal bureaucracy, not the party bureaucracy, would become the training ground for generations of future civilian leaders who received their education and many values at the National University in Mexico City. Furthermore, as de facto head of the party and the executive branch, Cárdenas effected an increasing centralization of power in the hands of the president, removing the possibility of competition from other sources, including dissident generals.

To implement this philosophy, Cárdenas startled many civilian politicians, as well as numerous officers, with his decision to rename the PNR (the Party of the Mexican Revolution, PRM) in 1938, and create four corporate sectors: labor, popular, agrarian, and military.[22] Many officers resisted direct incorporation into the government party because they supported the process initiated under Calles and reinforced under Cárdenas, of eliminating direct political participation. Now it seemed to them that Cárdenas had done an about-face,

reversing what they had learned in military schools, in their journals, and on
active duty since the early 1920s.[23] Even his own secretary of defense, Manuel
Avila Camacho, faithful ally and later presidential successor, privately feared
an eventual division within the armed forces over this decision. Avila Camacho
preferred the military's role as that of adviser rather than participant.[24]
Cárdenas explained publicly why he took this rather controversial step, announcing that he did not want the officers in the new military sector to
represent the armed forces as a special caste.[25] Again, Cárdenas seemed very
concerned that the military might differentiate itself socially; he believed such a
military would act in its own interests, possibly those of a single class, as
distinct from the interests of all Mexicans.

Under the original National Revolutionary Party statutes, individuals from
the army and navy were party members as citizens, not as representatives of the
armed forces, and should continue to function apart from all political affairs.[26]
In this period of the party's evolution, the military was not a separate sector.
Yet, when incorporated into regular party ranks, the government imposed
certain restrictions on military membership. Gradually, the party, similar to
other state institutions, developed a corporatist quality, integrating constituencies from various occupational categories. These groups, such as organized
labor, were deeply involved in political affairs, and their representatives,
although not accurately reflecting the wishes of their constituencies, spoke
precisely for those constituencies. According to another clause, all party
members except the military were required to pay regular and extraordinary
dues punctually; Jorge Alberto Lozoya argues that this suggests the military
entered the party unwillingly.[27] I argue that these clauses suggest that the
civilian leadership not only was sensitive to the military's resistance to joining
but could not make up its mind how to include the military within its corporatist framework. Unlike most other groups, the military already was incorporated directly into the state, and its political power during the formative years
of the party was decisive.

Both before and after the addition of a military sector in the government
party, officer participation in party leadership ranks added important elements
to the party's own value system for many decades. The military ethos of rank,
discipline, militancy, and loyalty, qualities that also are the hallmark of the
party, can be traced back to military participation.[28]

With the division of a new party into four sectors, including one representing the military, the officer corps had to choose its own representatives. The
Secretariat of National Defense selected forty delegates, one from each of
thirty-three military zones, one from each of the two naval zones, three from
the department level at the secretariat, and two as personal representatives of
Avila Camacho. The two leaders of the delegation, both loyal Cárdenistas,
were General Juan José Ríos and General Heriberto Jara. The assembled
delegates from all four party sectors chose three officers among their leaders,
men suggestive of the direction the army was headed. Predictably, they selected
Division General Heriberto Jara, representative of the revolutionary veterans,
an important military figure who had pursued a political career, as vice-

president of the assembly. They also selected Captain Alfonso Corona del Rosal, a young political-military officer critical to the future transformation and subordination of the military to civilian leadership, as secretary; and Brigadier General Edmundo M. Sánchez Cono, later the official military representative on the party's national executive committee in 1938, as a member of the statutes committee.[29] When the final composition of the constituent assembly of the new PRM became public, the military sector exceeded the other three sectors in strength.[30]

Even prior to Cárdenas's controversial decision, the party played a significant role in civil-military relations. Keeping in mind that political leadership during the 1920s collected around various personalities, typically a military figure, the most prominent of whom were Generals Obregón and Calles, the party helped to unify civilian and military elements, channeling their respective interests. The establishment of the party, primarily Calles's brainchild, regardless of his actual motivations, provided the postrevolutionary generation with a mechanism for forming a coalition.[31]

In anticipation of the presidential election of 1940, Cárdenas reinforced the channeling process, ordering all zone commanders to ban political activity at military installations and to participate through the party.[32] Enforcement of the orders was essential because the front-runners for the PRM presidential nomination, automatically Cárdenas's successor, were all military officers, among them Generals Manuel Avila Camacho, Juan Andreu Almazán, Rafael Sánchez Tapia, and Emilio J. Mújica.[33] As the government party strengthened its role in the presidential election process, dissident officers, supporting a candidate other than the party's choice, had to seek a leave. The military sector of the PRM formally backed Avila Camacho for the nomination, which of course he obtained. During the campaign, thirty-four officers on active duty received extended leave to lobby for General Almazán, Avila Camacho's strongest opponent.[34]

During the campaign Avila Camacho revealed publicly, for the first time, his private doubts about military participation in the party. In fact, in addition to his well-known posture as a national unification candidate, he personally represented the new nonpartisan military officer. According to José Piñeyro, he personified the military bureaucrat, an officer who earned his general's stars behind a desk, not on the battlefield. He bluntly told audiences that partisan participation of men in uniform would be a "return to the past."[35] Within a month of taking office in December 1940, he ordered the withdrawal of members of the army and navy from the organs "of political action to which they belong."[36]

Avila Camacho deserves equal credit with Cárdenas—perhaps greater credit than Cárdenas—for Mexico's transition to civilian leadership. He not only sensed strong dissatisfaction with Cárdenas's decision to incorporate the military within the government party but took immediate steps to reverse it. The officers already elected to the 1940-1943 legislature joined other sectorial groups. The president reinforced the move toward diminished military influence in politics first by retiring many revolutionary generals who lacked the technical qualifications for modern warfare, and second by reducing military expenditures from 21 to 15 percent of the national budget by the end of his administration. The reduction was in line with the pattern of decline over two decades but, as Walker suggests, is surprising considering the armed forces' increased activity during World War II.[37] Avila Camacho strengthened his position during the war years by taking the unusual step of appointing former President Cárdenas secretary of defense, the only time since 1932 that a president returned to the cabinet in that capacity.[38] World War II also made it possible for Mexican officers, in much larger numbers than previously, to take advanced training in the United States, thus increasing professionalization on a technical level among future generals.[39]

Interestingly, however, the president allowed his secretary of interior, Miguel Alemán, to alter the military's balance of power. Alemán created a presidential guard, which later developed into an elite unit within the armed forces. The guard, whose chain of command goes directly to the president, was designed to restrain ambitious generals in the regular army.[40] It is possible that Alemán anticipated if not his own selection as president, that of another civilian, and that chief executive's wanting an insurance policy in connection with the final transition from military to civilian rule.

Civilian Adjustments to the Military Heritage

The year 1946 marked the evolutionary process from military to civilian control in a symbolic and concrete fashion. General Avila Camacho, a revolutionary veteran and aide to General Cárdenas, selected Miguel Alemán, a young, civilian politician, as the party's presidential candidate. Ironically, Alemán's father, a revolutionary general, had died fighting against the government in the Escobar rebellion only eleven years earlier. The choice of Alemán represents a benchmark in civil-military relations. First, it was military leaders who were instrumental in turning over absolute political leadership to a younger generation of civilians. In fact, Avila Camacho himself was the last serious official precandidate to come from the Defense Secretariat. Second, Alemán's designation marked the advent of a new kind of professional politician: a university teacher, career bureaucrat, civilian.[41]

When Alemán took office in December 1946, he not only symbolized personally the new civilian political generation but surrounded himself with similar types in the most influential cabinet posts.[42] Parallel personnel changes occurred within the military. It has been asserted that Alemán promoted a new generation of officers to the rank of general: men, similar to civilian politicians, who had graduated from the reformed military academies in the 1920s and early 1930s. As will be illustrated in the analysis of promotions, Alemán also promoted many younger officers rapidly through the ranks, although older generals continued to hold the most influential posts. Nevertheless, the most important change in military leadership from 1946 through 1970 took place under Alemán. Symbolically, his appointment of Colonel Santiago Piña Soria

Exhibit 2-2
Presidents of Mexico and Their
Defense Secretaries, 1946–1994

President	Term	Defense Secretary and Educational Background
Carlos Salinas Gortari	1988–1994	Antonio Riviello Bazán HCM 1942-44; ESG 1950-52 Protégé of Roberto Yáñez V.
Miguel de la Madrid	1982–1988	Juan Arévalo Gardoqui HCM 1940-43; ESG 1948-50
José López Portillo	1976–1982	Félix Galván López HCM 1930-34; ESG 1941-44 Protégé of Marcelino García Barragán
Luis Echeverría Alvarez	1970–1976	Hermenegildo Cuenca Díaz HCM 1920-22; ESG 1940-42 Protégé of Gilberto Limón
Gustavo Díaz Ordaz	1964–1970	Marcelino García Barragán HCM 1921-23 (mustang); ESG None
Adolfo López Mateos	1958–1964	Agustín Olachea Aviles HCM None (mustang); ESG None No formal education
Adolfo Ruiz Cortines	1952–1958	Matías Ramos Santos HCM None (mustang); ESG None Completed secondary Protégé of Joaquín Amaro
Miguel Alemán	1946–1952	Gilberto Limón Márquez HCM None (mustang); ESG None Completed secondary Protégé of Francisco Urquizo

Key: HCM = Heroico Colegio Militar; (Heroic Military College); ESG = Escuela Superior de Guerra (Higher War College); Mustang = officer originally from enlisted ranks.

as chief of the presidential staff, and of General Hermenegildo Cuenca Díaz as assistant secretary of defense represented the ascendancy of the new generation, not, as some Mexican authors have asserted, the most significant change in the military structure since 1920.[43]

Strangely, indicative of a more troublesome pattern, Alemán combined military and police functions for internal security purposes. In fact, observers suggest that military repression expanded, especially against independent labor organizations.[44] This view implies that although Alemán reportedly reconstituted the military's leadership with a new breed of officer, his commitment was not necessarily to depoliticizing the military in the broadest sense of the term but, rather, to ensuring the military's loyalty to him and his administration. He used the armed forces, in tandem with civilian security forces, to carry out actions deemed necessary to guarantee the success of his political and economic programs.[45] Hence, while purging the military of its older, more politicized officers, veterans of a period when political intervention was the norm, Alemán was introducing the new generation of military leader to a different form of activity: the enforcement of internal security, politically defined by the president and his collaborators. Similiar military involvement into what typically had been civilian responsibilities did not recur until the first year of the Carlos Salinas administration, 1989.

The event that brought civil-military relations into sharper focus, as in Avila Camacho's administration, was the presidential succession. Two issues of importance to the armed forces came to the forefront in the 1952 presidential election. The first was whether Mexico should accept military aid from the United States. Alemán rejected a proposed bilateral military assistance pact; allegations that Mexico would subordinate itself to United States policies helped persuade the president.[46] It is also likely that Alemán did not sign the treaty because although the military favored United States assistance, he needed to appease the populist wing of the party in order to strengthen the victory of his presidential candidate, Adolfo Ruiz Cortines.[47]

The second issue was how to deal with officers opposed to Alemán's choice of a successor. A sizeable group of officers, many Revolution veterans, wanted General Miguel Henríquez Guzmán as president. When he did not receive the nomination from Alemán, he formed a popular electoral front to campaign openly for the office against the government party's candidate. Some observers suggest that support for the general went beyond a personal interest in him, and instead was a strategy among older military officers opposed to Alemán's policies to ensure the ascendancy of their views.[48] Alemán confronted them in an extremely inflexible manner, instructing his defense secretary to grant unlimited leaves—tantamount to discharging them from active duty—rather than the usual limited leave to campaign. It was a very plain message to the officer corps: support the government's candidate or leave the service. Military loyalists active in the campaign were handsomely rewarded. Among the generals, Alfonso Corona del Rosal became governor of Hidalgo; Jacinto B. Treviño, Ruiz Cortines's original patron, and Rafael Melgar, long prominent in political affairs, became senators; and Rafael Sánchez Taboada, one of the national directors of the campaign, became secretary of the navy. Since then no group of officers has ever "sought to fulfill its political ambitions outside the PRI."[49]

From 1952 until 1968 no presidential decision regarding civil-military relations compared to those implemented by Calles, Cárdenas, Avila Camacho, and Alemán. The military was called in by successive presidents in conflicts involving students and unions, most notably to occupy the National Polytechnic Institute in 1956, to replace striking telegraph workers in 1958, and to bring striking railroad workers into line in 1959. In the last instance, Military Camp No. 1 was virtually transformed into a huge political prison, a situation duplicated on a much smaller but still unsavory scale in the 1970s and early 1980s.[50]

1968, Where Did It Lead?

No single event from 1952 to the present has affected the military and civil-military relations more than the suppression of students activists in Tlatelolco Plaza during the summer of 1968, immediately prior to the Olympic Games in Mexico City. The events leading up to this move occurred over several months, which gave the government and the president opportunity to seek advice from numerous sources, including leading figures in the intellectual community.[51] According to some observers, the president ignored their counsel, taking a strong stance to forestall dissatisfaction with a softer attitude on the part of the military.[52] Much speculation about the decision itself has been offered in academic and popular accounts, but it is important to obtain as complete a picture as possible of the military's role in the decision, because it could serve as a case study both of military influence in political decision making and of the degree of clarity in the subordination of the military to the civilian sector.

The traditional view is that President Gustavo Díaz Ordaz decided upon force, specifically ordering troops, through his secretary of defense, General Marcelino García Barragán, to confront student demonstrators. This view, presented by Jorge Alberto Lozoya, is offered with no evidence or citations.[53] The opposite view is that the military was on the verge of reasserting itself in Mexican politics, but "a coup did not take place because of the personal following of Gustavo Díaz Ordaz among high-ranking officers and . . . it would be more fruitful to remilitarize the country gradually and through institutional channels."[54]

Other accounts, based more firmly on interviews with individuals present at the decision, or having access to those who were, give a fascinating and significant interpretation. Two basic versions exist: one with Díaz Ordaz out of the capital in order to avoid direct connection with the events; and one with Díaz Ordaz in the capital but unwilling to make the decision. The first version has been presented as follows:

> The situation was becoming serious, and it was decided that President Díaz Ordaz had to leave town. He was playing golf in a resort in Michoacán when the decision was made. General Barragán had arrayed the troops, and he was in the Presidential Palace. Echeverría, who was the Interior Minister at the time, was down on the street with General Ballesteros. Echeverría began giving orders to move the troops, and General Ballesteros interrupted him saying that General Barragán was commander of the troops and that these orders would need to be cleared through him. So General Ballesteros called General Barragán to explain the situation to him. General Barragán's response was that Echeverría should keep his hands off Army matters. General Ballesteros then put Echeverría on

the phone and that is when Barragán told Echeverría what he could do. After
that the order was given to clear the square. General Barragán then went down
to the golf course to tell Díaz Ordaz that the situation was all clear. Díaz Ordaz
was scared because he thought the Army was about to tell him they had taken
over. When he heard what General Barragán had to say, he gave him an
emotional embrace and told him he was a good soldier.[55]

The second version has Díaz Ordaz present but unable to make the decision, leaving it in the hands of his secretary of defense. Present were

> Echeverría, General Barragán, and three staff members. Reports of student
> strife were coming in. "OK, Mr. President, it is obvious something must be
> done. Unless you object, I am going to clear Tlatelolco." Then, General Bar-
> ragán turned to his two aides and said, "I want the place cleared out." After it
> was over, he reported to the president, "Mr. President, the situation is clear."[56]

As Michael Dziedzic concludes, although the details of these and supporting accounts vary somewhat, the essential characteristics are consistent. Most
important, it was the secretary of defense who took the initiative, not the
president or Echeverría. In fact, General Barragán was so disgusted with the
entire chain of events that he told Echeverría that he and the president "created
this mess, now let me clean it up my way."[57]

The repercussions of the decision were in many respects more important
than the decision itself in relations between the officer corps and the political
leadership. The consequences can be broadly categorized: altered views of the
military toward civilian leadership, altered views of the political leadership
toward the military, the views of younger officers toward older officers within
the military, and changed views of the role of the military in Mexican society.
One of the most important outcomes, influencing many aspects of civil-military relations long after 1968, is how the officer corps looked upon political
elites. As Dziedzic points out, although General Barragán acted in accord with
specific instructions from civilian elites, he did not need to be told not to
assume the powers of the presidency. In other words, the military recognized
the limits of its role. According to Dziedzic's sources, the officer corps proudly
cited its loyalty to the president, especially since it realized that it, not politicians, held the reins of power at that moment.

The retention of military subordination to civil authority was reaffirmed by
these events, which can be seen as one of many positive reinforcements of the
steadily evolving relationship since 1946. On the other hand, the overall image
of civilian leadership took a nosedive in the estimation of the officer corps,
especially among younger men. The new generation deemed the events of 1968
clear evidence of civilian bungling, increasingly viewing the leadership as
politically incompetent and illegitimate.[58] That outlook led to the cadets'
transfer from the Heroico Colegio Militar in Mexico City to Chetumal during
the summer. One officer who was a cadet at the time believed their commanders did not want them influenced negatively by events in the city; no mention

was made to the cadets about the military's role in the disturbance.[59] Future officers would not be inclined to repeat such actions against large numbers of Mexicans, taking the blame for civilian incompetence. The military's perception of civilian fallibility led it to reappraise its role in the internal security decision-making process. In other words, it opted for a larger voice in preventive measures in regard to civil unrest.

It is not known whether the military pushed this new emphasis on civilian political elites, or whether political elites invited the military's increased involvement. To some degree, it is likely that both groups' views coincided on a revised internal security role. What is evident is that the civilian leadership realized that it could not unilaterally ask the military to perpetrate the "horror of slaughtering large numbers of countrymen in the future."[60] Analysts conclude that a shift in direction in national security matters can be traced directly to Tlatelolco Plaza.[61]

The new national security orientation in practice involved increased political intelligence gathering on the part of the military against actual and perceived subversive groups. Also, joint cooperation between police, especially federal agents, and the military, became the norm. Most disturbing of all, elements of the military, with the knowledge and tolerance of the higher command, participated in paramilitary groups similar to those found throughout Latin America in the 1970s and 1980s. According to Stephen Wager, Mexico's version was referred to as the "Brigada Blanca" (White brigade), a counterforce—comprising select army and civilian personnel, and organized along military lines—to extreme left elements.[62]

An infusion of fresh leadership in the officer corps was another effect of 1968 on the military. Some changes happened naturally through attrition, as younger officers took control of decision-making positions in the National Defense Secretariat and in the zone commands. It also occurred, as will be demonstrated later, as a consequence of presidential promotion policies. Considerable dissension within the officer ranks existed, reflected by the fact that instead of the usual yearly ten to fifteen changes in medium- and high-level commands yearly, 1968 witnessed ninety-seven such appointments, including top commanders among the general staff and seven zone commanders.[63] The military, realizing the extent of damage to its institutional reputation wrought by its actions in Tlatelolco Plaza, demanded a high price from the government as compensation. That price is mostly apparent in structural and material changes within the armed forces. For the first time since Miguel Alemán's administration, the government created a new zone command, and it established three new battalions—infantry, parachute, and military police—as well as a new company of combat engineers in the presidential guards.[64] At the same time, half of the troops in the army were given new weapons, and the air force acquired thirty-seven new planes from the United States, twenty for training and seventeen for transport.[65]

The residue of 1968 tainted presidential attitudes toward the military throughout the next administration, primarily because Díaz Ordaz's successor was Luis Echeverría, intimately involved with those events. Specifically, Echeverría never forgave the military for its violence in the plaza, not only because of what happened but because his attempts at moderation had been thwarted. According to a firsthand account, Echeverría told the commander to "be kind to the students," whereupon General Barragán reportedly told Echeverría, through the president's aide, to "que se chinga su madre" (literally, to fuck his mother).[66] Elements in the military also intensely disliked the president. One source has it that when Echeverría was speaking at the University of Michoacán as a presidential candidate, he asked for a moment of silence in memory of the students killed in 1968. When officers learned of this, they reportedly asked Díaz Ordaz to withdraw his candidacy. President Echeverría's views of the military colored his attitudes not only toward technical modernization but toward his own political security vis-à-vis the military.

The officer corps, customarily acquiring little in the way of up-to-date weaponry, especially aircraft, tried to obtain new fighter planes during Echeverría's administration, a request the president consistently refused. Instead, the president concentrated on improving technical training, expanding military occupational specialty programs, and building new facilities.[67] He also increased the military's involvement in nonmilitary, civic action programs. Yet, despite these tendencies, the military rapidly increased its presence in national security matters, confronting and ultimately eliminating several guerrilla groups. As a consequence, it did obtain valuable combat training and some prestige.[68]

Echeverría himself was to have his own, much smaller version of Tlatelolco. On June 10, 1971, a paramilitary organization, Los Halcones, at the instigation of political opponents within the cabinet, brutally suppressed a group of student demonstrators. Echeverría appeared to have lost control over his own cabinet. In the midst of this crisis, the military's backing was critical, much more so than in 1968. Echeverría faced open treason within his own ranks, and without the military's support, he may not have had, or he may have presumed he did not have, sufficient political strength to move against his enemies. Martin Needler reports that he called an emergency meeting of senior army commanders, and after receiving their unanimous backing, he forced the head of the Federal District Department and the police chief of Mexico City to resign and had the commander of the paramilitary forces arrested. Army support saved Echeverría from being controlled by reactionary leaders in his administration.[69]

Despite the military's loyalty to the president during the crisis, Echeverría still viewed the officers not as potential future loyalists but, rather, as potential competitors for political power. The 1971 coup d'état against President Salvador Allende in Chile, during which a constitutionally elected president was overthrown and killed after more than forty years of military subordination to civilian rule, reinforced his attitude. Hence, instead of strengthening the military through expansion or new arms as a reward for its loyalty, Echeverría paid greater lip service publicly to its professionalism, patriotism, and popular roots, thereby emphasizing its nonpolitical role.[70]

To the military's focus on civic action and increased internal security responsibilities, the president added the most important customs posts, an assignment with economic as well as internal security implications. Judith Hellman believes that the threat of a military coup actually weighed on the president's mind. The possibility that the military might actually take the reins of power was most likely during the final months of Echeverría's administration. Despite the intensity of public rumors, including reports in the U.S. media, most authors considered this a feat of public imagination rather than a real possibility.[71] Nevertheless, the rumors are significant, because of the degree to which they reflected a decline in presidential legitimacy and the established relationship between the military and political leadership. The relationship was sorely in need of repair.

Echeverría's handpicked successor was a dark-horse candidate with extremely limited political influence. José López Portillo, a childhood friend, had only recently been recruited into public life. His choice as the PRI standard-bearer led many Mexicans to believe that Echeverría hoped to become the gray eminence, like Calles, of his successor. In fact, rumors abounded that Echeverría might try to remain in power; similar rumors had had even wider currency during the last months of Alemán's administration. Michael Dziedzic asserts that a group of generals became so concerned that they asked to see the president, whom they reportedly told, "'We serve you, Mr. president: however, we are also very loyal to the Constitution. We must pick the Constitution. Were you to do anything against the Constitution, we would be forced to defend the Constitution.' In other words, if you try to stay in power, the Army will push you aside."[72]

López Portillo came into office with his sovereignty guaranteed by the military. He created an ambience much more favorable to substantive changes within the armed forces. He may have chosen to implement these programs as a reward for the military's ending his predecessor's influence. On the other hand, it is very important that López Portillo was the son of a career officer, a military engineer, and graduate of the Colegio Militar. He remembered that his father had been transferred from post to post in the course of his duties, and expressed considerable respect for his father's loyalty to the institution.[73] Therefore, López Portillo's personal experience, more than that of any other president since 1946, may have inclined him to look favorably on military requests.

During the López Portillo administration, the official attitude toward the armed forces changed in four general respects. First, the president encouraged the army to consolidate and increase its role in the area of public security by taking over the protection of vital installations, including utilities and petroleum facilities. Second, he enlarged military involvement in the making of national security policy. Third, López Portillo advanced modernization, not just in education but in arms. Fourth, he enhanced the public presence of the army.[74] In all cases, López Portillo himself initiated these expenditures without any pressure from the military.

In practical terms, López Portillo facilitated the changes in various ways. He authorized spending for ground, air, and sea transportation systems, high-technology equipment such as computers and radar, administrative personnel, and new combat units. To further educational professionalization, incorporating a new integrated civil-military philosophy of national security, he built the Colegio de Defensa Nacional, which conferred master's degrees in national security and defense management.[75] In the policy decision-making process, hidden from public view, the president was careful to include the secretary of defense in all major consultations. In fact, the president informed the defense secretary of his decision to nationalize the banks before he informed the treasury secretary, the only cabinet member asked to vow his support for the measure the night before it was announced.[76] The military enhanced its image with an increased show of weaponry at military parades, although the president attributed this change to military leaders rather than to his office.[77] In his own public appearances, López Portillo praised the military more than his predecessor had. He defended it against an intellectual's accusation that some military men were corrupt, declaring he was proud of the armed forces, and that "no soldier of the Republic is corrupt."[78] His administration completely overhauled the basic structure of the military under the defense secretary, General Félix Galván López, who shifted responsibility for the national military service (draftees) from very old semiretirees in special units to young, aggressive battalion and regimental commanders. According to Alden Cunningham, this allowed the military's version of civic values and patriotism to reach a large portion of the nation's youth.[79] Finally, the López Portillo administration ended with the largest operation in the history of Mexican armed forces: twenty thousand troops and officers participated in a war game.[80]

When José López Portillo left office in November 1982, he left the political system, particularly the presidency, at its lowest ebb in many decades. His successor, Miguel de la Madrid, faced numerous problems, not the least of which was reviving the legitimacy of presidential and establishment leadership. It is not surprising, given these circumstances, that the president continued to curry favor with the military, perhaps in some respects more intensely than his two immediate predecessors. Again, the military's public presence became notable in what traditionally had been civilian parades, and presidential praise for the military incorporated such terms as "cornerstone" of internal stability and "guardian" of society.[81]

The increased role of the military in antidrug programs, activities begun under López Portillo, characterized the de la Madrid administration. Analysts of the drug trade suggest that de la Madrid stressed the military as the "honest, dedicated phalanx of Mexico's *campaña antidroga*" at the expense of the civilian attorney general's office.[82] The emphasis was part of growing participation by the military in internal security matters. Civilians formerly laid out the military's role in the *National Development Plan*.[83] Also, events in Guatemala and Central America as a whole intensified security concerns along the southern border, brought about a stronger military presence there, and gave the military a more influential voice in foreign policy matters.[84]

The stabilizing trend in relations between civilian and military leaders hit a snag of sorts when de la Madrid limited the military's part in emergency relief after Mexico City's major earthquake in 1985. Jorge Castañeda, a Mexican analyst, asserts that a split occurred between older and younger officers, and between the latter and civilian leaders, over the passive assignment.[85] The younger officers wanted a much greater share of the emergency effort, as defined in the national disaster plans. As suggested later in this book, de la Madrid's decision was expressive of the doubts many civilian leaders entertain in regard to the military's becoming prominent in the public arena: it can place civilian leadership in an unfavorable light and enhance the military's political potential.

Hidden behind many public displays and actions toward the military is the fact that the de la Madrid administration provided a stronger legal basis for military modernization than any previous administration. Measured in terms of new legislation governing the role and responsibilities of the military, de la Madrid's government exceeded even the efforts of Avila Camacho, who was so important in the transition from military to civilian political leadership. Calles initiated two statutes, and no changes occurred thereafter until Avila Camacho, who initiated three new pieces of legislation during his presidency. Alemán and Ruiz Cortines each formulated two sets of laws affecting the military, but Echeverría and López Portillo only passed one new law apiece. Under de la Madrid, six new laws were put on the books, three times those of any president since 1946.[86]

De la Madrid stabilized relations with the armed forces while simultaneously increasing their presence, but the political situation altered radically after 1988, when he left office. He had been able to restore some of the influence of the presidency lost by his predecessor, yet overall, civilian leadership's legitimacy had dropped to such a low level that for the first time since the party was formed, a dissident from within the PRI captured an extraordinary number of votes in the presidential election, and more important, forced official tallies to reflect a substantial portion of the ballots cast in his favor.

The consequences were many, but for civil-military relations they were threefold. First, de la Madrid's successor, Carlos Salinas de Gortari, faced the daunting task of assembling a new set of constituencies in 1989. The traditional amalgam of interest groups had been shattered by preelection maneuverings and policy debates among the three leading presidential contenders. Within the first few months of his administration, Salinas included the armed forces as an important element in his new political formula.

Second, in recognition of his redefined constituencies, Salinas made extensive use of the military in executing some of his decisions. For example, he had the army, not the police, move against a notorious drug trafficker, Miguel Angel Félix Gallardo.[87] In the largest such operation to date, he ordered a military takeover of the Cananea Corporation following an unresolved strike,

which according to Lorenzo Meyer, a Mexican commentator, involved heli-
copters and hundreds, possibly thousands, of soldiers.[88] Also, Salinas, like de
la Madrid, encouraged a military presence in government parades.

Third, as a consequence of well-organized opposition, local, state, and
national elections are being vigorously contested. Election violence, especially
at the state and local level, has become a hallmark of Salinas's administration.
The government has used troops to maintain order and, in some cases, to effect
election fraud. Salinas is expanding the internal security role of the military.
Most important, because of its implications for politicizing the military, he is
involving it in the electoral process. Salinas also gave prominence to a national
security group within his cabinet headed by former Colonel Jorge Carrillo
Olea, a longtime veteran of security affairs in the Secretariat of Government,
whom he shifted to the antidrug program in 1990.[89] He has increased the pace
of technological modernization; for example, on Naval Day, June 1, 1990, he
announced that Mexico required a modern navy to protect its national sovereignty.[90]

The Mexican historical record since the 1920s , from a presidential perspective, suggests a number of variables important to the gradual withdrawal of the
military from politics, and the ascendancy of and belief in civilian political
supremacy. Some of these variables can be found in other Latin American or
Third World contexts, but Mexico has developed its own formula for stable
civil-military relations. Most of these variables and their precise implications
are developed in considerable detail in succeeding chapters. It is worth summa-
rizing them here to keep their relationships in mind throughout the book.

Even this brief outline of presidential attitudes and behavior toward the
military suggests several important phenomena. One of the most significant is
the establishment of a major political organization, and its continued growth
and legitimacy. Interestingly, although the party's role in policy-making is
minimal, it provided an institutional means through which a coherent and
legitimate pool of political leaders could be identified. The degree of civilian
unity, as will be seen later, has been essential to the development of military
subordination to civilian authorities.

Second, the military's withdrawal and the imposition of civilian supremacy,
extending back many decades, are directly attributable to military, not civilian,
presidents. These men, unlike most of their peers elsewhere in the world, came
from guerrilla forces, and hence not only did not share roots with civilian
leaders but in many respects, had a civilian rather than an institutionalized
military mentality. Because many of them had fought against the Porfiriato's
militarism, and Victoriano Huerta's collaborators, they had a natural aversion
to instituting a new form of establishment militarism.

Third, even beginning with the administration of General Obregón, each
successive presidency encouraged and expanded military professionalization,
both in developing higher tactical skills and in imposing a strong sense of
loyalty to the presidency and the secretary of defense. The military's sense of
discipline concerning political participation or association with the opposition,
sometimes imposed through extreme measures, accompanied that of civilian

political leaders, who developed an almost untouchable loyalty to and discipline toward a single party, the PNR and its successors.

Fourth, although political leadership, initially through military men in the presidency, imposed certain forms of behavior on the military, civilian political leadership has allowed within the military a certain degree of autonomy, even though the overall resources made available to the armed forces have declined considerably over time.

Fifth, civilian leadership has increased its dependence on the military for support, especially in internal political matters, as the legitimacy of established political institutions, including the presidency itself, has declined. Publicly, whether civilian reliance on the military has been greater or lesser, each president has lauded the military's loyalty and patriotism, not only conveying to the military the importance of its fealty but reinforcing that value in the eyes of the general public. Both the officer corps and the average Mexican have come to view subordination of authority to civilian leadership as natural and legitimate.

Notes

1. Edwin Lieuwen, *Mexican Militarism* (Albuquerque: University of New Mexico Press, 1968), 2.

2. For support for this contention and for other useful parallels between Díaz and the postrevolutionary regimes, see Lorenzo Meyer's "Continuidades e innovaciones en la vida política mexicana del siglo xx, el antiguo y el nuevo régimen," *Foro Internacional* 16 (July–September, 1975): 37–63.

3. Roderic A. Camp, "Civilian Supremacy in Mexico, the Case of a Post-Revolutionary Military," in *Military Intervention and Withdrawal*, ed. Constantine P. Danopoulous, (London: Routledge, 1991), 3.

4. Gordon C. Schloming, "Civil-Military Relations in Mexico, 1910–1940: A Case Study" (Ph.D. diss., Columbia University, 1974), 321.

5. Camp, "Civilian Supremacy in Mexico," 5.

6. See Roderic A. Camp, *The Making of a Government: Political Leaders in Modern Mexico* (Tucson: University of Arizona Press, 1984), 40ff.

7. Lieuwen, *Mexican Militarism*, 71.

8. Ibid., 69.

9. Schloming, "Civil-Military Relations in Mexico," 225.

10. Ibid., 232–233.

11. Ibid., 241.

12. Lieuwen, *Mexican Militarism*, 110.

13. Phyllis Greene Walker, "The Modern Mexican Military: Political Influence and Institutional Interests in the 1980s" (M.A. thesis, American University, 1987), 4.

14. Ibid., 257.

15. Schloming, "Civil-Military Relations in Mexico," 289.

16. Donald F. Harrison, "United States-Mexican Military Collaboration During World War II" (Ph.D. diss., Georgetown University, 1976), 206.

17. Schloming, "Civil-Military Relations in Mexico," 297–298.

18. José Luis Piñeyro, "The Mexican Army and the State: Historical and Political Perspective," *Revue Internationale de Sociologie* 14 (April–August, 1978): 120.

19. Schloming, "Civil-Military Relations in Mexico," 297.

20. Walker, "The Modern Mexican Military," 21.

21. Schloming, "Civil-Military Relations in Mexico," 340.

22. Piñeyro, "The Mexican Army and the State," 121.

23. Jorge Albeto Lozoya documented these doubts through personal interviews with surviving officers. See his *El ejército mexicano (1911–1965)* (Mexico: El Colegio de México, 1970), 60.

24. Luis Javier Garrido, based on an interview with General Alfonso Corona del Rosal, in his *El partido de la revolución institucionalizada, la formación del nuevo estado en México (1928–1945)* (Mexico: Siglo XXI, 1982), 243.

25. Lieuwen, *Mexican Militarism*, 124.

26. Lozoya, *El ejército mexicano*, 61.

27. Ibid., 61.

28. John Bailey and Leopoldo Gómez, "The PRI and Liberalization in Mexico" (Unpublished paper, Georgetown University, October 1989), 11.

29. Lozoya, *El ejército mexicano*, 59–60.

30. Garrido, *El partido de la revolución institucionalizada*, 245.

31. Schloming, "Civil-Military Relations in Mexico," 243–244, 336.

32. Lieuwen, *Mexican Militarism*, 135.

33. Lozoya, *El ejército mexicano*, 63.

34. Virginia Prewett, "The Mexican Army," *Foreign Affairs* 19 (April 1941): 615.

35. Piñeyro, "The Mexican Army and the State," 121.

36. Lozoya, *El ejército mexicano*, 64.

37. Lieuwen, *Mexican Militarism*, 143; Walker, "The Modern Mexican Military," 25. Although not negating Avila Camacho's determination to pare down the military's influence, budget reductions could be made while actually increasing military expenditures, given the sizeable military aid Mexico accepted from the United States during the war years, which coincided with Avila Camacho's administration.

38. During the war years Avila Camacho also restructured his chain of command. According to Donald F. Harrison, he established a presidential general staff to carry out his direct orders as commander in chief to the field, and he consolidated the military zones into three military regions, Pacific, Gulf, and Isthmus, comprising land, sea, and air forces, with the authority to coordinate their actions with civilian officials. Each commander reported directly to the president through his general staff, and each had the authority to act independently in case of invasion. "United States-Mexican Military Collaboration During World War II," 211.

39. Guillermo Boils, *Los militares y la política en México 1915–1974* (Mexico: El Caballito, 1975), 76.

40. Luis Rubio and Roberto Newell, *Mexico's Dilemma: The Political Origins of Economic Crisis* (Boulder, Colo.: Westview Press, 1984), 82–83.

41. Camp, "Civilian Supremacy in Mexico," 8–9.

42. See Roderic A. Camp, "Education and Political Recruitment in Mexico: The Alemán Generation," *Journal of Inter-American Studies and World Affairs* 18 (August 1976): 295–321, and *Mexico's Leaders, Their Education and Recruitment* (Tucson: University of Arizona Press, 1980), 107ff.; Peter H. Smith, *Labyrinths of Power: Political Recruitment in Twentieth Century Mexico* (Princeton: Princeton University Press, 1979), 250.

43. See Lozoya, *El ejército mexicano*, 69, and Piñeyro, "The Mexican Army and the State," 122, for their views on Alemán's contributions.

44. Boils, *Los militares y la política en México*, 79.

45. Alemán's extreme need for the military's loyalty may go beyond the fact that he was the first civilian president since 1929, a circumstance that would give pause to anyone in his shoes. In part his need to ensure the loyalty may have some basis in his own personal experiences. Because his father had revolted against the government, indeed, had been killed by the very government Alemán ultimately led, he would naturally harbor some suspicions against the military generally, and individual officers specifically. Moreover, the military had nearly killed Alemán himself in 1929, when his father was in revolt, and he had been saved only by a safe conduct from a general, his father's friend, who had remained with forces loyal to the government. Alemán expressed these feelings to me personally in an interview in Mexico City, October 27, 1976.

46. Lyle N. McAlister, *The Military in Latin American Socio-political Evolution: Four Case Studies* (Washington, D.C.: Center for Research in Social Systems, 1970), 208.

47. Walker, "The Modern Mexican Military," 28.

48. Ibid., 29.

49. José Luis Piñeyro has researched this particular election's impact on the military most thoroughly in "The Mexican Army and the State," 125–127.

50. Boils, *Los militares y la política en México*, 82.

51. Roderic A. Camp, *Intellectuals and the State in Twentieth Century Mexico* (Austin: University of Texas Press, 1985), 208–212. Among the more interesting attempts to seek advice was through the Secretariat of Foreign Relations, whose head, Antonio Carrillo Flores, requested reports of student-government relations from various ambassadors stationed abroad, including Octavio Paz, then ambassador to India.

52. Martin C. Needler, *Politics and Society in Mexico* (Albuquerque: University of New Mexico Press, 1971), 71.

53. Jorge Alberto Lozoya, *El ejército mexicano*, 3d ed. (Mexico: Colegio de México, 1984), 125.

54. Kenneth F. Johnson, *Mexican Democracy: A Critical View*, rev. ed. (New York: Praeger, 1978), 106.

55. Michael J. Dziedzic, "The Essence of Decision in a Hegemonic Regime: The Case of Mexico's Acquisition of a Supersonic Fighter" (Ph.D. diss., University of Texas, Austin, 1986), 113.

56. Michael J. Dziedzic, "Mexico's Converging Challenges: Problems, Prospects, and Implications" (manuscript, U.S. Air Force Academy, April 21, 1989), 9.

57. Steven J. Wager, "The Mexican Military, 1968–1978: A Decade of Change" (unpublished paper, Stanford University, June 1979), 52. Yet at no time, according to a former president, despite the rumors, was García Barragán disloyal to the president.

58. Williams S. Ackroyd, "Descendants of the Revolution: Civil-Military Relations in Mexico" (Ph.D. diss., University of Arizona, 1988), 254, based on interviews with Mexican officers in 1982–1983.

59. Personal interview, Mexico City, 1990. The officer surmised that many young cadets, given their popular social roots, would have been upset with the level of repression against students and bystanders, thus explaining their removal.

60. Edward J. Williams, "The Evolution of the Mexican Military and Its Implications for Civil-Military Relations," in *Mexico's Political Stability: the Next Five Years*, ed. Roderic A. Camp (Boulder, Colo.: Westview Press, 1986), 156.

61. Alden M. Cunningham, "Mexico's National Security in the 1980s–1990s," in *The Modern Mexican Military: A Reassessment*, ed. David Ronfeldt (La Jolla: Center for United States-Mexican Studies, University of California, San Diego, 1984), 169; Edward J. Williams, "The Mexican Military and Foreign Policy: The Evolution of Influence," in *The Modern Mexican Military: A Reassessment*, ed. David Ronfeldt (La Jolla: Center for United States-Mexican Studies, University of California, San Diego, 1984), 186.

62. Wager, "The Mexican Military," 25.

63. Piñeyro, "The Mexican Army and the State," 134.

64. Guillermo Boils, "Los militares en México (1965–1985)," *Revista Mexicana de Sociología* 47 (January–February, 1985); 175.

65. Piñeyro, "The Mexican Army and the State," 135.

66. Dziedzic, "Mexico's Converging Challenges," 8.

67. *Revista de Ejército y Fuerza Aérea*, October 1974, 79.

68. Williams, "The Mexican Military and Foreign Policy," 9.

69. Martin C. Needler, "A Critical Time for Mexico," *Current History*, February 1972, 83.

70. Judith Adler Hellman, *Mexico in Crisis*, 2d ed. (New York: Holmes and Meier, 1983), 207.

71. Smith, *Labyrinths of Power*, 295.

72. Dziedzic, "The Essence of Decision in a Hegemonic Regime," 323.

73. Gloria Fuentes, *El ejército mexicano* (Mexico: Grijalbo, 1983), 309.

74. As López Portillo argued, "The military never has put pressure on me as president or when I was budget secretary to expand their budget. It is always the president who takes the initiative, not the secretary of defense. . . . I initiated this myself for my own reasons." Personal

interview, Mexico City, 1991. Otto Granados Roldán, "Regreso a las armas?" in *El desafío mexicano*, ed. Francisco de Alba et al. (Mexico: Ediciones Océano, 1982), 127.

75. José Luis Piñeyro, "The Modernization of the Mexican Armed Forces," in *Democracy under Siege: New Military Power in Latin America*, ed. Augusto Varas, (Westport, Conn.: Greenwood Press, 1989), 115.

76. Christopher Dickey, "Modernization Could Lead Mexican Military into Politics," *Washington Post*, September 23, 1982, 29A.

77. Fuentes, *El ejército mexicano*, 306.

78. *Proceso*, November 24, 1980, 14.

79. Cunningham, "Mexico's National Security in the 1980s–1990s," 170.

80. Boils, "Los militares en México," 176.

81. Brian Latell, *Mexico at the Crossroads: The Many Crises of the Political System* (Stanford: Hoover Institution, 1986), 29.

82. Richard B. Craig, "Mexican Narcotics Traffic: Binational Security Implications," in *The Latin American Narcotics Trade and U.S. National Security*, ed. Donald J. Mabry (Westport, Conn.: Greenwood Press, 1989), 35.

83. *National Development Plan* (Mexico: Ministry of Planning and Budget, 1983), 19.

84. Caesar Sereseres, "The Mexican Military Looks South," in *The Modern Mexican Military: A Reassessment*, ed. David Ronfeldt (La Jolla: Center for U.S.-Mexican Studies, University of California, San Diego, 1984), 212.

85. Jorge G. Castañeda, "Mexico at the Brink," *Foreign Affairs* 64 (Winter 1985–1986): 293.

86. Instituto Mexicano de Estrategias, "Evolución de la política militar de 1917 a 1989" (Mexico, 1989), 4.

87. Larry Rohter, "Use of Troops a Cause of Concern in Mexico," *New York Times*, November 5, 1989, A8.

88. Lorenzo Meyer, "Ejército y Cananeas del futuro," *Excélsior*, September 6, 1989, 12A.

89. Fernando del Villar, a civilian, replaced him in 1990, when Jorge Carrillo Olea took over the leadership of the government's antidrug program.

90. *El Nacional*, June 2, 1990, 5.

3

A Mirror Image: Professionalism and Values

The military, depending on how analysts evaluate its potential influence, is a large or small unknown quantity in Mexico's political formula. Large or small, questions remain primarily because few Mexicans or outside observers have a feel for officer corps attitudes, values, and beliefs. In the same vein, little attempt has been made to understand how political leaders view the military, and how their attitudes correspond to those of military officers. Because both the political and military leaderships are themselves products of the larger culture, it is important to understand the attitudes of the average Mexican toward the military as an institution and toward its mission.

Understanding the values of the officer corps is important in the larger context of Mexican politics because of the historic role of the corps in the political arena. Despite the military's having stayed directly out of the political arena since 1946 (that is, not controlling presidential leadership), most observers are unsure of what its conduct would be in a future crisis. According to one of the country's leading intellectuals, Daniel Cosío Villegas, many Mexicans believe that the military, like other Latin American militaries, might be inclined to impose its own authoritarian order should it deem such action necessary. They have reached this conclusion because of their ignorance of its leadership, suggesting a wide social separation between political, intellectual, and economic circles and the officer corps.[1]

Professionalism

In general, organizational theorists consider the military to be a profession, just like law and medicine. A profession must have five attributes: (1) it must be based upon a body of systematic theory (for example, theories of warfare); (2) its members must possess differentiating expertise (for example, knowledge of military strategy and weaponry); (3) it has certain powers and privileges granted by society (for example, the military exercises autonomous control over its admission, training, and standards); (4) it must subscribe to a code of ethics (the most critical variable for the military because a code governs intra-

39

and intergroup relationships); and (5) its culture, including values, norms, and symbols, must convey its mystique and distinctions.[2]

The degree to which the officer corps obeys higher civilian political authority, and the nature and scope of its attitudes toward political participation are incorporated into the military's code of ethics and culture. It is sometimes forgotten, however, in stressing the insularity of the officer corps in Latin American countries, that professional perspectives and values are not developed in a vacuum. As Sam Sarkesian has noted, "Military systems, to remain legitimate, reflect society and, thus, professional ethics, attitudes, and beliefs developed from roots deep within the political-social system.[3]

Officer attitudes are an element worth assessing. Another is whether one set of values can be attributed to the organization as a whole, which raises the question of the Mexican military's unity. Because of the low level of general familiarity with the military, it is extremely unlikely that any differences within it would become known to most outsiders. McAlister believed that in the 1960s a younger group of officers, whom he called *pencillinos*, were highly critical of government ineffectiveness in correcting important social and economic failures, and resentful of having to perform associated political and quasi-military tasks.[4] In the 1970s a military zone commander expressed similar frustration, complaining the military was utilizing its few resources to help the masses in civic action programs while civilian politicians, with an excess of resources, constantly misapplied them.[5] It is quite possible that younger officers do not share the attitudes of generals toward military and governmental policies. The process of officer formation in Mexico, however, does have far-reaching effects on moderating such differences.

Despite some evidence of earlier discontent in the officer corps, and the distinct possibility of its persistence for similar or different reasons today, the general notion, based on limited information, is of

> a unified and well-disciplined corps. Indeed, while factional divisiveness has sometimes appeared publicly within three major institutions responsible for Mexico's historical political stability (namely, the PRI, the executive administration, and the Catholic Church), the one national institution in which elite integration has consistently appeared to persist is the military.[6]

The level of military integration is an unknown quantity; this has important internal implications and external repercussions. As an institution and a profession, the military has its own priorities. It is, as one author suggests, very much part of the social matrix, but like the Catholic church, remains apart from the rest of society.[7] This separateness, according to some analysts, has nevertheless not led to a caste tradition. Those who support this interpretation argue that revolutionary and popular origins, notwithstanding subsequent professionalization, have imprinted themselves on officer corps values.[8] That self-image has been conveyed by Mexico's military leadership. For example, General Felíx Galván told an interviewer that "the Mexican army will respect whatever political regime that comes to power with popular support [the key phrase is *with popular support*]. Beyond phrases and postures, the armed forces come from the people. We are people of the people [*Somos pueblo-pueblo*]."[9] More recently, General Leobardo Pérez Ruiz, in a public address before the president, explained that the army and air force have popular origins, and it is from them that they derive a natural inclination to help the population during civil emergencies.[10]

Whether or not the officer corps shares its social origins with the people will be empirically examined later. A linkage to the lower classes, or as more recent analysts suggest, to the middle classes, is questionable. In the first place, members of organizations that are highly institutionalized, with rigorous prescriptions for behavior, tend to comply with the rules, regardless of their social background, and more often than not they internalize the rules.[11] Interestingly, Peter Smith applied this characterization to Mexican politicians' behavior, but it could also apply to the military.[12] Frederick Nunn suggests another weakness of the presumed military-class linkage. He argues that Mexican officers, "once professionalized, are remarkably critical of the bourgeoisie. Allegations of middle-sector origins notwithstanding, officers do not look kindly on the sociocultural regalia of the bourgeois world—this despite aspiring to the same economic lifestyles."[13] Although it has been said that the officer corps and the civilian political elite have a similar origin, ideology, and political trajectory, absolutely no evidence exists to support that assertion.[14]

The issue of unity extends beyond ideology and class origin to the corporate strength of the military, the degree to which Mexican officers operate in their own interests or the interests of their institution. Theoretically, as will be seen, Mexican military literature promotes group sacrifice for country, but the way in which the professionalization process actually works, as distinct from its content, suggests an opposing interpretation. Michael Dziedzic argues that the presence of group cheating at the Escuela Superior de Guerra (ESG), evidence of which is presented in the section on education, is more compatible with turning out individuals willing to break rules in return for personal advancement, than to sacrifice for their country.[15] In other words, the professionalization process does not necessarily instill a sense of corporate solidarity.

Dziedzic, a U.S. military officer, is one of the most informed analysts of the Mexican military, particularly the air force. His reasoning is convincing. Of course, the Mexican military is not alone in its infractions of codes of conduct. According to a study carried out by four teams of investigators at U.S. army posts, "Dishonesty is across the board," "Integrity was a luxury that a junior officer could not afford in today's army and survive." Junior officers believed "that the barrier to their integrity was the senior officers' lack of integrity." Officers resigned because "many senior officers, particularly lieutenant colonels and colonels in command positions were forced to abandon their scruples and ignore the precepts of duty and honor; and if necessary to lie and cheat in order to remain successful and competitive."[16] Incidents of small-group cheating at West Point have also been well documented. Such perceptions of the army appeared to be widespread at the time of the study, but do not seem to have been translated into a belief that the army had lost its sense of professionalism and corporate responsibility.

A circumstance that might help to explain professional dishonesty is the importance of self-interest and institutional integrity in the population as a whole. In other words, is such behavior tolerated or encouraged in civilian institutions, or in the nonmilitary culture? Is the environment of most civilians different from that of junior officers? The larger social context may exert far more influence on behavior than any other condition or experience.

Officer Values

Whatever the source of officer values, what governs officers' behavior, and especially their relationship to civilian authorities, obviously influences civil-military relations. Socialization becomes a key variable, indeed one of the hypotheses offered in the introduction, in explaining civilian supremacy. Perhaps most important in this respect are military attitudes toward discipline and loyalty. From an institutional point of view, the idea that the army should be changed from a vehicle for advancing individuals' political aims into a nonpolitical institution whose sole task would be to defend against internal and external threats stemmed from General Joaquín Amaro's modernizing mission in the 1920s. He sought, as Edwin Lieuwen suggests, to instill a new sense of discipline and of obedience to civil authority among younger officers.[17] Officers who increasingly achieved top rank in the military had been trained at the Escuela Superior de Guerra (ESG). The founding principles of the ESG, established under Amaro's supervision, include a description of the officer's respect for authority. Article 14 states:

> The professors will be particularly exacting with their students in the practice and exercise of all the habits that contribute to the development of an affection for the army and an enhancement of military spirit; any tendency to depreciate military studies or *put down the discipline and prestige of the army will be severely reprimanded* [italics added].[18]

The Heroico Colegio Militar (HCM) warns cadets that it expects similar discipline and loyalty. Citing the 1965 HCM admissions pamphlet, Lyle McAlister asserted that the cadet from admission until graduation as an officer of the Mexican army, from reveille to taps, lives in an environment in which his activities have been carefully planned to develop the personal qualities the institution wants to instill, particularly loyalty.[19] According to an officer who attended the HCM during that period, its fundamental goal was unquestioning subordination to authority: "The Heroico Colegio Militar is essentially a brainwashing school. Its most important goal is to produce unthinking officers who will obey authority; really robots I would say."[20] Fifteen years later the 1980 admissions pamphlet emphasized even more strongly that "discipline is the norm

to which the military must subject its conduct; it has as its foundation obedience . . . and the exact completion of those duties prescribed by military laws
and relations."[21]

In the discussion on educational socialization in this book, it will be
argued, on the basis of firsthand reports from U.S. officers in the Mexican
training program, that the officer corps, even by U.S. standards, is subject to
an extreme form of military discipline and authority. In the Mexican context,
military discipline means unquestioning, unyielding deference and obedience
to superiors. No order is questioned and no action is taken independently of a
superior.[22] The extent to which this attitude is imbued, both as a procedural
philosophy and general value, is illustrated by two recent examples.

One consequence of this exaggerated discipline is the centralization of
authority in the hands of a few superior officers. During General Félix
Galván's tenure as secretary of defense (1976–1982), the government allowed
the U.S. Air Force to fly over Mexican territory with permission, which only
General Galván could grant. Somewhat later the subsecretary of defense and
the chief of staff were allowed to authorize search-and-rescue missions. A
lower-ranking officer was actually jailed for three days because he authorized
an overflight without Galván's permission. According to Dziedzic's sources,
Galván even approved leave requests for captains; no lower officer would dare
to do so.[23] One officer explained,

> I remember once that the subsecretary of defense told me that I had a problem. I
> asked the general what my problem was. He said that "I was thinking too much,
> and that in this army we don't think." Really, in this country, the secretary of
> defense is like a small god in terms of how he can send someone here or send
> someone there, or change their assignment, without any appeal whatsoever."[24]

The procedural characteristics of internal military decision making not
only severely limit individual officer initiative but reinforce obedience to higher
authority. Officers who openly take issue with a decision of a superior are
blackballed for having an "attitude" problem. Such treatment can dog their
entire careers, and they either resign or accept the prospect of a severely limited
career.[25] Some Mexican officers believe "the right attitude" is essential to
promotion. One officer stated,

> Look, I was an aide to President ——— for many years. I had contacts with
> many important officers, and the president. But without the kind of attitude
> that the military hierarchy wishes to see, you will never rise up the promotion
> ladder, even if you are well thought of by an incumbent president. I have been in
> the service for twenty-five years and look at my present rank. I am an example
> of a nonconformist, and the harsh consequences that produces within the
> military in Mexico.[26]

The overall concept of discipline inevitably becomes paramount to a general's
own value systems. Anyone surviving and successfully operating in such an

environment for some thirty years cannot help but absorb unswerving discipline into his own beliefs.

Mexican officers expect such discipline not only in their peers and subordinates but in the populace. General Juan de Dios Calleros Aviña, a two-time zone commander and director of the national military service program under President Salinas, told a reporter that discipline is born in the home, is affirmed in the classroom, and should become a habit of the ordinary citizen, thus producing the most dignified, strongest, and progressive individuals and peoples.[27]

The importance of discipline in the cultural worlds of civilians and military officers has been noted by a leading Mexican intellectual. Of the many changes that have occurred in his country during the past two decades, he believes that one of the most signal is the extraordinary decline in respect for civilian authorities among civilians. He describes its impact in this way:

> But in the military, respect for authority remains very strong and traditional. For example, let's take the use of language as an illustration of this in civilian culture. The use of *usted* and *tu* has changed tremendously during this period. The use of these two forms of address is part of the culture of hierarchy in Mexico. The elimination of the *usted* and the use of the familiar form with people who are recent acquaintances is a change in the hierarchical structure within the civilian community. Let's take a comparison between the police and the military. The police are much more influenced by the civilian world and are also much more cynical about the level of corruption among their peers and their leaders. The police would believe anything is possible of one of their police chiefs. But the military, when confronted with this kind of information, reacts much more differently than the police because it does not have this cynical bias.[28]

It may be, as Morris Janowitz suggests, that outmoded forms of discipline are sometimes an expression of ideological beliefs among various officers, attitudes that are generally conservative.[29]

Intense discipline and loyalty are inextricably intertwined in the military. Acceptance of this level of discipline relies on absolute loyalty to the institution, and to superior officers who represent the institution's decisions. The loyalty of high-ranking officers to civilian authorities reinforces military loyalty to civilian leaders. This sense of loyalty to national political institutions has been repeatedly reinforced in the military textbooks and academies since the modernization program began in the early 1930s. The 1952 edition of the text on military morale and patriotism emphasized that it was the firm duty of the army to support the government, and above all, the soldier must never forget the loyalty he owes to national institutions.[30] Twenty-five years later, when General Cuenca Díaz dedicated the new HCM installations, he remarked that "the army is disciplined, it is loyal."[31]

The Mexican military is not alone in its demand for loyalty. Although all political systems have their version of the "team player," it can be argued that the Mexican political system, under the dominance of a single party and leadership group for many decades, encouraged a stronger sense of institutional loyalty than is found in many competitive political systems. Until very recently, only rarely would a politician within the Mexican system criticize it or its leadership publicly.[32] Generalized silence was not always the norm. Political arguments were intense. In fact, in the 1920s many politicians and intellectual figures were armed. One prominent federal deputy of that time, Praxedis Balboa, customarily wore a pistol to the lower chamber, and said he felt naked when he finally removed it at the end of the decade.[33] The subsequent self-imposed discipline of Mexican politicians is very likely to have impressed the officer corps, just as General Calleros Aviña alluded to societal discipline as an admirable quality. It is fair to suggest that the most influential element in retaining military loyalty is the officer's belief in the civilian leadership's ability to maintain order. As long as the government demonstrates that ability, and retains at least limited popular respect, the military will support civil authority.[34]

When an officer doubts civilian ability, as in certain crisis situations, and does so publicly, it leads to trouble. One of the most notable recent cases of an officer's openly questioning civilian competence, and by implication the army's loyalty, took place during the confrontation between the army and Lucio Cabañas's guerrillas in the 1970s. The officer in charge, Salvador Rangel Medina, told the press after he had been criticized repeatedly for not capturing Cabañas, that he would be happy to do just that as soon as he received a government order to that effect. The government immediately removed him from his post.[35] Not only the commander but many junior officers serving in the campaign against Cabañas questioned government policy, especially peasant repression. According to one source who fought the guerrillas, higher authorities were so disturbed by the officers' reactions that they ordered all of them to different assignments following their departure from Guerrero. The high command hoped to reduce or eliminate the potential for cohesion among a group of disillusioned officers.[36]

The military's attitude toward discipline impacts on its perception of order and societal behavior. "The military ethic emphasizes the permanence of irrationality, weakness, and evil in human nature. It stresses the supremacy of society over the individual and the importance of order, hierarchy, and division of function."[37] Acceptance of the importance of discipline, loyalty, and order to a degree typically not encountered in society as a whole is enhanced by a self-selection process as officers move up the ladder in rank. For example, most professional officers in the U.S. armed forces, those who enrolled in an academy with the intention of making the army a career, come from family backgrounds in which the father is conservative. In a survey of U.S. air force cadets only 2 percent perceived their fathers as liberal, and we learn that larger numbers of liberal than conservative cadets drop out.[38] Officers who remain in the services continue to characterize themselves largely as conservative; in another study nearly half describe their ideologies as conservative; a third are in the middle of the spectrum; and only 15 percent label their views liberal.[39] Other studies reveal that twice as many liberals resign their commissions as remain, whereas the majority of conservatives stay on active duty.[40] Thus, the higher one rises in the rank structure, proportionately, the more likely one is to be ideologically conservative.[41]

In the 1960s and 1970s, the attitudes of the Mexican officer corps toward discipline and order may also have been affected by family background. Unfortunately, we have no empirical data on how Mexican officers classify themselves or their parents' political views. An interesting pattern in the backgrounds of the most influential generals, which sheds some light on parental ideological influence and conservatism, was that junior officers promoted from enlisted ranks, "mustangs," reach the rank of general in disproportionate numbers, as will be seen from an analysis of their origins. I have argued that the reason is that they, more than any group of officers, experienced an extreme superior-subordinate relationship as enlisted soldiers. The usual thinking in regard to Mexican lower socioeconomic groups, the overwhelming origin of mustangs, is that within them family structure is hierarchical, extremely authoritarian, and socially conservative, suggesting that the enlisted officer may be more likely to possess the traditional military values, as does the U.S. conservative officer, and to be a more well-adjusted and career-oriented military professional.[42]

The average Mexican officer thinks of society in terms of order or stability, and an orderly society is the product of discipline and respect for authority. According to an officer interviewed by Ackroyd, "Authority is first, since order cannot exist if there is no authority which sustains and imposes it."[43] Ackroyd interpreted this and other statements to suggest that the Mexican officer corps may be tolerant of many conditions but can neither accept nor understand disorder. General Salvador Revueltas Olvera, former zone commander of Monterrey and senior member of the National Defense Committee of the 1988–1991 legislature, declared that the sole mission of the Mexican army is *to avoid instability* and bloodshed.[44]

Some scholars see a likelihood of political and social disintegration stemming from a class struggle. It is their view that the armed forces' size and political importance is directly correlated with degree of social integration.[45] The potential for a class uprising of some sort has made some analysts interested in the military's attitude toward Marxism and Mexican communists. Frederick Nunn, for example, believes that the Mexican army "is hostile to Marxism, especially to the Communist party, which is simply beyond the ideological pale of the century's paradigm. Officer recruitment still avails the corps of anti-Marxist, lower-middle-sector, upwardly aspirational material at all ranks."[46] Some Mexican officers surely fit his description. One such officer explained that communism implied the introduction of foreign ideas into Mexico, ideas that as far as he was concerned, had no place in the country. He felt it was necessary to get into the HCM, where he could continue his education and play a part "in helping to stamp out communism in Mexico."[47] Other scholars believe the military's anticommunism is so virulent that it influences Mexican foreign policy decision making, especially vis-à-vis Cuba, counteracting the leftist posturing common to civilian foreign policy rhetoric.[48]

Attitudes toward Political Involvement

The extent of the military's anti-Marxist posturing is much less important than its view of its role in relation to civilian authorities. The political events of 1987 and 1988 make it clear that splits in the civilian leadership, although coming from the left, have been engineered not by Marxists—even if many have latched onto the initial successes of Cuauhtémoc Cardenas's splinter movement—but by persons within the traditional, populist leadership. Also, as will be demonstrated later, many of the Mexican military, officers and enlisted alike, have personally voted for opposition parties of the Left and the Right, in spite of Marxist associations with the Mexican Left.

Of relevance here is the inclination of the officer corps to intervene militarily in civilian matters. In a society like that of the United States, where civilian political supremacy is accepted as the norm among citizens and political and military leaders, the military is not required to assure its continued loyalty to the same degree as occurs in Mexico.[49]

> Whereas other countries have also found political training useful for purposes of civilian control of the military and national integration, traditional civil-military relations in the United States preclude expanding into these roles. The deeply ingrained acceptance of civilian control by professional soldiers in the United States eliminates the need, in the absence of revolutionary circumstances, to use political training as a means of control.[50]

For example, throughout the 1960s the *Revista de Ejército y Fuerza Aérea* repeatedly featured the motto "Militar si, militarista nunca."

Lyle McAlister has gone so far as to argue that the Mexican army is an impartial institution, and as such, does not express opinions on political matters but only complies with the dispositions of the government, offering guarantees to all political parties and to all the citizenry.[51] Theoretically this statement is correct, and more important, it is the image the military conveys to its own future leaders, and to outside observers. To illustrate, General Alfonso Corona del Rosal, who for many years served as a significant bridge between the civilian and military leaderships, wrote in August 1982, assessing the potential for a military coup d'état:

> I can say that that possibility has not entered in the mind of any military man, whatever his rank or position. I know numerous companions of various ranks, I have shared a military life with many of them during long years. We treat each other with friendship, confidence and frankness; consequently, I am in the position of affirming that none of them have ever expressed to me that desire, nor much less intention.[52]

Corona del Rosal, of course, was making a personal statement.

In 1983, at the beginning of the de la Madrid administration, one of Mexico's leading generals, then chief of staff, used the Army Day official ceremony to criticize those within the military who believed it should assume a greater role in political decision making. According to General Vinicio Santoyo Fería, "In the army there is no place for anyone giving advice on national decisions because we are not and have no wish to be judges." [53] This strong statement, made in a public forum, can be interpreted two ways, both of which are accurate. One, the statement reinforces and repeats the military's official stance for at least the past four decades; it praises the status quo. Two, it can be deduced from the statement itself and the occasion that the leadership, military and civilian alike, sensed an undercurrent of opinion within the officer corps favoring a more activist military posture in political affairs.

To moderate the desire of the officer corps for an active political role and to inculcate disinterest in politics, the military uses its training programs and official journals to socialize officers to a position subordinate to civilian authority. Attempts to depoliticize the military through such means also affect officer interest regarding external political and social matters. In the United States most officers prefer to focus on social problems within the military itself and not on the broader range of social issues outside the military. [54] In fact, a comparative study of top officers and businessmen in the United States revealed that the former do not seem to be as interested in politics as the latter. [55] According to one analysis of the *Revista de Ejército y Fuerza Aérea*, only 2 percent of its articles had some political content; about 16 percent concentrated on the theme of loyalty to the nation and its institutions. [56] This emphasis can be altered in much the same way that a president concerned about political stability can alter the pattern of promotions among high-ranking officers. Boils reported a change in political and social content from 2 to 18 percent in the same magazine from 1968—the date of the student massacre in the Tlatelolco Plaza—to 1973. [57] By the mid-1970s, some analysts were detecting changes in the military's conceptualization of its political role. They see recent officer education and training as preparation for broader activities. Enhanced administrative skills made possible by development of the National Defense College in the early 1980s can lead to greater participation in the formulation of national security and development policies. [58]

The extent of the military's decision-making role will be analyzed later; here we are looking at the notion that the military's conceptualization of national security has changed. According to Luis Herrera, one of the few students of Mexico's national security policy, national security has meant defense of sovereignty. Sovereignty usually is thought of in terms of territorial integrity, but it also includes the independence to determine national priorities and objectives. In 1983, with announcement of the National Development Plan, national security gained another dimension when it was placed in the context of internal and international politics. Thereafter the military began to rethink its national security functions. [59]

The reconceptualization of national security has taken the military in two directions. First, into the foreign policy realm. As Mexico began to act as a regional broker between the United States and Nicaragua, and to express its views on U.S. policies in Central America and the Caribbean, the military, both materially and politically, appeared to demonstrate increasing interest in this external focus. Some viewed the military as prone to rising expectations.[60]

The national government's international forays could indirectly increase the scope of the military in political affairs. Changes in its conception of internal security are likely to produce quicker and deeper consequences for civil-military relations than heretofore. The importance of internal security to national security is given high visibility in the revised Organic Law of the Mexican Army and Air Force, Article 1, Section 2.[61] The emphasis is the consequence of the paradoxical contradiction between what the military has traditionally concentrated upon in its training programs and increasingly since the 1970s tasks civilian leaders have requested it to perform. For example, members of recent classes at the ESG believe their enemy is internal, not external: when they travel outside Mexico City, they are armed, and they accept election duty as the norm.[62] Civilian leadership runs two risks in ordering the military to perform tasks normally thought to be within the purview of the police or other civil authorities. First, "as officers trained primarily for military pursuits, they have been forced into the political task of containing extremist dissidence on a growing scale. The conflict between their apolitical training and their increasingly political role causes contradictions and doubts in the minds of the younger generations of officers."[63] Second, when the government calls upon the army to deal with civil disputes, for example, in connection with electoral fraud, it encourages the view of a politicized army.[64] If the populace comes to accept such an army, the officer corps, a product of that very populace, will also begin to be of that mind.

Civilian Views of the Military

The military's self-conceptualization of its role and the extent to which it might change in relation to its political activity are influenced by general societal norms, at both the popular and elite levels. In the long run, societal attitudes are most important because they provide the greatest reinforcement for the military ethos, particularly regarding its relationship to civil authority. According to Stephen Wesbrook, professional corporateness depends on a discernible professional ethos, yet in the United States, social and political ideologies conflict with the professional military's ideology. "The military ideology demands authority, honor, and obedience; the political ideology consensus, expediency, and compromise. . . . Moreover, the liberal ideology challenges the military profession directly by regarding professional soldiers as a threat to liberty, democracy, and economic prosperity."[65] Mexico, on the other hand, has not enjoyed a historical tradition conducive to these conflicting ideologies except in recent years.

I argue societal attitudes are the fundamental determinant of civil-military relations specifically and values engendered among the officer corps generally, but it is striking how little testing of this relationship has been reported in the Latin American military literature. The tendency is to examine the military isolated from its societal matrix. I suggested above that the officer corps is relatively self-selecting ideologically compared with society as a whole, but it is society that legitimizes the military through acceptance of its purpose and perception that social norms are closely linked to the military's professional ethics and behavior.[66]

Military Prestige in Civilian Eyes

Generally, how do Mexicans perceive the military? More particularly, how does the public view the military as an institution? How do young Mexicans view the military as a career? And how does the man in the street view the military as a component of society? In the last three decades or so of the nineteenth century the military did not conjure up a positive image in the minds of civilian leaders. According to one historian, "army" for them was synonymous with crime, venality, violence, and corruption.[67] As the army gradually left off overt political activities after 1950, becoming more insular, it has gained in anonymity, which can often lead to a positive or neutral image. On the other hand, lessened visibility means it cannot rally societal support.[68] John J. Johnson, who interviewed working- and middle-class Mexicans in the 1960s, found

> neither the man in the office nor the man in the street ordinarily know how many men are in uniform or even whether the military establishment is being reduced or expanded. The average person of some education, wealth, and status is befuddled when he is asked what share of national income goes to the armed forces.[69]

The situation Johnson described remains unchanged. Even prominent persons and intellectuals are woefully ignorant concerning the military and readily admit it.[70] Military funding and the military role are in large measure not part of the public discourse.

Coming into the 1980s, the military's institutional image in certain respects was quite favorable, especially compared with the images of civilian institutions. For example, when Mexicans were asked in a national poll to identify individuals most deserving of respect, they chose parents, teachers, and priests, thus indirectly praising family, school, and the church. The persons least deserving of respect were political bosses, politicians, military men, and bankers.[71] However, when Mexicans were asked to rank institutions, as distinct from individuals or occupations, the military scored more positively than all political organizations. Again, schools and the church were at the top of the list, well above other institutions, but strongly entrenched in the middle of the ranking, along with the legal system, was the military; 48 percent of the respondents expressed confidence in it. By comparison, legislators and bureaucrats received the confidence of only 25 percent or so.[72] A survey of younger Americans yielded a pattern similar to that obtaining in Mexico: the military ranked fourth, after colleges, churches, and the media but well above political institutions in levels of respect.[73] Expressed differently, Mexicans gave the military high marks for integrity. When asked in 1985 who would lie to the public, 59 percent of a survey's respondents named politicians; 26 percent, public officials, and 2 percent, the military.[74] Some observers believe the military had strengthened its institutional image in the early 1980s by its rescue operations during the El Chichón volcanic eruption and its campaign against drug traffickers.[75]

The military as a career and, more important, its prestige as an occupation indirectly affect how the institution is perceived compared with other organizations. The Mexican military has been a magnet for certain working-class groups for much of the period under study. The earliest survey of occupational preferences, conducted two years after Alemán entered the presidency, found that lower-income and lower-middle-income groups found business, as an owner or manager, and military careers the most attractive.[76] Becoming an officer would appeal to Mexicans from lower-income groups for two reasons. First, an officer is considered a professional, and professional status in a socially conscious society is important to upwardly mobile persons. Second, the military subsidizes higher education through a master's degree, enables career success through regularized promotions and provides exceptional job security, an especially rare attribute in a developing economy.[77] Similarly, in the United States young Americans enter the military for education benefits and security.[78]

Middle- and upper-middle-class Mexicans see a military career in an entirely different light. Johnson asserted that in the 1960s civilian leaders exhibited considerable prejudice against the military. He suggested that they considered military officers as "definite inferiors" who were socially unacceptable and with whom social contact ordinarily should be limited to official functions.[79] When asked whether they had thought of the military as a career, most had never so regarded it, believing it low in status and offering few economic rewards compared with other available occupations.[80] U.S. youth have similar reactions, ranking it lowest among their choices.[81] A 1982 survey of Mexican journalists, most of whom worked for centrist and right-of-center papers, asked whether they wanted their sons to pursue a military career. They replied in the negative, giving as reasons the military's suppression of the people, its corruption, and its lack of opportunity for advancement.[82] Nor do politicians encourage their sons to follow military careers. The names of sons of successful politicians cannot be found in the graduation lists of the HCM.[83] In contrast, children of successful officers can be found pursuing national political careers, including as members of President Salinas's cabinet. Interviews with prominent Mexicans, most of whom from middle-class backgrounds, affirm these findings. Their parents never encouraged them to consider the military as an option, and none of them did. In the case of one officer, the son of a high-ranking zone commander, his own father discouraged him from a military career, hoping he would obtain a university degree instead.[84]

For whatever reason, depending on class background, the educated Mexican sees the military officer as the social inferior of the civilian politician. As

Ackroyd suggests, one possible consequence of this inequality is the officer's tendency to defer to the socially superior civilian politician.[85] One source recalled meeting with a group of politicians in the 1960s. Leaving the gathering, one of the officers remarked that he and his fellows "only needed napkins on their arms" to complete their treatment as waiters.[86] This comment suggests that the officer believed they had been treated condescendingly. Generalized, such dealings reinforce the officers' perception that they are not thought of as professional equals. Psychologically, this puts them at a disadvantage.

A likely response is resentment, displayed individually or collectively. One officer recalled a policeman's stopping him on his way to work in Mexico City for a traffic violation, a pretext to exact a bribe. When informed that he was a lieutenant in the military, the policeman persisted. The officer pulled out his sidearm, ordered the policeman to get into the automobile, and took him to defense headquarters as a lesson "not to fool around with the military."[87] Such behavior, born of resentment, was intended to demonstrate to a civilian that the officer and his peers were to be accorded respect and deference.

A more telling incident, suggestive of collective resentment, occurred late at night on a major boulevard of the capital. To allow a column of military vehicles on maneuvers to proceed in orderly formation, military police temporarily halted traffic, among which were several cars from the Government Secretariat. Agents in these cars peremptorily told the guards to get out of the way. They refused and an altercation between the civilian agents and the commanding officer ensued. It reached a point where the soldiers released the safeties on their guns and snapped the bolts home.[88] This occasion does not represent simply machismo but different opinions on respective positions of authority. Such resentments, in a different arena, could lead to possible policy conflicts.

Citizen attitudes toward the military and its role in society are helpful to civilian political elites, who alone cannot impose hegemony over the military unless the citizenry is strongly supportive. As I have pointed out, the Mexican military has accepted a fairly narrow compass of responsibility up to the present. That society agrees with that limited role can be measured by the military's size and financial support compared to the militaries of other countries. For example, in the mid-1970s, only .13 percent of the total Mexican population was in the military, contrasted with 1.32 percent in the United States, and approximately .6 percent in most Latin American countries. In terms of expenditures, Mexico's military received .86 percent of GNP; that of the United States, nearly 7 percent; and most Latin American militaries, 2 to 3 percent.[89]

Civilian leaders historically have used the budget as a means to limit the military's size and political influence. In recent years civilian attitudes toward expanding military prestige have fluctuated. A case in point was President Miguel de la Madrid's decision not to allow the army to implement fully its DN-III (E) emergency plan in response to the September 19–20, 1985, earthquakes, even though the carefully devised scheme had worked well in other disasters, such as the 1982 El Chichón volcano eruption in Chiapas. Reportedly, the head of the Federal District Department, Ramón Aguirre Velázquez, persuaded the president to limit the role of the armed forces in a tragedy that consumed 20,000 lives lest an effective performance whet their appetite for greater political involvement.[90]

Although civilian leaders may have been concerned about enhancing the military's civic-action image and thereby reducing their own visible role in earthquake relief, they expanded the military's share of the antidrug effort. Shortly after Salinas became president, he increased the military's internal security work, which served to elevate its visibility and further politicize its functions. The president's repeated use of military units to carry out executive political decisions has attracted some criticism, but only from Mexico's most outspoken commentators. Very few elites comment publicly on the armed forces, especially depreciatively. Cartoonists, who usually take on almost any topic, are strangely silent about the military. Still, a leading intellectual, Lorenzo Meyer, raised a cautionary hand: "The health of the military and all of society requires that we be very careful with this peculiar political instrument . . . the armed forces."[91] In his opinion, few Mexicans believe soldiers should be closing industrial plants or imposing electoral results.

Citizen Views of Military Intervention

How do Mexicans view the military? A recent analysis argues that a strong antimilitary bias on the part of the general public—a characteristic distinguishing Mexico's political culture from that of many Latin American and Third World countries—has likely served to inhibit greater military participation in the political arena.[92] This and other assessments of public attitudes are largely informal and speculative, but two recent public opinion polls offer some hard evidence.

An April 1983 national survey of 7,051 Mexicans from fifteen occupational groups and thirty-two states (with a margin of error of less than 2 percent) discovered that 26 percent of the respondents thought the military should participate in government; 24 percent thought it should sometimes participate; and 50 percent thought it should never participate.[93] In 1987 the same question in a national poll of 9,028 Mexicans elicited these responses: 22 percent thought the military should participate in government; 16 percent, sometimes; and 62 percent, never, a fairly strong decline in support.[94] Class differences were apparent. It might be supposed that the wealthy would strongly favor military protection of private property in times of political instability, but they were the cohort most opposed to it both in 1983 and 1987. The other group definitely against military participation in government was the college-educated. The survey results correspond with the speculations cited above.

Strong sentiment against military involvement in the political arena, especially in the 1987 poll, is encouraging for continued limitation of the military's political activities. Nevertheless, between 40 and 50 percent of Mexicans in the past decade believed the military should have some political role; this sizeable body of public opinion might be more receptive to increased military participation. Interestingly, it is the least-educated, those with only a primary education, who take this stance, the same Mexicans who see the military as a potential career in a much more favorable light. It is quite possible that because the military enables opportunities for upward social mobility, they perceive military leaders as sharing their goals and concerns. Older Mexicans are also much more favorably inclined toward military involvement in government. Not surprisingly, Mexicans who have a positive image of the police, who are generally unrespected in Mexico, and those who care about security as a social issue lean more strongly in that direction.

The Mexicans who most endorse the present system are those more strongly supportive of military involvement. A dichotomy between occupation groups appears between peasants and laborers on one hand, ironically the most positive toward military intervention, and intellectuals, government officials, and private-sector management on the other, the most opposed. These breakdowns suggest how successful the military has been in sustaining its image as an institution of the masses. True, peasants had the most "don't know" responses, indicative of the possibility that their minds could change quickly if future personal experience were negative. The responses also suggest that the political leaders are very satisfied with the civil-military balance as it is now constituted. The satisfaction is likely to remain in the short term because graduates of the National University and National Polytechnic Institute, institutions producing the largest number of political leaders, are the most strongly opposed to expanded military involvement.

Some interesting political values affect Mexican responses to military participation in government. If attitudes toward bringing the Catholic church back into politics are taken into account, the results are significant. Remembering that the other key corporate institution, the Catholic church, has a long history of intervention in Mexico and the region, one could expect the same Mexicans to not differentiate the church's and military's corporate functions from fuzzier political ones. Of those strongly in favor of Church involvement, an overwhelming percentage favored military participation. However, the former group is a tiny percentage of the population. On the other hand, those most strongly opposed to Church involvement are equally opposed to military participation, which suggests that they see it as a much broader, sophisticated issue in governance.

It is also interesting that Mexicans were much more definite about the Church's than the military's staying out of politics. The comparison is important because it suggests the impact of educational socialization and experience. The much higher number of persons opposed to an expanded Church role is not surprising because several civil wars were fought over the issue. But more important, the 1917 Constitution incorporates numerous restrictions on the Church, political and economic, and denies it legal status. The Church is the only institution so treated; no comparable provisions constrain the military despite historical efforts to remove it from politics. The difference between how the two institutions are handled constitutionally and, I argue, societally, are conveyed by the fact that the Constitution says that a legislator cannot be a minister of a religious cult but can be a member of the armed forces. (Article 55, Section VI). The average Mexican's attitudes toward the military have been derived from experience, and have entered the value system over time.[95]

Many observers have made numerous assertions about alliances between certain institutions and Mexican opposition parties, the most common concerns an alliance between the National Action Party (PAN), the opposition party of the ideological Right, and the Catholic church. Much less clear, but occasionally implied, is that the potential for an alliance obtains between the Right and the military, and hence potential linkage with PAN. Poll data do not support such assertions. Basically, no difference on the issue of military intervention exists among PRI or PAN sympathizers, or party members. In fact, negative responses were higher among PAN members in 1987 than among PRI members. Interestingly, differences occur among leftist party members. In 1983 members of the Unified Mexican Socialist Party were strongly opposed to military involvement, as were members of the Revolutionary Workers Party (PRT). Four years later, members of the PRT actually were more favorably inclined toward a military political role than the average Mexican; the more active the party sympathizer or member, the more in favor of military involvement. An explanation might be twofold. First, leftist parties draw disproportionately from lower-income groups, the same groups supporting military political involvement more strongly. Second, although the poll was taken before the 1988 elections, more sophisticated leftist party members may have believed that the military might be more receptive to their interests, and more neutral in the electoral process, than the government and PRI leaders, who constantly engaged in and overlooked fraud.

Two other phenomena can have bearing on the self-conceptualization by the officer corps of its role and other professional values. A small number of civilians can have a direct influence on the military through involvement with the officer corps or through other means. In the history of the United States armed forces, the noncareer officer has lessened the potential for a caste mentality and "democratized" officer corps values. Mexico, of course, does not recruit officers outside the military academies. Like the United States, it does occasionally give direct commissions to individuals whose special expertise it requires. For example, Article 152 of the Organic Law states that "professional or technical personnel required on active duty whose specialties do not exist in schools or military formation courses should be recruited from graduates of civilian schools and universities."[96] In the navy, at least, individuals offered direct commissions are not indoctrinated in a special or regular training course but are assigned to units where they receive on-the-job professionalization.[97] Although a number of military lawyers have received law degrees from the National University, they pursued the degrees *after* completing their training at the HCM. Among the generals in our sample, there is only one with a direct commission. Enrique Lendo Pérez, who directed the Army, Navy, Air Force Bank from 1982 to 1988, earned several professional degrees from the National University and followed a professional career in the public sector until the Secretariat of National Defense recruited him as assistant director of the bank in 1981.[98]

The number of civilian professionals incorporated as officers are so few that their potential capacity to introduce civilian values into the value system of the officer corps is negligible. A more important vehicle for conveying civilian values is the president, especially because military subordination to him as the supreme commander is drilled into the junior officers. Presidents use public occasions to lavish encomiums upon the military as a loyal and patriotic institution, thereby reinforcing its self-conception. Franklin Margiotta found that many of the officers he interviewed were positive about presidential concern for their status; indeed, he stated that many officers expressed deep personal respect, at times approaching reverence, for individual presidents. "Presidential concern for military status seems to have had a salutary effect upon civil-military relations in Mexico and may have helped insure political stability,"[99] a hypothesis introduced earlier. Unlike many Latin American leaders, however, Mexican presidents have not encouraged or permitted visible displays of military power. Civilian leaders and most Mexicans still have an ingrained antipathy toward such displays.[100]

The other source of potential influence on officer corps values is external. The proximity of Mexico to the United States, despite historical conflicts even as recently as the Mexican Revolution, places the U.S. military in a position to have an effect through military assistance and training programs. A foreign country can influence a military's professionalization and value system in those and several other ways. In many Latin American countries, foreign military missions were an essential ingredient in bringing about self-definition and evolution.[101]

Great care should be taken in transferring the experience of South American militaries to that of Mexico's in the twentieth century. As Frederick Nunn suggests, the Mexican military's professionalization is unique. For example, unlike Brazil's, Mexico's professionalization was internally generated and focused, not a product of Europe or the United States.[102] Soon after the Revolution General Amaro sent his brightest lieutenants and captains to military academies in France, Spain, Italy, and the United States, as well as assigning them to embassies. On their return, as the chapter on education demonstrates, they planned and led a professional program without direct foreign assistance. During World War II, however, Mexico accepted Lend Lease credits of some $39 million for training scholarships, defense factories, and weaponry.[103]

The general literature on the Mexican military conveys the notion that the military itself has taken the initiative to insure an autonomous position vis-à-vis the U.S. military despite fairly friendly cooperation during World War II.[104] Edward Williams, for example, writes that the military has been fastidious in maintaining independence from its counterpart to the north, and across the board has had relatively little intercourse. He also cites Mexico's 1951 refusal to negotiate a defense assistance pact that would have channeled military aid to Mexico.[105] Mexico has no defense assistance pact with any foreign power, and since the 1960s, among the larger Latin American countries, only Mexico and

Cuba have not had a major U.S. military advisory group.[106] A profound nationalism explains why the military will not work with foreign powers.[107]

Although foreign military influence in Mexico compared to other countries in the region is not extensive, the United States has some weight in that regard. It is clear from top generals in our sample that many generals, especially more recent ones, have received technical training above the border: from 1950 to 1963, 240 officers; from 1964 to 1968, 306.[108] The training is given to the officers with the greatest potential for command, and consequently, a much higher proportion of officers reaching the rank of general are educated in the United States than the figures suggest for the entire officer corps. Moreover, the only foreign officers, other than Central Americans who have attended the ESG with the cream of Mexico's officers, are from the United States. José Luis Piñeyro believes that the lesser role of the United States in Mexico compared with that of other countries does not signify no political-ideological penetration; it simply means that it is difficult to measure.[109]

There are two important elements to consider. The first is the degree to which the military actually desired isolation from the United States. The second is the results of U.S. influence. Some of the historic examples of the military's desire to stand on its own are misleading. In 1948 the United States proposed a hemispheric defense council at the Organization of American States meeting in Bogota, Colombia. Mexico's officer corps supported the proposal, but civilian authorities vetoed it. According to John C. Drier,

> After others had spoken [in support of the proposal] at the small meeting it was the turn of the Mexican general. Standing behind him in the crowded room was the Mexican Foreign Minister, who headed his country's delegation. Quietly, the Mexican said that, while he personally was in agreement with his military colleagues from the other countries, his government had adopted a contrary position and that, as Mexico's representative, he must oppose the creation of a permanent military body.[110]

In 1951 the United States offered mutual defense assistance pacts to eight Latin American nations, under which they were to receive military assistance in exchange for assuming hemisphere defense responsibilities. Lieuwen points out that although Mexico's armed forces welcomed the offer, the civilian-dominated administration of Miguel Alemán refused.[111] Mexico was the only Latin American nation to do so. Both the 1948 and 1951 incidents occurred, of course, under Alemán, the president who introduced the most radical changes in civil-military relations. It may be that the incidents do not reflect subsequent military attitudes, but they do point up the fact that since 1946 it has been civilian, not military, leaders who have insisted on the military's formal and informal independence from outside influences.

Most analysts are in agreement that the Mexican military is not under the sway of the United States in the sense that the officer corps has accepted either attitudes of the U.S. government or attitudes of U.S. officers toward civil-military relations.[112] The military does maintain, according to General Antonio Riviello Bazán, secretary of defense, close ties and communication with U.S. military attachés.[113] On the other hand, the United States, willingly or unwillingly, had an unexpected impact on the Mexican military and on civil-military relations by the 1980s.

Corrupting Influences

Drug trafficking in Mexico and U.S. influence in determining the Mexican government's antidrug strategies have, in my opinion, something to do with the attitudes of the officer corps, and are likely to affect values and behavior for decades to come. Corruption has tainted the political world for many decades, and in many respects contributed to the declining legitimacy of political institutions and the rise of political opposition. The military, while having its own problems with corruption, has until very recently been able to maintain a generally favorable public image, at least more so than civilian political institutions. One danger of increased corruption is its potential contribution to the military's declining prestige as an institution. A second danger is that increased internal corruption will bring greater civilian interest and involvement in the military, altering the autonomy the military has earned since the Revolution. A third danger is the growing dissatisfaction among honest officers with institutional immorality and questionable leadership, factors that can quickly demoralize from within. The pervasiveness of corruption introduced by drug trafficking threatens Mexico's military in all these ways.

In a sense, the demand in the United States for drugs, even without U.S. interference in drug interdiction policy on Mexican territory, would have affected Mexico's society, internal security, and national defense strategies. Although the secretary of defense declared in 1990 that the "Mexican army is at the margin of all anti-drug trafficking; we help only in those zones in which there are insufficient federal judicial police personnel," the impact on the military itself up to 1988 was in no way marginal.[114] The military is primarily involved in destroying drug caches, yet in June of 1990 it caught and arrested 89 presumed traffickers, destroyed 96 secret airfields, and confiscated 312 arms and 26 vehicles.[115] The navy installed radar equipment on Isla Mujeres, Quintana Roo, to identify and intercept ships transporting drugs from South America to Florida.[116]

Even by the mid-1970s drugs were a significant part of Mexican-United States relations. From 1973 to 1978, Mexico received $47,567,000 in assistance under the International Narcotics Control Program, more than any other Latin American nation. It is not unlikely that some of the money and equipment found its way to the military, and as Stephen Wager speculates, such equipment can be used for other activities.[117] More important, however, the spread of drugs redefines the military's potential role, and exposes it to forces that can threaten its internal cohesiveness and loyalty. One analyst holds that the rapid expansion of the drug trade has meant greater involvement of national and foreign actors in Mexico.[118] U.S. drug consumption has without doubt compromised Mexican national security. As will be suggested in an analysis of Mexico's new form of combat—antidrug campaigns—the Condor program used substantial military forces in direct action: 15,000 soldiers, 1,225 officers, and 20 generals.[119]

The Mexican press is strangely quiet on the subject of corruption in the military, especially in regard to the drug trade, but certain allegations have recently come to light. Presentation of evidence to a California grand jury coincided with an unpublicized, limited housecleaning in the Mexican military's hierarchy, including the transfer of Brigade General Juan Poblano Silva and his chief of staff. The U.S. attorney's office in San Diego issued warrants for their arrest. One of the defendants in the case listed the home and business numbers of General Arturo Cardona, president Salinas's chief of staff. According to a Washington *Post* reporter, an officer at the National Defense Secretariat said the two generals were "still in the army, because there has not been any conclusive proof against them."[120] Mexican civil authorities were incensed at the newspaper's article, and in a letter to the editor from the president's office explained that Mexico's attorney general and the National Defense Secretariat found no proof of drug involvement in the San Diego evidence, only that both men were mentioned by the drug dealers.[121] In Los Angeles, California, in a federal court trying a murder charge in connection with the killing of U.S. Drug Enforcement Administration agent "Kiki" Camarena, one witness mentioned former Secretary of Defense Juan Arévalo among other government officials, alleging complicity.[122]

Recently, the extent of drug-related corruption in the military became far more visible. The secretary of the navy, Admiral Mauricio Schleske Sánchez, resigned in June 1990, giving family reasons. His departure was not voluntary; he and other top officers had been fired by the president. The naval figures, including Admiral José Luis Cubría, director general of the merchant marine, have been accused of possessing "inexplicable wealth," assets unreported on their statements to the controller general, the source of which is said to be drugs. Among the holdings are large homes in Houston, Texas.[123] A group of naval officers arrested for trafficking in drugs accused the former secretary of using naval intelligence as a clandestine police force under his personal command.[124] In late 1988 and early 1989 *Excélsior*, Mexico's leading daily, published the names of some prominent political and private-sector *sacadolares* (persons transferring large sums of money to the United States) among them were several military zone commanders.[125] Other criminal activity within the military is coming to light. According to the government's own newspaper, in 1990 twenty-seven military men in the 1st Naval Zone were convicted for cocaine possession and for shipping drugs to Tampico and Veracruz.[126]

A source within the Mexican military suggested that General Riviello Bazán is so concerned with drug corruption that he is rotating zone commanders more frequently to prevent senior officers from having sustained contact with the same people.[127] The National Defense Secretariat has increased internal military intelligence, and expanded phone surveillance.[128] The government has reacted to pressures from the United States beyond accusations in criminal court cases. President de la Madrid reassigned General Vinicio Santoyo Fería, the National Defense Secretariat's highly respected chief of staff and first director of the National Defense College, to the 15th (Jalisco) military zone, one of the principal drug-trafficking regions, to demonstrate the government's concern and to ease strained relations with the United States over prosecution of the antidrug program.[129] Recently, the two countries quietly attempted to establish a U.S. military counternarcotics team at the U.S. embassy in Mexico City to relay intelligence information and help plan operations.[130] When it became public knowledge, heated debate erupted.

The military's image is complex and fragile, formed through its extensive professionalization process and within the context of societal attitudes toward the officer corps as a profession and the military as an institution. One of the most noteworthy consequences of professionalization is the extreme level of discipline and subordination to authority imposed on young officers. The structure not only washes out officers who lack the "right attitude" but insures unquestioning loyalty to commanding officers. It has also socialized officers, as part of the larger professionalization process, to accept civilian control, and discourages interest in political affairs. Despite continuation of traditional civil-military patterns, both societal values and residual nonmilitary roles demanded of the military open the possibility for an increasingly active military in political affairs.

Notes

1. David Ronfeldt, *The Mexican Army and Political Order since 1940* (Santa Monica: Rand Corporation, 1973), citing Daniel Cosío Villegas, *Visión*, April 8, 1972, 8.

2. Martin Edmonds, *Armed Services and Society* (Leicester, U.K.: University Press, 1988), 38–41.

3. Sam C. Sarkesian, *Beyond the Battlefield: The New Military Professionalism* (New York: Pergamon Press, 1981), 13.

4. Lyle N. McAlister, *The Military in Latin American Socio-political Evolution: Four Case Studies* (Washington, D.C.: Center for Research in Social Systems, 1970), 245.

5. Personal conversation, Mérida, Yucatán, October 1973. Leon Padgett also noted that in 1975 younger officers were given the opportunity to express themselves in a public forum in a new publication entitled *Insignia*. See his *The Mexican Political System*, 2d ed. (Boston: Houghton Mifflin, 1976), 98.

6. David F. Ronfeldt, "The Mexican Army and Political Order since 1940," in *Armies and Politics in Latin America*, ed. Abraham F. Lowenthal (New York: Holmes and Meier, 1976), 301.

7. Frederick M. Nunn, "On the Role of the Military in Twentieth-Century Latin America: The Mexican Case," in *The Modern Mexican Military: A Reassessment*, ed. David Ronfeldt (La Jolla: Center for U.S.-Mexican Studies, University of California, San Diego, 1984), 42.

8. Guillermo Boils, "Los militares en México (1965–1985)," *Revista Mexicana de Sociología* 47 (January–February 1985): 171.

9. Oscar Hinojosa, "Cualquier régimen de gobierno, con apoyo popular, será respetado por el Ejército," *Proceso*, March 1982, 6.

10. *El Nacional*, August 5, 1990, 6.

11. Peter H. Smith, *Labyrinths of Power: Political Recruitment in Twentieth-Century Mexico* (Princeton: Princeton University Press, 1979), 14.

12. In one respect, this is not surprising because, as Manuel Camacho points out, the political bureaucracy itself originally was a product of military and civil influences, both in personnel and culture. See his "La cohesión del grupo gobernante," *Vuelta* 1 (October 1977): 29.

13. Nunn, "On the Role of the Military in Twentieth-Century Latin America," 42.

14. Julio Labastida Martín del Campo, "Los grupos dominantes frente a las alternativas de cambio," *El pérfil de México en 1980*, vol. 3 (Mexico: Siglo XXI, 1972), 137.

15. Michael J. Dziedzic, "The Essence of Decision in a Hegemonic Regime: The Case of Mexico's Acquisition of a Supersonic Fighter" (Ph.D. diss., University of Texas, Austin, 1986), 28.

16. Sam C. Sarkesian, "An Empirical Reassessment of Military Professionalism," in *The Changing World of the American Military*, ed. Franklin D. Margiotta (Boulder, Colo.: Westview Press, 1978), 49.

17. Edwin Lieuwen, *Mexican Militarism* (Albuquerque: University of New Mexico Press, 1968), 93.

18. Luis G. Franco, *Glosa del periodo de gobierno del C. Gral. e Ing. Pascual Ortiz Rubio, 1930-32, 3 años de historia del ejército de México* (Mexico, 1946), 67.

19. McAlister, *The Military in Latin American Socio-political Evolution*, 230.

20. Interview with a Mexican army officer, Mexico City, 1990.

21. William S. Ackroyd, "Descendants of the Revolution: Civil-Military Relations in Mexico" (Ph.D. diss., University of Arizona, 1988), 112.

22. Ibid., 113.

23. Dziedzic, "The Essence of Decision in a Hegemonic Regime," 383.

24. Personal interview, Mexico City, summer 1990.

25. Interview with a Mexican army officer, 1990.

26. Personal interview, Mexico City, summer 1990.

27. *El Nacional*, January 28, 1990, 14.

28. Personal interview, Mexico City, summer 1990.

29. Morris Janowitz, *The Professional Soldier* (Glencoe, Ill.: Free Press, 1960), 48.

30. Jorge Alberto Lozoya, "The Mexican Army Today," *International Journal of Politics* 1 (Summer-Fall 1971): 285.

31. José Luis Piñeyro, *Ejército y sociedad en México: Pasado y presente* (Puebla: Universidad Autónoma de Puebla, 1985), 118.

32. For a discussion of loyalty in Mexican political culture, see my *Intellectuals and the State in Twentieth-Century Mexico* (Austin: University of Texas Press, 1985), 18ff.

33. Interview with the author, Mexico City, July 4, 1975; also see Daniel Casío Villegas's autobiography, *Memorias* (Mexico: Joaquín Mortiz, 1976).

34. Roderic A. Camp, "Civilian Supremacy in Mexico, the Case of a Post-Revolutionary Military," in *Military Intervention and Withdrawal*, ed. Constantine P. Danopoulous (London: Routledge, 1991), 13.

35. Personal interview with Luis Herrera, Mexico City, June 24, 1989.

36. Personal interview in Mexico City, 1990.

37. Samuel P. Huntington, *The Soldier and the State: The Theory and Politics of Civil-Military Relations* (Cambridge: Harvard University Press, 1964), 79.

38. R. F. Schloemer and G. E. Myers, "Making It at the Air Force Academy: Who Stays? Who Succeeds?" in *The Changing World of the American Military*, ed. Franklin D. Margiotta (Boulder, Colo.: Westview Press, 1978), 327.

39. Sarkesian, "An Empirical Reassessment of Military Professionalism," 46.

40. Gary Spencer, "Methodological Issues in the Study of Bureaucratic Elites," *Social Problems* 21 (Summer 1973): 92.

41. However, in a comparative study of businessmen and officers, Bruce Russett found that U.S. officers were not "markedly more conservative on other kinds of issues or in their basic human nature, as some observers would have us believe." The possibility does exist that businessmen, as a group, are just as conservative as officers, thus revealing very little about officers' values compared to society as a whole. "Political Perspectives of U.S. Military and Business Elites," *Armed Forces and Society* 1 (Fall 1974): 87.

42. Roderic A. Camp, "Generals and Politicians in Mexico: A Preliminary Comparison," in *The Modern Mexican Military: A Reassessment*, ed. David Ronfeldt (La Jolla: Center for U.S.-Mexican Studies, University of California, San Diego, 1984), 153.

43. William S. Ackroyd, "The Military in Mexican Politics: The Impact of Professionalism,

Civilian Behavior, and the Revolution," *Pacific Coast Council of Latin American Studies Proceedings*, 12 (1985–1986), 101.

44. *El Nacional*, April 6, 1990.

45. For an excellent example, see Boils, "Los militares en México," 171.

46. Nunn, "On the Role of the Military in Twentieth-Century Latin America," 49.

47. Daniel Mora, "Profile of the Mexican Company Grade Officer" (Paper presented at the Rocky Mountain States Latin American Conference, Tucson, February 1984), 3–4. In Russett's comparative study, he concluded that U.S. officers were not particularly concerned about any internal threat from communism. "Political Perspectives of U.S. Military and Political Elites," 88.

48. Edward J. Williams, "The Mexican Military and Foreign Policy: The Evolution of Influence," in *The Modern Mexican Military: A Reassessment*, ed. David Ronfeldt (La Jolla: Center for U.S.-Mexican Studies, University of California, San Diego, 1984), 38.

49. Despite my argument here, it is very important to remind the reader that a significant distinction exists between antimilitary sentiments versus sentiments against the use of violence. Marion Levy, Jr., brings out this point very lucidly, arguing that "the social history of the United States has shown no recalcitrance [concerning] violence, but the emphasis has been on individualistic applications of violence rather than carefully regimented ones." See his imaginative essay, "Armed Forces Organization," in *The Military and Modernization*, ed. Henry Bienen (Chicago: Aldine-Atherton, 1971), 75. This explains why the U.S. murder rate from guns is the highest of industrialized nations in the world, seven times that of Canada in 1990.

50. Stephen D. Wesbrook, "Historical Notes," in *The Political Education of Soldiers*, ed. Morris Janowitz and Stephen D. Wesbrook (Beverly Hills: Sage Publications, 1983), 274. According to Wesbrook, on only one occasion, immediately after World War II, did the army attempt to become involved in national integration in advocating universal military training.

51. McAlister, *The Military in Latin American Socio-political Evolution*, 235.

52. "Introdución," in Gloria Fuentes, *El ejército mexicano* (Mexico: Grijalbo, 1983), v.

53. Phyllis Greene Walker, "The Modern Mexican Military: Political Influence and Institutional Interests in the 1980s" (M.A. thesis, American University, 1987), 88.

54. Sarkesian, "An Empirical Reassessment of Military Professionalism," 43.

55. Russett, "Political Perspectives of U.S. Military and Business Elites," 97.

56. Ackroyd, "Descendants of the Revolution," 124.

57. Guillermo Boils, *Los militares y la política en México, 1915–1974* (Mexico: El Caballito, 1975).

58. David Ronfeldt, "The Modern Mexican Military," in *Armies and Politics in Latin America*, ed. Abraham Lowenthal and J. Samuel Fitch (New York: Holmes and Meier, 1986), 234. But as Sarkesian has argued, it is necessary for the professional officer "to become more politically astute, knowledgable, and sensitive to political imperatives of domestic and international societies." *Beyond the Battlefield*, 185.

59. Luis Herrera-Lasso and Guadalupe González G., "Balance y perspectiva en el uso del concepto de la seguridad nacional en el caso de México" (unpublished paper, 1989), 4–5.

60. Edward J. Williams, "Mexico's Central American Policy: National Security Considerations," In *Rift and Revolution: the Central American Imbroglio*, ed. Howard J. Wiarda (Washington, D.C.: American Enterprise Institute, 1984), 303–328; Stephen J. Wager, "Basic Characteristics of the Modern Mexican Military," in *The Modern Mexican Military: A Reassessment*, ed. David Ronfeldt (La Jolla: Center for U.S.-Mexican Studies, University of California, San Diego, 1984), 89.

61. *Diario Oficial*, December 26, 1986, 2.

62. Personal interview, Mexico City, 1991.

63. Leon Padgett, *The Mexican Political System*, 97; Boils, "Los militares en México," 179.

64. Jorge Alberto Lozoya, *El ejército mexicano*, 3d ed. (Mexico: El Colegio de México, 1984), 126.

65. Wesbrook, "Historical Notes," 275–276.

66. Sarkesian, *Beyond the Battlefield*, 124.

67. Lieuwen, *Mexican Militarism*, xii.

68. This overwhelming emphasis on secrecy is revealed nicely by the fact that in the late 1970s,

a magazine reporter called the Secretariat of National Defense for the name of the head of the Escuela Superior de Guerra, which is public information. In more than two dozen calls, she was stonewalled by officials.

69. John J. Johnson, *The Military and Society in Latin America* (Stanford: Stanford University Press, 1964), 164.

70. Personal interviews, Mexico City, 1989, 1990.

71. Enrique Aldúncin Abitia, *Los valores de los Mexicanos, México: Entre la tradición y la modernidad* (Mexico: Fondo Cultural Banamex, 1986), 176.

72. Alberto Hernández Medina et al., *Como somos los mexicanos* (Mexico: Centro de Estudios Educativos, 1987), 110.

73. John D. Blair, "Emerging Youth Attitudes and the Military," in *The Changing World of the American Military*, ed. Franklin D. Margiotta (Boulder, Colo.: Westview Press, 1978), 159.

74. Brian Latell, *Mexico at the Crossroads: The Many Crises of the Political System* (Stanford: Hoover Institution, 1986), 30.

75. Christopher Dickey, "Modernization Could Lead Mexican Military into Politics," *Washington Post*, September 23, 1982, 29A.

76. McAlister, *The Military in Latin American Socio-political Evolution*, 222.

77. Ibid., 221.

78. Janowitz, *The Professional Soldier*, 109.

79. Johnson, *The Military and Society in Latin America*, 171.

80. McAlister, *The Military in Latin American Socio-political Evolution*, 222.

81. Blair, "Emerging Youth Attitudes and the Military," 167.

82. Ackroyd, "Descendants of the Revolution," 172.

83. The only exception I recognized from 1922 through 1970 was Alvaro Elías Calles Sáenz, son of Plutarco Elías Calles and grandson of President Calles, who graduated from engineering school in 1957. *Memoria gráfica del cincuentenario de la reapertura del Heroico Colegio Militar* (Mexico: SHCP, 1970), 482. The only other example is Federico Amaya Rodríguez Morales, also a 1957 engineering graduate, the son of former Senator Federico Amaya Rodríguez, who eventually ended up in the civilian executive branch. However, both examples are clouded by the fact that Calles's father was a graduate of a military preparatory school, and his grandfather was a major postrevolutionary military and political figure. Amaya Rodríguez Morales's father is career military, and former chief of staff, his Senate post coming at the end of a long career.

84. Personal interviews, Mexico City, 1990. This is not an isolated case. Another individual, a granddaughter of a prominent revolutionary figure, and the daughter of an important general officer, recalled her father's desire that her brothers not enter the service. The most notable example is that of Miguel Alemán. As a teenager, he wanted to pursue the same career as his father, a revolutionary general. His father was dead set against his son's interest, and told him that "he didn't want him to become a military officer because it had no future." He encouraged him to go to college and pursue a legal career. Personal interview, Mexico City, 1990.

85. Ackroyd, "Descendants of the Revolution," 171.

86. As told to my source by an army general, personal interview, Mexico City, 1990.

87. Personal conversation with a brigadier general, Mexico City, May 1965.

88. Personal interview with a Mexican politician, Washington, D.C., June 1987.

89. Camp, "Civilian Supremacy in Mexico," 18.

90. Roderic A. Camp, "The Military," in *Prospects for Mexico*, ed. George Grayson (Washington, D.C.: Foreign Service Institute, 1988), 87.

91. Lorenzo Meyer, "Ejército y Cananeas del futuro," *Excélsior*, September 6, 1989, 12A.

92. Walker, "The Modern Mexican Military," 89–90.

93. Partido Revolucionario Institucional, *Encuesta Nacional*, April 1983. I am indebted to Miguel Basáñez, who directed both polls, for posing a question about the military's role in politics, and for running extensive cross-tabulations of the military question with other questions in the 1983 and 1987 surveys.

94. The straightforward results of this and the 1983 poll, without cross-tabulations, have been published in Miguel Basáñez's *El pulso de los sexenios, 20 años de crisis en México* (Mexico: Siglo XXI, 1990), 238–240.

95. Camp, "Civilian Supremacy in Mexico," 19–20.

96. *Diario Oficial*, December 26, 1986, 14.

97. Vicente Ernesto Pérez Mendoza, "The Role of the Armed Forces in the Mexican Economy in the 1980s" (M. A. thesis, Naval Postgraduate School, Monterey, California, June 1981), 21.

98. *Diccionario biográfico del gobierno mexicano* (Mexico: Presidencia de la República, 1987), 209.

99. Franklin D. Margiotta, "Civilian Control and the Mexican Military: Changing Patterns of Political Influence," in *Civilian Control of the Military: Theories and Cases from Developing Countries*, ed. Claude E. Welch, Jr. (Albany: State University of New York Press, 1976), 221.

100. Rodney W. Jones and Steven A. Hildreth, *Emerging Powers: Defense and Security in the Third World* (New York: Praeger, 1986), 393.

101. For the thrust of this argument, see Frederick Nunn, *Yesterday's Soldiers: European Military Professionalism in South America, 1890–1940* (Lincoln: University of Nebraska Press, 1983).

102. Nunn, "On the Role of the Military in Twentieth-Century Latin America: The Mexican Case," 33.

103. Donald F. Harrison, "United States-Mexican Military Collaboration during World War II" (Ph.D. diss., Georgetown University, 1976), introduction.

104. Walker suggests that their relations were closest during this period until the 1980s, "The Modern Mexican Military," 23.

105. Williams, "The Mexican Military and Foreign Policy," 40.

106. Jones and Hildreth, *Emerging Powers*, 389.

107. Miguel Basáñez, *La lucha por la hegemonia en México, 1968–1980* (Mexico: Siglo XXI, 1981), 58.

108. José Luis Piñeyro, "The Mexican Army and the State: Historical and Political Perspective," *Revue Internationale de Sociologie* 14 (April–August 1978): 134.

109. José Luis Piñeyro, "Presencia política militar nacional y en el Distrito Federal: propuestas de análisis," in *Distrito Federal, Gobierno y Sociedad Civil*, ed. Pablo González Casanova (Mexico: El Caballito, 1987), 78.

110. John C. Dreier, *The Organization of American States and the Hemisphere Crisis* (Baltimore: Johns Hopkins University Press, 1962), 47. Dreier was the U.S. representative at the time. For details about the civilian position, and how the conflict was resolved, see the memoirs of Jaime Torres Bodet, the then-secretary of foreign relations, who himself, with President Alemán's approval, handpicked General Manuel Cabrera Carrasquedo as the military representative. *La victoria sin alas* (Mexico: Fondo de Cultura Económica, 1970), 293ff. General Cabrera was oficial mayor of national defense, 1946–1948, and was a brigade general during the conference. He reached three-star rank in 1949, and substituted as governor of Oaxaca in 1955. *Hispano Americano*, October 10, 1955, 15; Ronald Hilton, *Who's Who in Latin America, Mexico* (Stanford: Stanford University Press, 1946), 17.

111. Edwin Lieuwen, "Depolitization of the Mexican Revolutionary Army, 1915–1940," in *The Modern Mexican Military: A Reassessment*, ed. David Ronfeldt (La Jolla: Center for United States-Mexican Studies, University of California, San Diego, 1984), 61.

112. Boils, "Los militares en México," 182; Nunn, "On the Role of the Military in Twentieth Century Latin America," 40.

113. *El Nacional*, June 9, 1990, 3.

114. Ibid.

115. Ibid., July 2, 1990.

116. Ricardo Blanco Velázquez, "Instaló la Armada un sofisticado equipo antinarco en Isla Mujeres," *El Nacional*, August 26, 1990, 20.

117. Stephen J. Wager, "The Mexican Military 1968–1978: A Decade of Change" (unpublished paper, Stanford University, June 1979), 22.

118. Herrera-Lasso and González G., "Balance y perspectiva en el uso del concepto de la seguridad nacional en el caso de México," 31.

119. José Luis Piñeyro, "The Modernization of the Mexican Armed Forces," in *Democracy*

under Seige: New Military Power in Latin America, ed. Augusto Varas, (Westport, Conn.: Greenwood Press, 1989), 120.

120. *Washington Post*, August 15, 1989.

121. Ibid., August 24, 1989.

122. See Beatriz Johnston Hernández, "El gran acusado en el juicio por el asesinato de Camarena de gobierno mexicano," *Proceso*, July 16, 1990, 18.

123. Carlos Marín, "Inexplicablemente rico, Schleske omitió declarar sus residencias en Houston," *Proceso*, August 3, 1990, 8–13.

124. See Ortiz Pinchetti, "Actividades de narcos de las que Schleske debio estar enterado," *Proceso*, July 23, 1990, 8.

125. *Excélsior*, December 31, 1988, 27A, and January 2, 1989, 30A. One source said he had recognized more than a dozen high-ranking officers on the list.

126. *El Nacional*, May 19, 1990, 34.

127. *Washington Post*, August 15, 1989.

128. Personal interview with an army officer, Mexico City, 1990.

129. Piñeyro, "The Modernization of the Mexican Armed Forces," 124; this is ironic because his name appears on the *Excélsior* list.

130. *Los Angeles Times*, June 7, 1990.

4

Military-Civilian Interlocks

Numerous interpretations have been offered of the level of interchange between military officers and the political system, and its impact on civil-military relations. It has been asserted that a limited but important presence of the military in political roles has actually guaranteed, in Mexico's case, military subservience to civilian leadership. Many variations on this general theme exist. Basically, if one considers the Mexican political system since Lázaro Cárdenas's presidency to have taken on corporatist qualities, then various forms of military interlocks might be viewed as formal means of civilian co-optation.

Political Officeholding

Franklin Margiotta first offered the theory that political officeholding by the military explained the persistence of civilian supremacy in Mexico.[1] Essentially, he contended that the political system, by design, allocated a certain percentage of positions to high-ranking military officers, thereby providing an open but limited channel for politically ambitious officers. It was his belief that this "informal, individualized military representation has been sustained at fairly even levels in the last twenty years, thus giving the military a direct stake in the political system and personal ties to their political counterparts."[2] As will be demonstrated, Margiotta's thesis was valid through the early 1960s, but data he used to support his argument after that date are flawed, for that argument is based on absolute numbers of officers in high political office, not the percentage of the military's representation. Although the number of men remained the same over short periods, the number of such offices doubled or even tripled in many areas.

Historically, political officeholding by military officers in Mexico was quite common. This is not surprising because during many periods of the country's history, as elsewhere in Latin America, military men were in charge of the presidency. Beginning with General Porfirio Díaz in 1884 until 1988, of 2,612 nationally prominent politicians and state governors, one in five had risen to the rank of lieutenant colonel or higher in the National Guard or armed forces. Politicians who were themselves in the military recruited other military figures. Of the influential political generations, Díaz's (1820–1839), which fought

66

against U.S. troops and in the internecine Liberal-Conservative conflicts, came most strongly from career military backgrounds. Two-thirds of the cohort were officers. However, of politicians in the next generation (1840–1859), fewer than half as many (29 percent) were career officers. The following generation (1860–1879), best represented by Francisco I. Madero, the first revolutionary president, did not increase the military's representation.

It is the next generation (1880–1899), that of Generals Alvaro Obregón and Plutarco Elías Calles,[3] who had participated in the Revolution, that again increased the military's representation, if only slightly: 37 percent. The postrevolutionary generation (1900–1919), led by Miguel Alemán, the first elected civilian President since Madero, marked a significant drop to 8 percent.

The *administrative* pattern of military representation can be seen in table 4-1. The military's presence in Díaz's administration decreases consistently each time he is elected president, from an initial 55 percent to only 25 percent in 1911. Actually, Madero did not alter Díaz's pattern. Instead, it was Madero's murder, initiating the truly violent phase of the Revolution, that renewed the cycle of a direct military presence. General Victoriano Huerta, who in 1913 attained the presidency through a bloody coup, reintroduced the level of military officeholding that characterized Díaz's 1884 administration. The level was exceeded by the Convention government, an ineffectual military junta dominated by victorious Villistas and Zapatistas. Venustiano Carranza (1914–1920), Madero's civilian heir, whose own legitimacy is never fully recognized, found it necessary to keep a strong military presence. After his ouster by General Obregón, a fairly consistent pattern of military officeholding obtained in the postrevolutionary governments from 1920 through 1940. General Avila

TABLE 4-1. Mexican Military Officeholders by Administration, 1884–1988

Years	Percentage	Years	Percentage
1885–1888	55	1924–1928	34
1888–1892	51	1928–1930	29
1892–1896	44	1930–1932	32
1896–1900	34	1932–1934	33
1900–1904	30	1935	24
1905–1910	26	1935–1940	27
1911	25	1940–1946	19
1911	22	1946–1952	8
1911–1913	24	1952–1958	14
1913–1914	50	1958–1964	15
1914–1915	64	1964–1970	7
1914–1920	46	1970–1976	10
1920	35	1976–1982	6
1920–1924	40	1982–1988	5

Camacho, Cárdenas's personal choice as his successor in 1940, is himself seen as a staff officer, rather than a typical revolutionary. As Mexico's last military president, his transitional role was crucial in reducing the military's political presence to only one-fifth of political officeholders. As generational data imply, it is Alemán who actually drastically reduced the military to less than 10 percent of his appointees, a figure not equaled until 1964.

Alemán is the perfect figure to carry out this task. Many of his supporters expected him to institute such a policy, and recall with pride his appointment of young, well-educated civilian professionals, like themselves, to political office.[4] This anti-military attitude stems from the 1929 presidential campaign, during which many of Alemán's collaborators were supporters of José Vasconcelos, the civilian opponent.[5] As noted earlier, Alemán himself, the son of a revolutionary general, nearly lost his life in 1929 because his father rebelled against the government, in opposition to Obregón's presidential candidacy. The elder Alemán was killed during the rebellion.[6] Interestingly, although Alemán was most responsible for the dramatic reduction of career officers in political posts, he initiated a structural change at the presidential level that had repercussions for civil-military relations. A presidential chief of staff had existed since the time of Cárdenas, but Alemán initiated a military presidential staff, which had as one of its functions maintaining closer liaison between the chief executive and the armed forces.[7]

Military officers hold fewer than 2 percent of all important political posts in Mexico in the 1990s. In the executive branch, from midlevel to the top, only 4 percent claim service in the army, air force, or navy as their occupation.[8] Qualitatively, the influence of military officers has declined even further than Margiotta's thesis would suggest. Military officers have found certain types of political posts more attractive or available than others—those having the least say in policy-making (see table 4-2). Excluding the Secretaries of National Defense and of the Navy and the Department of the Air Force, military men have not been significant in cabinet-level agencies for years, basically since Alemán's administration. On the state level they have persisted much longer as governors, accounting for one in four state chief executives from 1953 through 1964. Again Alemán accounted for a precipitous drop, from 40 to 13 percent. Whereas Alemán reduced the military's presence across the board in the legislative and executive branches, his successors revived the military's presence in the legislative branch, especially the Senate, to pre-1946 levels. The Senate, the least influential of the two legislative bodies, retained the military presence longest. In the 1960s, 15 percent of top officerholders were career military officers. For a comparative perspective, concurrently in the United States only 2 percent of top executive branch officials were career military.[9] By 1976, when Luis Echeverría took office, the military, in terms of holding political office, essentially had disappeared from the political scene.

Peter Smith, in his excellent work on political recruitment, offered a more accurate but different version of Margiotta's thesis for the period 1946 through 1971. Although he correctly noted the drop in military officers after 1946, he argued that when "they've entered the elite, they have come in at levels of

TABLE 4-2. Political Offices Held by Mexican Military Officers

Administration	Cabinet %	Governor %	Senator %	Deputy %
1935–1940	12	48	18	—
1940–1946	12	40	20	—
1946–1952	0	13	5	3
1952–1958	2	23	17	11
1958–1964	0	23	20	11
1964–1970	4	3	15	3
1970–1976	2	5	12	2
1976–1982	0	3	5	3
1982–1988	1	5	3	1
1988–1994	0	0	2	1

Note: Governors are placed in the administration during which they were elected or appointed, thus more accurately indicating the president responsible. Both military secretariats are excluded.

substantial prestige and prominence."[10] His sample was small, including secretaries and subsecretaries of military agencies, thus distorting representation at those levels in relation to other positions, giving the false impression that as their percentages declined elsewhere, they retained importance at the highest levels.

The qualitative distribution of military officers by positions of influence has a long history in Mexico. From 1884 to 1934, officers accounted for only 14 percent of the cabinet posts (including defense agencies), not much different from the figures for the post-1935 era (12 percent). Officers were also well represented among national elective offices: 38 percent of the deputies and 21 percent of the senators came from military backgrounds. Military officers actually dominated politics at the state level. Two-thirds of military officers who rose to national political office had held state political office. More important, of the 365 officers during this period who were prominent politically, 57 percent were state governors. Of the officers who reached national political office after 1935, 39 percent had been governors, compared to only 18 percent of the civilian politicians.

Political-military types have always had greater access to governorships. During various periods of Mexico's history states have been characterized by the most turbulent politics and violence, often requiring a military commander as well as a skilled politician. In their own right, military zone commanders are important figures in state politics. Even in the 1980s, when a military man became governor of Chiapas, a state with a range of difficult political problems, the primary reason was internal security.[11] In this individual case, the then-secretary of defense, General Félix Galván, remarked that the governor, whether military or civilian, had no authority to direct troops, indicating that in his mind, his status as a career officer had little political importance.[12] It is

interesting that no analysts, Mexican or foreign, have pointed to Miguel Angel
Barberena, governor of Aguascalientes (1986–1992), as a military representative. A rear admiral, and graduate of the Heroico Colegio Naval, he has spent
most of his career in government, party, and elective offices. He has never held
a command position, yet was a member of the presidential military staff in
1989.[13]

Not only have officers declined proportionately among political elites, no
longer holding important political posts, but the kinds of officers who occupy
legislative posts are different. In the 1982 legislature, four deputies were career
officers, all brigadier generals or higher; two other officers also held seats, but
they were no longer on active duty. Several former enlisted men were in the
lower chamber, two of whom were members of the Mexican Communist Party
(PCM) and the Unified Socialist Party of Mexico (PSUM). Only two senators
had military backgrounds: one was a former cavalry major, the other an active
duty naval officer with the rank of corvette captain (lieutenant colonel).[14]

In the 1985 legislature five deputies had military backgrounds, but only
three were known to be on active duty, two of whom were senior officers,
including Alonso Aguirre Ramos, who as a zone commander, department
head, and contender for secretary of defense in 1982, could be considered an
influential general.[15] The other two were majors, including Germán Corona del
Rosal, son of Alfonso Corona del Rosal, one of Mexico's influential political-
military officers, the last career officer to become president of PRI.[16]

In the 1988 legislature only two active duty officers were deputies: one was a
captain and military lawyer; the other was an air force graduate of the Colegio
de Defensa Nacional. There were also two engineers who had left the service,
and one retired division general, Salvador Revueltas Olvera, a former zone
commander who was president of the National Defense Committee in the
Chamber of Deputies.[17] The military had only three officers in the Senate: one
retired, the second a brigadier general and Colegio de Defensa Nacional
(CDN) graduate, and the third an active duty admiral. In sum, high-ranking,
active duty officers in Mexico are rarely present in either legislative house.
Most significant, they have lost control over the national defense committees
in both chambers, whose members since the 1930s typically had been active
duty or retired military officers.

The political activities of Mexico's generals since 1946 suggest some interesting patterns about which top officers have chosen political careers and the
political offices they have held. Among the generals in our sample, 37 percent
held some type of political office. Of officers born before 1910, more than half
successfully pursued political careers. Of those born after 1920, the proportion
was one-tenth, although men born after 1920 account for more than two-fifths
of the generals in our sample. Mexico's generals more commonly held appointive (25 percent) than elective offices (21 percent).

It is not surprising that generals having sufficient political skills to become
department heads or chief of staff also were more likely to pursue political
careers. Interestingly, officers from certain military occupational specialties
followed political interests in larger numbers. The most politicized divisions

were the army medical corps and infantry. The least politicized among generals have been specialists in administration and communications, none of whom have held political office, and generals in the artillery and air force. It is understandable that the infantry is overrepresented because older officers were more likely to be in the infantry, and they followed political interests in numbers much greater than their younger counterparts. The reasons for the medical corps as the source of the most generals in politics is less explicable, other than the fact that it, more than any military specialty, has greater contacts with civilians, thus making its members more receptive to experimenting with a civilian job during their careers.

The army medical corps plays a very important role in the interchange between politicians and military officers, somewhat analogous to the role bankers played between the private sector and public officials. (Among businesspeople, bankers were a key channel for communication with the political world, and more of them occupied political positions than did members of any other private-sector group.) Its impact is limited by its members' importance in the officer corps itself. A significant initial link was provided by Gustavo Baz, a distinguished physician who interrupted his studies at the Military Medical School to fight in the Revolution, and then returned to the National Medical School to complete his program with a generation of distinguished physicians and politicians. Baz, who later directed both of his alma maters, had become a friend of General Cárdenas's earlier in his career, and served as president of the National University during the Cárdenas administration. As a teacher, he produced many disciples. He was personal physician to the family of Avila Camacho, who, as president, asked Baz to leave the university to become his secretary of public health in 1940. The importance of the Military Medical School as a special channel for political contacts remains to this day.[18] Jesús Kumate Rodríguez, one of Mexico's leading medical researchers, graduated from the Military Medical School in 1946, taught there in the 1940s and 1950s, and was appointed secretary of public health in 1988, following in Baz's footsteps.[19]

Contrary to Margiotta and others, some analysts believe that military officeholding since 1946 is not indicative of military political influence. Lyle McAlister, an advocate of this point of view, suggests that the "decisive question is whether the officer is selected by and represents the military institutions or whether he seeks or holds office because of his personal motivations and acts according to impulses from the party and/or a civilian constituency."[20] There is no evidence that the National Defense Secretariat pressures civilian leadership to include officers in any political posts. If one accepted this as true, the decline in military representation would be indicative of the level of its influence. In the 1950s and 1960s Edwin Lieuwen believed that gubernatorial and congressional political posts went to certain military men because they had personal followings in their home states or congressional districts, not because the military exerted pressure as an interest group.[21] In the 1970s Margiotta quoted an officer who learned that he had been asked to run for Congress because the local zone commander requested PRI officials to select a military candidate.[22]

The most recent case of a career army officer being designated a PRI candidate for governor is that of Absalón Castellanos Domínguez, who administered his home state from 1982 to 1988. An experienced field commander, he was the grandson of Belisario Domínguez, one of the most revered martyred political figures of the Revolution, and the uncle of Jorge de la Vega Domínguez, former party president and prominent politician. In 1982, while zone commander of Nayarit, General Castellanos Domínguez was approached to become the PRI's gubernatorial candidate. The general himself explains how it happened:

Pedro Ojeda Paullada, then president of the CEN of PRI, called me to join the working trip of the PRI candidate Miguel de la Madrid Hurtado in the state of Chiapas.

He called me three or four times, but I explained that I was a soldier, chief of a zone, and that first I had to speak with my superior, the secretary of defense. Finally I did this, and the then secretary, Félix Galván, spoke to me and told me that if I would call back they would give me the authorization. . . . This is how it happened. I traveled to Chiapas and met Miguel de la Madrid. I greeted him. But we didn't talk to each other, never.

One day Ojeda Paullada called me again and told me he wished to speak with me, and asked if he could see me in Mexico City. He didn't say why, and I didn't ask him. Again I explained that I couldn't travel there without the authorization of the secretary of defense, my immediate superior. He called two, three times and I repeated this. Finally General Galván called me and told me he had spoken with him and I could visit Mexico. We were sitting in his [Ojeda's] office, . . . and he told me, "Well, the party has chosen you as precandidate for the governorship of Chiapas. . . ."

I had a moment of doubt, of indecision. I felt a great satisfaction for the opportunity they gave me, but my doubt was: had they consulted anyone or what. . . . One of the things that soldiers have in their head is that their superior has to know about it before they make a decision. This is a logical thing, no? But I said, well, I am a zone commander and I can decide. That is how I decided in that moment and I told Ojeda. . . .[23]

This anecdote is extremely revealing of Mexican military culture. It not only implies that civilian leaders made up their own minds about the general's candidacy but also demonstrates at the highest possible level the degree of subordination within the military hierarchy—even a zone commander, the most important field officer, must receive permission to travel elsewhere in Mexico.

Political officeholding by military officers may be more important theoretically not because the military has historically had some role in determining its level of representation but because of its long-term impact on military professionalism. It could be argued, for example, that the persistence of politically active officers reduces the potential of the military's becoming caste conscious.[24] Some prominent politicians believe this is the case, including recent presidents. Miguel de la Madrid wanted to have more military officers in the Chamber of Deputies, and several more as governors.

Unfortunately, I had to remove General Alpuche [governor of Yucatán] because the party said it would never be able to win the elections after his continued performance in office. I wasn't able to replace him with someone else from the military, and I never received any pressure from the military to replace him with one of its own. I personally believe that *having some officers in political office is very helpful to the relationship*. [Emphasis added.][25]

The gradual but persistent decline of important officers in politics increases the potential for greater isolation of the military from other groups, including politicians, and the development of a caste mentality.

Other Civilian-Military Linkages

Fewer military officers in top political offices eliminates the military's direct influence in policy-making and decreases ties between political and military figures at the highest levels, but these effects may be tempered by the presence of junior officers as aides to high-level politicians and as moonlighters. For example, a cabinet secretary may ask the presidential chief of staff for a major or lieutenant colonel to act as a liaison between the secretary and the staff— this is by special request; it is not a general rule. One former secretary remarked, "I thought this was silly and unnecessary myself. . . . I think it has to do with the presidential relationship. In other words, the closer the relationship between the secretary and the president, the less need to have a special link to presidential military staff."[26]

It has been said that moonlighting is common among younger officers, especially in the public sector. Although moonlighting is illegal, one source asserted that an officer had estimated in the mid-1960s that as many as one-fourth or more of the officer corps held second jobs.[27] A secretary of planning and budgeting who attempted to stop double employment in the public sector in the late 1970s, was told to desist.[28] The military condoned the practice, probably because large numbers of younger officers resign their commissions over low pay. Some civilian officials believe low pay tends to lead military men into other activities. A former secretary of government properties was so concerned about inadequate military compensation that he gave military aides in his agency a separate salary.[29] Today, moonlighting is not widespread but is practiced by certain specialists, such as military physicians, who work in non-military hospitals after completing their daily assignments. Other officers who are unassigned often take additional jobs or start small family businesses.[30]

Another important channel for political-military communication in the civilian world is embassies abroad. The linkage is especially important at the Mexican embassy in Washington, D.C. As later evidence suggests, these assignments are career plums for would-be generals. One prominent political figure who has served in an embassy remarked that of the five or six officers he came to know personally, one became the secretary of defense, and another the subsecretary. Because of the level of formal socializing, there is a very close relationship between the ambassador and the military staff. Such socializing produces strong friendships.[31] In recent years the military has developed a good relationship with the Secretariat of Foreign Relations. Attachés have become a critical means of cementing ties between that secretariat and the defense ministries.[32] As if to reinforce the significance of these informal contacts, the *Diario Oficial* announced in 1990 that as part of the military's enhanced responsibilities for national development, the selection of military attachés would thenceforth be more formalized, and that they would come more directly under the authority of the Secretariat of Foreign Relations.[33] Although not compromising attachés' obedience to naval or defense regulations, the ruling marks a basic shift in ties between the secretariat and the military and, more important, between the civilian political world and the officer corps.

According to Article 174 of the military code, special leaves are given to officers (1) to hold popularly elected posts; (2) to carry out a presidentially designated activity outside military service; and (3) to carry out civil activities or employment in executive agencies of the national government, state governments, the Department of the Federal District, municipalities, decentralized agencies, or state-owned enterprises and other public institutions.[34] According to José Luis Piñeyro, of the fourteen thousand officers on active duty in the mid-1980s, probably no more than 8 percent had leaves to work in government agencies or the PRI.[35]

The leave policy has been abused in several ways. Although leave time is not to be counted toward time in grade, William S. Ackroyd, on the basis of interviews with several military officers, declares that many officers are given credit for time spent in civilian jobs when they return to active duty.[36] Rear Admiral Miguel Angel Barbarena, who has held civilian posts for twenty-two of the past twenty-six years, is a case in point. According to the Organic Law, officers are not permitted leaves for party positions, unless they are appointed by the president. In the 1988 presidential campaign, Salinas's military presidential staff had not obtained required official leaves.[37] Other reported instances of active duty leave abuse involve the legal requirements of individual states. To illustrate, General Fernando Pámanes Escobedo in 1974 left his position as zone commander of Chihuahua to become governor of his home state, Zacatecas. Section 5 of the state constitution requires a military officer to take leave from active duty *at least one year* prior to the gubernatorial election, a provision the general honored in the breach.[38] A more notable figure violated a similar provision: General Hermenegildo Cuenca Díaz, upon leaving the National Defense Secretariat in 1976, became the PRI candidate for governor of Baja California (he died in midcampaign).[39]

Although the number of high-ranking officers who now occupy political posts is minuscule, the practice by younger officers during early stages of their careers has important implications for the military. The exchange, because it involves low-level officers, does not carry as much weight, but it does serve as a personal and communications bridge between the officer corps and civilian politicians. On the other hand, the more widespread the practice, the more difficult it becomes for the corps to instill a sense of professionalism.[40] As long as many officers are financially dependent on temporary jobs, especially in the public sector, their loyalty to the military is somewhat compromised.

Social and Kinship Ties

Another means of establishing closer ties between the military and the political leadership is through personal rather than positional connections. In other words, if the military is recruited from a selected pool, its potential for a stronger caste mentality is enhanced. Still, in terms of civil-military relations, an argument can be made that the more isolated the military from other leadership groups, the more limited its opportunities for direct intervention in politics.

The institutional character of the armed forces has limited its ties with nonstate power sectors, especially economic groups. Ties to private-sector leaders are significant because in the majority of countries where the military has intervened politically, alliances between businesspeople and the military have been fundamental.[41] Miguel Basáñez believes the Mexican military will not engineer a coup because it lacks strong ties with leading entrepreneurs.[42] More generally, no evidence supports the view that nonstate conservative interests have penetrated the armed forces.[43] An interesting alteration in the public's political perception has taken place recently, however, that may affect the military's behavior vis-à-vis the political leadership. Small but vociferous prolife groups, complaining about art shows and plays they find religiously offensive, have been sending protest letters since 1988 to the Secretariat of National Defense rather than to the Secretariat of Government.[44] If Mexicans generally begin to channel complaints to the military instead of to civilian agencies, it will increase popular pressure on the officer corps.

Historically, the military has had ties, at least on a personal level, with the political world. Prior to 1935, when the military was the dominant force in politics, nearly one in three officers was related to a prominent political figure, but very few had kinship ties with other leadership groups, including entrepreneurs and intellectuals. And fewer than one in ten had ties to more than one group. One-tenth of the officers were sons of political notables. Since 1935 the proportion of officers related to intellectual and entrepreneurial groups has slipped to less than 3 percent. However, the percentage of those with relatives in politics remains strong: 38 percent.

The potential importance of informal ties with the civilian political leadership, in terms of maintaining or altering civil-military relations, is a matter for speculation. The actual importance can be seen empirically in a different context. The officers most likely to pursue political careers come from politically active families. In fact, of generals with known family backgrounds, three in four who held national political office were related to someone who held an equivalent post. Many older officers, some of whom dabbled in politics themselves, produced sons who are now in politics but following a civilian, professional career. Recent examples are Héctor Hernández Cervantes, director general of Bancomer; Renato Vega Alvarado, subsecretary of agrarian affairs, son of General Renato Vega Amador, a zone commander and former chief of police of the Federal District; Miguel González Avelar, director of Mexico's foreign service institute; Emilio Lozoya Thalmann, whose father, General Jesús Lozoya Solís, was also governor of his home state; and Guillermo Ortíz Martínez, subsecretary of the treasury. At the cabinet level, such children include Manuel Camacho, head of the Federal District Department, son of a medical officer. The last president to have such a close connection with the military was José López Portillo, whose father, a distinguished engineer, graduated from the Colegio Militar. However, Luis Echeverría could boast numerous connections, including his father-in-law, General José Guadalupe Zuno, an important regional figure; his own father, who represented the Treasury Secretariat as an army paymaster for many years; and his mentor, General Rodolfo Sánchez Taboada. Regardless of the nature of the personal relationship, it is a valuable communication channel between the political and military worlds.

Not only scholars have pointed to the importance of such interlocks. In 1974 President Echeverría called for the new generation of public officials to multiply "their ties with the younger military officer formed in the institutions created by the Mexican Revolution, who will be, undoubtedly, the guarantee of the constitutional life of our country."[45]

The interlock, on both the institutional and personal levels, between the military and the civilian leaderships, can be examined from another perspective. Political figures, for reasons explained elsewhere, do not produce military offspring. Of the 1,113 individuals in top executive-branch positions under President Salinas, only 43, or fewer than 4 percent, had career military fathers. In the legislative branch only 1 percent had fathers in the military. And of the more than 200 federal judges, only 1 came from a military background. Two percent of governors and their top personnel had fathers who were in the military.[46]

More important, whereas the military maintained some visibility in public political offices, at least until the 1970s, civilians rarely have been allowed to hold posts reserved for the military. In other words, unlike the U.S. Department of Defense, the Secretariats of the Navy and of Defense do not fill decision-making or advisory posts with civilians. In fact, the navy led the way in culling the political-military officer from its leadership. In that sense, it could be said to be the first service to have achieved control by orthodox career officers. On the other hand, it is the only service since 1946 to have been led, however briefly, by a civilian. Not surprisingly, President Alemán was the one to experiment. In the last year of his administration he appointed a close friend from preparatory school, Raúl López Sánchez, the son of an important revolutionary general, Mariano López Ortíz—which probably made the choice more acceptable to the navy. In 1964 the navy actually had a civilian *oficial mayor*, the third-ranked position in the secretariat. It is very likely that Fernando Castro y Castro had impressed his future superior, Admiral Antonio Vázquez del Mercado, when the latter held a civilian post as director general of fishing industries and Castro y Castro was secretary of the National Advisory Commission on Fishing.[47]

The other means by which civilians can come in contact with the Mexican officer corps is education. In the United States prominent political figures frequently are alumni of the service academies, often having studied there during wartime. Jimmy Carter, for one, an engineering graduate of Annapolis, had close personal ties to navy brass. In Mexico, however, few civilian politicians are products of the service academies. Only 7 percent of Salinas's appointees are alumni of military schools, roughly divided between the ESG and the Escuela Naval Militar. All but ten (1 percent) are in the National Defense or Navy Secretariats. Fewer than 3 percent pursued graduate studies at the Centro de Estudios Navales Superiores, the Colegio de Defensa Nacional (CDN), and the Escuela Médico Militar.

The CDN since 1989 has enabled excellent contact between civilian and military students. Lieutenant colonels are among the faculty, and colonels and generals are among the student body. According to the instructors, civilian and military students, and civilian and military instructors frequently socialize. Although a few civilians have been attending only since 1989, many civilians have taught there for many years, and directors general, assistant secretaries, and secretaries lecture regularly.[48] The importance of educational contacts are discussed in chapter 6.

The only area in which considerable contact between officers and civilians is maintained through higher education is military law. A small percentage of officers pursuing careers in military law graduate from the National University after completing their military education. A notable example is General Max Notholt Rosales, who even as a retired officer was director general of naval legal affairs under two secretaries of the navy, from 1977 to 1988. He graduated from the HCM in 1947 and from the National School of Law in 1967.[49] Civilian lawyers from the National University have taught at the Center for Higher Naval Studies, the navy's equivalent of the Escuela Superior de Guerra, at least since the 1950s.[50]

The lack of substantial military contact with civilians has many possible consequences. It is charged, for instance, that military officers tend to have a uniform point of view in regard to social problems, and often are at odds with the majority of the population. The homogeneity, observers say, originates in military discipline and/or indoctrination at the military academies. Marion Levy argues that it is the absence of general social contact and isolation from civilian settings that may be at the root of the uniformity, not the training.[51]

The insularity of the Mexican military not only limits civilian occupancy of top posts in the secretariats, and the benefits that might flow therefrom, but impacts on the continuity of top military leadership. As I have stated elsewhere,

It is worth noting that the secretariat of national defense is the only cabinet agency since 1946 which has not had a change in secretary mid-way through an administration. The top leadership of the military is characterized by extraordinary stability, and the secretary of defense always [is a] senior officer.[52]

This is just one illustration of how the political elite discourages military intervention. It hopes that by not politicizing officer corps leadership, it eliminates a possible reason for military intervention. The continuity in military leadership suggests that the president, who frequently plays musical chairs with or removes other cabinet figures, does not tinker with the armed forces. Salinas's abrupt dismissal of Admiral Scheskle as secretary of the navy in 1990 was an exceptional, necessary intervention. However, in granting the military autonomy in personnel matters, the civilian leadership simultaneously encourages the artificial separation of the military and civilian leaderships. The lack of contact between the two groups increases some risks associated with military intervention, and the distance civil leadership has maintained from internal military affairs has decreased other risks.

Party and Electoral Activity

Mexico's civilian leadership involved the military politically through one other means. At the same time that President Cárdenas and other revolutionary leaders were reducing the politically active officer corps, Cárdenas altered the structure of the government party—the Mexican Revolutionary Party (PRM)—to incorporate the military as a special sector, as discussed in detail earlier. Previously, the party had three sectors, agrarian, labor, and popular, and the military was one of many groups in the popular sector. Cárdenas created the military sector to bring the officers into the open and force them to channel their political activities through the party, where they could be kept in check by other sectors.[53] One analyst declared that fortunately for Mexico, ambitious generals responded to Cárdenas's challenge and chose to engage in combat on the electoral level.[54]

Cárdenas, of course, was criticized for deliberately trying to involve the military in party politics. His motivations seem clear in his response: "We are not involving the army in politics, it is already involved. In fact, it has dominated the situation, and we are reducing its influence to one out of four votes."[55]

Although the military sector was short-lived, from 1938 to 1940, it is not its potential policy influence as a separate party sector that is important to consider.[56] In the first place, the party per se was not a vehicle for that kind of policy influence, which instead occurred within the executive branch. Making the military a visible component of the corporatist structure through the party was important more for psychological reasons. Although Cárdenas's reasoning makes sense, an argument could be made that by highlighting its influence in such fashion, the government gave the military much more prestige, recognizing it as an equal of the larger, traditional sectors. Strategically, this was a serious political error. The case of the private sector is instructive. The entrepreneurial leadership has always felt politically limited and inferior to other groups, especially labor, because it has never been formally incorporated within the party.[57] It participates individually as part of the popular sector, which since 1943 the military does too. In terms of civil-military relations, elimination that year of the military's sectorial representation in the party sent a message to the populace that the military had no legitimate reason to be involved in electoral politics, and that the system did not recognize its formal participation as acceptable. The socialization of succeeding generations of Mexicans, civilians and military alike, to the fact that the military's task fundamentally was nonpolitical benefited from this perception.

When the government withdrew the military's sectorial status in the party, it did so with great care, leaving a talented and politically ambitious officer in the position of secretary of popular action, the party's top representative of the popular sector. The officer, Major Antonio Nava Castillo, cofounded and later served as first secretary general of the National Federation of Popular Organizations, the most influential umbrella organization in the popular sector. He was a military aide to Manuel Avila Camacho, ultimately rising to the rank of division general in 1961.[58] Later, Leandro Valle, an organization made up almost entirely of retired and active officers, or their closest relatives, informally replaced the abolished military sector. Many of Mexico's leading political-military officers, such as Generals Hermenegildo Cuenca Díaz and Fernando Pámanes Escobedo, were its members or leaders. It has never had much visibility or any influence within the party leadership.[59] In 1954 those officers, looking for an electoral vehicle more to their liking, established the Authentic Party of the Mexican Revolution (PARM), a co-opted offshoot of the PRI (which replaced PRM in 1946) financed by the government. The PARM has generally been led by retired army officers and, in recent years, admirals. It joined Cuauhtémoc Cárdenas's alliance, becoming part of the populist opposition in 1988.[60]

When Alemán ran for the presidency in 1946, he tried to impose his "civilianizing" pattern on the party too. He not only revised its name but imposed an unknown and unpopular president of the National Executive Committee president. In less than a year he appointed General Rodolfo Sánchez Taboada, a former aide to Lázaro Cárdenas, to the post. From December 1946 to December 1964, four generals, among Mexico's most important political-military officers, directed the government's party: Rodolfo Sánchez Taboada, Gabriel Leyva Velázquez, Agustín Olachea Aviles, and Alfonso Corona del Rosal. It is also no accident that military officers led the party during the same years the military was most prominently represented in national political office after 1946. Even if only symbolically, the military was better represented in the party leadership (six of its twenty-one presidents since 1935) than in the leadership of the executive branch.

Piñeyro believes that a liaison group of prominent military officers evolved as a substitute for the military sector after 1952. In his opinion, General Corona del Rosal, along with other high-ranking officers, headed this group within the PRI for years, and the group was the only link between the army and the bureaucratic-political apparatus, especially the PRI, through which top officers could voice personal and institutional demands.[61] This pattern has been formalized in more recent years in the military's selection of talented and ambitious young officers as assistants on the PRI president's staff, but they have no input, practically speaking.[62]

The military has tended to remain aloof from party activities, especially since 1952. Opposition groups do not have special ties to, nor do they attempt to elicit support from, the military. In part, of course, this is a by-product of a modified one-party state, and the continuous relationship between an established civilian leadership and the officer corps.[63] Until 1987 an opposition party with widespread support among various sectors of the population did not exist, and hence the government party was unchallenged in its co-opting of the military. Among military officers in national political office between 1935 and 1987, only one was a member of the National Action Party (PAN), the Mexican Democratic Party, the Mexican Socialist Party, the Revolutionary Workers Party, or the Unified Socialist Party of Mexico. In this respect Mexico has been unique among most Latin American countries. As Ackroyd suggests, co-optation "in a multiparty system encourages military intervention," but in a single-dominant-party system, intervention is discouraged.[64]

After the Revolution elements of the military, in alliance with civilian groups, tried to wrest control from established political leadership, but the efforts tapered off gradually until 1952. Military leadership has employed various socializing means to convey a message of nonparticipation. For example, the May 1927 issue of *Revista del Ejército* reprinted an editorial from the government-controlled newspaper *El Universal* that condemned the political ambitions of Generals Arnulfo R. Gómez and Francisco R. Serrano, both of whom were presidential hopefuls.[65] Obregón, who ran a second time, forced Gómez to rebel, capturing and executing him. Serrano, Obregón's relative and political disciple, and Serrano's closest civilian aides were murdered on Obregón's orders.

Serrano's death is extremely important because it served as a severely cautionary message to officers present and future who might consider pursuing political ambitions "outside" the system. The ruthless massacre of Serrano's campaign staff also sent a chilling message to civilians giving thought to associating themselves with military political opponents of the regime. It is often forgotten that the key figure in establishing many aspects of current civil-military relations, Miguel Alemán, was a student supporter of General Gómez, and that Alemán and many of his peers went on to become important figures in politics from 1946 through 1970.[66] Their antimilitarism stemmed from the events associated with the 1929 presidential campaign.

Although a military rebellion occurred in 1929 and again on a minuscule scale in 1939, forces loyal to the political elite easily suppressed both attempts. It was not until 1940 that an important faction within the officer corps joined a splinter group from the political establishment to support General Juan Almazán's presidential candidacy. Inevitably, although Almazán attracted supporters from other sectors as well, he was unsuccessful in his bid. Officers who supported Almazán were granted a leave to campaign for him, but the defense secretary announced on September 13 that they had until October 1 to return to active duty or face charges of desertion—an order that considerably circumscribed their political choices.[67]

The last presidential hopeful to attract followers from within the officer corps was General Miguel Henríquez Guzmán, who tried for the official party nomination in 1945 and 1951. Having failed twice, he ran against the civilian elite's choice in 1952. The general, who could claim personal ties to martyred President Francisco I. Madero, ironically, had helped suppress Almazán's supporters as the Monterrey zone commander. Civilian elites were not even tolerant of his 1945 precandidacy; they removed one of his supporters, General Marcelino García Barragán, who was on leave from active duty and serving as governor of Jalisco, from office nearly a year early—in February 1947—as punishment for supporting Henríquez Guzmán.[68] In 1951 Henríquez Guzmán formed his own party, the Federation of Peoples Party of Mexico, which García Barragán headed. Interestingly, Cuauhtémoc Cárdenas, the only Mexican to produce a popular opposition movement in many decades, was a student supporter of Henríquez Guzmán in 1951.[69] Henríquez Guzmán had been chief of staff to Cárdenas's father in 1929.[70]

According to Piñeyro, since 1952 almost no officers have spoken out against the government, or supported a political candidate or opposition party. The exceptions, such as a brigadier general who as principal speaker at PAN's closing election meeting in 1985 criticized the government, and former Colonel Leopoldo de Gyves, who served as a federal deputy from the Unified Socialist Party of Mexico (PSUM), are rare, and have either left the service or do not have active commands.[71]

The military and civilian leaderships' success in limiting officer political activity can be illustrated empirically. Given the presence of opposition parties after 1920 and the establishment elite's limited legitimacy, one might expect many civilian and military leaders alike to have joined those parties. Yet, from 1920 to 1934 only 5 percent of the politically active officers were leaders of opposition parties, and fewer than 6 percent were members. Among politically active civilians, the proportions were even smaller. Officers who joined opposition parties were not sympathizers of Díaz or Huerta but, rather, were revolutionaries who supported alternative choices. However, joining opposition parties quickly disappeared as a career experience among successful generals; since 1946 only 3 percent have done so, and of those, all but one were born before 1900. No general born after 1910 has been an active member or leader of an opposition party until the announcement of Alberto Quintanar López on September 20, 1990, that he had joined the Democratic Revolutionary Party (PRD) as an adviser. The son of a chauffeur, the former troop commander and director general of infantry under de la Madrid was on retired status.[72]

The government and the military seem to have an informal rule preventing military officers, even on leave, from involving themselves with parties other than the PRI. In fact, since 1952, only one active duty general has worked for an opposition civilian presidential hopeful (Vicente Lombardo Toledano, candidate of the Popular Party, forerunner of the Popular Socialist Party [PPS]). Octavio Véjar Vázquez, who had become vice-president of the party in 1951, was tried under Article 17 of the 1945 law of military discipline, which held that "the military on active duty is strictly prohibited from involving himself in political affairs or work, directly or indirectly, without losing the rights given by the Constitution. . . ."[73] According to Lieuwen, the many officers who participated in the PRI campaign equally violated Article 17.[74] Véjar Vázquez was detained in the Tlatelolco military prison for disobeying a superior's order. His trial raised the question of whether career officers with leave really were free to participate in politics, that is, opposition politics.[75]

Observers of the Mexican political scene have witnessed the military's involvement in successive presidential campaigns. In regard to the 1981 presidential contest, for example, Michael Dziedzic cites a U.S. exchange officer's description of the activity:

"When we arrived there were four DINA buses parked behind the mess hall. In the morning the purpose of the buses became evident; they were to transport troops to the towns where PRI candidate Miguel de la Madrid was to visit starting Friday 18 Dec 81. The troops were formed up at about 0630 to prepare for the trip. They were in civilian clothes and were to serve as extra guards and crowd fillers. I asked some of my classmates about this and if they didn't find it strange that this happens. They said it happens every election year and although they didn't agree with the practice, [they] knew there was nothing they could do about it."[76]

These troops and junior officers obviously were not on leave to perform these activities, directly contrary to the prohibitions set forth in the organic military law.

De la Madrid's presidential campaign staff, according to several of its members, were on leave.[77] Generally, an important officer, known to the candidate, directs presidential campaign security. In the case of de la Madrid, the officer in charge was General Carlos Humberto Dávila Bermúdez, whose career is instructive of this type of officer. Bermúdez demonstrated an interest in politics at a young age, having served as an auxiliary secretary to Alfonso Corona del Rosal, who was president of the National Executive Committee of the PRI from 1963 to 1964. Much of his career was spent with the presidential staff. Under Echeverría, he was in charge of military aides; under López Portillo, he was subchief of the presidential staff; and under de la Madrid, he became chief of the presidential staff in 1982.

When Salinas ran for president in 1988, one author asserted that one general, four colonels, and one hundred other officers and troops were working for the PRI.[78] These security people were known euphemistically in the media as the Logistic Assistance Group. The cozy relationship between the military and the PRI not only is important to civil-military relations in general, but gives certain officers leadership advantages within the service itself. It is the president who designates the secretary of defense, and because officers with political interests can exercise them only under the PRI umbrella, those officers become known to men who may become president. Juan Arévalo Gardoqui, for example, rose from chief of security in Adolfo López Mateos's campaign, to chief of aides in 1958, giving him contact as a junior officer with many future leading politicians.

Traditionally, the only long-lived opposition party with which the military might have some ongoing contact, and possibly some ideological affinity, is the PAN. Some analysts, Edward J. Williams among them, have speculated about a possible alliance between the PAN and conservative military officers, but there is no empirical evidence of such a connection.[79] Williams argues that the military has no love for the Left, a statement made, of course, before the Cuauhtémoc Cárdenas candidacy in 1987. Cárdenas himself, of course, is a populist. His desertion from PRI ranks and his creation of an opposition alliance (the National Democratic Front [FDN]) combining populist and left elements from outside and within the party produced a new environment in military-opposition party relations. It threatens what Salinas's defense minister calls the military's political neutrality: military personnel as an institution do not have a party.[80]

Cárdenas told the press in 1988 that he was not looking for an open and direct relationship with those in command of the armed forces in spite of the fact that "when any military person expresses his sympathy with the FDN [now the Democratic Revolutionary Party, the PRD], he is removed from his post and various charges are brought against him."[81] However, in early 1990, after political violence in Michoacán and Guerrero, Cárdenas did call for the military to prevent such actions and to protect his sympathizers. Although PAN representatives made no public declaration, the other parties represented in the lower chamber, including the PRI, PARM, PPS, and the Cardenista splinter group, the Party of the Cardenista Front of National Reconstruction (PFCRN), rejected his call for intervention, saying it would cause political instability.[82] In response to Cárdenas, the secretary of defense professed that the military intervenes in political conflict only when constitutional order disappears. It was taking preventive measures, he said, in Acapulco and Zihuantanejo, Guerrero, two trouble spots, to preserve order and keep public transportation operational.[83] However, on April 5, 1990, the army declared a state of seige, and military police in armored vehicles began routing PRDistas from various Michoacán state halls.[84]

Although no officers have shown any inclination go counter to informal military policy by involving themselves with the PRD, there is substantial evidence that numerous officers and enlisted men are sympathetic to Cárdenas's program. Some observers indirectly hold that elements in all the services, at the highest levels, are demanding an end to corruption and the implementation of policies beneficial to the people's basic needs.[85] Moreover, it has been asserted that many officers and enlisted men alike voted for Cárdenas in 1988.[86] In urban areas the military tended to vote for both the Left and the Right rather than for the PRI.[87] The first evidence of military voting for opposition parties actually occurred before Cárdenas's candidacy. According to a former member of the PRI National Executive Committee, officers and enlisted men voted in the late 1970s in larger numbers for opposition parties, primarily on the left, than for the PRI, in polling booths on military bases in the Federal District.[88] Interestingly, the secretary general of the Socialist Workers Party (PST), one of the leftist opposition organizations during this period, was Luis Graco Ramírez Garrido Abreu, coordinator of the PST congressional delegation and son of a prominent general.[89] According to newspaperman Luis Angel Garza, in 1976 the polling booth at the Monterrey military zone headquarters, one of the most influential zones in Mexico, went for the Panistas, and one of the battalions was transferred to Sinaloa in consequence.[90]

In the 1988 elections the leftist magazine *Proceso* placed a number of its reporters at individual polling stations serving largely military voters. In Cárdenas's home state, Michoacán, in the polling station adjacent to the general barracks of the military zone command in Morelia, the general's son received 502 votes to 156 for Salinas and 156 for Clouthier, the PAN candidate. On the air base in Zapopan, Jalisco, the location of the air force academy, Salinas received 752 votes to 193 for Clouthier and 77 for Cárdenas. In a number of Oaxacan polling stations covered by the magazine, including those in military residential zones, Cárdenas received more votes than Salinas.[91]

There is one other feature of military involvement in elections: the military itself is in charge of ballot packets, which means that in cases of fraud or alleged fraud, the military's representatives must know the real results, or in some cases may even be a party to electoral manipulation. Because of the military's socialization and training, if excessive fraud is reverted to in the immediate future, and public outcry cannot go unanswered, the military may no longer be a willing silent partner in civilian-directed machinations.

Civic Action and Disaster Relief

Civic action is another element in what David Ronfeldt labeled the residual political roles of the military. Civic action, generally composed of a variety of developmental-type projects, brings the officer corps in contact with rural poverty and ordinary Mexicans. The specific nature of civic action programs depends on the needs and priorities given to them by individual states. The military is the entity representative of the federal government in the hinterland, and in that sense performs a political function for the political leadership.[92]

The scope of the military's civic action, including its responsibilities in the antidrug campaign, are prescribed by the Mexican Constitution:

> No military authority may, in time of peace, perform any functions other than those that are directly connected with military affairs. There shall be fixed and permanent military commands only in the castles, forts, and warehouses

immediately subordinate to the Government of the Union; or in encampments, barracks, or arsenals established for the quartering of troops outside towns.[93]

Strictly speaking, the military has been violating portions of this article since 1920. Its programs have included health education; applied medicine, from dentistry to minor surgery; school and road construction and repairs; dispensing food supplies and utensils; and reforestation.[94]

Military civic action did not originate as counterinsurgency measures but as a component of the armed forces revolutionary tradition. According to historians, in 1921 General Obregón created nineteen labor battalions to be employed in road construction, irrigation projects, railroad maintenance, and telegraph repairs. These functions were continued under his successor and legitimized in the army's organic law, as long as they had some connection to military needs.[95] Considering the military's actual activities, "needs" obviously have been broadly defined.

The military itself, however, gives various forms of civic action high priority. The idea, according to one analyst, is to convey a benign image to the public. The army and air force assigns it significant attention in the official *Revista Ejército y Fuerza Aérea*.[96] By the 1950s the military was involved in such public relations functions as Little League baseball and transportation of antimalaria drugs. And even in that decade it was already cooperating with civilian police against drug smuggling and sales.[97] In the 1960s, 60 percent of its budget was devoted to these types of projects. During the following decade, military officers with engineering and communications skills were recruited to a pilot developmental program known as Plan Huicot.[98] In the 1990s the military continued its health programs, which in addition to checkups and innoculations, also involved the distribution of potable water, veterinary checkups, and actual surgical procedures. In March 1990, in the state of México alone, 1,500 troops were engaged in these activities.[99]

The army was put in charge of coordinating disaster relief in 1966, reflected in the aforementioned DN-III-E national security plan. In the 1980s two major emergency relief programs received national attention. One was the effort subsequent to the eruption of the Chichonal volcano in 1982, during which the secretary of national defense took personal charge of the operations. According to Alden Cunningham, the move suggested the military's ascendancy over civilian elements in disaster situations, and the increased esteem thereby accorded the military added legitimacy to and respect for the government.[100] In contrast, during the major earthquake in Mexico City the following fall, instead of giving the military overall responsibility, civilian authorities took control. The military's role was to provide security, and

in so doing, it occasionally impeded spontaneous civilian ventures, thereby damaging its reputation—a fact that embittered many generals toward the *técnicos* who had restrained them. At the same time, the navy's image sparkled because after its ministry building collapsed, blue-uniformed officers were seen relentlessly hunting for survivors in the ruins of its own and nearby buildings.[101]

The National Security Role

Although the military's participation in campaigns, elections, and opposition parties is its most obvious means of political involvement in Mexico, indirect means equally affect its self-image and potential political participation. Among the most important, suggested by one of the working hypotheses, is the manner in which civilian and military leaderships define national security. A hypothesis has been offered by Phyllis Walker, who argues that

> the national security doctrines designed by the armed forces of other Latin American countries—in particular, those of the Southern Cone—to deal with perceived threats were not developed in Mexico. Moreover, the absence of such a doctrine may represent a partial explanation for the military's continuing non-intervention in political affairs throughout the post-World War II era.[102]

It has been suggested that in other countries, notably Brazil from 1964 to 1974, its primary concern was domestic subversion and that the officers educated in this "ideology of internal warfare" at the Higher War College were the primary architects of the March 1964 coup against the civilian government.[103]

The trend toward an armed forces national security function is universal. Some theorists expect it to become a primary function of the military in most countries.[104] This orientation in Mexico is complicated by the fact that the United States, in its relations with Latin America, has not articulated a notion of internal security that incorporates level of development.[105] Proximity to the United States and the long history of U.S. aggression against Mexico, and the fact that Mexico is the only country in which the majority of U.S. officers say they would fight against domestic insurgents, encouraged Mexico to pursue an external defense strategy.[106] Nevertheless, Mexico too has moved in the direction of the military's playing a larger national security role.

Mexico's definition of national security was influenced by the cold war mentality of the United States in the postwar era. The 1952 edition of the basic text on military ethics changed the order of Mexico's military objectives, placing preservation of internal order first and defense of national territory third.[107] In 1965, after an armed group attempted to assault the military barracks in Ciudad Madera, Chihuahua, references to special or guerrilla warfare began to appear in military publications.[108] Colonel Jorge Carrillo Olea, former director of Mexico's Department of Federal Security defined it:

> Number one, Mexico does not have external military enemies. This permits us to set aside a series of matters. . . . The unsatisfied demands of the people are the first element to attend to: services, education, justice. . . . To ignore these will produce a more polarized society.
>
> Mexico's problems are inside its borders, recognizing that the source of many of these originate from outside the country and have a great deal to do with social justice. Which are the groups on the margin at truly insupportable extremes? Where is the government not capable of guaranteeing average stan-

dard measures and norms of justice and of democracy? This is the problem of national security.[109]

Despite the military's reorientation from external defense to internal security affairs, national security experts suggest that the military itself had little to do with the change. According to Olga Pellicer, "One outstanding feature of the national security issue in Mexico is the slight participation of the military sector both in the definition of the concept of national security itself and in the decision as to the most appropriate means of confronting the dangers that threaten it."[110] In an interview granted by General Félix Galván López, defense secretary from 1976 to 1982, he suggested that the essence of national security, the ideology that inspires it, the relations among the classes that facilitate it, and the respective share of power to each group were not matters for the army to decide.[111]

In 1985, as if to reinforce this interpretation, the Secretariat of Government quietly established an agency known as the General Directorate of Investigation and National Security. Its first head was Pedro Vásquez Colmenares, a veteran civilian politician. Phyllis Walker observed that his appointment signaled the military's inability to translate its influence into a more active role in national security policy-making.[112] Her reasoning appears logical, but closer examination of this agency and other security-oriented agencies since 1985 suggests a somewhat different picture.

Within a week of taking office in 1988, Salinas appointed José Córdoba to direct a technical cabinet comprising five sections. Four of the sections—economic, agricultural, social welfare, and foreign relations—had been established by de la Madrid, but Salinas added a fifth: national security, composed of the Secretariat of National Defense; the Secretariat of the Navy; the Secretariat of Government; the Secretariat of Foreign Relations; and the attorney general.[113] Although Vázquez Colmenares's appointment might seem to reflect civilian dominance over security affairs, it is worth noting that his immediate superior was Jorge Carrillo Olea, a colonel and subsecretary in charge of all secretariat security-oriented agencies. Carrillo Olea was the only active duty officer holding a position at that level in a civilian government agency from 1982 to 1988. In 1988 he was appointed to replace Vázquez Colmenares as director of the new agency, the only active duty officer holding a civilian directorship's post or higher.[114] Carrillo Olea, unlike previous active duty officers on leave or retired, uses his military title. He was not a typical cadet, having been the outstanding student of his HCM generation in 1957, and having commanded the 3rd Company of Cadets at HCM from 1959 to 1962. A graduate of the Escuela Superior de Guerra, he trained in the United States at Fort Knox. He held the key military intelligence post as head of the intelligence section at national defense headquarters, where he served with five future generals, including Miguel Angel Godínez Bravo and Carlos H. Bermúdez Davila, presidential chiefs of staff, 1976–82 and 1982–88 respectively. His personal values are illustrated by the fact that he once arrested himself as an example to his subordinates. He has ties to the present senior officer corps because his cadet peers are now generals, and he has been linked personally to General Jesús Castañeda Gutiérrez, Echeverría's presidential chief of staff.[115]

Carrillo Olea's predecessor as subsecretary, Fernando Gutiérrez Barrios, went on to become the government secretary in 1988, after a long history in the Department of Federal Security. Gutiérrez Barrios, of course, is a former officer, the son of a Revolutionary colonel, and a graduate of HCM who resigned his commission as a captain in 1959.[116] An internal security focus has also taken hold in the Defense Secretariat at the higher echelons. The new oficial mayor of the secretariat, General Raúl Juárez Carreño, received advanced training in intelligence gathering, counter insurgency, and psychological warfare in the United States.[117]

These men who are responsible for the implementation of national security policy have closer ties to the military than their typical civilian peers. The switch from a civilian to military head of the General Directorate of Investigation and National Security may have been an indication of the military's increasing role in defining national security, a role that only a few years earlier it had eschewed. On the other hand, typically, its antecedent agency, the Federal Security Department (DFS), which disbanded in 1985,[118] had been headed since 1946 by an active duty or retired officer holding the rank of colonel.[119] It is important to note that the agency was founded in 1946 in the Alemán administration. The president ordered the secretary of defense to pick four or five top young officers to organize the DFS.[120] Its first director, General Marcelino Iñurreta, who had studied with the U.S. Federal Bureau of Investigation, having been a federal deputy, organized the department.[121] Once again, Alemán, while reducing the military's overt role in politics, simultaneously provided the means for insuring its involvement in national security issues, at least at the enforcement level.[122]

Indirectly, the military's regular representation in the Directorate of Federal Security and subsequently in the National Security Directorate gives it some access to political intelligence information. Cunningham believes that although junior officers assigned as aides in various agencies and to state governors are not required to report in any organized fashion to the secretary of national defense on information they obtain, "at higher levels, especially among security agencies, the coordination and information exchange is clearly facilitated by military men who operate in or take charge of civilian police forces or work in the Government Secretariat."[123]

Ties to security agencies have involved the military with civilian leaders and agencies, providing a special channel of communication. On the other hand, the security agencies' unsavory reputation, especially the DFS and the federal judicial police, with whom the military has associated, taints the military.[124] None other than former Defense Secretary Félix Galván López recognized this effect. When he was zone commander, he told the governor of Chihuahua that the military should not serve with the federal police against drug traffickers because he had witnessed police agents abusing prisoners.[125] However, according to the 1990 Americas Watch *Report on Mexico*, "torture and political killings are still institutionalized in the military" and by federal and state police.[126] In reponse to this characterization the Salinas administration created the National Commission on Human Rights.[127] Of the seventy formal complaints processed in its first two months, only one involved the military: the detention and torture on August 12, 1988, of Australian citizen Phillip Edward Hastings, who had been detained by four members of the army in Puerto Vallarta and later interrogated by judicial police. He had been examined by Captain Mario Sánchez Jiménez, an army surgeon, and certified as being in good health and having been subjected to no maltreatment. Yet, when he arrived at a hospital the same day, he had six fractures on his nose and hands, and marks over his entire body. Hastings identified his aggressors as two members of the Mexican army. The commission recommended to the Secretariat of National Defense that the soldiers and the physician be discharged, and that criminal proceedings be brought against them.[128] Following that report, the Catholic church's Centro de Derechos Humanos Fray Bartolomé de las Casas alleged that soldiers interrogated and beat peasants in search of marijuana fields. Bishop Samuel Ruíz García formally requested an investigation from General Miguel Angel Godínez Bravo, commander of the 31st zone.[129]

Hardware specialists, examining Mexico's acquisitions program since the mid-1980s, also detect an emphasis on national security as part of military modernization. They believe that the greater prominence of national security considerations parallels the growing foreign policy assertiveness, and that civilian and military leaderships are both reevaluating the armed forces' traditional role.[130] The military's mission is delineated in three defense plans known as DN-I, DN-II, and DN-III. DN-I sets forth the Secretariat of Defense's strategy in case of invasion, an approach relying on a people's militia and protracted guerrilla warfare. DN-II responds to internal problems, including insurgencies, strikes, and other civil disturbances, and calls for an immediate reaction and isolation of the instigators. DN-III, which has been put into effect on several occasions, responds to natural disasters to avert the country's becoming vulnerable to internal or external enemies.[131]

The Mexican military plays a significant internal political role as part of the national security formula. Its scope includes civic action projects, drug eradication, and political suppression. When the civilian leadership fails to negotiate a satisfactory solution in a political dispute, and failing the use of other threats, it may take recourse in a military solution. Typically, Mexican politicians have not resorted to the military except in extreme cases; however, such cases occur far more often than one might think. The more civilian leadership relies on the military to carry out politicized, internal police functions, the more the military itself expects to have a voice in political decision making, and equally important, the more society, including future civilian and military leaders, defines intervention as a legitimate military responsibility.

The military's ability to suppress opposition groups and individual leaders is critical to the system's stability. Elite divisions are a potential source of regime instability. However, as the secession of the Cardenistas from the PRI illustrates, as long as the masses remain relatively undisturbed, elite splits will not destabilize Mexico. On the other hand, mass movements will not endanger the system as long as the elites remain relatively cohesive. The military is more likely to intervene when mass movements and elite splits occur simultaneously.[132] Irving Louis Horowitz believes the military's police function is a form of militarization. Although he does not provide concrete evidence of such a relationship, he argues that the "military receives special benefits for its internal management of order," and that among various co-opted groups, it is one of the largest beneficiaries of Mexico's centralized system.[133] Piñeyro, however, suggests that especially after 1961 the military obtained concessions in payment for its political activities, including promulgation of an armed forces social security law.[134]

Beginning in the late 1950s the military played a primary role in suppressing the railroad workers strikes in 1958–1959, the telephone and postal workers movement in 1960, and a student movement in Mexico City in 1961. It was also implicated in the death of an important peasant leader, Rúben Jaramillo, but as Karl Schmitt notes, the case was hushed up, and the involvement of the army high command and the national leadership was impossible to ascertain.[135] The military has been used to shut down critical presses too. The presidential guard arrested the editor of *Política*, a left-wing publication, in the early 1960s.

The military's most frequent use, and least documented, has been to control numerous rural political disturbances. To maintain order in the countryside, it uses small detachments of soldiers, each generally led by a lieutenant, that are assigned to the more inaccessible regions.[136] A U.S. officer's report in the early 1980s noted that a detachment's most common task is to mediate land disputes in small Indian villages, and to investigate murders and other potentially explosive situations.[137] In the late 1970s General Galván strengthened this system by expanding patroling from a fixed base.[138]

In the late 1960s the military subdued electoral unrest in Mérida and Tijuana, provoked by strong competition from the National Action Party.[139] Its most notable intervention in suppression of a mass movement is, of course, the student massacre at Tlatelolco Plaza in 1968, spoken of earlier.

When Echeverría became president in 1970, the military involved itself in an internal political dispute, probably inadvertently coming close to supporting a dissident faction in a high-level power struggle. As discussed previously, his political enemy, Alfonso Martínez Domínguez, then head of the Federal District, used a group of paramilitary forces known as the Halcones, under the command of Colonel Manuel Díaz Escobar, to attack a student group in the capital, hoping to destabilize the government and force Echeverría's resignation. The president survived the incident and in an emergency meeting obtained the backing of his senior commanders, after which he fired Martínez Domínguez and the police chief, and arrested Díaz Escobar. Reportedly, Díaz Escobar was not well liked in the military. Nevertheless, remarkably, his reported arrest and his involvement in such an event did not result in his being blackballed in his career;[140] he reached the rank of brigadier general in 1975, went on to head at least three zone commands after 1976, and retired as a division general in 1984. The president's actions implicitly absolved the military or its representative of any complicity in the political plot.

The military received national attention shortly afterward when the PRI candidate for governor of Guerrero, Rúben Figueroa, was kidnapped by an active guerrilla group led by Lucio Cabañas Barrientos, who under murky circumstances was killed by the military in December 1974, several months after Figueroa had gained his freedom. Military censorship prevailed over other activities in the antiguerrilla campaign too. As one participant recalled, "One incident that has never been revealed publicly, . . . someone accidentally set off a firefight between a parachute battalion and an infantry group, and a number of soldiers were killed by our own troops."[141]

Since 1977 the military's police role, with internal security implications, has focused largely on the drug trade. And under Salinas the military has functioned as a sort of an independent, presidential SWAT team. The government used the military twice for strike duty: first to replace striking Mexico City bus drivers rather than suppress them, and later to occupy the Cananea mining company after negotiations broke down with the workers' union.[142]

In the past decade the single most important linkage between the military and the political leadership is the cooperation of both in the fight against the drug trade. Salinas reinforced the importance of drugs as a national security issue in his first state of the union address: "The drug trafficker has become a grave risk for the national security and the health of Mexicans." He committed the state to combating it forcefully.[143] The military's involvement, especially since implementation of the Condor Plan in 1977, has serious implications for Mexico's political leadership and for the military's political role. Among the issues raised are interinstitutional coordination, since the program is in the hands of the attorney general; exposure of the army to the extensive corruption that accompanies the drug trade; increased contact between U.S. officers and government officials and the Mexican officer corps; constitutional questions raised by the military's strategy; supremacy of the military over civilian control in various regions; and enhancement of the military's public image compared to that of civilian politicians.[144]

In 1985, 20 generals, 120 high-ranking officers, and 25,000 soldiers—18 percent of the active duty army—were engaged in antidrug work. As of that date, 315 military men had died in the antidrug campaign.[145] In 1990 the government paper *El Nacional* quoted Secretariat of Defense figures of 12,000 soldiers on full-time duty against drug trafficking.[146] Reportedly a majority of officers would prefer to devote themselves to traditional military pursuits, but instead they were facing internal challengers to power, within and outside the political and military elites.[147] Sensing the officers' resentment, Salinas has narrowed the scope of military antidrug work to destroying drugs rather than combating dealers.[148]

General Roberto Heine Rangel is a typical high-ranking officer deeply involved in the drug eradication program. He completed courses at Fort Leavenworth, Kansas, and Fort Benning, Georgia, wrote a book on guerrilla warfare, and taught a course on the subject at the HCM. He commanded field operations in the Condor program, and served as a zone commander in Sonora, 1978–1979, and Guerrero, 1987.[149] His career suggests the use of antiguerrilla combat techniques learned in the United States against drug traffickers. He and his peers are a pool of veterans whose experience may have had or will have an impact on promotions.

According to some observers, drug-driven corruption undermined the government's credibility in the late 1980s.[150] The linkage became more visible in the first year of the Salinas administration, when the former head of the Department of Federal Security, indicted for journalist Manuel Buendía's murder, was said to have ties to the drug trade. The problem reached even more serious levels in the military high command. The military is so concerned with drugs corrupting its leadership that it has stepped up internal intelligence, including increased tapping of phones. One officer remarked that an unforeseen consequence of such measures has limited conversations about, and criticisms of, military policy among officers.[151]

The antidrug campaign has made the military the supreme authority, or in some cases, the only authority in parts of such states as Oaxaca, Sinaloa, Jalisco, and Guerrero.[152] The long-term effect of this is, of course, to subvert civilian political supremacy, and give the military a taste of political control on a regional level. Its increased visibility has largely been positive, and there does not seem to be public resistance to its exercising such a role, opening up the possibility of engaging in other nontraditional roles in the future.[153] On the other hand, the inability of the combined efforts of the attorney general's office, state police, and the armed forces to rein in drug trafficking suggests that the government has its own security problem, and that its territorial hegemony is incomplete. Richard Craig asserts that either through intimidation or corruption, drug lords exercise de facto power in portions of Sinaloa, Durango, Chihuahua, Guerrero, Veracruz, and Oaxaca.[154]

Whether the armed forces are in control or not in several regions, they are operating twenty-four hours a day. Many of the techniques they use, which one might logically expect in wartime, especially on foreign soil, are in violation of Article 129 of the Constitution, which confines the army to certain locations, thus limiting its ability to subvert civilian control. Permanent military roadblocks, for example, are constitutionally questionable.[155]

The image of the military in the provinces is affected by its role in drug eradication. It is somewhat ironic that use of marijuana by troops and officers has been associated with the military since the Revolution. It probably began when officers gave marijuana to drafted civilians in the old Federal Army. Its use was popularized in the revolutionary song "La Cucaracha," which schoolchildren in the United States sing, substituting a less offensive phrase for "marijuana que fumar." Although the military has been involved in eradicating drug production for many decades, until the 1970s it had to cope only with individual farmers, not cartels. More important, the number of peasants growing the associated crops has increased tremendously, complicating the military's relationship with the rural population. Because the military likes to think of itself as deriving from the masses, and it realizes that most peasants are trying only to survive, not to profit from criminality, it becomes difficult to destroy crops.[156]

The officer corps has involved itself politically in many ways, both in structural roles assigned to it by the civilian leadership and in extramilitary posts held by officers. As the latter have declined, which in recent years can hardly be seen as representative of military versus individual officer interests, the military has widened its nontraditional activities, most notably in the antidrug campaigns. Any new departures from its residual political roles have implications for the growth or decline of military influence in the political system, and the scope of civil-military interlocks.[157]

Notes

1. Franklin D. Margiotta, "The Mexican Military: A Case Study in Non-intervention" (M.A. thesis, Georgetown University, 1968).

2. Roderic A. Camp, "Generals and Politicians in Mexico: A Preliminary Comparison," in *The Modern Mexican Military: A Reassessment*, ed. David Ronfeldt (La Jolla: Center for U.S.-Mexican Studies, University of California, San Diego, 1984), 148.

3. Calles was actually born in 1877, but because of his formative experience and background, belongs to this significant political generation.

4. Roderic A. Camp, "Mexican Military Leadership in Statistical Perspective since the 1930s," in *Statistical Abstract of Latin America*, vol. 20, ed. James W. Wilkie and Peter Reich (Los Angeles: Latin American Center Publications, University of California, Los Angeles, 1980), 602.

5. Personal letter from Eduardo Bustamante, Mexico City, December 16, 1975.

6. Personal interview with Miguel Alemán, Mexico City, October 27, 1976.

7. Lyle N. McAlister, *The Military in Latin American Socio-political Evolution: Four Case Studies* (Washington, D.C.: Center for Research in Social Systems, 1970), 241. General Ignacio Maria Beteta, brother of Ramón Beteta, was only a thirty-six-year-old lieutenant colonel when he took the post.

8. *Diccionario biográfico del gobierno mexicano* (Mexico: Presidencia de la República, 1989), 961.

9. Lloyd W. Warner et. al., *The American Federal Executive: A Study of the Social and Personal Characteristics of the Civilian and Military Leaders of the United States* (New Haven: Yale University Press, 1963), 379. The important difference is, of course, that many U.S. officers served on active duty in the military for two to four years.

10. Peter H. Smith, *Labyrinths of Power: Political Recruitment in Twentieth-Century Mexico* (Princeton: Princeton University Press, 1979), 93, 121.

11. Phyllis Greene Walker, "The Modern Mexican Military: Political Influence and Institutional Interests in the 1980s" (M.A. thesis, American University, 1987), 43.

12. Oscar Hinojosa, "Cualquier régimen de gobierno, con apoyo popular, será respetado por el Ejército," *Proceso*, March 1982, 7.

13. Roderic Ai Camp, *Mexican Political Biographies, 1935-1981* (Tucson: University of Arizona Press, 1982), 24–25; *Diccionario biográfico del gobierno mexicano*, 663.

14. Volker G. Lehr, *Manual biográfico del Congreso de la Unión* (Mexico: UNAM, 1984).

15. *Washington Post*, September 23, 1982, 29A. One observer suggested that placing him in the Congress was a means of isolating him from other active duty officers. Personal interview, Mexico City, 1991.

16. *Directorio del 53 legislatura, 1985-1988* (Mexico, 1986), 200-202. A sixth such deputy would have been Rear Admiral Miguel Angel Barberena, who resigned his congressional seat to become governor of Aguascalientes.

17. *Diccionario biográfico del gobierno mexicano* (Mexico: Presidencia de la República, 1987), 322.

18. Alicia Olivera de Bonfil and Eugenia Meyer, *Gustavo Baz y sus juicios como revolucionario, médico y político* (Mexico: INAH, 1971), 43–44.

19. Colegio Nacional, *Memorias* 8, no. 1 (1974): 265–267.

20. McAlister, *The Military in Latin American Socio-political Evolution*, 237; Martin C. Needler expresses it somewhat differently: "Individual military officers may take active political roles, but this does not mean that the armed forces *as an institution* are an independent political factor." *Politics and Society in Mexico* (Albuquerque: University of New Mexico Press, 1971), 71.

21. Edwin Lieuwen, *Mexican Militarism* (Albuquerque: University of New Mexico Press, 1968), 148.

22. Franklin D. Margiotta, "Civilian Control and the Mexican Military: Changing Patterns of Political Influence," in *Civilian Control of the Military: Theories and Cases from Developing Countries*, ed. Claude E. Welch, Jr. (Albany: State University of New York Press, 1976), 239.

23. *Proceso*, March 13, 1989.

24. George Philip, *The Military in South American Politics* (London: Croom-Helm, 1985), 17.

25. Personal interview, Mexico City, August 23, 1990.

26. Personal interview, Mexico City, 1990.

27. Thomas E. Weil, "The Armed Forces," *Area Handbook for Mexico* (Washington, D.C.: GPO, 1975), 368–369.

28. Personal interview with Carlos Tello, Washington, D.C., April 1984.

29. Personal interview, Mexico City, 1990.

30. Personal interviews, Mexico City, 1990.

31. Personal interview, Mexico City, 1990.

32. Personal interview, general, Mexico City, 1990.

33. *Diario Oficial*, August 21, 1990, 3–4.

34. Ibid., December 26, 1986, 16.

35. José Luis Piñeyro, "Presencia política militar nacional y en el Distrito Federal: Propuestas de análisis," in *Distrito Federal, gobierno y sociedad civil*, ed. Pablo González Casanova (Mexico: El Caballito, 1987), 64.

36. William S. Ackroyd, "Descendants of the Revolution: Civil-Military Relations in Mexico" (Ph.D. diss., University of Arizona, 1988), 198–199.

37. Oscar Hinojosa, "Con licencia o sin licencia, están en campaña," *Proceso*, May 2, 1988, 9.

38. *Excélsior*, February 5, 1974, 9.

39. For further comments on this, see Elisur Arteaga, "Maquiavelo, poder y constitución" (unpublished manuscript), 39.

40. Michael J. Dziedzic, "Civil-Military Relations in Mexico: The Politics of Co-optation" (unpublished paper, University of Texas, Austin, 1983), 29–30.

41. Luis Herrera-Lasso and Guadalupe González G., "Balance y perspectiva en el uso del concepto de la seguridad nacional en el caso de México" (unpublished paper, 1989), 29.

42. Miguel Basáñez, *La lucha por la hegemonía en México, 1968–80* (Mexico: Siglo XXI, 1981), 58.

43. Guillermo Boils, "Los militares en México (1965–1985)," *Revista Mexicana de Sociología* 47 (January–February 1985): 182.

44. *Mexico Journal*, March 14, 1988, 24–26.

45. Jorge Alberto Lozoya, "El ejército mexicano," in *Lecturas de política mexicana*, Centro de Estudios Internacionales (Mexico: El Colegio de México, 1977), 375.

46. *Diccionario biográfico del gobierno mexicano* (1989), 961, 977, 985, 995.

47. *Hispano Americano*, December 7, 1964, 18; *Quien es quien en la administración pública de México* (Mexico: Presidencia de la República, 1982), 409.

48. Based on interviews with six instructors, Mexico City, summers, 1989 and 1990.

49. *Diccionario biográfico del gobierno mexicano* (1987), 276.

50. Personal interview, former civilian instructor, Mexico City, 1990.

51. Marion J. Levy, Jr., "Armed Forces Organization," in *The Military and Modernization,* ed. Henry Bienen (Chicago: Aldine-Atherton, 1971), 64.

52. Roderic A. Camp, "Civilian Supremacy in Mexico, the Case of a Post-Revolutionary Military," in *Military Intervention and Withdrawal,* ed. Constantine P. Danopoulous (London: Routledge, 1991), 20.

53. Evelyn P. Stevens, "Mexico's PRI: The Institutionalization of Corporatism?" in *Authoritarianism and Corporatism in Latin America,* ed. James Malloy (Pittsburgh: University of Pittsburgh Press, 1977), 233.

54. Talukder Maniruzzaman, *Military Withdrawal from Politics: A Comparative Study* (Cambridge, Mass.: Ballinger, 1987), 97.

55. José Luis Piñeyro, *Ejército y sociedad en México: Pasado y presente* (Puebla: Universidad Autónomo de Puebla, 1985), 56.

56. Avila Camacho ordered this change less than two weeks after taking office on December 10, 1940, in a communiqué to the Secretariat of National Defense. For details on the impact of his decision on the party, see Luis Javier Garrido, *El partido de la revolución institucionalizada* (Mexico: Siglo XXI, 1982), 303ff.

57. Roderic A. Camp, *Entrepreneurs and Politics in Twentieth Century Mexico* (New York: Oxford University Press, 1989), 125.

58. *Revista del Ejército y Fuerza Aérea,* August 1975, 142; *Hispano Americano,* April 11, 1983, 6; *Excélsior,* March 30, 1983, 18.

59. "Autopostulado, Cuenca será gobernador," *Proceso,* December 25, 1976, 6-9; Elías Chávez, "El ejército, desprestigiado por gobernantes sin autoridad moral," *Proceso,* May 15, 1978, 18.

60. Its leaders have included Generals Jacinto B. Treviño and Juan Barragán Rodríguez, and Admiral Antonio Gómez Velasco.

61. José Luis Piñeyro, "The Mexican Army and the State: Historical and Political Perspective," *Revue Internationale de Sociologie* 14 (April–August 1978), 127.

62. Margiotta, "The Mexican Military," 24.

63. Camp, "Civilian Supremacy in Mexico," 17.

64. Ackroyd, "Descendants of the Revolution," 200.

65. Lieuwen, *Mexican Militarism,* 98.

66. Personal letter from Manuel R. Palacios, Mexico City, February 1, 1973. Also see my *Mexico's Leaders, Their Education and Recruitment* (Tucson: University of Arizona Press, 1980), 135ff., and my article on the 1929 campaign, "La campaña presidencial de 1929 y el liderazgo político en México," *Historia Mexicana* 27 (1977): 231-259.

67. Edwin Lieuwen, "Depolitization of the Mexican Revolutionary Army, 1915-1940," in *The Modern Mexican Military, A Reassessment,* ed. David Ronfeldt (La Jolla: Center for U.S.-Mexican Studies, University of California, San Diego, 1984), 60.

68. *New York Times,* February 18, 1947, 15; Luis Medina, *Historia de la revolución mexicana, periodo 1940-1952, civilismo y modernización del autoritarismo,* no. 20 (Mexico: Colegio de México, 1979), 97. For more details, see Elisa Servin, "Crónica de una disidencia: Miguel Henríquez Guzmán" (unpublished paper, 1990).

69. Olga Pellicer de Brody, "La oposición en México: El caso del henriquismo," in *Las crisis en el sistema político mexicano, 1928-1977,* Centro de Estudios Internacionales (Mexico: El Colegio de México, 1977), 36-37.

70. José María Dávila, *El ejército de la revolución* (Mexico: SLYSE, 1938), 109.

71. Piñeyro, "Presencia política militar nacional y en el Distrito Federal," 65.

72. "Mexico's 'New' PRI Looks Like Old," *Miami Herald,* October 1, 1990.

73. Oscar Hinojosa, "Con licencia o sin licencía, están en campaña," 10.

74. Lieuwen, *Mexican Militarism,* 145.

75. *Hispano Americano,* November 18, 1974, 10; *Excélsior,* November 11, 1974, 20; *New York Times,* April 15, 1952, 5, and April 18, 1952, 5.

76. Dziedzic, "Civil-Military Relations in Mexico," 7.

77. Hinojosa, "Cualquier régimen de gobierno," 9.

78. Ibid., 6.

79. Edward J. Williams, "The Evolution of the Mexican Military and Its Implications for Civil-Military Relations," in *Mexico's Political Stability: The Next Five Years*, ed. Roderic A. Camp (Boulder, Colo.: Westview Press, 1986), 154.

80. *El Nacional*, June 9, 1990, 3.

81. Oscar Hinojosa, "Su voto demonstro que los militares no son homogeneamente gobiernis-tas," *Proceso*, August 8, 1988, 19.

82. *El Nacional*, March 13, 1990, 7. Earlier, a corporal had been charged with firing on a group of PRD sympathizers. In a rare news conference, General Antonio Riviello Bazán, the secretary of defense, told reporters that the corporal had been turned over to civil authorities for prosecution. See Larry Rohter, "Use of Troops Cause of Concern in Mexico," *New York Times*, November 5, 1989, 8.

83. *El Nacional*, March 1, 1990, 3.

84. *Los Angeles Times*, April 6, 1990; Pascal Beltrán del Rio, "Militares y judiciales, juntos evauaron las alcaldías en Michoacán," *Proceso*, April 9, 1990, 6–11.

85. Hinojosa, "Su voto demonstro que los militares no son homogenamente gobiernistas," 19.

86. Herrera-Lasso and González, G. "Balance y perspectiva en el uso del concepto de la seguridad nacional en el caso de México," 30.

87. José Luis Piñeyro, "The Modernization of the Mexican Armed Forces," in *Democracy under Seige: New Military Power in Latin America*, ed. Augusto Varas (Westport, Conn.: Green-wood Press, 1989), 126.

88. Personal interview, April 18, 1986.

89. *Diccionario biográfico del gobierno mexicano* (1987), 544.

90. Hinojosa, "Su voto demonstro," 18.

91. Ibid., 18.

92. Dziedzic, "Civil-Military Relations in Mexico," 12; Wager, "Civic Action and the Mexican Military," 19.

93. *Constitution of the United Mexican States* (Washington, D.C.: Pan American Union, 1964), 59.

94. David F. Ronfeldt, "The Mexican Army and Political Order Since 1940," in *Armies and Politics in Latin America*, ed. Abraham F. Lowenthal (New York: Holmes and Meier, 1976), 293.

95. McAlister, *The Military in Latin American Socio-political Evolution*, 209; Lieuwen, *Mexican Militarism*, 72.

96. Wager, "Civic Action and the Mexican Military," 19.

97. Schmitt, "The Role of the Military in Contemporary Mexico," 55.

98. Stephen J. Wager, "The Mexican Military, 1968–1978: A Decade of Change" (unpub-lished paper, Stanford University, June 1979), 15.

99. *El Nacional*, March 19, 1990, 14.

100. Cunningham, "Mexico's National Security in the 1980s–1990s," 174.

101. Roderic A. Camp, "The Military," in *Prospects for Mexico*, ed. George W. Grayson (Washington, D.C.: Foreign Service Institute, 1988), 87.

102. Walker, "The Modern Mexican Military," 75.

103. Stanley E. Hilton, "The Brazilian Military: Changing Strategic Perceptions and the Question of Mission," *Armed Forces and Society* 13 (Spring 1987): 330, 346.

104. Levy, "Armed Forces Organization," 47.

105. Gabriel Marcella, "Latin American in the 1980s: The Strategic Environment and Inter-American Security" (Carlisle Barracks, Pa.: Strategic Studies Institute, U.S. Army War College, June 15, 1981), 31.

106. Bruce M. Russett, "Political Perspectives of U.S. Military and Business Elites," *Armed Forces and Society* 1 (Fall 1974): 87.

107. Needler, *Politics and Society in Mexico*, 66, citing Alfonso Corona del Rosal, *Moral militar y civilismo*, 2d ed. (Mexico: Estado Mayor Presidencial, 1952).

108. Guillermo Boils, "Fuerzas armadas y armamentismo en México," *Nueva Política* 2 (April–September 1977): 357.

109. *El Nacional, Suplemento Especial*, October 27, 1990, 1.

110. Olga Pellicer de Brody, "National Security Concerns in Mexico: Traditional Notions and New Preoccupations," in *U.S.-Mexico Relations, Economic and Social Aspects*, ed. Clark W. Reynolds and Carlos Tello (Stanford: Stanford University Press, 1983), 187.

111. Ibid., 188.

112. Walker, "The Modern Mexican Military," 76.

113. *Diario Oficial*, December 7, 1988, 4.

114. A civilian, Fernando del Villar, replaced Colonel Carrillo Olea in 1990, when the president placed him in charge of all antidrug activities.

115. *Proceso*, November 9, 1987, 18; *Quien es quien en la administración pública*, 26; *Diccionario biográfico del gobierno mexicano* (1987), 79; *Excélsior*, February 27, 1976, 4A.

116. He served as a civilian employee of the Federal Security Police, Secretariat of Government, 1950-1952, then was chief of information of the same agency until 1958. He was promoted to Subdirector in charge of the Federal Security Department, which he held until 1964, after which he became director under Luis Echeverría, who was the secretary of government. In 1970 he reached the subsecretary of government post, remaining there for twelve years. See *Hispano Americano*, May 6, 1986, 7; *Mexico Journal*, December 16, 1988, 16; *Diccionario biográfico del gobierno mexicano* (Mexico: Presidencia de la República, 1984), 201.

117. *Diccionario biográfico del gobierno mexicano* (1989), 187.

118. The Department of Federal Security (DFS) was in league with the drug cartels and cooperated with the Central Intelligence Agency. It was disbanded in an effort to root out corruption and to repair Mexico's intelligence image. See William Brannigan, "With Friends Like These, Who Needs Enemies," *Washington Post, National Weekly Edition*, July 23-29, 1990, 31. The prosecution in the murder trial of Kiki Camarena in Los Angeles, California, accused Javier García Paniagua of having attended an October 1984 meeting to plan Camarena's murder. See the *Los Angeles Times*, May 16, 1990.

119. General Marcelino Iñurreta founded the Department of Federal Security in 1946 and was its first director; the subdirector was a lieutenant colonel. Iñurreta was replaced in 1952 by Colonel Leandro Castillo Venegas, whose second in command was Gilberto Suárez Torres, lawyer, special federal agent, and later attorney general of the Federal District. In 1958 Colonel Manuel Rangel Escamilla, who had relatives among senior officers, took over, with Gutiérrez Barrios as his assistant. He was followed in 1964 by Gutiérrez Barrios. Captain Luis de la Barreda Moreno replaced Gutiérrez Barrios in 1970, with another officer, Miguel Nazar Haro, as his subdirector. In 1976 the first experienced politician, Javier García Paniagua, was appointed director. He left after two years to become subsecretary of government. (He later became president of the PRI, labor secretary, and briefly, a precandidate for president. However, he has strong connections with the military, having been a friend of Lázaro Cárdenas for many years; a student supporter, with Cárdenas's son, of General Miguel Hernández in 1952; and most important of all, is the son of General Marcelino García Barragán, secretary of defense, 1964-1970. In 1988 Manuel Camacho appointed him director of the Federal District police.) Miguel Nazar Haro, then a lieutenant colonel, took over the post in 1978. There has been some dispute as to his having military rank. I find no record of his having graduated from the Heroico Colegio Militar, but he is listed in a government organization manual with the rank of lieutenant colonel, and a Government Secretariat source asserts he does have military rank. His successor, José Antonio Zorrilla Pérez, the second civilian to head the agency and its last head, took charge in 1982. Both Zorrilla Pérez, charged as the intellectual author of the murder of newspaperman Manuel Buendía, and Nazar Haro, indicted by a U.S. grand jury on a list of charges including grand theft auto, imparted an unsavory image to the agency.

120. Personal interview, Mexico City, 1990.

121. Arturo R. Blancas and Tomás L. Vidrio, *Indice biográfico de la XLIII Legislatura Federal* (Mexico, 1956), 88-89.

122. In contrast, the Brazilians created the first National Intelligence Service under the first military president, 1964-1967. See Hilton, "The Brazilian Military," 331.

123. Alden M. Cunningham, "Mexico's National Security in the 1980s-1990s," in *The Modern Mexican Military: A Reassessment*, ed. David Ronfeldt (La Jolla: Center for U.S.-Mexico Studies, University of California, San Diego, 1984), 173n26.

124. Larry Rohter points out that recent threats against notable commentators, such as Jorge Castañeda, may suggest a loss of presidential authority over groups associated with security services and the federal judicial police. See his "Government Critics Harassed in Mexico, Setting Off a Storm," *New York Times*, June 21, 1990, A1. This and other problems led to the replacement of the attorney general in mid-1991.

125. *Proceso*, August 15, 1988, 31–32.

126. Americas Watch, *Report on Mexico* (New York: Americas Watch, 1990), 17; *Los Angeles Times*, June 14, 1990. The most specific evidence ever presented against the military is the testimony of a former enlisted man, Zacarías Osorio Cruz, who testified to the Canadian Immigration Board that he took part in executions ordered by senior Mexican army and air force officers between 1977 and 1982, during which time he lined up hooded and handcuffed prisoners on a military firing range near Mexico City and riddled their bodies with gunfire. See Americas Watch, *Report on Mexico*, 35–36.

127. *Diario Oficial*, June 6, 1990, 3–4; August 1, 1990, 2–9.

128. Consejo Nacional de Derechos Humanos, recommendation 4-90, July 25, 1990, addressed to General Antonio Riviello Bazán; interview with Jorge Carpizo, director of the new commission, Mexico City, 1990.

129. *El Nacional*, October 25, 1990, 13; Americas Watch also concluded that "it is not in the long-term interests of human rights in Mexico for the United States to be encouraging the Mexican military to step in to 'solve' the drug trafficking problem." *Report on Mexico*, 84.

130. Rodney W. Jones and Steven A. Hildreth, eds., *Emerging Powers: Defense and Security in the Third World* (New York: Praeger, 1986), 382–83.

131. Piñeyro, "The Modernization of the Mexican Armed Forces," 118–119.

132. Ibid., 125.

133. Irving Louis Horowitz, "Militarism and Civil-Military Relationships in Latin America: Implications for the Third World," in *Research in Political Sociology*, vol. 1 (Greenwich, Conn.: JAI Press, 1985), 86.

134. Piñeyro, "The Mexican Army and the State," 132.

135. Karl Schmitt, "The Role of the Military in Contemporary Mexico," in *The Caribbean: Mexico Today*, ed. Curtis A. Wilgus (Gainesville: University of Florida Press, 1964), 60.

136. Stephen J. Wager, "Civic Action and the Mexican Military" (unpublished paper, Department of History, U.S. Military Academy, 1982), 7.

137. Michael J. Dziedzic, "Mexico's Converging Challenges: Problems, Prospects, and Implications" (unpublished manuscript, U.S. Air Force Academy, April 21, 1989), 13, citing a report from Oaxaca, September 3, 1981.

138. Edward J. Williams, "The Mexican Military and Foreign Policy: The Evolution of Influence," in *The Modern Mexican Military: A Reassessment*, ed. David Ronfeldt (La Jolla: Center for U.S.-Mexico Studies, University of California, San Diego, 1984), 187.

139. David Ronfeldt, "The Mexican Army and Political Order since 1940" (Santa Monica: Rand Corporation, 1973), 2.

140. Julio Scherer García, *Los presidentes* (Mexico: Grijalbo, 1986), 62. Scherer García is quoting an extraordinary interview in March 1986 with a former defense secretary, General Félix Galván, one officer who would know most of the details. For his subsequent career, see pp. 62ff. For his early career, see *Revista de Ejército y Fuerza Aérea*, November 1975, 139; *Revista de Ejército y Fuerza Aérea*, August 1977, 94.

141. Personal interview, Mexico City, 1990.

142. Lorenzo Meyer, "Ejército y Cananeas del futuro," *Excélsior*, September 6, 1989, 1, 12A.

143. *Unomásuno*, December 2, 1988, III.

144. Herrera-Lasso and González, G. "Balance y perspectiva en el uso del concepto de la seguridad nacional en el caso de México," 26.

145. Boils, "Los militares en México," 180.

146. *El Nacional*, March 1, 1990, 3.

147. Camp, "The Military," 90.

148. Personal interviews, Mexico City, 1990.

149. *Revista de Ejército y Fuerza Aérea*, October, 1975, 125; *Quien es quien en la administración pública en México*, 77.

150. Richard B. Craig, "Mexican Narcotics Traffic: Binational Security Implications," in *The Latin American Narcotics Trade and U.S. National Security*, ed. Donald J. Mabry (Westport, Conn.: Greenwood Press, 1989), 35.

151. Personal interview, Mexico City, 1990.

152. Guillermo M. Boils, "Los militares en México (1965-1985)," *Revista Mexicana de Sociología* 47 (January-February, 1985): 180.

153. Walker, "The Modern Mexican Military," 112. Craig also argues that the military's role and increased influence have the potential to change the political balance of power in Mexico, a security concern for civilian leadership and for the United States. "Mexican Narcotics Traffic," 35.

154. Ibid., 31.

155. Boils, "Los militares en México," 188.

156. Personal interviews, Mexico City, 1990.

157. Williams, "The Mexican Military and Foreign Policy," 16.

5

Officer Origins

Theorists have argued for more than three decades that leaders' social and geographic origins are critical variables in understanding elites' composition and behavior. C. Wright Mills was one of the first social scientists to articulate this interpretation for political elites. Essentially, he believed that

> all the structural coincidences of their interests as well as the intricate, psychological facts of their origins and their education, their careers and their associations make possible the psychological affinities that prevail among them, affinities that make it possible for them to say of one another: He is, of course, one of us. And all of this points to the basic, psychological meaning of class consciousness.[1]

Homogeneous backgrounds may have for elites not only a psychological effect on their sense of community, but an effect on their recruitment too. If Mexican political leaders are an indicator of generational criteria in elite recruitment, it becomes apparent that stable leadership recruits like types. In countries split by sharp ethnic or religious divisions, the distribution of leaders from each background can be crucial to regime stability. Mexican society is not fractured along such lines, but a strong sense of regionalism prevails; those differences never have been the primary basis of conflict among contemporary politicians. In Mexico, however, urban and rural origins are becoming increasingly significant in terms of divisions in cultural traditions and values. It is as though two Mexicos exist side by side.

The significance of background to the officer corps, whether one considers career experience, social class, geographic origin, age, or family characteristics, is its potential to foster a military caste mentality. Such a mentality would separate the military from not only the population, but from political and other leadership groups. It would be a critical variable in civil-military relations if the military were to develop an identity of its own and in that separateness come to believe that it is superior to the civilian components of the society. Mexican observers do not believe that the present officer corps displays a caste mentality, although little attention has been paid to this issue, largely because its roots can be traced to the guerrilla armies during the Revolution (1910–1920). However, some scholars believe the potential for the officer corps to develop such a mentality in the 1990s is present as it takes on attributes differentiating it from the population and other leadership groups.[2]

Political-Military Officer

Since the 1920s Mexico's military has been characterized by three types of officers: *political-military, mustang,* and *orthodox professional.* The qualities of each significantly influence the homogeneity of the officer corps, its caste mentality, and the civil-military relationship. One of the most interesting features of the twentieth century military is the presence of the political-military officer, historically an individual who straddles two careers, one in the army and another in state and national politics. Unlike his orthodox or regular military counterpart, he has an interest in and skills appropriate to politics. He is an officer whose career in politics is as important as a career in the military. Older political-military officers were combat veterans of the Revolution who typically alternated between political posts and military commands.

In the nineteenth century military officers holding political posts were the norm, especially in the initial phases of the Díaz administration, as our analysis of political-military interlocks makes clear. For example, among national officeholders who were contemporaries of Porfirio Díaz, who were born in the 1820s, 55 percent were career military officers with a rank of lieutenant colonel or higher. For the 1830s generation, the proportion was 67 percent; the 1840s generation, 35 percent; and the 1850s generation, 25 percent. For the 1880s generation, the most important during the Revolution, the proportion was 53 percent, and for the 1890s generation, 36 percent.

During the nineteenth century, under the Porfiriato (1884–1911), a military career was somewhat of a plus in politics. Slightly over half of all politically prominent figures, regardless of their military or civilian background, served only once in a national political post. Among two-time officeholders, military officers had an advantage: 29 percent had managed a second post, compared with 19 percent of civilians. Officers and civilians serving in three or more offices were on a par. After the 1930s, repetitive officeholding declined among all national politicians, with six out of ten, regardless of background, holding office only once. Although military officers did somewhat better at obtaining a second post than civilians, about twice as many civilians as officers secured three or more posts over their entire political careers.

After the Revolution a paradoxical situation emerged in the officer corps. The political leadership, victorious revolutionary generals, especially such men as Alvaro Obregón, Plutarco Elías Calles, and Lázaro Cárdenas, decided to professionalize the military by removing their peers, generals, from the officer corps. Despite the purges, the political-military officer, having revolutionary credentials, remained remarkably persistent in top military posts well into the late 1960s and early 1970s. From the point of view of officer homogeneity, they added significant diversity to the officer corps itself, and served as a critical bridge between the post-1946 professional politician and the pre-1946 politicized officer corps.

Presidents Obregón (1920–1924) and Calles (1924–1928), and Calles as a gray eminence in the early thirties, stiffened professional requirements through increasingly demanding educational programs, but it was President Cárdenas who in 1936 moved decisively to weed out large numbers of revolutionary officers, including many with political ambitions. He saw to legislation that shortened an officer's career span from thirty-five to twenty-five years. It meant that all officers who had served before 1911 would be automatically retired, and that by 1940, at the end of Cárdenas's term, all officers who had served before 1915 would be gone.[3] If the legislation continued in effect, by 1946 no officers who had taken part in the Revolution would be among the military leadership.[4]

In reality, however, revolutionary generals did not disappear after 1945. Nonpolitical officers who opted for advanced military training and political-military officers, both with revolutionary combat records, remained. The political-military officer survived much longer than expected for a variety of reasons, necessity being the foremost. One significant structural means for accomplishing this end, not previously recognized, is that political leave time is excluded from computation regarding rank or retirement. In other words, political-military officers into the 1950s and 1960s were more likely to have had combat experience than their younger, orthodox peers. Of the 466 generals about whom we have combat information, 176 or 38 percent were political-military officers (defined as having held a high-level national political office or a state governorship). Of those officers, nearly two-thirds had seen combat, almost all during the Revolution. Among nonpolitical officers, only 21 percent possessed combat records. Thus, leave time extended the influence of an older generation of political-military officers ten to fifteen years beyond their expected career span.

Phyllis Walker believes that after Miguel Alemán's administration (1946–1952), top leaders of the National Defense Secretariat were selected on the basis of their revolutionary credentials, bypassing younger officers. She asserts that such selections insured the military's support for political leadership after 1952 and its continued nonintervention in political affairs.[5] An examination of military leadership bears this out. Of the top regional zones' nine military commanders in 1951, seven were officers with revolutionary credentials, and all but one had entered politics; we have information on only eight of the ten commanders in 1956, but seven of those were revolutionaries, and six held political office.[6] In other words, there was essentially no change in that regard between Alemán's and Adolfo Ruiz Cortines's (1952–1958) administrations.

Revolutionary officers have been most visibly represented among secretaries of defense, the last of whom was Hermenegildo Cuenca Díaz (1970–1976)—which is stretching the connection, because he had only accompanied President Carranza as a cadet in 1920. His predecessor, Marcelino García Barragán, had joined the Juárez Brigade, Division of the North, on May 14, 1915, as a second lieutenant under General Obregón, thus having served in the army for forty-nine years, excepting 1943 to 1947, when he was a state governor, and 1950 to 1958, when he left the army to twice support the revolutionaries' candidate for president, Miguel Henríquez Guzmán. Walker believes that the political elite relied so heavily on the revolutionary presence among the military's leadership that it actually underwent "considerable consternation" attempting to decide on National Defense Secretariat appointments for the López Portillo administration.[7]

The political-military officer introduced two features into the officer corps. The first, and most obvious, is the persistence of the commander with revolutionary roots or credentials. The second feature is brought by this type of officer: a politically interested and skilled individual. Normally, as Morris Janowitz suggests,

> the military bureaucracy, like any other bureaucracy, has its own political leaders. These political leaders are not only concerned with internal management but also serve to relate the military to external elites and to the variety of publics with whom it must deal. These select military leaders have more of the symbolic negotiating and bargaining skills appropriate for domestic politics.[8]

Mexico's military went beyond Janowitz's description of organic leadership. Although it developed a cadre of career officers who through staff positions have gained these political skills, and have dominated command positions for some time, Janowitz's "select military leaders" in Mexico were for many decades largely political-military officers, men who obtained hands-on political experience in elective and appointive offices. This is why this group is so important to examine.

A division between officers whose careers lie with field command, especially if their careers entail active combat, and those who are primarily staff officers, who administer troops from behind a desk, develops in many militaries. In Mexico, the division is complicated in two ways. First, Mexico opened up career opportunities for developing political *skills outside* the armed forces, thereby expanding the number of opportunities available to its potential commanders beyond those found in the U.S. Army.[9] Second, the political officers were veterans with premier combat credentials, that is, they had fought in the 1910 Revolution. These credentials were as important to the military officer's career in the 1940s and 1950s as World War II combat was to the U.S. officer's leadership potential after 1945. However, the revolutionary combat veteran in Mexico who also pursued political ambitions helped blur the separation between the desk and field officer in that he often occupied posts in both the military and civilian sectors.

The importance of the revolutionary credential and the extended influence of the politically experienced commander in the armed forces delayed the rise of the orthodox career officer. They also created resentment on the part of the young professional officers of older combat veterans. Edwin Lieuwen argues that the division between the two cohorts occurred quite soon after the Revolution, in fact under President Cárdenas, himself the prototype of the political-military combat veteran. According to Lieuwen,

His professionalization and modernization program loosened the bonds between the revolutionary generals on the one hand and the junior officers and
enlisted men on the other. The *oficiales* were interested in professional military
careers. They came to feel that they were better qualified to command—than
the *divisionarios* [division generals], who were politicians rather than soldiers.[10]

From the 1940s through the early 1970s, the existence of this division in the
military leadership, particularly the army, had potential repercussions. Some
scholars believe that the political officer, a combat veteran, was not well
respected by his more orthodox peers. They suggest that the political officer,
lacking prestige among his more "professional" colleagues, could not serve as a
significant political link between civilian and military elites.[11] This raises the
possibility that in a serious crisis, the professional officers might not have
sufficient respect for their politically oriented leaders to obey specific commands.[12] Although that potential existed for many years, it did not materialize.

Since the mid-1970s the division in leadership has disappeared as the
political-military officer has left the scene. During the 1970s high-ranking
officers with political experience in top defense posts stabilized at about 25
percent of the total.[13] In 1982 no officers with direct political experience
outside the military bureaucracy, with one exception, were appointed to top
posts. That exception held a National Defense Secretariat department headship: Luis Garfias Magaña directed the archives. In 1988 no politically experienced officers were appointed to National Defense Secretariat posts under
President Salinas. The same can be seen clearly in the data on military zone
commanders (Appendix D). Political-military officers often dominated certain
zone commands, especially in the 1940s and 1950s, and even well into the 1960s
and 1970s. After the late 1970s, however, they ceased to appear among influential field commands.

The political-military officer disappears from the top staff and command
posts because his type no longer exists in Mexico. The fading away of active
duty generals with direct political experience reduced the likelihood of an
internal military conflict but opened the door to a different, potentially more
debilitating weakness, one seemingly present within the political leadership.[14]
As I suggested elsewhere:

> As Mexican politicians and military officers have become more technically
> proficient and specialized, the generalist is disappearing. Among politicians, he
> is represented by the lawyer, but among military officers, he is represented by
> the political-military officer. The only officer who generally retains these more
> diverse political skills is the zone commander. Of the institutional alternatives
> to the bureaucratic elite in Mexico, only the zone commanders within the
> military have some comparable skills. But in general, in a crisis demanding
> leaders with substantial mass group skills, neither Mexican politicians or mili-
> tary officers offer strong preparation in the 1980s.[15]

The replacement for the traditional political-military officer is currently a
junior officer who temporarily serves as an aide to a prominent political figure

in the executive branch or as a gubernatorial appointee. He is generally a captain or major. Some observers say that many junior officers hold lower-level positions in the federal bureaucracy. An examination of middle-level posts in 1983, 1987, and 1989 reveals only one or two career military officers. No empirical evidence exists on how many junior officers serve as aides; one officer estimated several hundred in the mid-1980s.[16] However, vestiges of political experience lacking in prestige must still be present within the military, because the smaller numbers of high-ranking officers who have served as politicians' aides never mention it in their public biographies.

Political-military officers added a number of characteristics to military leadership not found among contemporary officers. For most of the period since 1946 the political-military officer contributed substantially to the aging of Mexico's officer corps. Top officers were older than the leading politicians. Only 17 percent of top civilian politicians after 1935 had been born before 1900, compared to 58 percent of all political-military officers after 1946. Broken down by decade born, the differences become apparent. Top political and military leaders born in the 1880s accounted for nearly a fifth of all political-military officers, but only 4 percent of civilian politicians. Those born in the 1890s accounted for 13 percent among civilian politicians and nearly 40 percent of political-military officers. The first decade of the twentieth century was a critical one for civilian leadership—the first important decade for the post-1940s era: the political-military general is essentially extinct by 1980. Whereas more than a sixth of all prominent politicians have been born since 1930, the century's first decade is represented by only 1 percent of politically experienced generals.

Generational differences between political-military and regular officers have two consequences: they provide a generational division within the civilian leadership, and a generational division within the military leadership. In the latter case, the division has implications for military officers, and military and civilian leadership. For example, a survey of all national political leaders from 1935 to 1985, categorized by pursuit of military or civilian careers, suggests that the military's presence in national political offices can be divided into three important generational periods (see table 5-1). The breaks occur between the 1890s and 1900s decades and the 1920s and 1930s decades. Officers account for a third of the political leaders born during the two earlier decades. After 1900 the military's presence drops precipitously, stabilizing at 8 percent, a level more or less maintained through the formative years of the political system. The 1930s generation, however, presages the military's withdrawal from political leadership. Mexico's future political leadership in the late 1990s and the early twenty-first century will come largely from the post-1940s generation. By 1989, 39 percent of all middle- and top-level officeholders had been born between 1940 to 1949; 33 percent after 1950.[17]

The political-military officer's age created a second division, but within the military itself. A comparable examination of generations *within the military* suggests an equally divided leadership by career experience (table 5-2). The political-military officer, at least among generals in top command posts,

TABLE 5-1.   Mexican Politicians' Careers, by Generation

| Decade of birth | Officeholder (%) | |
	Military	Civilian
1880s	39	61
1890s	29	71
1900s	9	91
1910s	8	92
1920s	7	93
1930s	1	99
1940s	0	100

retained substantial influence for a long period, and among younger generations. By the 1900s generation, generals did not exercise much influence over
civilian political offices. Among the 1900s regular officer generation, however,
more than half of the generals were transitional political-military careerists.
Even among the 1910s generation, the politically experienced officer continued
to exercise considerable influence within the military.

Not until the 1920s generation does the political-military officer become a
relic among his regular peers. In terms of generational background, the top
officers have become younger and more homogeneous. Nevertheless, in the
foreseeable future they will remain nearly a decade in age behind their civilian
counterparts, if Salinas's generation is indicative of future political leadership.
Although they begin their careers at a very young age, time in rank now
requires approximately thirty years to reach the rank of brigadier general, and
longer for two- and three-star ranks. Consequently, top officers are likely to be
ten years older than prominent politicians, having more in common with an
older than with the youngest generation of political elites.

TABLE 5-2.   Mexican Military Officers' Political Careers, by Generation

| Decade of birth | Officer career type (%) | |
	Regular	Political
1880s	14	86
1890s	28	72
1900s	48	52
1910s	71	29
1920s	90	10
1930s	94	6
1940s	100	0

Regionalism and Class

Regionalism has played a historic role in Mexico, more so than generational differences, at least through the 1940s. The centralization of political power in Mexico City, especially in the postrevolutionary period, eliminated regionalism's national political impact relatively quickly, measured in terms of states' or regions' abilities to operate autonomously from the center. Cárdenas's suppression of the last military rebellion, in San Luis Potosí in 1939, consolidated, once and for all, military power in the hands of the federal government. Nevertheless, political events beginning in the mid-1980s suggest that regionalism is likely to reassert itself, not through independent military means but, rather, through electoral participation and violence. Considerable resentment exists in various regions toward the federal government and toward politicians in Mexico City.[18] The resentment is not likely to disappear as civilian leaders are increasingly Mexico City-born.

Political-military officers helped temper the dominance of Mexico City natives among national political leaders and in the officer corps itself. Because they were older, naturally they better represented the regional prerevolutionary distribution of the population. For example, 18 percent of all prominent civilian politicians since 1935 have been from the Federal District, a proportion not much different from the proportion of the general population now resident there. However, in this century, at least since the 1930s, the capital has been overrepresented, measured by politicians' backgrounds. Among politicians who were career military officers, only 8 percent were from the Federal District, the only region producing a significantly different level among political and political-military leaders. Political-military officers tended to give stronger representation to the West and the North, thus providing those regions with a fairer share of representation. The political-military officer's elimination has served to swell the figures of recent politicians born in the capital. Among younger, middle-level individuals in the federal bureaucracy, a whopping 51 percent come from Mexico City. In fact, foreign-born politicians, a mere 1.62 percent of the total, exceed the percentage of politicians from each of fourteen states.[19]

Regional strengths introduced by politically active military officers are repeated within the officer corps itself. Regular officers reaching the rank of general come from three regions; in descending order of importance, the Federal District, the North, and the Gulf. In fact, regular officers are more strongly from the Federal District than are national politicians generally: 26 percent, half again as much as the percentage for civilian leaders. The North is somewhat overrepresented too because of its importance to the Revolution and the dominance of two generations of political-military leaders from northern states, especially Coahuila, Sonora, and Chihuahua. The Gulf is well represented because an extraordinary number of naval officers come from Veracruz, Mexico's principal port. Although political-military officers contributed to exaggerating the North's importance—one out of five came from that region—they provided a strong counterbalance to generals from the east-central and western states.

Political-military officers also introduced another source of diversity of origin into the military and political leaderships. Mexico has been characterized by increasing urbanization; hence leadership, regardless of sector, has increasingly tended to come disproportionately from metropolitan areas. Again, political-military officers were more representative of the general population, specifically the rural population. Among all politicians, fewer than one in three comes from a rural area, and among nonpolitical officers, fewer than one in four does so. Half of all political-military officers grew up in rural surroundings, in part, of course, because they were from an older generation. Other consequences will be further developed in our analysis of the regular, orthodox officer.

The political-military officer also represented a different social class among civilian and military leaders. Perhaps more than any background variable, class has potential impact on the development of a caste mentality. In the first place, whether one looks at regular military or civilian politicians, the political-military officer is socially atypical. Over the years, 55 percent came from working-class backgrounds. Among orthodox officers, only 15 percent are known to have come from such backgrounds, and among politicians, 35 percent come from the masses. In terms of political connections, however, or ties to important revolutionary or Porfiriato families, political-military officers could offer nothing different from their civilian peers. The only other significant difference between the tiny percentages of political-military officers and civilian leaders with prominent well-to-do and intellectual relatives, is that among the former most had relatives from prominent financial families, whereas civilian politicians were equally divided as to intellectual and financially secure families.

The political-military officer contributed to the heterogeneity of civilian and military leadership because of differences in his educational background. For the military, these differences were important because they delayed the impact of military academies on both the socialization and recruitment of the officer corps—especially considering the fact that many of the generals controlled command posts necessary to career advancement, whether in the field or as staff heads. One out of three political-military officers never went beyond preparatory school, a characteristic shared by only 2 percent of regular officers. In other words, by the 1890s generation, all regular army officers had graduated from the Colegio Militar, or had pursued further professional military studies; for only two-thirds of political-military officers was this the case.

Thus, for early generations, a political-military career was the means by which the self-made battlefield commander without formal education could climb the military and political ladder. By the 1900s generation, with revolutionary experience eliminated from their backgrounds, political-military officers increasingly blended in educationally with their regular counterparts. Although only a third of the officers from this generation can be considered political, 97 percent were graduates of the Colegio Militar and nearly half completed the staff and command school at the Escuela Superior de Guerra

(ESG). All regular officers were graduates, and nearly two-thirds had completed the advanced course. By the 1920s and 1930s generations, although political-military men had declined to about 20 and 10 percent, respectively, of all generals, actually a higher proportion, three-quarters, were ESG graduates. This suggests that the younger political officer was the product of a homogeneous military training, and that to achieve a political career, he would also require a level of education competitive with that of successful civilian politicians.

Educationally, the political-military officer added diversity to civilian leadership. Basically, as was true within the military, the political-military officer allowed a politically ambitious man, usually from a lower socioeconomic background, to rise to the top of the political ladder. Without the political-military officer's presence in national politics, the leadership would have been further restricted to college-educated, middle- and upper-class individuals. Furthermore, none of the political-military officers who reached national political office, with the exception of physicians, had advanced degrees, a credential possessed by 12 percent of the civilian leadership. Obviously, among the college-educated officers in national politics, most had studied military curricula, the content of which will be analyzed later, whereas among civilians, education had been primarily in law, with a heavy concentration in liberal arts.

Without political-military officers in Mexican politics, increasingly the case, the likelihood of a civilian politician's having a military degree is slim. Of the more than fifteen hundred national *civilian* political figures about whom we have information, only 1 percent graduated from the Heroico Colegio Militar; they had resigned their commissions to pursue other careers. Economics as a field second only to law in politicians' education is absent altogether in military officers' preparation. Only two officers holding national political office have some background in public accounting or economics; this suggests a lack of emphasis on, as well as a need for, such training. Their particularized education bars military men from moving into many of the most influential cabinet agencies, including Treasury, Planning and Budgeting, and Commerce, and stands in the way of their flexibility as generalists.

The sharp decline of the political-military officer has numerous consequences for the military and for civil-military relations. The working hypothesis offered by Franklin Margiotta, discussed in the introduction—that the limited but consistent political representation of military officers serves as an important bridge between politicians and the officer corps—lost validity in the 1970s, which suggests that other variables are more important in explaining Mexico's continued civil-military relations. The disappearance of the political-military officer also increased the homogeneity of backgrounds in the officer corps.

Mustangs

One of the remarkable characteristics of the Mexican officer corps since 1946 has been the presence of the "mustang," an individual, similar to his U.S. Army counterpart, who achieves a commission after starting out in the enlisted ranks, generally as an ordinary soldier. Nearly one in four men reaching the rank of general began in the military as an enlisted soldier, a fact giving substantial credence to the belief of observers, and of officers themselves, that officers are a product of the masses. Although analysts point to revolutionary origins as the source of the popular roots of the officer corps, mustangs have had greater long-term effects.

The surviving revolutionary officer, more often than not a political-military general, and the enlisted soldier who makes officer rank are often one and the same in the early years. That is, among officers born in the 1880s and 1890s who saw combat in the Revolution, nearly half joined the revolutionary forces as ordinary soldiers. They were promoted on the basis of leadership and combat skills, essentially battlefield promotions. This type of officer in the next generation, that is, born in the first decade of the century, some of whom had the opportunity to fight in the Revolution, declined to 17 percent. In other words, increased professionalization in the 1920s further separated officers from the enlisted ranks. Had this pattern continued, the number of mustangs might have disappeared altogether.

Instead, President Cárdenas instituted formally what had happened informally during the revolutionary decade. In 1935, in an address to the Colegio Militar, he explained to the cadets that officers "should not think of ourselves as professional soldiers . . . but rather as armed auxiliaries organized from the humble classes."[20] He also announced that a substantial number of the Colegio's cadets would thenceforth be drawn from enlisted ranks. Two years later, when the government realized that sufficient junior officers were not available for police duty in remote rural regions, the Centro de Instrución de Jefes y Oficiales was set up to train noncommissioned officers of proven ability for service as officers.[21]

The enrollment of enlisted soldiers as cadets at the Heroico Colegio Militar lasted until 1944.[22] The program led to two influential generations of mustangs in the officer corps, men born from 1910 through 1929. Generals born during these two decades dominated the armed forces in the 1960s, 1970s and 1980s. Of their numbers, nearly one in four could claim mustang status. This is an even more remarkable figure given the fact that during the years this program was in effect at the military academy, only 12 to 16 percent of the cadets enrolled had begun their careers as enlisted soldiers. The percentages indicate that the success rate of cadets from enlisted backgrounds was far higher than that of the usual cadets.

Termination of the program in 1944 resulted in eliminating mustangs among general officers born after 1930. In 1955 after much debate, the Secretariat of National Defense instituted a limited version of the original program. For the first time a select number of first sergeants who had graduated from the noncommissioned officers school and who had demonstrated exceptional leadership ability were chosen for a one-year program at the Heroico Colegio Militar.[23] In 1966 another change occurred. The regular cadet program was extended to four years. From 1966 to 1978 first sergeants selected for the program were required to enroll for four years. After 1978 first sergeants were allowed to take one year of special training and then a one-year program at the Heroico Colegio Militar to become second lieutenants. That program occasioned resentment on the part of regular cadet officers, who perceived its graduates as adversely affecting their own promotion rates.[24] However, I have found among generals no graduates of the 1955 program.[25] An expanded program was instituted in the 1980s, when de la Madrid's modest modernization program produced a unmet need for officer cadets.[26] One communications officer in our study, enrolled as an enlisted cadet in 1949; he is the last example of a true mustang reaching the rank of general.[27]

With the exception of revolutionary mustangs, the largest group of enlisted men who became generals in the past fifty years joined the army in the late 1930s. Typical of the career of the enlisted officer from this generation is that of General Ulises Beltrán Tenorio, who joined the army as an ordinary soldier in the 1st Combat Engineer Battalion in 1939. Three years later he enrolled in the Heroico Colegio Militar in the artillery class, completing his training in 1943, after which he joined a mechanized brigade's transportation company. He rejoined the army cartographic section in 1949, later serving in the Presidential Guards and on the National Defense Secretariat staff. He trained twice in the Panama Canal Zone, in photography and artillery, and completed the Higher Arms curriculum at the Escuela Superior de Guerra in 1961. He was appointed director of the Cartographic Services in 1982 by his HCM classmate Juan Arévalo Gardoqui.[28]

Mustangs not only have risen to the rank of general but have achieved other top posts in the armed forces. They often take several years longer to achieve generalships but are no less successful than typical cadets. "In fact, as a percentage of all officer candidates at the Heroic Military College, the cadet who entered the army originally as an enlisted man has, in the past, greater success reaching the rank of general than his peers."[29] One reason for the accomplishment may be that their completion rate is higher than their civilian counterparts who enlist directly as cadets at the HCM and customarily have had no previous exposure to military life. The discipline and generally authoritarian environment at the HCM and later at the ESG are more difficult hurdles than the academic challenge, and enlisted men, as suggested above, often cope more easily than do relative novices with the former.

Mustangs reached their heyday in the 1982–1988 administration, especially in holding top posts in the National Defense Secretariat. Although four secretaries of national defense from 1946 to 1964 can claim enlisted origins, Juan Arévalo Gardoqui's colleagues best exemplify their success. Among his twenty-seven upper-echelon colleagues, ten were mustangs. Such predominance is attributable not to Arévalo Gardoqui's personal preferance—he himself was not a mustang—but to that of his second- and third-ranking officials. Marco Antonio Guerrero Mendoza, his subsecretary, joined the 47th Infantry Battalion as a private in 1938, and Arturo López Flores, his oficial mayor, entered the military as an infantryman in 1937. Both enrolled as cadets a year after their enlistments.

Mustangs have been important to the officer corps for several reasons. The socioeconomic makeup of the officer corps owes them a significant debt. A much larger percentage of mustangs, because of their enlisted origins, come from the working class. In fact, although the majority of officers whose social origins are known have been middle class, the proportion of officers from these origins who enlist in the military as cadets is much higher. If mustangs are excluded from the ranks of generals, only 14 percent come from lower socio-economic classes. Among mustangs alone, however, half come from such classes. The disappearance of mustangs from the officer corps increases the social homogeneity of the generals. It also helps to distance officers further from the masses in terms of roots, thus contributing to the potential of a new caste mentality. As one of our original hypotheses suggested, a caste mentality significantly affects civil-military relations and military subordination to civil authority.

The military, in contrast to civilian structures, provides an important channel for upward social mobility through the enlisted officer program. The civilian with political ambitions who comes from a working-class background comparable to that of the mustang must survive financially and intellectually in a middle-class academic environment. Few do. Although civilian institutions of higher education are numerous and diverse, and many working-class applicants enroll in them, not many graduate.[30] Why, then, did the Secretariat of National Defense drop the enlisted officer program? No official explanation has been given, but several possibilities come to mind. One, political authorities were trying, by the mid-1940s, to reduce the size of the officer corps; closing off one possible channel for recruits was a means of limiting the size of the cadet pool. Second, Cárdenas's definition of the officer corps was part of his larger populist political platform advocating stronger ties between the state and the masses, incorporated into a sophisticated, corporatist political structure. A residue of his philosophy has been a fixture of the political system ever since, but his successor, General Manuel Avila Camacho, deemphasized this orientation on many fronts, including state-military relations, and possibly the program was a victim of the new direction.

John J. Johnson offers a more practical assessment, based on an interview with an officer:

> One of the chief reasons his nation felt obliged to suspend the practice of permitting able non-commissioned officers to win regular commissions was that their wives simply could not make the social transition: this made them unacceptable to the wives of the regular commissioned officers and an embarrassment to their own husbands, all of which led to family difficulties.[31]

If Johnson's source is correct, it explains why the military quietly eliminated the program. It could never be discussed publicly because the rationale contradicts the military's projected populist image, and the lack of class conflict that Mexican leadership stresses.

The mustang's elimination also alters the geographical composition of the officer corps. Proportionately, mustangs provide much stronger representation for rural Mexicans than do high-ranking officers generally. Enlisted men are drawn from many regions, but cadets have to transport themselves to Mexico City. Consequently, only 28 percent of the officers from cadet origins were born in rural villages compared with nearly half of the officers who enlisted before becoming cadets. Elimination of the mustang not only has increased the urban bias of the officer corps but has emphasized certain regions. Most important, like political-military officers, mustangs did not come disproportionately from the Federal District, as does the officer corps as a whole. Nearly twice as many regular officers as mustangs, one in four, were born in the Federal District. Mustangs provided stronger representation for both the North and the East Central regions *and* overrepresented the South, the poorest region and the least-well-represented among politicians and other leadership groups. Also, the officer corps, because of the influence of naval officer candidates, who are not mustangs, overrepresents the Gulf, a region significantly underrepresented among mustangs. In other words, without mustangs, generals as a whole take on many of the social and geographic background variables, including both strengths and weaknesses, of Mexican politicians.

Within the armed forces, mustangs affect the prominence of career military occupational specialties (MOS) among its leadership. Interestingly, combat plays no special role in the mustang's background once the revolutionary generations have disappeared. Specific career choices within the service typify mustangs. Two patterns become clear. First, because many of them emerged from the Revolution, more than half were infantry. Generally speaking, the more sophisticated the training, the less likely mustangs will be found. For example, they are underrepresented in artillery, and most significant, five times as many regular officers as mustangs pursue engineering and medicine. The air force, unlike the navy, provided equal opportunities for mustangs; however, mustangs overwhelmingly dominate one specialty, communications, among army officers reaching the rank of general. Nearly three-quarters of all generals in our sample with a communications background are mustangs, which suggests a second pattern. In the early years mustangs were extremely well represented in the infantry, the core of the army. As the army professionalized educationally and technically, cavalry, artillery, and engineering increased in importance. Communications, on the other hand, never had the critical mass of the other three fields, thus affecting its generals' potential to influence future policy decisions.

Regular Career (Orthodox Professional) Officers

The political-military officers and mustangs, two subgroups with special characteristics, have affected the officer corps, especially at the upper ranks. However, it is the officer corps as a whole that must be analyzed in order to understand the image it projects and its composition. Because the political-military officer and the mustang officer are no longer presences among Mexican generals, age, geography, class, and family military background among the typical officer group require examination.

Why look at the generals on the basis of age? Generational experiences, especially in a society that has undergone significant changes politically and structurally in the twentieth century, can affect the outlook of leadership groups. In the case of Mexico, the Revolution is a natural dividing line between pre- and post-1910 generations. Some of Mexico's most astute historians believe that individuals born after 1920 "do not have the slightest idea of the difficult realities which the Revolution brought."[32] A man who has taught for a number of years at the Colegio de Defensa Nacional (CDN) believes the military, as distinct from the population in general, is divided into four groups or generations: the first consists of revolutionary generals; the second is the generation formed during World War II; the third is graduates of the staff and command school at the ESG; and the fourth is a new generation of graduates of the CDN. In his opinion the new generation has quite different ideas about what should happen in society and where Mexico should go politically; it is much more influenced by what is happening generally in Mexican society than was the previous generation.[33]

Some of these distinctions are valuable, but the rationales for the distinctions are somewhat different from that provided above. For so many reasons, including those that differentiated the political-military general from the rest of the generals, the pre-1900 generations constitute a clear grouping of men who shared the comradeship of combat, a very special quality. That experience is all pervasive when one considers that only 2 of the more than 134 generals born before 1900 had not actually fought in the Revolution. That shared experience itself helped to serve as a bridge to civilian politicians, many of whom participated in the Revolution but did not choose the military as a career.

The pre-1900 generation put its stamp on the officer corps and, as suggested above, flavored both the composition and the self-image of the military far beyond its own expected lifespan. Like their peers who had fought in the Liberal-Conservative conflicts and during the French intervention, its members were politically ambitious. Hence, three-quarters of their numbers also successfully pursued political office at the highest levels. Typical of this type of officer is Matías Ramos Santos, who grew up in Zacatecas in the 1890s but never went beyond the first grade in school. He joined the revolutionaries as a private on March 18, 1911, and fought under Captain Gertrudis Sánchez, later a major military figure. Ramos Santos became an officer in 1912, and rose rapidly to the rank of brigade general. Retired in 1921, he was reactivated to command troops against the de la Huerta rebellion in 1923, after which he led numerous troops in the field and military zones throughout the 1920s. Ramos Santos was a field commander par excellence, but had little experience at staff headquarters. He had his first taste of politics in 1918 as a federal deputy from his home state; took another leave in 1931, after rising to be subsecretary of the Secretariat of War, to serve his home state as governor from 1932 to 1934; after which Cárdenas appointed him president of the national executive committee of the National Revolutionary Party. Subsequently, he commanded six different military zones from 1938 to 1952, taking charge of the National Defense Secretariat in 1952.[34]

The second group of officers (born from 1900 to 1919) is more difficult to describe. Many of them were the first to be trained not only in the HCM but also in the ESG. About 20 percent fought in the Revolution, but most of them with combat experience (34 percent) earned their spurs against the rebellions of 1923, 1927, 1929, and 1939. Roberto Salido Beltrán, who commanded the Mexican Air Force in the early 1970s, is representative of the group. He enrolled in the Colegio Militar in 1929 at the age of seventeen, graduating as a second lieutenant of artillery. He graduated from the Military Aviation School as a pilot in 1937. Shortly after he joined the forces opposing the Cedillo rebellion in 1938, and was promoted to captain for his services. He followed a staff career, the wave of the future, including several stints as an instructor at the ESG and the Military Aviation School. Selected for the ESG's air force course, he graduated in 1953, after which he served as subdirector of the air force, founding director of the Colegio Aire, and in the 1960s, military attaché in the Mexican embassy in Washington, D.C.[35] His peers were a transitional generation, reflecting the qualities of officers to come, and they dominate the armed forces in the 1950s and 1960s (see Exhibit 5-1). They were molded during the political system's adolescence, many being called to defend the state against fellow officers, commonly from the pre-1900 generation, whose vision of the political model differed or who were struggling for a share of the power.

The third generation, born in the 1920s, was shaped almost completely through higher military education and through technical training abroad. Nearly all its members were graduates of the ESG, the most universal of their

Exhibit 5-1
Generational Representation among Presidents
and Defense Secretaries, 1890s–1940s

President	Generation (Birth Date)	Defense Secretary	Generation (Birth Date)
Carlos Salinas Gortari	1940s	Antonio Riviello Bazán	1920s
Miguel de la Madrid	1930s	Juan Arévalo Gardoqui	1920s
José López Portillo	1920s	Félix Galván López	1910s
Luis Echeverría	1920s	Hermenegildo Cuenca Díaz	1900s
Gustavo Díaz Ordaz	1910s	Marcelino García Barragán	1890s
Adolfo López Mateos	1910s	Agustín Olachea Aviles	1890s
Adolfo Ruiz Cortines	1890s	Matías Ramos Santos	1890s
Miguel Alemán	1900s	Gilberto Limón Márquez	1890s

shared environmental experiences. In that sense, surviving the rigors of ESG, which has a dropout rate no less severe than combat mortality rates, replaced combat as a key experience. Whereas 98 percent of the pre-1900 generation had combat in the Revolution, exactly 98 percent of the 1920s generation had no combat. Many also were mustangs, having started their careers in the enlisted ranks. Edmundo Castro Villarreal, an exemplar of this group, was born in 1927, and joined the cavalry at age fifteen. He completed the HCM's infantry course in 1947, and seven years later graduated from the ESG. He continued his training in Argentina, where he completed the Argentine staff and command course in 1959. A diploma was granted him by the Inter-American Defense College in Washington, D.C., in 1966. During the interlude he had served as a section head at defense headquarters, followed by various staff and command positions, including two stints as an ESG instructor. In the 1980s he became a zone commander, and in 1987, a department head.[36]

Contemporary observers of this generation thought that as these officers moved into positions of influence, militarily and politically, anything could happen.[37] Basically, however, their predecessors had already provided an evolutionary bridge. Although it is true that many were trained or grew up during World War II, the war itself had little impact on their formation,[38] other than increasing the prestige of the U.S. military in Mexico, and probably influencing Mexican security concerns within the context of the post-1945 cold war mentality. They were a decisive generation in post-1946 leadership because they accounted for a fourth of all commanding generals, controlling top posts in the 1970s and 1980s.

The fourth generation, the 1930s generation, which has been called the Colegio de Defensa Nacional group, is the one we understand least. Its members are the officers now in control of the armed forces and likely to dominate into the twenty-first century. Their full impact on the military and civil-military relations is yet to come. They tend to have urban middle-class backgrounds, to have lived in Mexico City, and to have followed staff careers. José Gómez Salazar, the son of a Mexico City businessman, typifies this group. A graduate of the HCM in the 1950s and the ESG in the early 1970s, he was selected as a member of the first generation to graduate from the Colegio de Defensa Nacional, where he completed his master's thesis on national security policy in 1982. His ideas were surely influenced by his experience as a military attaché in the Mexican embassay in El Salvador in the 1970s, following a decade of staff positions at the regimental and zone levels. From 1984 to 1988 he directed the Department of Military Transportation at defense headquarters in Mexico City.[39]

An artificial separation between the military and civilian leaderships in Mexico has been sustained by the difference in the ages of the two cohorts. Conservatism and a strong association with the values arising from the shared experiences of the revolutionary and postrevolutionary generations naturally persisted longer among the military leaders than the political leaders because of age differences. Also, different age groups emphasize other elite background characteristics more strongly, including regional origins, birthplace, and education. If these varying backgrounds produce differing ideas, as some authors have asserted, then an older generation of officers at the top of the military hierarchy may have contributed to a source of friction between the two groups.[40] A trend toward younger senior officers, at least since the late 1970s, was brought about by the elimination of the political-military officer and the officer with revolutionary roots. It may well increase the military's influence, as Cunningham suggests, because "younger officers will have more in common with the generally younger civilian leadership."[41] The trade-off for bringing the two groups closer together in terms of age, implying shared backgrounds and generational experiences, is that the traditional political-military leadership interlock is done away with.

In addition to generational differences, geography has a potentially signifi-cant influence. For example, in some Latin American countries certain regions dominate political and military leadership, and are resented by other regions. Frank McCann found an extremely influential geographical pattern in Brazil. By comparing the geographical distribution of military students with that of generals, he discovered a sharp distortion. For example, at the turn of the century only 5 percent of the students came from the politically important state of Río Grande do Sul, but 49 percent of the officers of that generation who became generals were from Río Grande do Sul. On the other hand, the Federal District produced 29 percent of the students but only 8 percent of the gener-als.[42] McCann's data suggest that promotion can be affected by origin. That is to say, generals, similar to national politicians, tend to recruit and promote like types.

Prior to the 1940s only one significant geographic pattern is present among Mexican military officers: overrepresentation of the North. More than a fourth of all officers came from the North, a statistic explained by the fact that nearly one in three revolutionary generals did so. But an analysis of the post-1946 military leadership suggests three regional patterns: continued overrepresenta-tion of the North; increasing dominance of the Federal District; and under-representation of the west central region.

Among Mexican generals in the past four decades the North continued to dominate as a birthplace. General population figures, taken from the 1910 census, the closest to the average birth year of all generals in the sample, suggest the degree of the North's overrepresentation; however, the information presented in Table 5-3 indicates conclusively that overall overrepresentation is due primarily to the 1880s, 1890s, and 1900s generations, those who would have fought in the Revolution. The North no longer is influential among generals' backgrounds, nor is it likely to be so in the future. The only exception to this is air force generals: nearly one in three is from the North, whereas this is true of only 18 percent of all generals.

Far more important, geographically speaking, in generals' birthplaces is Mexico City. The predominance of the capital city is a phenomenon found among other Latin American militaries. Imaz found that approximately 38 to 47 percent of each Argentine military graduating class were from the Buenos Aires metropolitan area.[43] Mexican data from the mid-1950s suggest a com-

TABLE 5-3.   Birthplaces of Mexican Generals, by Generation

Birthplace Region	Generation (%)						Average	General Population
	1880s	1890s	1900s	1910s	1920s	1930s		
Federal District	0	3	24	24	23	36	19	5
East Central	22	23	17	12	10	8	15	22
West	14	20	10	15	14	11	14	16
North	27	28	19	10	16	11	18	11
South	6	8	5	10	16	5	9	14
Gulf	19	8	14	17	15	24	15	12
West Central	11	10	12	12	5	7	9	21
Total	99	100	101	100	99	102	99	101

Note: Totals do not add up to 100 due to rounding.

parable figure: 39 percent of cadet aspirants were from the Federal District.[44] Forty-one percent of Brazil's current cadets are from Río de Janeiro, the historic capital, rather than Brasilia.[45] Although the comparative figures relate to aspirants and cadets, figures in table 5-3 for Mexican generals reveal the capital's importance among those who rise to higher ranks. In fact, over the history of the officer corps, the proportion of officers from Mexico City has been several times the proportion of the population living there (19 percent and 5 percent). Figures for generals born since 1930—in 1930 only 7 percent of the population lived in Mexico City—show a ratio of 5 to 1. It appears that the military has become sensitive to the imbalance; of the 245 spaces for cadets in the 1991 Heroico Colegio Militar class, only 18 percent have been allotted to the Federal District.[46] This may effect a decline in Federal District birthplace among generals in 2020 or, as McCann discovered in Brazil, officers from the capital may be promoted disproportionately. Members of the 1992 Escuela Superior de Guerra class, who will become the next generals, overrepresent the Federal District at 39 percent of the class.[47]

Generational data for Federal District birthplace demonstrate that the 1900 generation is a key group because the capital origin escalates from 3 percent to 24 percent, an eightfold increase in ten years, and remains at a quarter of high-ranking generals until the 1930s generation. Scholars argue that in Mexico and elsewhere the geographic concentration of military units affects recruitment of enlisted men.[48] Prospective Mexican officers have to apply in the capital, thus imposing a financial and geographic hurdle for applicants from more distant regions. Also, it has been said that the availability of superior preparatory education and the visible presence of the academies in Mexico City have contributed to attracting greater numbers of applications from the Federal District.[49]

The dominance of Mexico City in the backgrounds of Mexico's generals has several implications. All Mexican elite groups seriously underrepresent other regions. Considerable provincial resentment exists against Mexico City, or the center, because of its authoritarian exercise of political and economic power. That is translated into resentment against people from Mexico City too. In the past the military, more than other leadership groups, provided broader geographic representation and alternative channels for upward mobility to ambitious provincials, who typically found other doors closed. Thus,

> exaggerated figures for military officers from Mexico City carries with it the risk that the military, as an alternative career for the upwardly socially mobile provincial, has been sharply restricted, moreso than among their political and cultural counterparts. If access by provincial groups to bureaucratic, intellectual, and military careers is a determinant of political stability in the future, there are likely to be difficulties in meeting that demand.[50]

The third geographical trend with considerable significance revealed by data regarding the birthplaces of Mexican generals is the great underrepresentation of the west central region, one of Mexico's most populous. Although 21 percent of the population lived there in 1910, it accounted for only 9 percent of the top officers. Although not explaining why this might be so for early generations, one possible interpretation for low representation among subsequent groups of generals is the role of the army in suppressing the bitter Cristero rebellion against the government in the 1920s. An oral history of peasants in the region suggests that they see military zone commanders as opponents of land reform.[51] According to contemporary military observers, the military purposely maintains a low profile there. From a 1981 Foreign Area Officer Trip Report covering León, Aguascalientes, Irapuato, and Zacatecas, Michael Dziedzic concluded that a

> major contributing factor to the army's limited role within the state is religious in nature . . . the population is deeply religious, and there still exists some latent resentment against the military . . . since the late 1920s when the army brutally put down the Cristero revolts. Consequently, an understanding has been reached between the state and the military that low visibility on the part of the latter would be in the best interests of both parties.[52]

The military, as an institution, reinforces its historic role in the region as part of its self-image. An examination of individual officer records and the military's own publications suggests that the suppression of the Cristeros was considered an important contribution to national unification and a demonstration of military loyalty to the state.[53] As if to mirror the revolt's importance in the generals' formation, it plays a similar role, for opposite reasons, among Mexican clergy. Mexican bishops come disproportionately from the West Central region, but surviving priests and bishops remember well their persecution as seminary students in the late 1920s.[54]

One other region stands out in the birthplaces of high-ranking Mexican officers: the Gulf, which was overrepresented, although not significantly so

until the post- 1930s generation. This because naval officers have been disproportionately represented in that Veracruz, home of the primary naval academy,
is located in that region. Of the military officers from the Gulf in the 1900,
1910, and 1920 generations, 38, 71 and 53 percent, respectively, were navy
officers. Of all naval officers in our sample, nearly half are from the Gulf, most
from Veracruz; 7 percent are from the Federal District, and the remainder are
from all other regions combined. Veracruz is to the navy what the Federal
District is to the army. Thus, officers in each service come disproportionately
from a particular region, and each is substantially different from the other in
terms of geographic composition. There is no evidence that these circumstances exacerbate interservice rivalries, but they create some potential in that
direction. More important, younger generals and admirals, like politicians, are
coming from these two regions in increasing numbers. Half of the national
executive branch division heads, the lieutenant colonels and colonels of the
civilian political elite, come from the Federal District in the 1990s, and Veracruz was the only other state with a reasonably strong representation in their
birthplaces.[55]

A second geographic variable in regard to birthplace and early residence of
military officers is size of native town. Studies of Third World countries reveal
that most elites have rural backgrounds because the societies are rural. Proportionately, however, rural birthplaces among the military have been overrepresented. Officers' birthplaces worldwide tend to overrepresent smaller cities.[56]
Janowitz believed that the typical officer comes from what he described as a
"hinterland," and is of petty middle-class social origin. A combination of the
provincial lower-middle-class origins contributes to the military's "fundamen-
talist" orientation and lack of integration with other elites, especially the
political elite.[57]

Although our empirical data do not allow for a precise conceptualization of
"hinterland," a basic generational picture of urban and rural origins can be
drawn. The trends shown in Table 5-4 imply a contrast between Mexican
political and military elites.

Mexico's military leadership, in contrast to what Janowitz found elsewhere, is not a rural-based elite, nor does it differ substantially from the
civilian leadership.[58] Historically, the officer corps has always been disproportionately urban, although much less so than political leadership. Prior to 1935,

TABLE 5-4. Rural Birthplaces of Mexican Generals and Politicians

Leader Type	Generation (%)						
	1880s	1890s	1900s	1910s	1920s	1930s	1940s
Politician	47	44	37	29	24	21	05
General	62	52	34	16	25	21	*

*The 1940 cohort of generals is too small for statistical accuracy and has been combined with the 1930 cohort.

during most of the Porfiriato, only slightly more than half the officers came from rural backgrounds, and with few exceptions, that figure was relatively consistent from the 1820s generations to the turn of the century. Only two-fifths of their civilian counterparts were from rural communities. In fact, rather than a natural decline in rural birthplaces because of urbanization, the 1910 Revolution provided many ambitious rural men with an opportunity to use popular armies as a channel for upward mobility, especially those from the 1880s generation, and to a lesser extent, the 1890s generation. Again, the 1900s generation becomes a benchmark generation for both politicians and general officers, as a sudden drop in rural birthplaces becomes apparent for the post-revolutionary generation.

Contrary to popular belief, the military urbanized at a faster rate than the civilian political leadership. Sixty-seven percent of all generals in our study came from urban communities. From 1900 to 1910, an extraordinary decline in military rural backgrounds to only 16 percent occurred; fewer than half as many as the previous generation, a change not equaled or exceeded by either leadership group until the present (1940s) leadership generation. The military's rural backgrounds increased again in the 1920s generation, equal to its political counterpart, largely because President Cárdenas introduced the mustang in the 1930s. It is also interesting that a select number of states—Zacatecas, Durango, Hidalgo, Tabasco, Michoacán, and Guerrero—have largely accounted for the rural birthplaces of Mexico's generals.

Morris Janowitz offered the thesis that many professional armies, as a consequence of constituents' rural birthplaces, have an anti-urban outlook, and that the officer corps develops a critical attitude toward upper-class urban values.[59] Of course, because the Mexican officer corps has been predominantly urban, it does not have such an attitude, but one could say that the military has had an antirural prejudice, or at least has rarely identified with peasant or rural interests. The traditional view, shared among the officer corps, is a positive association with rural groups.[60] This bias is, typically, attributed to political elites too. Urban backgrounds, then, contribute to similar dispositions among both political and military leaders.

Generational and geographic differences within and between the officer corps and the political leadership have received relatively little attention in Latin America. In contrast, the general literature since José Nun's theory regarding the middle-class military coup has paid close attention to social origins as a source of divisions within the military, and as a basis for political intervention.[61] Several variations on these theories exist. The first is that the military is likely to support, or intervene in support of, policies advocated by its own class. In Mexico, this is not, as will be demonstrated, a likely source of division between the two leadership groups. More important, some scholars believe that social origin contributes strongly to the social and political attitudes of the officers.

The importance of social origins to the military has best been expressed by Marion Levy, Jr.:

Given the general isolation of armed force personnel and given the special emphasis on this isolation until basic training, at least, can be imposed upon the new members, the general social origin of the personnel has a special relevance for their behavior while members. After all, their origins constitute the source of the nonarmed-force opinions of members of the armed force organizations. These opinions are of great importance when members of the armed force organizations operate in contexts other than those strictly military ones.[62]

In the Kourvetaris and Dobratz survey, the authors could not find a universal relationship in the officer corps between social origin and political participation.[63] Nevertheless, persuasive arguments suggest that comparable class origins within the military and political leaderships eliminate social-class differences as a source of friction between the two groups.[64] But in Mexico, the caste mentality of the military, potentially enhanced by class differences, becomes particularly significant, given the military's defense strategy. The strategy against the United States is based on the concept of a people's war, which requires close collaboration between the masses and the armed forces.

The 1910 Revolution created some shared roots between the military and the masses. The military's modernization since the 1940s has gradually increased the distance, social and otherwise, between the officer corps and the ordinary Mexican. One expert suggests that in the past few years, the

overall thrust of the military's modernization, however, has been to build its self- sufficiency, both in terms of food supplies and technical and professional personnel. Some analysts have emphasized that modernization is also giving the military a distinctive social status which tends to isolate soldiers from the rest of society. It does this by creating a centralized command structure, full-time soldiers, bureaucratization, specialized high esprit de corps, technical sophistication, a corporate identity, and professional responsibility.[65]

Still another reason that class origin is thought to be important is its ideological implications, especially in terms of attitudes toward democracy versus authoritarianism. It is probably true, as Janowitz suggested many years ago, that social origin seems to be more consequential in Third World countries than in industrialized nations in shaping the military's political perspectives.[66] Nevertheless, a general assumption is that individuals from lower socioeconomic backgrounds, people who typically are victims of the military's "political" activities, would be strongly opposed to such authoritarian abuses. Frederick Nunn is not convinced that lower-class officers would evince ideals any more democratic than officers from different social backgrounds.[67] However, a study of authoritarian attitudes among Mexican children conducted by Rafael Segovia unequivocally found that as socioeconomic status increases, authoritarianism decreases.[68] Segovia also discovered that as education increases, authoritarianism decreases. In Mexico, as in most other societies, increased education would be associated with individuals of higher socioeconomic status. For military officers, the level of education is not likely to be associated with a decline in authoritarianism but, rather, its increase. First, the content of the education is more important than level, especially in terms of obedience to authority. Second, the higher the educational level in the Mexican military system, as will be demonstrated elsewhere, the more complete the subordination to authority.

Social origin is not particularly important to Latin American military officers because of the socialization process through which all officers must pass, not only in the military academies but during their entire careers. The process instills obliviousness to class, a strong set of values that determines organizational behavior, and most important, the primacy of institutional over personal or political interests.[69] Socialization processes can eliminate the significance of social class origin; on the other hand, the Mexican military can stress values and organizational behavior that give officers a closer identification with the masses, and build a strong sense of subordination to civil authority.

More important, the lower-middle-class origins of the Mexican officer corps and the middle- and upper-middle-class origins of politicians have fundamentally affected civil-military relations. Several generals have indicated that they believe middle-class professionals in the public sector perceive them as ignorant. One officer who served in the Chamber of Deputies concluded, "My fellow members in the chamber seemed to think that military officers couldn't think or write."[70] Numerous anecdotes suggest that they are seen as socially inferior. This phenomenon, perhaps more than any other variable, has encouraged distance between civilian and military groups and has considerably affected civil-military relations.

The Mexican officer corps, like any elite group, has never been representative of the population. Prior to 1935, only 38 percent of the officers came from the working class, whereas more than 91 percent of the population were working class. During the same period, 46 percent of the officers came from the middle classes, from which no more than 8 percent of the population were drawn; 15 percent came from the upper class, the class of only 1 percent of the population. In percentage terms, of course, the upper class was most over-represented in the officer corps.

The Mexican Revolution temporarily altered the socioeconomic composition of the officer corps. The 1880s generation was most important, and of this age cohort, nearly two-thirds of the officers came from working-class families compared with nine-tenths of the population. At no other time in the past century has the working class been better represented, numerically or proportionately, in the corps. Even in the following generation, although their numbers declined, working-class officers still accounted for almost half of those reaching the rank of general. As has been true of all other background characteristics, a sharp distinction occurs between the nineteenth and twentieth centuries (table 5-5). In the 1900s cohort nearly four-fifths came from the middle and upper classes (upper-class origins were negligible), at a time when only one-tenth of the population was classified as middle or upper class. Politicians have been much more representative of the population as a whole than have top military officers, except the oldest generations, who are not numerically significant among post-1940s leaders. The youngest political

TABLE 5-5. Middle-Class Socioeconomic Origins of Mexican Generals
and Politicians, by Generation

Leader Type	Generation (%)							
	1880s	1890s	1900s	1910s	1920s	1930s	1940s	1950s
Generals	27	53	79	80	88	88	85	100[a]
Politicians	77	67	58	62	56	75	95	100

[a]For the military, this is based on a small sample of lieutenant colonels because forty years of age is too young to become a general.

generations, like the military, bear witness to the nearly complete disappearance of leaders from the working class, even though in the 1940s and 1950s the working class was 80 percent of the population.[71] For most of the two decades individuals desirous of upward social mobility would have found greater opportunities in a political rather than a military career.

The figures regarding the socioeconomic background of military officers are extremely important, given the military's attitude about who it is and what it represents socially in Mexico. General Félix Galván, secretary of defense, best expresses this view:

The army comes from the people. I myself am a product of *campesinos*. We, truthfully—this isn't a word, a phrase or posture—truthfully, we are the people of the people. The enlisted men are campesino boys who we recruit; the officers also come from the popular classes. I myself, from the highest rank, am a product of campesinos. And my family members are people of the people.[72]

William S. Ackroyd found that officers he interviewed considered their social identity to be toward the lower end of the socioeconomic scale.[73] The discrepancy between actual and perceived class backgrounds can be explained in two ways. First, a wide range exists in the empirical categorization of the middle classes. Although the same criteria were applied to both politicians and officers, it is fair to say that a far greater number of politicians come from upper-middle-class backgrounds, whereas officers come from the bottom of the middle class.[74] Second, an increasingly large percentage of middle-class officers are the children of career military. Their parents' incomes, however, do not put them in the same category as politicians' children. Although middle class, these men share their fathers' perception that they too are from the "people."

It is also possible that the socioeconomic backgrounds of the officer corps as a whole do not accurately reflect those of high-ranking generals. A study of U.S. officers found this to be the case; although working-class backgrounds were underrepresented in the U.S. military, the discrepancy was much less among all officers, suggesting that middle-class origins, for whatever reason, assist officers in reaching the top ranks.[75] Ackroyd offered some data to confirm this pattern for Mexican officers: graduates of the Escuela Superior de

Guerra were disproportionately from the middle class relative to cadets graduating from the Heroico Colegio Militar.[76] As will be demonstrated later, graduation from the ESG is typical of almost all general officers.

The overrepresentation of the lower middle class in the backgrounds of the Mexican officer corps can be explained largely by the economic advantages offered by the corps. Edwin Lieuwen believed that admission fees of both the Heroico Colegio Militar and the Colegio Aire initially screened out lower-income applicants. Because applicants are tested in the Federal District, they must also be able to pay travel expenses to get there.[77] Also, the required competitive examination is a social screening device. Whereas members of the lower middle class can more readily obtain the preparatory education necessary to pass the examination, those from lower socioeconomic backgrounds often cannot.[78]

It is possible that in the future the officer corps will become more rather than less representative of the population, something that has already occurred in the United States.[79] Since World War II sons of the lower-middle and working classes have had greater opportunities to become officers.[80] The reason for this is that as the economy grew, lower-middle-class children had a wider range of opportunities for upward social mobility, and working-class children received better education, which enabled them to compete more effectively. Lyle McAlister expected this to happen in Mexico, especially because the middle class was nearly 30 percent of the population in 1970.[81] However, less prosperous times since the late 1970s have considerably reduced middle-class growth. In consequence, the foreseeable future will bring little change in the social composition of the officer corps.

Studies of other nations suggest that most individuals join the military as a means of upward social and economic mobility. Most newly independent nations recruit for the military among the middle and lower-middle classes. The United States, with the smallest working class, recruits two-thirds of its military officers from the lower-middle and working classes,[82] and the officer's social background is likely to determine his or her persistence in the military. Lifetime careerists tend to come from lower socioeconomic strata than do those who resign their commissions. Thus, "the striking implication was that young men from less privileged social backgrounds are finding opportunities for increased social status in the military career more attractive than in civilian careers."[83]

Upward social mobility as a basis for choosing a military career has been important for those with little formal education but with political ambitions. They have a greater chance for success in the military than did their civilian counterparts with equivalent educational credentials.[84] This circumstance applied only to the revolutionary generation. In other words, individuals from the 1880s and 1890s without advanced education had fewer chances of rising to the top of the political ladder through a career in politics than through a career in the officer corps. Many officers believe that this "revolutionary" origin alters the social composition of the Mexican officer corps, especially relative to other Latin American militaries.[85]

For the revolutionary generation, especially those who chose politics, the military was attractive to the lower socioeconomic classes and to men in rural areas. Peter Smith believes that at "that specific historic juncture, then, the military appears to have provided routes of access for socially deprived *campesinos*" to the political elite.[86] But looking at high-ranking officers in general rather than just political-military officers, one sees a military more open to urban than rural poor, even though more mustangs (who are generally from the working classes) come from rural areas. Rural working-class Mexicans are less likely than their urban counterparts to pursue a military career because the latter have greater access to primary and secondary education.[87]

One additional background variable, whether or not an individual's father is in the military, has significant bearing on the characteristics of the officer corps, in terms of both self-image and relationship to political leadership. In fact, other than upward social mobility, the reason given by the largest remaining number of officer aspirants to the HCM is to follow in the footsteps of the father or other relatives.[88] In Brazil, for example, Alfred Stepan found that 30 percent of the cadets at the army academy were sons of career military personnel.[89] Cadets entering the HCM because of an intrinsic desire for a service career are for the most part sons of army personnel.

Second- or even third-generation army men are extremely important because they indicate the emergence of a self-perpetuating officer corps.[90] The same danger exists among the political leadership, which is drawing, especially at the upper levels, increasingly on a pool of sons and daughters of prominent political figures. This is not the case in the United States, where sons of federal personages are barely present among political leaders.[91] Politicians' parentage affects the Mexican recruitment process, and indeed the ability of each individual to climb the political ladder. In the Salinas cabinet, political parentage is one of the most common background variables, nicely illustrated by the fact that both the president and his strongest competitor, Cuauhtémoc Cárdenas, are the sons of national political figures.[92]

Military fathers have always been well represented in the backgrounds of the Mexican officer corps. The fathers of prominent officers from the 1880s through the 1930s came primarily from three important backgrounds: peasant or laborer (33 percent), military (18 percent), and professional (16 percent). The figure for working-class parents, however, is deceptive. Revolutionary officers account for four-fifths of the fathers who were peasants or laborers; this means that among all other generations of top officers prior to 1935, fewer than one in ten had a working-class father. What these figures suggest is that the revolutionary generation was extremely important in contributing to the contemporary military's popular roots, but that its contribution was short-lived. Also, although the military accounts for 18 percent of officer fathers during the whole period, for the revolutionary generation alone, it drops to 7 percent, practically eliminating military parentage as a contributor to a caste mentality.[93] Instead, fathers with professional careers assumed second place in importance.

The pre-1935 generations, except for the revolutionary group, not only were the children of military fathers but often came from prominent military, political, or landowning families (14 percent). A larger percentage also were otherwise related to prominent political figures (23 percent) or military figures (5 percent). Although the revolutionary generation gave birth to a new military, most of whose members had no familial roots in the established military, it did not, as might be expected, eliminate the caste aspect of the military. Rather, it initiated an entirely new set of parental sources for officers in the second half of the twentieth century. In the mid-1950s, one in five parents of aspirants to the HCM was in the military.[94] Analysts assume that the military accepted aspirants in percentages approximating the distribution of fathers' backgrounds. Stephen Wager estimated that military families constituted about 20 percent of the total number of cadets, and that double that figure had extended family members serving in or affiliated with the armed forces.[95]

Data from our survey of Mexican generals reveal that one in three is the child of a career military father, typically an officer.[96] General Antonio Riviello Bazán, secretary of defense under Salinas, is not only the son of a division general but the brother and step-brother of two other generals. Because only a few ever reach the position of secretary of defense, a more typical example in the current administration is General Genaro Ambia Martínez, whose father, a military engineer, graduated from the Colegio Militar's School of Administration in 1925. Genaro himself specialized in engineering, following his father's MOS, and after graduating from the CDN in 1982, became director of the cartographic service at the beginning of the Salinas administration.[97] These and many other examples illustrate that the generals are themselves sons of the postrevolutionary professional officer corps; and in addition to reestablishing the importance of military parentage, generals with military fathers since 1946 are more numerous than in any previous period. The phenomenon does not appear to be unusual for Latin America. Frank McCann found that 40 percent of the entering cadets in Brazil's Academia Militar das Agulhas Negras (AMAN) were sons of military men in the 1960s; nearly three-quarters of them were sons of corporals or sergeants.[98] It is likely that the educational and financial status of higher-ranking officers permits their children to take up more prestigious and lucrative civilian vocations. The military offers attractive opportunities to children of NCOs, but Mexico's military has never had a well-developed noncomissioned officer corps.

If about one in five Mexican cadets has a career military father, the fact that one in three of such cadets actually reaches the rank of general is significant.[99] U.S. military observers suggest that one aid to surviving the rigors of the ESG, a hurdle that most officers who go on to generalships must overcome, is kinship with a prominent officer. If junior officers who are the children of officers are more likely to achieve highest ranks, whether on their own merits or those of a father, a potential for resentment among officers without such blood ties exists. Among U.S. military cadets, a direct correlation exists between career military parentage, academic success, and lower attrition rates.[100] Nevertheless, two in three Mexican officers do not have officer fathers, hence substantial upward mobility within the service still is the norm for them.

The gradual decline and nearly complete elimination of political-military and mustang officers among Mexican generals has considerable impact on the officer corps. No longer does a large percentage of officers having personal experience with and ties among civilian politicians, serve as a bridge between the two leadership groups. Other means will have to substitute for maintaining adequate communication and exchange. The absence of political-military officers and mustangs affects the caste quality of the military, encouraging it to become more isolated. Differences in social origins, and in some cases geography, helped to diversify the military and, in some cases, increased its comparability to the political leadership. The increasing homogeneity in officer backgrounds facilitates the military's tilt toward developing a stronger caste mentality, differentiating it from, and complicating its relations with, civilian leaders. The military, like politicians, suffers from various representational weaknesses in its leadership.

Notes

1. C. Wright Mills, *The Power Elite* (New York: Oxford University Press, 1959), 283.

2. José Luis Piñeyro, "The Mexican Army and the State: Historical and Political Perspective," *Revue Internationale de Sociologie* 14 (April–August, 1978): 154.

3. Gavin Kennedy, *The Military in the Third World* (New York: Scribner's, 1974), 129.

4. Actually, it was his successor, General Manuel Avila Camacho, who implemented the law; he retired 550 officers during the first year of his administration, 1941. See Talukder Maniruzzaman, *Military Withdrawal from Politics: A Comparative Study* (Cambridge, Mass.: Ballinger, 1987), 97.

5. Phyllis Greene Walker, "The Modern Mexican Military: Political Influence and Institutional Interests in the 1980s" (M.A. thesis, American University, 1987), 29.

6. México, Dirección Técnica de Organización, *Directorio del gobierno federal*, 1951, 182–83; *Directorio del gobierno federal*, 1956, 201.

7. Walker, "The Modern Mexican Military," 30.

8. Morris Janowitz, *The Military in the Development of New Nations* (Chicago: University of Chicago Press, 1964), 45.

9. Ibid., 40.

10. Edwin Lieuwen, *Mexican Militarism* (Albuquerque: University of New Mexico Press, 1968), 122.

11. Lyle N. McAlister, *The Military in Latin American Socio-political Evolution: Four Case Studies* (Washington, D.C.: Center for Research in Social Systems, 1970), 241.

12. Roderic A. Camp, "Mexican Military Leadership in Statistical Perspective Since the 1930s," in *Statistical Abstract of Latin America*, vol. 20, ed. James W. Wilkie and Peter Reich (Los Ageles: Latin American Center, University of California, Los Angeles, 1980), 604.

13. Ibid.

14. Roderic A. Camp, "The Political Technocrat in Mexico and the Survival of the Political System," *Latin American Research Review* 20, no. 1 (1985): 112.

15. Roderic A. Camp, "Generals and Politicians in Mexico: A Preliminary Comparison," in *The Modern Mexican Military: A Reassessment*, ed. David Ronfeldt (La Jolla: Center for U.S. Mexican Studies, University of California, San Diego, 1984), 155.

16. Personal interview with a general, United States, 1984.

17. *Diccionario biográfico del gobierno mexicano* (Mexico: Presidencia de la República, 1989), 955.

18. For examples from northern Mexico, see Edward J. Williams, "The Resurgent North and Contemporary Mexican Regionalism," *Mexican Studies* 6 (Summer 1990): 299–323.

19. *Diccionario biográfico del gobierno mexicano*, 955.

20. Lieuwen, *Mexican Militarism*, 120.

21. Virginia Prewett, "The Mexican Army," *Foreign Affairs* 19 (April 1941): 614.

22. Comments by General Luis Garfías Magaña, Workshop on the Modern Mexican Military, Center for U.S.-Mexican Studies, University of California, San Diego, La Jolla, March 21, 1984.

23. For background on this controversy, see "Editorial," *Revista de Ejército y Fuerza Aérea*, September 1955, 3; Raúl Díaz de León Durán, "Bienvenidos los sargentos primeros al H. Colegio militar," *Revista de Ejército y Fuerza Aérea*, August 1955, 64–65; S. Rangel Medina, "El nuevo curso de formación de officiales en el H. Colegio Militar," *Revista de Ejército y Fuerza Aérea*, June 1955, 3–5. Phyllis Greene Walker, "National Security," in *Mexico: A Country Study*, ed. James D. Rudolph (Washington, D.C.: GPO, 1985), 352; Stephen J. Wager, "The Mexican Military" (unpublished paper, 1983), 9, much of which is incorporated into Robert Wesson's section on Mexico in his *The Latin American Military* (Westport, Conn.: Greenwood Press, 1986), suggests such a program was instituted in 1948, but I can find no evidence of an earlier version.

24. Personal interview, Mexico City, 1990. Of course, first sergeants already had put in considerable time in grade as enlisted men. In terms of actual promotions, these first sergeants have not had much success, remaining at the lower ranks.

25. Generals suggest that these men rarely rise beyond the rank of major because of their shortened HCM training and regular graduates' resentment against them. Personal interviews, Mexico City, 1990.

26. Personal interview, Mexico City, 1990.

27. Salinas's appointee as head of the air force appeared to be a mustang too. However, an officer explained to me that sometimes officers will encourage their sons to enlist in the military as one would take a temporary job, to earn some money. The head of the air force had not enlisted as a means of social advancement; rather, his officer father had started him off as an enlisted soldier, after which he decided to pursue a military career. Personal interview, Mexico City, 1990.

28. *Revista de Ejército y Fuerza Aérea*, February 1973; *Quien es quien en la administración pública en México* (Mexico: Presidencia de la República, 1982), 75; *Diccionario biográfico del gobierno mexicano*, 1984 (Mexico: Presidencia de la República), 58.

29. Camp, "Generals and Politicians in Mexico," 141.

30. Ibid.

31. John J. Johnson, *The Military and Society in Latin America* (Stanford: Stanford University Press, 1964), 172.

32. Daniel Cosío Villegas, *Memorias* (Mexico City: Joaquín Mortiz, 1976), 57.

33. Personal interview, Mexico City, June 24, 1989.

34. *Revista de Ejército y Fuerza Aérea*, April 1962, 50–52.

35. *Revista de Ejército y Fuerza Aérea*, September 1972, 114; *Enciclopedia de México, Annual*, 1977, 596; Secretaria de Defensa Nacional, *Memorias* (Mexico: SDN, 1964–1965), 37.

36. *Diccionario biográfico del gobierno mexicano* (Mexico: Presidencia de la República, 1987), 87; *Revista de Ejército y Fuerza Aérea*, June 1976, 131.

37. Frank Brandenburg, *Making of Modern Mexico* (Englewood Cliffs, N.J.: Prentice-Hall, 1964), 160.

38. Although a small group of air force officers served in the Philippines during World War II, and many held top command positions after 1945, the impact on their ideology is unknown. They are such a small group numerically that whatever influences they carried probably were limited within the armed services.

39. *Diccionario biográfico del gobierno mexicano*, 1987, 159.

40. Camp, "Mexican Military Leadership in Statistical Perspective Since the 1930s," 598.

41. Alden M. Cunningham, "Mexico's National Security in the 1980s–1990s," in *The Modern*

Mexican Military: A Reassessment, ed. David Ronfeldt (La Jolla: Center for U.S.-Mexican Studies, University of California, San Diego, 1984), 172.

42. Frank D. McCann, "Brazilian Army Officers Biography Project" (Paper presented at the National Latin American Studies Association, Miami, December 1989), 6.

43. José de Imaz, *Los Que Mandan* (Albany: State University of New York, 1970), 58.

44. Javier Romero, *Aspectos psicobiométricos y sociales de una muestra de la juventud mexicana* (Mexico: Dirección de Investigaciones Antropológicas, 1956), 47.

45. McCann, "Brazilian Army Officers Biography Project," 22.

46. Personal interview, Mexico City, 1990.

47. Personal interview, Mexico City, 1991. Half of the states were not represented at all.

48. Wager, "The Mexican Military," 8; McCann, "Brazilian Army Officers Biography Project," 5.

49. McAlister, *The Military in Latin American Socio-political Evolution*, 221.

50. Camp, "Generals and Politicians in Mexico," 112.

51. Ann L. Craig, *The First Agraristas: An Oral History of a Mexican Agrarian Reform Movement* (Berkeley: University of California Press, 1983), 77.

52. Michael J. Dziedzic, "Civil-military Relations in Mexico: The Politics of Co-optation" (unpublished paper, University of Texas, Austin, 1983), 11. Stephen J. Wager, "Civic Action and the Mexican Military" (unpublished paper, Department of History, U.S. Military Academy, 1982), 7, reported exactly the same pattern in the Bajio region, which includes Guanajuato and Michoacán.

53. Survey of *Revista de Ejército y Fuerza Aérea*, 1943 to 1989.

54. Roderic A. Camp, "Religious Elites in Mexico—Some Preliminary Observations" (Paper presented at the National Latin American Studies Association, Miami, 1989), 11; personal interviews, 1987, 1988, and 1989.

55. *Diccionario biográfico del gobierno mexicano*, 1989, 955.

56. George Kourvetaris and Betty Dobratz, *Social Origins and Political Orientations of Officer Corps in a World Perspective* (Denver: Graduate School of International Studies, University of Denver, 1973), 11.

57. Janowitz, *The Military in the Development of New Nations*, 58.

58. See, for example, his conclusions in *The Professional Soldier* (Glencoe, Ill.: Free Press, 1960), 86.

59. Ibid., 58.

60. Personal interviews, Mexico City, 1990.

61. See his "The Middle-Class Military Coup Revisited," in *Armies and Politics in Latin America*, ed. Abraham Lowenthal (New York: Holmes and Meier, 1976), 49–86.

62. Marion Levy, Jr., "Armed Forces Organizations," in *The Military and Modernization*, ed. Henry Bienen (Chicago: Aldine-Atherton, 1971, 63.

63. Kourvetaris and Dobratz, *Social Origins and Political Orientations of Officer Corps in a World Perspective*, 78.

64. Gordon C. Schloming, "Civil-Military Relations in Mexico, 1910–1940: A Case Study" (Ph.D. diss., Columbia University, 1974), 317.

65. José Luis Piñeyro, "The Modernization of the Mexican Armed Forces," in *Democracy under Siege, New Military Power in Latin America*, ed. Augusto Varas (Westport, Conn.: Greenwood Press, 1989), 127.

66. Janowitz, *The Military in the Development of New Nations*, 56.

67. Frederick M. Nunn, "On the Role of the Military in Twentieth-Century Latin America: The Mexican Case," in *The Modern Mexican Military: A Reassessment*, ed. David Ronfeldt (La Jolla: Center for U.S.-Mexican Studies, University of California, San Diego, 1984), 41.

68. Rafael Segovia, *La politización del niño mexicano* (Mexico: El Colegio de México, 1975), 68.

69. José Nerique Miguens, "The New Latin American Military Coup," in *Militarism in Developing Countries*, ed. Kenneth Fidel (New Brunswick, N.J.: Transaction, 1975), 99–123.

70. Personal interview, Mexico City, 1990.

71. James W. Wilkie and Paul D. Wilkins, "Quantifying the Class Structure of Mexico, 1895–

1970," in *Statistical Abstract of Latin America*, vol. 21, ed. James W. Wilkie and Stephen Haber (Los Angeles: Latin American Center, University of California, Los Angeles, 1982), 585.

72. Oscar Hinojosa, "Cualquier régimen de gobierno, con apoyo popular, será repetado por el Ejército," *Proceso*, no. 29, March 1982, 9.

73. William S. Ackroyd, "Descendants of the Revolution: Civil-Military Relations in Mexico" (Ph.D. diss., University of Arizona, 1988), 154–155.

74. Universal agreement among politicians and generals existed on this point. Personal interviews, Mexico City, 1989–1990.

75. Kourvetaris and Dobratz, *Social Origins and Political Orientations of Officer Corps in a World Perspective*, 10.

76. William S. Ackroyd, "Civil-Military Relations in Mexico: A Study of Mexican Military Perceptions and Behavior" (Paper presented at the Rocky Mountain States Conference of Latin American Studies, Las Cruces, 1980), 15.

77. Lieuwen, *Mexican Militarism*, 147.

78. McAlister, *The Military in Latin American Socio-political Evolution*, 222.

79. Nevertheless, in the 1950s and 1960s, top U.S. officers were very well represented in the upper-middle classes. For example, in Lloyd Warner's study of colonels to four-star generals in 1963, 13 percent of their fathers were in big business; 15 percent were professionals; 16 percent were in small business; and 12 percent were white collar. *The American Federal Executive: A Study of the Social and Personal Characteristics of the Civilian and Military Leaders of the United States* (New Haven: Yale University Press, 1963). Among air force generals in a 1950 study, 30 percent were upper middle class; 62 percent, lower middle class; and 8 percent, upper lower class. R. F. Schloemer, and G. E. Myers, "Making It at the Air Force Academy: Who Stays? Who Succeeds?" in *The Changing World of the American Military*, ed. Franklin D. Margiotta (Boulder, Colo.: Westview Press, 1978), 335.

80. Janowitz, *The Professional Soldier*. Frank McCann discovered that in Brazil cadets from middle-class families also increased, but officers from both upper- and lower-class families have decreased since World War II. See his "Brazilian Army Officers Biography Project," 13.

81. Wilkie and Wilkins, "Quantifying the Class Structure of Mexico, 1895–1970," 589.

82. Charles H. Coates, "America's New Officer Corps," in *The American Military*, ed. Martin Oppenheimer (Chicago: Aldine, 1971), 50. Alfred Stepan found in Brazil that in the early 1960s 78 percent were from the middle class; 6 percent, upper class; and 9 percent, lower classes. *The Military in Politics: Changing Patterns in Brazil* (Princeton: Princeton University Press, 1971), 33.

83. Coates, "America's New Officer Corps," 51.

84. Camp, "Mexican Military Leadership in Statistical Perspective," 599.

85. Piñeyro, "The Mexican Army and the State," 154–155.

86. Peter H. Smith, *Labyrinths of Power: Political Recruitment in Twentieth Century Mexico* (Princeton: Princeton University Press, 1979), 95–96.

87. Camp, "Generals and Politicians in Mexico," 116.

88. Daniel Mora, "Profile of the Mexican Company Grade Officer" (Paper presented at the Rocky Mountain States Latin American Conference, Tucson, February 1984), 5.

89. Stepan, *The Military in Politics*, 33.

90. Camp, "Generals and Politicians in Mexico," 120.

91. Warner et al., *The American Federal Executive*, 33.

92. Roderic A. Camp, "Camarillas in Mexican Politics: The Case of the Salinas Cabinet," *Mexican Studies* 6 (Winter 1990): 96–97.

93. Interestingly, even in a society like the United States, war can broaden the career military backgrounds of an officer corps. Among Air War College graduates shortly after Vietnam, the percentage of graduates whose fathers were career military declined to only 5 percent, indicating the impact of war on breaking down caste qualities. See Schloemer, "Making It at the Air Force Academy," 339.

94. Romero, *Aspectos psicobiométricos y sociales de una muestra de la juventud mexicana*, 49.

95. Wager, "Civic Action and the Mexican Military," 12.

96. Figures for all U.S. Air Force Academy graduates are somewhat similar. One in four

officers had a father who was career military, and 2 percent had fathers and grandfathers with military backgrounds. See Schloemer, "Making It at the Air Force Academy," 338.

97. *Memoria gráfica del cincuentenario de la reapertura del Heroico Colegio Militar* (Mexico: SHCP, 1970), 447; *Diccionario biográfico del gobierno mexicano*, 1989, 30.

98. McCann, "Brazilian Army Officers Biography Project," 14, 16.

99. John F. Fitzgerald found that 25 percent of naval cadets at Annapolis were the children of career military fathers. See his article with Charles L. Cochran, "Who Goes to the United States Naval Academy?," in *The Changing World of the American Military*, ed. Franklin D. Margiotta (Boulder, Colo.: Westview Press, 1978), 362.

100. Schloemer, "Making It at the Air Force Academy," 338.

6

Education and Command

Formal training is integral to the professionalization of the career officer. Military academies perform three interrelated functions: to increase professional competence, a cognitive function; to mold values among cadets and lower-ranking officers, a socialization function; and to establish personal ties and peer trust crucial to future command, a recruitment function. The general literature presents considerable discussion on the cognitive function; a cursory examination of the socialization function, and almost no analysis or empirical evidence of the recruitment function.

This chapter evaluates the changing trends in military education, comparing new directions with patterns occurring among Mexican civilian leadership. Although useful conclusions can be drawn from the levels of military education, the primary focus of the analysis is on the socialization and recruitment functions, their implications for the successful career officer, and their contrasts with civil political leadership.

Evolution of Formal Education in the Military

Historically, Mexico's military educational system had little prestige. The majority of officers in the federal army, or its antecedent national guard in the nineteenth century were not graduates of specialized military training programs. Frederick Nunn, one of the few students of Latin American military education, declared that between "1876 and 1910 the army fared little better in the institutional, professional sense; the *porfiriato* did little to perpetuate the military past—and less to assure the army's future. Officers were only marginally prepared."[1] Furthermore, those reaching the rank of general could be distinguished educationally from all officers in the army; according to one historian, nearly all of the generals were nonprofessionals, and most of them were quite elderly by 1900.[2] In the broadest sense of professionalization, Nunn and Edwin Lieuwen are correct. Nevertheless, the number of officers attending the Colegio Militar did increase gradually from the 1870s through 1900.

From a recent historical perspective, it would be fairer to say that Porfirio Díaz contributed to the institutionalization of the military during his administration. His officers increasingly were trained at the Colegio Militar, where they actually pursued four years of technical studies in the arts of modern

warfare, a length of military education unequaled until the 1940s. Furthermore, under Díaz, enrollments at the Colegio Militar averaged 300, with 60
cadets graduating annually. It has been estimated that by 1892, 30 percent of
all officers were graduates of the Colegio Militar; by 1900, approximately 50
percent.[3] It is important to remember that the Colegio Militar began operation
in 1869. This explains to a great degree why many officers were graduates, and
why most generals, who began their careers before the 1860s, were without
formal military education. In 1882, after fourteen years in operation, only 19,
or 11 percent, of the 170 army generals were graduates, and 48, or 7 percent, of
the colonels.[4]

The education of top Mexican military figures has always lagged behind that
of civilian politicians. During many earlier periods military officers occupied
political offices, and in many administrations, actually held more posts than
civilians. However, if we compare top military political figures with their civilian
counterparts, the educational disparity become apparent (see Table 6-1).

The crucial difference is that 39 percent of generals have only a normal
(teaching certificate; in Mexico, less than high school during this period)
education or below; this was true for only 12 percent of civilian leaders.
Furthermore, the generals' university education is highly exaggerated in these
figures. For purposes of comparison, graduates of the Colegio Militar were
included in the university-level category. In terms of actual educational preparation, they should be placed in the preparatory or secondary category. Hence,
if those graduates are removed from the category, generals with a college
education or higher decline from 48 percent of the total to only 29 percent,
compared with 72 percent of the civilians. Even assuming these were the most
successful generals politically, only 16 percent were graduates of the Colegio
Militar. Of the generals who received professional or college training, most
attended the Colegio Militar, followed by the National University (8 percent)

TABLE 6-1. Educational Levels of Mexican Generals
and Civilian Politicians, 1884–1935

Educational level	Generals (%)	Civilian Politicians (%)
Primary	29	5
Secondary	7	4
Normal	3	3
Preparatory	12	12
University	45	62
Ph.D.	0.4	1
M.D. or D.D.S.	3	9
Total	99.4	96

Source: Mexican Political Biography Project

Note: Percentages do not add up to 100 due to rounding.

and state universities. A small group, 5 percent, attended Latin American, European, or United States institutions, and 1 percent graduated from Mexican seminaries. In contrast, most civilian leaders from 1884 to 1935 graduated from the National University or its antecedents (42 percent), and only 1 percent attended the Colegio Militar.

After the Revolution, renewed emphasis was placed on military education. The evolution of each military academy and its individual role in officer education, formation, and recruitment are examined subsequently, but it is important here to identify the general educational trends. Both the military and political leaderships increasingly have valued technical expertise. As indicated by their informal recruitment practices, the leaders have sought out and promoted disciples with specific, formal credentials, although institutionally such credentials have never been specified legally as necessary for advancement.

This upward educational trend can be seen quite clearly through a generational analysis of generals since 1940. Among revolutionary contemporaries of Generals Alvaro Obrégon and Plutarco Elías Calles, who continued to hold command positions after 1940, only a third obtained formal military training or university education. Of those, more than half were graduates of the Colegio Militar, some attending as higher-ranking officers. For example, Adrían Castrejón, who first joined the Maderistas as a guerrilla on July 2, 1911, matriculated in the Colegio Militar's cavalry program as a brigadier general on April 11, 1921. He graduated in 1923, and was promoted to brigade general in 1924 while serving as commander of the 24th military zone in Guerrero.[5]

A key change in educational patterns among high-ranking military officers occurs between the 1890s and 1900s generations. More than half the officers born during the 1890s attended a military or civilian college; of that number, 63 percent attended the Colegio Militar, and 14 percent graduated from the naval academy in Veracruz. Characteristics of the 1890s generation suggest not only an increase in level of education but an important shift in alma maters, from civilian to purely military. It is the postrevolutionary generation, those born in the first decade of the twentieth century, who mark the future nature of officer corps composition. Only one of the officers in our sample of sixty had not attended a military school or civilian university. More important, 90 percent had graduated from a military school. This figure alone does not tell the entire story. Half of all officers from the 1900s generation are graduates of the Escuela Superior de Guerra (ESG), compared with only 2 percent of the 1890s generation. The ESG, founded to prepare junior officers for staff and command positions, suddenly became an extraordinary presence in the educational background of Mexico's generals; ten years previously scarcely any could count it as part of their training. This can be explained by the fact that it was established in the early 1930s, and forerunner generations were too old to be eligible for admission.

The 1900s generation is a key group among generals and politicians for other reasons. In our discussion of civilian and military interlocks, it was shown that educational institutions—particularly the Heroico Colegio Militar and the National University—played a principal role. For example, among college-educated generals of the 1880s generation, 25 percent were graduates of the National University; by the 1900s generation, 15 percent. It was the last generation in which a larger minority of officers, other than those who are military lawyers, were National University alumni. Only 6 percent of all generals have attended the National University, the most important institution in politicians' education.

Finally, the 1900s generation can be considered a crucial generation for the military because the transitional professional soldier reached an apex among that cohort. The transitional professional soldier was an individual characterized by many professional qualities, not the least of which were training and advanced studies. At the same time, however, as I suggested earlier, these men were politicized, pursuing successful political careers. A decisive change occurs when the best-educated officers reaching the rank of general and who have political ambitions fade away and are replaced by more orthodox career officers, equally well educated, the military professionals. Accordingly, after 1910 superior education is the mark not of the political-military officer but of the true professional. It is the highly educated political-military officer in control of the military bureaucracy who raises fellow officers to this educational level, serving as an important bridge in the education of the officer corps.

From the 1900 generation onward, all officers of the rank of general had attained similar educational levels. In effect, officers born after 1910 who hope to become generals must attend the military academies or a civilian university. At the war college level, figures remain nearly constant among the three successive generations: about 60 percent of the generals have staff and command diplomas from the Escuela Superior de Guerra or its foreign equivalent. Such military education is high even by industrialized countries' standards. For example, in the mid-1960s only 28 percent and 24 percent of Czechoslovakia and Poland's officers were academy graduates.[6] By the 1960s, when Mexicans born in the 1940s entered the officer corps as cadets, another educational change occurred: attending the Escuela Superior de Guerra replaced attending the Heroico Colegio Militar as a new, informal credential in obtaining the rank of general. The 1940s generation, few of which are senior officers at this point, has graduated in much larger numbers—75 to 85 percent—from the Escuela Superior de Guerra.

By the 1980s, according to secretary of defense figures, during a typical year 2,080 soldiers were enrolled in military schools, 614 cadets in officer-training academies, 512 noncommissioned and junior officers in applied schools, 396 officers, colonels, and generals in higher war schools, including 7 naval officers, 38 civilians, and 12 foreigners.[7] Military analysts have argued that 90 percent of all officers (not just generals) were the products of officer-training schools. The remainder of the officers either obtained a direct commission or come "from a select group of NCO's [mustangs] with demonstrated ability who attend an officer preparatory course at one of the academies."[8]

The National Defense Secretariat, in recognition of the importance of its various military training programs, on January 1, 1976, established the Army and Air Force University to coordinate the army and air force academies and specialty schools. The reason for its departmental status in the ministry is "to lend continuity, uniformity and congruence to the doctrine and ideology of the military education programs."[9] One analyst sees the university's creation as representing the high point of armed forces professionalization.[10] By 1985 the military's umbrella university supervised twenty-three schools. Some observers believe that such diversity and technical competence enhance the military's capacity to perform political functions if the need were to arise.[11] Perhaps more than anything else the complexity and quality of military education suggest its increasing prestige compared with civilian institutions, which always have dominated Mexican educational life. Outside evaluators recently ranked the Escuela Médico Militar, which has had a strong reputation for many years, as number one among Mexican medical schools, ahead of the University of La Salle, the Autonomous University of Guadalajara, and the National University. In engineering, the Heroico Escuela Naval Militar Antón Lizardo ranks number five, after the Monterrey Institute of Higher Studies, the National Polytechnic Institute, the Autonomous Technological Institute of Mexico, and the University of Puebla.[12]

As officers' educational attainments rose, the military budget fell, from which one could infer an inverse relationship between professionalization and the military's political influence.[13] However, there is no evidence that the two trends are associated. In fact, the literature on the Latin American military repeatedly demonstrates that as professionalization (measured in terms of education) increases, so do budgetary allotments. Is Mexico an exception?

Mexico's civil-military relations are unique for many reasons, and serve to set Mexico apart. Higher levels of military education did not in and of themselves eventuate in less political influence. Rather, the political leadership (who at the time of growing professionalization were military men) decided on a course of action that included reducing the size of the military, cutting government outlays, and producing well-qualified officers without ties to revolutionary generals. The policy led to a new kind of officer corps, the post-1910 generations. However, it was not the increasing *levels* of education, from the Heroico Colegio Militar to the Escuela Superior de Guerra to the Colegio de Defensa Nacional, that contributed to diminished political influence but, rather, their curricula. Only in the sense that each level of education repeated its antecedent's message could it be argued that more education produced greater subordination to civilian authorities.

A look at the educations of politicians and generals in the 1990s reveals one significant difference. The more extensive the education of the politicians, the more diverse it became. In contrast, the more extensive the education of the military, for example, the separate Colegio Aire for pilots and the Colegio de Defensa Nacional for national security training, all officers generally still had to "advance through a fixed set of educational choices."[14] As the political leadership chooses among Mexican private and public institutions of higher education and foreign universities, the military is receiving more education as well, but within a domestic, mandated curriculum, thus enhancing its homogeneity.

Boils' comparison of the two sets of leaders since the 1970s reveals that military commanders were better educated in many respects than their counterparts in the government bureaucracy.[15] He goes on to suggest that the superiority has considerable importance for the military's future, implicitly in politics. As is true for some Third World countries, especially Africa, Boils holds that Mexico's military may have political potential because of its educational and technical superiority over competing civilian elites.[16] Absolutely no empirical evidence supports such a possibility.

All elite groups in Mexican life, intellectual, economic, political, and religious, are highly educated, relative to the general population.[17] By level and *quality* of education politicians are superior to military leaders. For example, among the youngest generals, those born in the 1930s, 29 percent have advanced graduate work; among civilians, 40 percent, or nearly 40 percent more than that of generals. Among the 1890s generation of officers, 11 percent had advanced training or the equivalent of the ESG (university); among the parallel political cohort, 71 percent had university training or above. The gap closed considerably in the 1980s, with establishment of the Colegio de Defensa Nacional. Nearly half of all top naval leaders now have advanced work, the majority from the CDN. Civilians are likely to retain their educational edge for years to come.

Teaching in the Military

The other aspect of education that has criticality in the knowledge, socialization, and recruitment functions is teaching. The military acknowledges the importance of teaching in two ways. First, and most obvious, service as an instructor, particularly at the Heroico Colegio Militar and the Escuela Superior de Guerra, is important to the officer's career. Second, and less obvious, service as an administrator, especially as director and subdirector, at either institution is prestigious.

Teaching is a significant responsibility in the military, and its prevalence in the careers of Mexican officers is striking (see table 6.2).[18] Nearly two-thirds of top generals since 1940 have taught, compared with 45 percent of all political leaders since 1935. The percentages are higher for generals in certain areas.

Teaching has not always been valued by the military. In the pre-1930s generations, only one in ten officers taught. For civilian politicians, in contrast, teaching has been a consistent experience over generations, extending well back into the nineteenth century. In fact, among the pre-1935 political leaders, 41 percent taught, a figure comparable to the military's post-1930s generations. Of the small number among older military generations who taught, slightly more than half were instructors at the Colegio Militar; the remainder were

TABLE 6-2. Teaching Experience of Mexican Generals, by Generation, 1880–1940

Schools	1880s	1890s	1900s	1910s	1920s	1930s	1940s
HCM, ENM, ESG	13	22	63	53	51	56	83
Applied	3	1	——	11	10	9	17
HCM, ENM, ESG, and applied	——	4	10	11	8	11	——
Other	——	4	4	——	1	5	——
None	84	69	23	25	30	19	0

Key: HCM = Heroico Colegio Militar; ENM = Heroico Escuela Naval Militar; ESG = Escuela Superior de Guerra.

instructors at state universities, the National University, and the National Preparatory School. Of the civilians who taught, over a fourth were professors at the National University.[19]

Teaching as an experience acquired importance within the officer corps with the 1900s generation (table 6-2). Again, we see that generals who had been born in the first decade of the twentieth century are the swing cohort in the evolution of the military's educational training and instruction. An examination by generations suggests the decisiveness of the change. The pattern in the 1880s to the 1890s generations, the revolutionary generals who remained after 1940, is predictive of future trends, given that only 10 percent of the pre-1880s generations taught, followed by 16 and 21 percent in the succeeding generations. Even the moderate increase indicates the value placed on professionalization by the National Defense Secretariat leadership. To survive, the older generals in top command posts took on the characteristics of the new generation, those born after 1900. The change from pre-1900 to post-1900 is marked: about three-quarters of the surviving revolutionary generals had never taught but were replaced by a group half of which had taught—a dramatic switch. The teaching pattern held for years, changing only with the present generation of generals, those fifty and younger, for whom teaching is a universal experience.

When the teaching experiences of all prominent generals since 1940 are looked at in the aggregate, an important aspect becomes apparent. Slightly more than half of the nearly two-thirds of all generals since World War II who have taught did so at the three major military schools; one in ten, at an applied school; and 2 percent, elsewhere. Teaching is more common among officers than politicians, but it is extremely narrow in scope. The generals have rarely taught outside military schools, rendering teaching as a channel for civilian contacts negligible. In terms of teaching's recruitment and advancement function, it is limited to the military's own institutions.

The early prestige of the military teaching experience is exemplified most obviously in the careers of the officers who have directed the Heroico Colegio Militar. Between 1940 to 1973, as the data in Exhibit 6-1 suggest, all ten directors reached the highest positions in the National Defense Secretariat. Two secretaries of defense, two subsecretaries, and three chiefs of staff directed

Exhibit 6-1
Directors of the Heroico Colegio Militar, 1920–1990

Name	Tenure
Joaquín Mucel Acereto	1920
Marcelino Murrieta Murrieta	1920–1921
Víctor Hernández Covarrubias	1921–1923
J. Domínguez Ramírez Garrido	1923–1923
Miguel Angel Peralta	1923–1925
Manuel Mendoza Sarabia	1925
Amado Aguirre	1925 (closed)
Miguel M. Acosta Guajardo	1925–1927
Juan José Rios Rios	1927–1928
Gilberto R. Limón Márquez	1928–1931
Joaquín Amaro Domínguez	1931–1935
Rafael Cházaro Pérez	1935–1936
Manuel C. Rojas Rasso	1936
Othón León Lobato	1936–1938
Alberto Zuno Hernández	1939–1941
Marcelino García Barragán	1941–1942
Gilberto R. Limón Márquez	1942–1945
Luis Alamillo Flores	1945–1948
Rafael Avila Camacho	1948–1950
Tomás Sánchez Hernández	1950–1953
Leobardo C. Ruiz Camarillo	1953–1955
Francisco J. Grajales Godoy	1955–1959
Jerónimo Gómar Suástegui	1959–1965
Roberto Yáñez Vázquez	1965–1970
Miguel Rivera Becerra	1971–1973
Salvador Revueltas Olvera	1973–1976
Absalón Castellanos Domínguez	1976–1980
Enrique Cervantes Aguirre	1980–1982
Jaime Contreras Guerrero	1983–1985
Carlos Cisneros Montes de Oca	1985–1988
Carlos Duarte Sacramento	1988-1990

Note: Between 1940 to 1973, all ten directors reached top positions in the National Defense Secretariat, including two secretaries (Marcelino García Barragán and Gilberto Limón Márquez), two subsecretaries (Gilberto Limón Márquez and Jerónimo Gómar Suástegui), and three chiefs of staff (Luis Alamillo Flores, Tomás Sánchez Hernández, and Roberto Yáñez Vázquez). Rafael Avila Camacho had already served as oficial mayor, and Francisco Grajales Godoy and Leobardo C. Ruiz Camarillo were chiefs of staff earlier.

the HCM. Also, officers who have already held top administrative positions often are selected to administer the college.

An officer's being made director of the Heroico Colegio Militar is somewhat analogous to a civilian's being chosen rector of the National University. Although the latter institution is not integrated formally into the political structure as an approved or required training site for future political leaders, the fact is that the majority of leading politicians are its alumni. Its president, consequently, has considerable status within the political and intellectual community. Although fewer individuals have moved back and forth between the National University presidency and politics in recent years than heretofore, it too has often served as a significant career step for the politically ambitious, most recently when Guillermo Soberón (rector 1973–1981) became secretary of health in 1982.

Heroico Colegio Militar

Initially, the Colegio Militar was the most important military educational experience for successive generations of cadets. President Obregón reopened the Colegio Militar, after it had been closed under his predecessor, but it closed temporarily in 1925 for repairs to its physical plant. The school reopened in 1926 with a new staff of instructors who had been trained in the United States or Europe, or who were former members of the Federal Army who had joined the revolutionaries after 1911.[20] The word *Heroico* was added to the name Colegio Militar in 1949[21] because the school (although not all its cadets) has always remained loyal to the president; its devotion was especially noteworthy in 1920, when cadets accompanied President Venustiano Carranza to Veracruz.[22]

The potential influence of the Heroico Colegio Militar as a locus of recruitment is enhanced by its relatively limited student body. If we think of it as a university, comparable to the National University attended by most politicians, its small size becomes apparent. Like the National School of Law, which graduates most future politicians, the Heroico Colegio Militar parallels a small, liberal arts college in the United States. In 1925 it graduated 200 officers, mostly second lieutenants. In 1930 its enrollment was 575: 483 had matriculated as civilians and 92 had been members of the military at matriculation. In 1935 only 137 cadets graduated; in 1944, 289. In 1945, enrollment was 617 students (very similar to the numbers fifteen years earlier), 488 civilians and 129 officer recruits. In 1954 enrollment was 589, and in 1955, 166 cadets graduated. During the 1960s graduating classes ranged from 200 to 290; for example, in middecade, 204 officer cadets graduated, 18 percent of whom were first sergeants (mustangs). In 1970, the last year a graduate of HCM could reach the rank of general by the early 1990s, 250 cadets were admitted and 252 graduated.[23] The relative balance has been a consistent pattern (245 slots were made available in the 1991 class).

A new facility opened in 1976 enabled a capacity of three thousand cadets, but enrollments in the 1990s filled less than half that capacity.[24] Although most men in a single class know one another personally after three years of training together, cadet groups by military occupational specialty (MOS) are small. For example, throughout the 1960s graduating classes in cavalry numbered no more than fifty; artillery second lieutenants, in the twenties; and administrative specialists, fewer than twenty.

The Heroico Colegio Militar recruits from a constituency different from that of civilian universities. Most applicants have only a secondary education; in one study, only a handful of aspirants had a preparatory education.[25] In Mexico, a preparatory education is the first requisite to pursue a college degree. Briefly, in 1947 a cadet with a secondary education who studied at the HCM for four years would receive the equivalent of a preparatory degree from the National University. The military dropped the program the following year, not reestablishing a preparatory equivalent until 1966.[26] However, on March 1, 1948, the Secretariat of National Defense initiated the Escuela Militar de Clases General Mariano Matamoros at Military Camp No. 1 in Mexico City. By the following November first sergeants enrolled in infantry and cavalry courses could graduate as second lieutenants if they satisfactorily completed the program.[27] Today the Heroico Colegio Militar diploma is the equivalent to a preparatory education. The only exception is pilots, who complete two years at the HCM and two years at the Colegio de Aire in Guadalajara and thereby earn a college degree.

Today an HCM applicant need be only a secondary school graduate, or a graduate of a private military academy.[28] For example, among top naval officers in 1990, excluding lawyers and physicians, only one in ten had a preparatory education; among army and air force officers, only one man had a preparatory degree. One top officer, in communications, had only a primary education. Some of the officers had attended private primary or secondary schools, but the vast majority were public school or vocational school graduates.[29] Prospective cadets are selected on the basis of examinations. In the mid-1950s, of 450 applicants, 223 were admitted[30]—a rate comparable to Brazil's leading military academy.[31] By 1965, however, according to one source, applicants to Mexico's military and naval academies outnumbered admissions by proportions of six to one and fifteen to one, respectively.[32]

Course content at the Heroico Colegio Militar is significant not only because nearly all army and air force officers pass through HCM classrooms but because of the time spent there. Most cadets enter the academy between the ages of fifteen and nineteen. In the case of generals, I found the typical age to have been close to seventeen to eighteen. During the four-year program, the cadet is provided food, clothing, and shelter, and the academy controls about four-fifths of the cadet's time, seven days a week. Visitors are permitted only Thursday evenings from 6:00 to 9:00; on Sundays the cadet may visit family or friends, or sightsee.[33]

The preparatory education of politicians, who typically live at home or with a guardian, is much more open than the officers, both in and out of the classroom, comparable to the education of a public high school student or a day student at a private preparatory school in the United States. One of the most important differences between the educations of politicians and officers is that the environment of the former is more varied and intellectual. Politicians have pointed to the significance of learning experiences in the homes of other students and professors, as well as in the larger ambience of the capital.[34] Officers rarely share these type of experiences since their free time is more limited. As William Ackroyd and others have suggested, the impact of the HCM is intensified by the fact that cadets are almost wholly removed from their families and other civilians, isolation typically reinforced by assignment after graduation to the provinces. Unlike the Brazilian model, it is not just the formal education, per se, but also imposition of a common set of experiences for all army and air force officers that are critical.[35] The military controls cadets and young officers during their late teens and early twenties, a period when values and behavior are being formed.[36]

The HCM experience is shared by a group of young men (women serve in the army but are not allowed at the academies) who have other things in common. Many, as discussed earlier, come from provincial, lower-middle-class backgrounds.[37] Unlike Brazilian cadets, most of whom come from secondary military academies where they have been educated from twelve to fourteen years of age, their educational backgrounds are diverse.[38]

According to one source, based on conversations over eighteen months with some forty field grade officers at the Escuela Superior de Guerra, the typical rural applicant has "seen notices and heard about the Military College in Mexico City. The military often advertised over the radio or distributed flyers extolling the merits of the Military College."[39] The hope is improved economic and social status. Another reason is familial, to follow in the footsteps of a father or uncle.[40] This is not an unusual pattern at the National University. Many future politicians attend the same institution as their fathers did, and those graduating through the late 1960s, comparable to the youngest generals in our sample, often majored in the same disciplines, especially law, economics, and medicine. In the late 1960s Daniel Mora encountered officers who had joined for ideological reasons. One officer reported, "Labor problems that Mexico City was experiencing were being fueled by communist agitators. Communism was beginning to take hold in Mexico and I foresaw problems in Mexico's future."[41] Communism has reemerged as an issue at the ESG since 1988, especially since the appearance of a strong left-of-center political movement and the rise of the PRD.

When the Colegio Militar was reestablished after the Revolution, the training program was expanded from eighteen months to three years, with separate courses for infantry, cavalry, and artillery.[42] In the mid-1920s, the National Defense Secretariat began sending officers to study in the United States, Spain, France, and Italy, and they often became instructors. By 1929 the Colegio Militar had a professoriate composed of seventy-eight officers and forty-eight civilians.[43] Although the typical cadet was exposed to civilian professors, most of these provided instruction in a limited number of courses in philosophy and language. By the 1990s the majority of instructors was still career military officers. From the 1920s though the 1970s military education remained virtually static, and according to Steven Wager, confined to strictly military subjects.[44] For example, in 1952, at the educational midpoint of most of our generals, their curriculum, with the exception of general culture, geography, history, and civics, consisted exclusively of military science.[45] Unlike future political leaders, most of whom carried a broad range of liberal arts courses, often with a heavy dose of political science and economics, officers received little exposure to such subjects.

Today a cadet's four-year program has a larger component of liberal and general studies but not much in the way of economics and political science. In the "first year a common program is studied; during the remaining years the cadet engages in specialized study for entry to the infantry, cavalry, artillery, combat engineers, or administration."[46] Ackroyd, who analyzed the content of the Heroico Colegio Militar curriculum in the 1980s, concluded that only approximately 10 percent of the courses are devoted to the social sciences, and only 5 percent have any political content. Another 5 percent are devoted to the behavior of officers in relation to the military and society.[47]

The other source of diversity in civilian education not found in the military is course materials. Although the military makes use of U.S. Army field manuals, the texts used in the regular courses are by Mexicans. In the 1950s no texts by foreign authors were used, a situation less likely now at the ESG but still the case at the HCM. In 1991, all ESG texts, except constitutional law, were foreign, with Mexican covers, but edited by an ESG graduate. Since the 1920s many of the texts used in institutions attended by future politicians have been foreign in origin, especially from France, the United States, and Spain.[48] Thus, by means of curriculum and staff, Mexico's military provides an extremely homogeneous environment for the officer's educational socialization, far more hermetic than the environment in which the politician's educational socialization takes place. It is likely that the Heroico Escuela Naval in Veracruz, which educates a small percentage of Mexico's high-ranking naval and marine officers, is somewhat more open in curriculum and staff, if its direct commission and foreign training policies are indicative of its educational philosophy. Nevertheless, there is no question that Mexican officers, regardless of rank, pass through a more nationalistic educational process than do their civilian counterparts.

The implications of the Heroico Colegio Militar's philosophy for the socialization of the officer corps are significant. As I have argued elsewhere,

> Over time, each generation claims a shared experience affecting professional outlook and behavior unmarred by curricular changes. A lack of non-military subjects and the static condition of the curriculum has been criticized by many observers, but a positive feature of these characteristics is to build cohesion among those officers sharing a Heroic Military College education.[49]

What exactly does this type of training produce? Each officer is reminded that he is a member of a corporate body that possesses an extensive degree of self-regulatory power, a mechanism for self-perpetuation, and a monopoly on a set of specialized and complex skills.[50] Most important, the training imparts values that shape officers' behavior, especially their attitudes toward political institutions.

Of all the means of professionalization, military education most deeply affects behavior. Cadets learn behavior from their military superiors. Nearly all of junior officers' superiors, whether in the barracks or in the classroom, are professional military men who have already passed through the same environment. In the civilian sector some professors are politicians, or intellectuals with political ambitions. Hence, civilian politicians, too, have achieved a remarkable cohesiveness in regard to values passed from one generation to the next from the 1920s through the 1970s, values that have contributed markedly to pragmatism and comity. In that sense, they share certain qualities with their military peers, perhaps more so than do some other Latin American militaries with the Mexican officer corps. Take the Brazilian military as an illustration.

Officers in the Brazilian military during the twentieth century attended many different schools. Changes in location, number, and function of the schools, according to Frank McCann, were matched by changes in curricula, instructors, and training facilities. McCann believes that such variety made "it difficult to develop lasting traditions and a sense of commonality in the officer corps. The changes and the variety of educational backgrounds necessarily deepened generational divisions."[51] And further, he believes that the pattern may have contributed to the junior officers' rebelling against their seniors in the 1920s. Such internal division would be highly unlikely in Mexico. As will be demonstrated, as the junior officer advances, he learns the value of discipline and obedience to authority, not altogether unlike the Mexican politician, who has acquired from his superiors a similar set of values through experiential socialization in a semiauthoritarian, one-party system.

If, as Ackroyd suggests, the "key to understanding military behavior, therefore, resides in the Mexican military educational system, the country's primary agent of military professionalization," the Heroico Colegio Militar is only the first step in a well-established process.[52] Three other Mexican institutions play a role in army and air force training and socialization processes: the applied schools, the Escuela Superior de Guerra, and the Colegio de Defensa Nacional. For naval officers, the educational experience is somewhat less homogeneous, not because most officers do not pass through the naval college, followed by the equivalent of the ESG, the Centro de Estudios Superiores Navales, and the Colegio de Defensa Nacional. Approximately one in six high-ranking military officers is a navy officer. The navy, as I mentioned, "accepts lateral entry for both enlisted and officer ranks from civilians, giving them a rank on the basis of their education and/or skill. The professionals are usually dentists, engineers, accountants, and lawyers. The army and air force only in special situations accept lateral entry for officers."[53] The navy lateral entry program introduces the potential for diverse influences on the mission of the officer corps, influences likely to be somewhat liberalizing. Because the number of lateral entrants is small, and because often they are not in main-line command positions, they are not apt to impact greatly on officer values as a whole.

Educational institutions have long been thought to play important roles in elite cognitive skills and the formation of values.[54] Only on the basis of recent scholarship has it been shown that universities, more than party organizations or even the bureaucracy, were critical to the initial recruitment of future politicians.[55] In the case of military officers, scholars have suspected the importance of military academies in the upward mobility of career officers for years. In the United States, it is no accident that 90 percent of all generals with two or more stars are West Point graduates.[56] In the case of Latin America, Glen Dealy has argued that both the universities and military academies provide "an ideal setting for the aggregation of a following which may sooner or later prove useful."[57] Similarly, it has been supposed that military schools are crucial to the formation of officer coteries in Mexico, but no evidence has documented the supposition because military careers and relationships are not discussed in the Mexican press.[58]

Historically, the Colegio Militar functioned as a locus of leadership recruitment. Among the military leaders who commanded troops in the field, headed military zones, and took on cabinet and gubernatorial posts in the early part of the Porfiriato, combat was their training ground and means of establishing ties of trust and friendship. An examination of battlefield commands under Porfirio Díaz himself makes the origins of his later political loyalties quite clear.[59] The peace of the Porfiriato, as I suggested above, augmented the relative importance of the Colegio Militar in the backgrounds of the Mexican officer corps, both as a training center and as a source of recruitment. Consequently, when General Victoriano Huerta came to power in 1913 after murdering the constitutional president, he naturally recruited his loyalists from Federal Army officers—many of whom, like him, were Colegio Militar graduates—including his own cadet class of combat engineers.[60]

After 1920 the same pattern continued. The military academy took on the recruitment function because "one of the most important things that one gets out of four years at the HCM is a lasting relationship with his classmates. A fraternal bond is developed among the individuals who persevere through four years together. It is a bond that lasts throughout a career."[61] The most important group in an officer's career is his own graduating class, particularly in his own specialty. It is clear from an analysis of leading generals that the key specializations are infantry, cavalry, and artillery, followed to a lesser extent by combat engineering. For example, since 1947, not one graduate of the Heroico Colegio Militar administration school among our sample of generals has held a top post. Some authors have speculated that promotions are improved by these personal relationships and ties to a graduating class, but they have offered no supportive evidence.[62] It does appear, however, that whom one knows clearly affects where and when an officer holds certain influential or prestigious posts.

Personal ties can be ascertained by analyzing the friendships of selected defense secretaries and their top associates. Such analysis of three of the four most recent defense secretaries revealed important characteristics of officer recruitment. It is not the class ties of the secretary that are important but those of his second and third in command, the subsecretary and *oficial mayor*. These take on added importance when the secretary of defense is from a generation older than most of his active duty contemporaries. This can be seen with General Hermenegildo Cuenca Díaz (1970–1976), who was twenty years older than the president who appointed him, and who attended the Colegio Militar from 1920 to 1922, ten to fifteen years before most of his top subordinates (see Appendix A). He was the last secretary of national defense to serve in the Secretariat of national defense who had served in the Revolution, as a young cadet having accompanied President Carranza on his flight from the capital to Veracruz. One of his zone commanders, Agustín Carreño Gutiérrez, a fellow student with Cuenca Díaz, also accompanied Carranza. But the vast majority of his subordinates attended the Heroico Colegio Militar at the same time as his two closest collaborators, his subsecretary and *oficial mayor*. His contacts with the two oficial mayores occurred through attending the ESG together[63] (see table 6-3).

As the notes to table 6-3 suggest, recruitment at the HCM occurs through peers and through teaching. Such patterns are equally true among politicians. Generally, fellow students are important collaborators in a very successful peer's administration, notably a president, but teachers are more important in initiating the budding politician into a successful career.[64] For example, Miguel de la Madrid obtained his first post at the Bank of Mexico through his economics professor, Daniel J. Bello. However, military officer recruitment differs from political recruitment because of the homogeneous environment of the educational institution. In other words, all individuals attending the Heroico Colegio Militar already have chosen the same career, and most of their instructors are themselves successful officers. Among students at the National University, and other schools important to politicians' recruitment, future public officials are a minority, as are their politically ambitious professors.

Educational patterns also have an impact on cross-career recruitment. As I argued in the analysis of military-political interlocks, education separates the two careers in Mexico. During the Revolution, future political leaders and military officers came together on the battlefield or in the bureaucracy. For example, Emilio Portes Gil, the only civilian president among a long line of Revolutionary generals from 1920 to 1946, first worked in the Ministry of War and Navy in 1914, then in the Department of Military Justice in 1915, and as a judge of the Sonora superior court, where he met General Plutarco Elías Calles, his most important political mentor.[65] President Adolfo Ruiz Cortines, the last of Mexico's presidents to have participated in the Revolution—in the paymaster corps—was an aide or private secretary to three important generals, Alfredo Robles Domínguez, Jacinto B. Treviño, and Heriberto Jara, all of whom pursued political careers.

For later generations, among college-educated officers, some exceptional cases of contact having future career implications occur. For example, Alfonso Corona del Rosal, later secretary of government properties and head of the Federal District, attended the National Preparatory School in 1930–1931, after

TABLE 6-3.   Class and Career Ties in the Mexican Secretariat
of National Defense, 1970–1976

Name, Office	Class	
	Heróico Colegio Militar (HMC)	Escuela Superior de Guerra (ESG)
Hermenegildo Cuenca Díaz (secretary)[a]	1920–1922	1939–1942
Jerónimo Gómar Suástegui (subsecretary)[b, c]	1928–1930	1934–1936
Enrique Sandoval Castarrica (subsecretary)[a, d]	—	1933–1935
Héctor Camargo Figueroa (subsecretary)[a]	1925–1927	—
Arturo Corona Mendioroz (oficial mayor)[c, e]	1931–1935	1939–1942
Leopoldo Garduño Canizal (oficial mayor)	DNA	1938–1941
Graciliano Alpuche Pinzón[f]	1937–1939	1944–1947
Jesús Castañeda Gutiérrez[e, f]	1937–1939	1949–1952
Guillermo Silva Medrano[c, f]	1930–1932	1943–1946
Joaquín Orozco Camacho	1928–1931	1937–1940
José del Carmen Zetina Brito	1926–1930	1933–1936
Roberto Salido Beltrán (air force)[g]	1931–1933	—
José Miguel Ortega Casanova	1926–1928	—
Rodolfo Mejía Chaparro[c]	1930–1932	—
Agustín Carreño Gutiérrez[a]	1920–1922	—
Maximiliano del Valle Huerta[e]	1925–1929	1939–1942
Rosendo Flores Cital[a]	1923–1925	1939–1942
Israel Cuéllar Layseca	1925–1927	—
Antonio Ramírez Barrera	1931–1935	1939–1942

[a]General Cuenca Díaz and Carreño Gutiérrez not only were cadets together but shared combat in that capacity, acting as a guard for President Venustiano Carranza when he fled to Aljibes, Puebla, in 1920; Héctor Camargo Figueroa, Rosendo Flores Cital and Enrique Sandoval Castarrica served in combat against the Cristeros, 1927–1929.

[b]General Gómar Suástegui was an alternate senator at the same time Cuenca Díaz served in the Senate.

[c]Héctor Camargo Figueroa commanded the 1st Company of cadets, Heroico Colegio Militar, 1930–1931, when Generals Gómar Suástegui, Corona Mendioroz, Silva Medrano, and Mejía Chaparro were students.

[d]General Sandoval Castarrica was on the presidential staff with Cuenca Díaz in the 1940s.

[e]Leopoldo Garduño Canizal, Arturo Corona Mendioroz, and Enrique Sandoval Castarrica taught together at the Heroico Colegio Militar; Jesús Castañeda Gutiérrez was commander of cadets under Jerónimo Gómar Suástegui's directorship, 1958–1964; and Maximiliano del Valle Huerta and Arturo Corona Mendioroz attended West Point together in 1950.

[f]General Silva Medrano commanded the 3rd Company of cadets at the Heroico Colegio Militar in 1939, when Alpuche Pinzón and Castañeda Gutiérrez were students.

[g]Roberto Salido Beltrán and Enrique Sandoval Castarrica were squadron commander and assistant chief of staff, respectively, in the small Air Force Expeditionary Force to the Philippines in 1945.

having graduated from the Colegio Militar in 1923 as a second lieutenant of cavalry. (The class of 1923 is the only one in the history of the Heroico Colegio Militar that produced two cabinet members, the secretary of defense, Marcelino García Barragán, and Corona del Rosal, who held office simultaneously (see Appendix A). He matriculated in the law school at the National University in 1932, where he became active in politics as secretary of the student society. After graduating with honors in 1937, he taught political economy there. He joined the government party's youth sector, and then became a member of the political publicity committee for General Avila Camacho's presidential campaign, which brought him into contact with many of the future political greats of his day. A cadet classmate, Antonio Nava Castillo, joined him in his political ambitions, becoming Avila Camacho's military aide and later a governor when Corona del Rosal was in the cabinet.[66]

In the United States corporate executives and, to a lesser extent, military officers often hold top political posts. C. Wright Mills argued that the explanation for this interchange among the three careers was the lack of a genuine U.S. civil service with its own training and recruitment program, which meant the government needed to seek out talent from many professions.[67] In Mexico the government created its own informal training and recruitment facility in the guise of the National University, where its careerists taught and recruited the best and brightest. Educationally, it produced a professional politician, or better said, political bureaucrat. Unlike the United States, which recruits many officers through the Reserve Officer Training Corps (ROTC) on college campuses, Mexican military officers and corporate figures are largely trained in separate institutions. For officers, that means strictly within the military academies, and although some HCM graduates resign their commissions because of an attraction to politics, they rarely persuade their peers to do likewise. In the 1920s and 1930s, leading entrepreneurs had much more contact with future political peers, as did the military, but as the private sector expanded and modernized, it financed institutions whose ideology and methodology were more to its liking and appropriate to new skills. Thus, businesspeople, like officers, have decreased their educational linkages over time.[68]

The potential of schools to serve as recruitment centers for career officers and politicians is reduced by the extent of preuniversity or professional training. José de Imáz found in Argentina that the future officer, having entered the military academy early, "after one or two years of high school, has had less time to build close bonds of friendship with those who (after the passage of time) might come to occupy responsible positions in the economic, political, or intellectual leadership of the country."[69] In Mexico in the early part of the century, preparatory education provided a key shared experience for many future leaders. Even as university education became more diverse, private preparatory schools became increasingly common in future politicians' and top businesspeople's backgrounds. Military officers, however, because cadets require only secondary education, attended an "exclusive" preparatory school, the Heroico Colegio Militar. Hence, because they embark on a separate educational track at a younger age, their opportunities for contacts with future politicians and businessmen are fewer.

The Heroico Colegio Militar in its early years included additional characteristics advantageous to future military careers. During a brief but important period, from 1923 to 1940, many higher-ranking officers attended the Colegio Militar. For example, the class of 1923, that of future Secretary of Defense Marcelino García Barragán (1964–1970), who himself was a major, graduated six colonels and one brigadier general, Adrián Castrejón.[70] Naturally, an older officer who assumed command positions very soon after graduating would have the opportunity to request fellow cadets as his subordinates. In a recruiting sense, older officer cadets functioned similar to teachers rather than as fellow students.

The HCM temporarily closed in 1925, thereby collapsing the cadet classes entering in 1923 and 1924. As a result, the 1925 graduating class produced an extraordinarily large and important generation. Some individuals, hoping to obtain more than one military occupational specialty, actually graduated in two separate classes. Javier Jiménez Segura, for example, a premier early model of a military technocrat, graduated both as an artillery lieutenant on December 21, 1924, and then as a military industrial engineer on October 1, 1925, later to guide the National Defense Secretariat's military industry in the 1970s. Other officers, such as Luis Alamillo Flores, founding director of the ESG, graduated with his 1924 class while in combat, returning to complete his formal training as a captain with the 1925 class.[71]

Teachers or cadet troop commanders at the HCM were equally important in the recruitment process. Military instructors often assist favored students later in their careers. For example, as the data in table 6-3 suggest, Héctor Camargo Figueroa, who was subsecretary in the 1970s, commanded the 1st Company of cadets in 1930–1931, when four members of Cuenca Díaz's administrative team were students. The HCM also serves to link instructors together who were in different graduating classes as students. Two of Cuenca Díaz's subsecretaries, Jerónimo Gómar Suástegui and Jesús Castañeda Gutíerrez, served together at the HCM as director and cadet commander, respectively, and three department heads actually taught together.

A more recent administration, that of Juan Arévalo Gardoqui, the secretary of defense under Miguel de la Madrid, suggests even more overwhelmingly the importance of HMC class ties to future defense posts. Of the twenty-seven top posts in the Secretariat of National Defense from 1982 to 1988, fifteen, or 56 percent, were held by generals who had overlapped as cadets with him at the HCM, including his subsecretary and oficial mayor, both of whom were in subsequent cadet classes (table 6-4). Three officers, Generals Manuel Vallejo Montiel, Ulises Beltrán Tenorio, and Gonzalo Ortiz Segura, were actually part of Arévalo Gardoqui's 1940–1943 class. Again, teaching at the HCM expanded contacts among other officers. For example, Generals Arévalo Gardoqui and Revuelta Olvera taught at the HCM together, and General Oliver Bustamante was a student when Arévalo Gardoqui was a cadet officer (table 6-4).

TABLE 6-4.   Class and Career Ties in the Mexican Secretariat
of National Defense, 1982–1988

| | Class | |
Name, Office	Heroico Colegio Militar (HMC)	Escuela Superior de Guerra (ESG)
Juan Arévalo Gardoqui (secretary)[a]	1940–1943	1947–1949
Marco Antonio Guerrero Mendoza (subsecretary)[b]	1941–1942	1946–1949 enl
Arturo Lopez Flores (oficial mayor)[b, c]	1938–1941	1952–1954 enl
Vicencio Santoyo Fería (chief of staff)	1948–1951	1963–1966
Juan Manuel Madrigal Magallón[d]	1945–1948	1953–1955
Mario Pérez Torres[e]	1946–1949	1955–1958
Víctor Luis Revueltas Olvera[f]	1947–1950	—
Armando M. Ortiz Salgado[d]	1948–1951	1954–1957
Salvador López Matamoros[g]	1938–1941	1945–1948
Ernesto Gutiérrez Gómez Tagle	1939–1942	—
Manuel Vallejo Montiel[d]	1940–1943	1947–1949
Arturo Zepeda Venegas[g]	1941–1942	1946–1949 enl
José María Rios de Hoyos	1942–1944	1952–1955
Alonso Aguirre Ramos[d]	1937–1942	1945–1958
José María Alva Valles	1938–1941	1951–1953 enl
Ulises Beltrán Tenorio	1940–1943	— enl
José Espejel Flores	1938–1941	— enl
Jorge Gustavo Grajales	1939–1942	1953–1956 enl
Roberto Heine Rangel	1942–1944	— enl
Alger León Moreno	1938–1941	—
Tomás Mancera Segura	1939–1941	—
José Moguel Cal y Mayor	1936–1939	1947–1949 enl
Mario Oliver Bustamante[d]	1943–1947	1951–1954
Gonzalo Ortiz Segura	1940–1943	— enl
Edmundo Antonio Paredes[d]	1953–1956	1962–1965
Alberto Quintanar López[g]	1942–1944	—
Antonio Riviello Bazán[g]	1942–1944	1950–1953
José Hernández Toledo	1942–1944	1948–1949 AC

[a]This group is extremely close in age: Arévalo Gardoqui was born in 1921, Guerrero and López Flores in 1919. Most other appointees were born within several years of those two dates.

[b]Most of López Flores and Guerrero's companions are mustangs, men who began their careers as enlisted soldiers, another shared exceptional experience that would bring them closer together as a group.

[c]Generals Arturo López Flores and Marco Antonio Guerrero, in addition to being classmates at the HCM, served with each other on the general staff at Secretariat of National Defense headquarters, 1956–1957; in Washington, D.C., as aides to the military attaché, 1962–1963; and again on the general staff in 1966.

[d]General Vallejo Montiel served as a garrison commander under General Arévalo Gardoqui in Chihuahua and was the head of Section 6, Staff, National Defense in 1965 when Marco Antonio Guerrero was his counterpart in Section 1; General Madrigal Magallón was subchief of Section 3, under General Guerrero in early 1965, and

In the 1988–1994 administration, Secretary of National Defense, Antonio Riviello Bazán, returns to the more traditional pattern, in which the secretary of defense is older than most of his collaborators, and therefore, as under Cuenca Díaz, it is his subsecretary and oficial mayor who recruit his collaborators from their cadet classes.[72] Fifteen of the thirty-two top officials in Riviello Bazán's administration overlapped HCM education with his two immediate collaborators (table 6-5).

Cadet friendship at the HCM not only has consequences for personnel decisions later in an officer's career but, equally important, may have policy implications. Michael Dziedzic cites a significant instance. General Félix Galván, secretary of defense from 1976 to 1982, appointed General Pérez Mejilla as director of the ESG during his administration; their friendship went back to their days at the HCM, and Pérez Mejilla used that friendship to obtain special funds to construct a new ESG building.[73]

During the year the HCM was closed, 1925, the National Defense Secretariat created several military specialty schools. The two most notable were the Escuela Médico Militar and the Escuela Militar de Transmisiones. The medical school is one of the most important in Mexico, graduating military physicians who practice at the Central Military Hospital in Mexico City, among other institutions. Recently, the school has been graduating approximately fifty physicians yearly.[74] Because of the school's prestige, its graduates have easy access to lateral transfers into the civilian medical community. More important from a recruitment perspective, these military officers have more interlocks with politicians, familial and professional. For example, in the Salinas administration, two important politicians are the sons of career military physicians, Manuel Camacho, head of the Federal District Department, and Emilio Lozoya Thalmann, director general of the federal workers social security institute.[75] As I argued earlier,

---

became chief of the same section when Guerrero headed Section 1 from 1965 to 1966; he also served under Guerrero in 1957 in Section 3; General Alonso Aguirre Ramos was also a section head in 1967 at the general staff with General Guerrero; General Arturo López Flores was also on the general staff in 1966; General Oliver Bustamante was the executive officer to General Arévalo Gardoqui in Chihuahua in 1976, and was a student at the HCM when General Arévalo Gardoqui was cadet officer; General Paredes served in General Arévalo Gardoqui's cavalry regiment in 1971, and was on the general staff from 1966 to 1967 with Guerrero and López Flores.

[e]Mario Pérez Torres was López Flores's chief of staff as zone commander of the 29th military zone, Oaxaca, Oaxaca, 1981–1982, and both were on staff together at the Secretariat of National Defense, 1959.

[f]General Revueltas Olvera served under Juan Arévalo Gardoqui as an adjutant to President Adolfo López Mateos. Both were cadet officers at the HCM. Also, his brother Salvador, a prominent zone commander and director of the HCM, graduated with many figures in this administration.

[g]Generals Arturo Zepeda Venegas and Guerrero Mendoza attended the HCM and the Escuela Superior de Guerra (ESG) together. Generals Riviello Bazán and Guerrero Mendoza were teaching colleagues in 1950. Generals Quintanar López and Guerrero were administrative colleagues as chief of instruction and subdirector of the ESG, respectively, in 1967. Generals López Flores and López Matamoros were in the same artillery class at the HCM, 1938–1941.

Note: Of the eight generals without a diploma from the ESG, two graduated from the National University, one in law and one in diplomatic sciences; two continued their military education, one at the military medical school and the other graduated a second time from the HCM in engineering; and the other four took the combat arms course at the ESG.

TABLE 6-5. Class and Career Ties in the Mexican Secretariat
of National Defense, 1988–1994

Name, Office	Heroico Colegio Militar (HMC)	Escuela Superior de Guerra (ESG)	Colegio de Defensa Nacional (CDN)
Antonio Riviello Bazán (secretary)[a, b]	1942–1944	1950–1953	—
Alfredo Ochoa Toledo (subsecretary)[c, d]	1948–1951	1954–1956	—
Raúl Juárez Carreño (oficial mayor)[e, f]	1945–1948	1954–1956	—
Fermín Acosta Jiménez (air force)	DNA	1953–1955	—
Genaro Ambia Martínez	1952–1955	DNA	1981
Juan José Ballesteros Beltrán	1948–1951	—	—
Juan de Dios Calleros Aviña	1948–1951	1967–1969	1984
Enrique Cervantes Aguirre	1951–1954	1960–1962	—
Carlos Cisneros Montes de Oca[e]	1949–1951	1957–1959	—
Antonio Clemente Fernández Peniche[a]	1946–1949	1965–1967	—
Rolando Gutiérrez López[c]	1951–1954	1958–1960	1982
Andrés Hiram Hernández Plascencia	1946–1949	—	—
Adolfo Hernández Razo[d]	1947–1950	1960–1962	—
Francisco Islas López[c]	1951–1954	1958–1960	1983
Héctor López Mestres	DNA	—	—
Manuel Martínez Arrellano	1946–1949	1955–1957	—
Joel Martínez Montero[e]	1947–1950	1955–1957	1982
Odelín Morales Pérez	1953–1958	—	—
Federico Niño Martínez		—	—
Jaime Palacios Guerrero[c, e]	1951–1954	1959–1961	—
Mario Pérez Torres[b]	1946–1949	1955–1957	—
Juan Poblano Silva	1951–1954	1969–1972	1982
Francisco Quirós Hermosillo	1952–1955	1960–1962	
Sergio Ramírez Michel	1947–1950	—	—
Leobardo Carlos Ruiz Pérez	DNA	DNA	—
Enrique Tomás Salgado Cordero[a]	1953–1956	1962–1964	1986
Héctor Luis Sánchez Chan		1968–1970	1983
Juan Félix Tapía García	1948–1951	1956–1958	—
Tito Valencia Ortiz[b]	1953–1956	1959–1961	1983
Jacobo Wittman Rojano[c]	1943–1947	—	1984
Agustín Eduardo Zárate Guerrero[c]	1947–1950	1966–1968	—

[a]General Riviello Bazán was an instructor at the ESG when Enrique Tomás Salgado and Antonio Clemente Fernández Peniche were students, 1965. When General Salgado graduated, he joined the 43rd Infantry Battalion under Riviello Bazán's command.

[b]General Wittman Rojano was commanding officer of the 1st Company of cadets, HCM, when Generals Pérez Torres, Zárate Guerrero, and Hernández Plascencia were students, 1947.

[c]General Ochoa Toledo was an instructor at the ESG when Generals Gutiérrez López, Islas López, Palacios Guerrero, and Valencia Ortiz were students.

[d]General Alfredo Ochoa Toledo served with Hernández Razo on the general staff at the National Defense Secretariat when the latter was assistant chief of staff.

these linkages have been important to civil-military relations. The School of Communications is the most prestigious in Mexico; every officer who rose through the ranks in the communications field was a graduate.

At the same time that the ESG was established in 1932, the Secretariat of National Defense created an intermediate training program above the HCM but not equivalent to the ESG. Called applied schools, they were established for officers of the rank of captain who were about to be promoted to major. In 1935 the National Defense Ministry required all infantry officers below the rank of colonel to take an examination; those who failed were put on a mandatory list for the schools.[76] In recent years attendance in their specialty courses have become required for advancement. However, an examination of officers who have completed the curriculum in higher combat arms, one of many applied courses, does not reveal that it has the same level of importance as the HCM and the ESG on officer recruitment and advancement. A graduate of the ESG in the 1980s described his experience in the cavalry application course in Querétaro:

> It was one year in length, with the emphasis on learning about my specialty. Its purpose was to further prepare and familiarize me with battalion/regimental operations, as well as prepare me for command. All the other branches have a similar combined military application course. Their course is only six months long though, since they have a larger number of officers to contend with.[77]

Escuela Superior de Guerra

The role of the HCM has been altered gradually since the founding of the Escuela Superior de Guerra in 1932. As Lyle McAlister has suggested, General Amaro, a key revolutionary officer, and the single-most-important figure in officer educational professionalization, organized the ESG while serving as director of military education in 1932. Succinctly, its purpose was to train company and field grade officers for battalion or higher command and staff duties, and to develop and disseminate tactical and strategic doctrine.[78] The individual given the responsibility for actually setting up the program and designing the curriculum was Major Luis Alamillo Flores, who went on a study mission to United States military schools.[79] Like a select group of other officers, he had taken the initiative to study abroad. He had spent three years at the Higher War College in Paris, where he obtained a staff and command diploma in 1931. He also studied at the Sorbonne and the Engineering School

---

[e]Antonio Riviello Bazán served as assistant chief of staff at the Secretariat of National Defense under his original mentor. His section chiefs were Raúl Juárez Carreño, Carlos Cisneros Montes de Oca, Jaime Palacios Guerrero, and Joel Martínez Montero. Of the six section heads under General Riviello Bazán, four joined him when he became secretary in 1988.

[f]Raúl Juárez Carreño has a special contact with Fernando Gutiérrez Barrios, secretary of government, who was an HCM cadet from 1944 to 1947. Because both ministries often work closely together, this tie is very useful to intersectorial communication.

of Versailles.[80] Before the ESG's founding, any officer desirous of advanced military training studied in France. Tomás Sánchez Hernández, who followed Alamillo Flores as the ESG's second director in 1934, trained at the Higher War College in Paris and at the Fontainebleau artillery school.[81]

The original ESG staff of nine instructors included officers from the rank of captain through colonel and one civilian. Three of the original instructors had studied in France, and all three later directed the ESG; and two also directed the HCM.[82] The ESG program attracted the cream of the officer corps, as both instructors and students, particularly officers interested in teaching the technical fields of artillery, engineering, communications, and the like. According to the Secretariat of National Defense, of seventy-eight applicants, five senior and twenty-six junior officers were accepted.[83]

The ESG acquired immediate prestige in the military community. Joaquín Amaro aided its image by publicly labeling its students as a "real elite."[84] Graduating from the ESG gradually took on greater importance for officers wishing to obtain the rank of general. The school's standing within the Mexican officer corps parallels an attitude expressed about the Brazilian Higher War College in 1949; attendance there became "added insurance for upward mobility."[85] Students of other Latin American militaries have suggested that higher military education in itself altered the level of confidence of military officers when in the company of better-educated civilians. Christopher Brogan asserts that Peruvian officers, prior to attending such an institution, felt themselves to be culturally inferior.[86]

The benefits of attending the ESG are several. A graduate of the ESG, so designated by the acronym DEM (Diplomado de Estado Mayor) after his name, and everyday use with his name, receives an additional 10 to 25 percent of his regular monthly income, depending on rank, which continues throughout active duty years. More important than financial considerations according to several Mexican and U.S. analysts is enhanced potential for promotion. Stephen Wager wrote: "It is generally recognized within military circles that without a diploma from the Superior War College, the highest rank an officer can hope to attain is Lt. Col. On the other hand, most graduates are practically guaranteed the rank of Colonel, and many eventually become general officers."[87] For U.S. Army generals, war college attendance is equally significant; in 1973 95 percent were war college graduates.[88] High figures for U.S. graduates are tempered by the fact that our war college is for colonels; thus they share a higher probability of reaching the rank of general.

It has been suggested that the change from graduation from the HMC to graduation from the ESG as a requirement for higher rank in the Mexican military occurred in the past twenty years. According to Guillermo Boils, the army and navy have been commanded nearly by all graduates from the higher military schools. Until the mid-1970s, of the twenty-one high-level staff and administrative command positions, only four had been held by graduates of the ESG; less than a year later the number was 12. Equally significant, Boils suggests, twelve of the thirty-five zone commanders in 1970 were graduates; the number was twenty-four a year later. Boils attributes the change not only to an increased emphasis on technical training but to a wholesale removal of senior officers, many of whom had no advanced training, by President Echeverría.[89]

Echeverría's political motivations aside, the number of higher-ranking army and air force officers with diplomas from the ESG has risen steadily over time, a fact that may be lost sight of if one considers only the statistics for the two years discussed by Boils. A more complete picture is available from promotion records (Exhibit 6-2). From November 1970 to November 1976, ESG-educated brigadier generals increased from only 49 to 51 percent, but the consistently upward pattern from 1958 to 1990 is apparent, the most significant changes occurring in the late 1970s and 1980s. It is also important to note that by 1990 all but one colonel each in the major army fields of infantry and cavalry were ESG graduates.[90]

In the 1980s analysts argued that department heads and zone commanders, reserved only for brigade and division ranks, and brigadier generals per se were required to graduate from the ESG.[91] This was not actually the case. Among field commanders the figures are even less comprehensive than for national defense staff. For example, in 1983, of the fifteen garrison commanders, a third did not have their DEMs. Among zone commanders, the most important field position, 17 percent in 1987 did not. It is clear that even in the 1990s, it is still possible to reach the rank of general and to hold top defense posts and not be an ESG graduate.

It was not until 1982 that a diploma from the ESG was the equivalent of a college degree. Ackroyd believes that despite formal certification as a licenciatura (a professional degree), an ESG diploma still carries less prestige than its civilian equivalent.[92] Officers who had attended the National University considered the ESG curriculum inferior. The ESG discourages officers from attending civilian universities. Many civilians consider the ESG degree a joke. Nevertheless, among officers themselves, the DEM is a key credential for advancement.

Exhibit 6-2
Colonels Promoted to General, Selected Years, 1954–1990

Year	Promotion, Colonel to General	Percentage with Diplomado de Estado Mayor (DEM)
1958	15	33
1964	45	37
1970	35	49
1976	80	51
1981	22	59
1990	45	67

Note: 1970 was the first year all brigade generals promoted to three-star rank (division general) were DEM holders.

The ESG came into legal being on January 18, 1929. Its articles of formation were very precise about the two-year curriculum and instruction. The mission, according to Article 1, was simply "to impart to the officers and commanders of the Army military knowledge of a higher quality, enabling them to exercise higher command."[93] It also made clear that instructors were to be military officers exclusively. Current regulations allow civilians who have taught for two years and have graduate education to teach; few have. Interestingly, Article 12 stated that the curriculum was designed to promote ample initiative on the part of the student officers.[94]

Contrary to Article 12, observers and graduates of the ESG have always characterized it as a program stressing rote memorization.[95] Stephen Wager tells us that more modern forms of training, such as war games adapted from United States models, were introduced in the 1980s.[96] However, war games were not being used in the 1990s. It has also been said that course work is increasingly oriented toward administrative, managerial, and technocratic approaches. David Ronfeldt believes this direction may dispose younger officers to define national problems in much the same way as does the new generation of civilian elites, especially those who make up the bureaucratic cadres, rather than in the fashion of the party leadership.[97]

In the mid-1970s the ESG lengthened its program to three years. Its purpose, according to one analyst, was "to prepare combat officers for command staff duties and officers of the supporting services for technical staff duties. In a separate course, air officers were trained for corresponding assignments."[98] Two other important changes occurred. First, the ESG opened a special one-year course in higher war studies to selected civilians as well as to officers of the rank of lieutenant colonel and above.[99] This could have significant implications for the socialization and recruitment of military officers. For example, commandants of the Brazilian Higher War College, believing the aim of their school was to train those who would influence government, had graduated 599 officers, 224 businessmen, 200 civil servants, and 107 professionals, of whom 39 were politicians, by 1966.[100] In Mexico, however, although civilians were to be given selected access, no evidence in the graduation records or information about the educational backgrounds of leading politicians suggests that any civilians have attended the ESG. The primary source of diversity among ESG personnel is not civilian students but military officers from other countries, including the United States.[101]

Because the ESG has not promoted officer contacts with influential civilians, its primary means of influencing officer attitudes about social and political issues, and possibly interest in political activities, is curriculum content and values. The values emphasized have been critical to officer socialization, a quality to be analyzed shortly. On the other hand, some commentators hold that content has contributed to shifting officer interests.

In the 1970s the ESG introduced greater diversity in curriculum and staffing, adding many new courses and inviting distinguished lecturers from the academic, political, and business worlds. In 1973 a course in military and humanities juridical investigation was offered to further high-level command-

ers' understanding of "National Doctrines."[102] However, most military doctrine, at least through the 1990s, according to reports by visiting military
officers, is not integrated into their system, having been based on out-of-date
U.S. Army manuals.[103]

Interestingly, however, it is only the third year of the curriculum that is
critical to the political formation of the officer. As Ackroyd has demonstrated,
only 6 percent of the first-year courses and 5 percent of the second-year
courses focus on general strategy or other sociopolitical subjects. The first two
years, in his opinion, reinforce discipline and group behavior but distance
officers from nonpolitical studies.[104] Officers in the second-year in the 1990s
agree with the assessment.[105] Members of the third-year class, however, who
have been well-screened at the ESG, are exposed to an entirely different
emphasis. Course content devoted to strategy and related subjects rises to 30
percent. Civilian lecturers exist, but are rare. The graduating class as a whole
produces a study of a sociopolitical problem, actually traveling to a field
location. According to Ackroyd, each such study is sent to the chief of staff
and classified for future use.[106]

The potential impact of the ESG is affected by the percentage of active duty
officers who actually pass through its classrooms. Officers who enter the ESG
are graduates of other military academies, nearly all the HCM. Student
officers are also required to have had two years of experience commanding
troops, but few actually have held command positions. Over the years, class
size has been quite limited, both in terms of who is accepted and, equally
important, who graduates. In the 1947 class, for example, twenty-four officers
began the program but only nineteen graduated. In the 1960s and 1970s,
average class size was twenty-four; in the early to mid-1980s, 34.[107] The 1989
entering class, scheduled to graduate in 1992, began with eighty-one officers;
one year later only forty-one were still around, and some of those will have
washed out by the end of the year.[108] Ackroyd estimates that in the 1980s only
7 percent of the officer corps were ESG graduates,[109] the only officers who
have received some exposure to political and social issues in the classroom.

Although the percentages of ESG graduates in the entire officer corps are
small, their presence among the higher ranks and top defense posts is more
important. For example, if we take the 1956 graduating class as representative
of the halfway point for most of the generals in our sample and examine their
careers, we find that of twenty-two lieutenants, captains, and majors (including
air college), fourteen were known to have reached the rank of brigadier general
or higher, and two, the rank of colonel. This means that an ESG diploma is
extremely useful to career advancement, especially compared to graduation
from the HCM. Only a small percentage of HCM graduates ever attain the
rank of general, but on the basis of such attainment by the members of one
randomly selected class, nearly two-thirds of ESG graduates will do so. If we
examine generals in important defense posts (see tables 6-3, 6-4, and 6-5), it is
clear how important the ESG experience has been for military decision makers. Of officers whose full educational backgrounds are known and who
enrolled in the ESG rather than a legal or medical program, figures are

strikingly similar for the 1970–1976, 1982–1988, and 1988–1994 administrations: 76, 73, and 76 percent, respectively, were ESG graduates.

Because attrition rates at the ESG in the three-year program are rather substantial, it is helpful to know what type of officer persists. For example, Mora reported that approximately 59 percent of the 1982 graduating class had dropped out by the third year. The officer who makes it through the program is one who is "willing to totally subordinate himself to the system, and is willing to make the ultimate sacrifice, is an individual who knows what rewards the system has to offer."[110] Mora also believes that the officers sure to make it through are sons of, or family friends of, generals. Of the officers completing the first year in the 1989 entering class, seven of the remaining forty are the sons of generals.[111] In the United States, children of military officers also have lower attrition rates.[112] An examination of the generals in our sample reveals some support for the statement in Mexico. Nearly a third of all generals in our sample had fathers in the military. However, among generals who were ESG graduates, the figure was substantially higher: nearly half. If Mora is correct, and he limited his description to graduates with ties to *high-ranking officers*, it is an important indication of how the officer corps, at the very highest levels, becomes more self-selecting. Among Mexican politicians, having highly placed relatives is commonplace, but the characteristic does not seem to increase in importance as one moves up the national political ladder. Ackroyd also believes that the ESG filters out officers from the lowest socioeconomic backgrounds.[113] However, an analysis of background data of generals on the basis of graduation from the HCM only versus HCM and ESG combined reveals that 90 percent of the ESG graduates were middle and/or upper class, compared with 85 percent from such backgrounds who did not attend the ESG.

Although the military and political content of the ESG curriculum is important to a complete picture of the future general officer, the impact of the program on officer discipline is even more important. Even the founding philosophy of the ESG, as laid out in Article 13 of its articles of formation, implies that the staff are to be behavior models for the students.[114] There is no question that

> the most significant contribution made by the Superior War College to the education of the officer corps is to enhance obedience to authority and self-discipline. Comparisons can be drawn with the political leadership. Nowhere do Mexican politicians formally learn that they must subordinate their views and their behavior to their superiors. Many observers note the self-discipline and silence maintained by the political leadership at times of personal and systemic crises. To be successful in the Mexican political system, an individual takes the blame for the benefit of the established institutions. It can be argued that the informally learned, self-disciplined behavior demanded by the political establishment is a value shared with military officers who receive it from the Higher War College.[115]

The level of subordination learned at the ESG, however, is far more severe than the discipline politicians learn through practical experience. U.S. officers who have attended the ESG provide an insightful, cohesive view of the experience. They suggest that the officer who becomes "part of the system" meets three conditions:

> First, the dominant value would be the individual's willingness to subordinate himself totally to those in authority over him. Coupled with this would be the expectation that submission will be rewarded and independence will be severely punished. Finally, the officer's primary motivation would be to secure the rewards that the system has to offer.[116]

How is subordinate behavior instilled in these officers? According to observers, many instructors teach in an arrogant style. One officer-observer who attended the ESG in the early 1980s reported that the instructors often "strutted onto the platform much like peacocks."[117] The instructor conveys to the class that he alone is the supreme authority. Students who offer differing or contradictory opinions are criticized or belittled in front of their classmates. Students are not encouraged to take the initiative intellectually. For example, instructors often show slides of U.S. weaponry or technology about which they know very little or nothing. Foreign guest officers who offer an explanation of the weaponry or technology are told they are mistaken or that the instructor does not wish to take up the offer.[118] Students are not evaluated on their subject matter knowledge but on their willingness to subordinate themselves to authority, that is, to the instructors. One officer told of the experience of a student who refused to drink with an instructor: he had not failed any examinations up to that point but promptly failed the next seven. The instructor, with the support of six colleagues, washed the student out of the program.[119] Classes since 1988 have reported an even higher level of instructor harassment that is intended to weed out all but the truly loyal.[120]

The personal influence of instructors is overwhelming. A class soon learns that the members must make sacrifices as a group to ensure their instructors have a positive attitude toward them as a group. Dziedzic provided an example of students in one class trying to decide how much of their instructors' meals and drinks they should pay for on a training exercise. The discussion was not about whether the class should offer something but, rather, how much.[121] Such a climate leads to another unprofessional characteristic. Group work and cheating on examinations or individual projects are the norm rather than the exception. Student officers at the ESG do not consider this to be unethical but simply a means of surviving.[122] Instructors share the same attitude. According to Article 129 of the new internal ESG code, such behavior is strictly forbidden.[123] Students pay other officers or NCOs to do assignments that are physically impossible to complete, given the workload.

Students who drop out of the ESG program are those who refuse to subordinate themselves to the instructors, or who find some of the norms unacceptable. As one ESG instructor observed, "Those who do not conform to the way of thinking—those who want to rebel—are weeded out."[124] The consequence of this emphasis is to produce an officer who obeys orders without question, and without regard to the order's legality. As one officer of a current ESG class described it, "Our classmates are, for the most part, articulate, intelligent, and professional in their own minds; the system is grinding them down *to complete obedient servants incapable of making a decision* while at the same time coopting them with financial rewards" [emphasis added].[125] The program also encourages a military culture in which relatively high ranking officers do not take the initiative in making recommendations, nor are they directly involved in the decision-making process. Because a hallmark of the military culture is subordination to civilian authority, a concept repeated constantly in armed forces literature, the implication is that officers will remain loyal to the president. On the other hand, a weakness in this arrangement is that if the supreme military commander, were to deviate from presidential authority, he would be able to control his subordinates, given their unquestioning acceptance of the hierarchical structure.[126]

The likelihood of such a happening has increased in recent years as the attitudes of younger officers toward civil authority appears to have grown more critical. One source argued that many officers in the army say that large numbers of their colleagues could outperform civilian counterparts in cabinet-level agencies.[127] Recent ESG classes give the impression that they are not very loyal to the political leaders, and when asked in class to rank their most important object of their loyalty, army places above country.[128] The formal oath taken by ESG graduates, expressed in the December 1987 ESG regulations, states that a staff officer's loyalty, honesty, dedication, and other qualities redound to the benefit of the armed forces first and country second.[129]

The ESG experience, translated into personal contact, becomes significant to recruitment and career advancement. It is not surprising, given the almost combatlike antagonism and survival rate of the officers who complete the ESG, that this experience, for the elite of Mexico's office corps, replaces the HCM in importance. In this connection a Mexican officer recalled:

> At the HCM a bond had been developed among the members of my class and this had been maintained during our early years of commissioned service. It lost its importance, however, when I became a War College graduate. My War College classmates became more important to me. My War College bond replaces the HCM bond. I haven't forgotten my HCM friends, but they are not as important as my War College friends. Having graduated from the War College we now have an advantage over non-graduates. It is like being a member of an exclusive fraternity. The personal relations that are created serve to keep us informed of what is happening within the military, help us to obtain personal favors, favorable future assignments, and it will serve to help us in future advancements.[130]

The same type of personal relationships grow among Mexican politicians at the National University. As with military officers, as educational credentials increased, graduate programs become more significant. However, a difference exists between the officers' ESG experience and politician's graduate-school training. Nearly all high-ranking officers pass through only one program, but politicians not only attend more than one institution but, increasingly attend school abroad. Thus to Mexican politicians, being a member of an exclusive fraternity frequently means having a master's degree from Harvard, Yale, or Cambridge. Such shared experience out of the country just like the earlier shared experience at the National University, not only brings individual politicians closer together, developing the close bonds of trust essential to political *equipos*, but also is given special recognition by older mentors with similar credentials. For example, it is no accident that President Miguel de la Madrid, who graduated from Harvard University with an M.A. in public administration, recruited Carlos Salinas, who has three degrees from Harvard University, including one in the same field. Politicians, like military officers, look more favorably on persons who have trod the same path.

The data in tables 6-3, 6-4, and 6-5 suggest the weight of the ESG in the careers of Mexican officers. The same pattern occurred among U.S. officers.[131] To illustrate, President Cuenca Díaz (1970–1976) selected only one classmate from his HCM generation among his collaborators (table 6-3); four of his top staff were in his 1942 ESG graduating class, accounting for 38 percent of the known ESG graduates in his administration. In Juan Arévalo Gardoqui's administration (1982–1988), the importance of the ESG years is enhanced by the fact that two classes graduated in 1949, the 1947 and 1946 classes (table 6-4). Further, the secretary and subsecretary were members of these two classes. Consequently, seven members, or 25 percent, of the top staff were 1949 ESG graduates. For the 1988–1994 administration, the ESG is important in two ways. First, General Riviello Bazán's two most important collaborators, his subsecretary and oficial mayor, are 1956 graduates. His subsecretary, General Alfredo Ochoa Toledo, was an instructor of at least four of Riviello Bazán's subordinates in the Secretariat of National Defense. Riviello Bazán himself taught two other collaborators when they attended the ESG in 1965.

Teaching at the ESG enhances the personal contacts of an officer by associating him with a select group of colleagues who as students are very likely to make field grade, and with a smaller group of instructors who also have increased opportunities for advancement.[132] The importance of teaching at the ESG, both in terms of career prestige and contacts, can be demonstrated by an analysis of ESG directors from 1932 to 1980 (see Exhibit 6-3). Of the twenty-one directors, eleven are known to have risen to top positions after their tenure, among them two subsecretaries, two chiefs of staff, two oficiales mayores, two department heads, and three zone commanders, and two were chiefs of staff prior to their appointments.

Colegio de Defensa Nacional

For a Mexican military officer today, the culmination of educational professionalization occurs at the Colegio de Defensa Nacional (CDN), inaugurated September 1981 in the old Colegio Militar in Popotla, Federal District.

Exhibit 6-3
Directors of the Escuela Superior de Guerra, 1932-1990

Name	Tenure in Office
Luis Alamillo Flores	1932-1935
Tomás Sánchez Hernández	1936-1940
Luis Rivas López	1940-1944
Luis Amezcua Figueroa	1944-1945
Daniel Somuano López	1945-1947
Rubén Calderón Aguilar	1947-1953
Juan Beristaín Ladrón	1953
Alberto Violante Pérez	1953-1954
Alfonso Gurza Falfán	1955-1957
Cristobal Guzmán Cárdenas	1957-1959
Francisco J. Grajales Godoy	1959-1960
Raúl Rivera Flandez	1960-1961
Antonio Ramírez Barrera	1961-1966
Arturo Corona Mendióroz	1966-1970
Esteban Aguilar Gómez	1970-1972
Juan Antonio de la Fuente Rodríguez	1972-1973
Alonso Aguirre Ramos	1973-1975
Mario Carballo Pazos	1975-1976
Pedro Fería Rivera	1976-1978
Marco Antonio Guerrero Mendoza	1978-1980
Alfonso Pérez Mejía	1980-1982
Joel Martínez Montero	1982
Rodrigo Montelongo Moreno	1982-1985
Rafael Macedo Figueroa	1985-1988
Daniel Velázquez Cordona	1988-1989
Alfredo Hernández Pimentel	1989-1990

General Félix Galván provided the initiative for the CDN after expressing concern that his top military collaborators were typically uninformed about broader social, economic, and political issues. The CDN was to provide skills in national defense strategy formulation, force development, international affairs, economics, and politics to a select group of senior colonels and generals who are marked for service in the highest military posts.[133] He assigned five officers, under the leadership of Vinicio Santoyo Feria, to design and implement the curriculum.[134] The curriculum is divided into five sections—politics, economics, international affairs, society, and national security—a lieutenant colonel is in charge of each. The first class of about twenty army, navy, and air force officers graduated in 1982.

By the time an officer reaches the defense college, his career pattern generally is determined. Consequently, CDN does not perform the same type of recruitment function possible through the HCM and the ESG experiences.

It nevertheless brings together officers who otherwise would not have crossed paths at either the HCM or the ESG. For example, among the generals reaching top posts in the 1988–1994 administration, three were members of the second graduating class, that of 1982. Although two of the officers had attended the HCM together in the 1950s, none had been at the ESG at the same time. The CDN brought the three together rather than only reinforcing the previous contacts of two officers.

The importance of the CDN, after less than eight years in operation, can be seen in its remarkable presence in the backgrounds of the most influential generals by 1988. Of the thirty-one top staff officers at the National Defense Secretariat, ten graduated with M.A. degrees in national security from the CDN (table 6-5). The majority of zone commanders in 1990 passed through its classes. Some two hundred officers have graduated from it since its founding, and nearly all division generals are alumni. Graduates of advanced war colleges in South American countries are more influential because they often end up in high *political offices*. This is the case with alumni, for example, of the Brazilian Escola Superior de Guerra, after which the CDN was patterned.[135] CDN directors will also achieve prestigious career posts. Vinicio Santoyo Fería, who served as first head from 1981 to 1982, was a veteran instructor and chief of first-year classes at the ESG, having served as subdirector of his alma mater in the 1970s. He quickly joined the 1982 administration as chief of staff after completing the CDN course simultaneously with his directorship.[136]

The CDN experience has important implications for the training and orientation of the general staff. In the opinion of Edward Williams, for the first time in recent history Mexican elites have begun to think through the formulation of an overarching national security policy.[137] The content of national security themes is considered elsewhere, but what is most important is the exposure of generals to a heavy dose of political topics and to civilian instructors. This brings Peru to mind; of the articles its Center for Higher Military Studies (CAEM) published between 1954 and 1957, only 1.7 percent dealt with social unrest, economics, politics, and guerrilla warfare. But immediately prior to the military takeover in Peru, the proportion of such articles rose to half.[138]

According to one source, the CDN during a single year in the 1980s devoted thirty-nine conferences to national and international situations, thirteen to national policy, ten to national security, fifteen to administration of the respective secretariats, and twelve to high-level staff studies—and those were only a portion of the overall offerings.[139] The CDN got off to a rocky start, its mission unclear and lacking in continuity. Eight directors in as few years headed the program, several for as little as three months. Since 1988 it has emphasized a broad curriculum, recruiting many civilian specialists to teach a wide range of topics from public administration to student movements.

The type of civilians invited to serve as lecturers at the CDN are intellectuals or professors respected in their fields. One of the striking characteristics of the program is that even individuals who have been known to have direct connections with Central American guerrillas have been asked to address the students; instructors report no automatic prejudice against contrary ideological views. The CDN does have a policy of not inviting speakers who are actively involved in electoral politics.

The key factor in choosing a civilian instructor is the degree to which the military trusts the individual. Three criteria appear to apply. A person's position might favor his inclusion in the program; for example, curriculum content might relate to the purview of the agency with which he is associated. The second criteria, trust, is typically determined by a personal relationship: kinship or professional ties. The third criteria is expertise: professional or intellectual merit.[140]

Recent CDN theses reveal the extent to which its graduates consider important and concrete social and political issues. Among them are "Diagnosis of the National Social Situation" (1982); "The Role of the CDN in National Security" (1984); "Pressure Groups in Mexico" (1984); "The Social Field in National Security" (1985); and "The Philosophy of National Security and External Security in Mexico" (1986).[141] Theses involve field research, and each officer is required to write one. Each class writes a collaborative work on a single broad theme; these are passed on to the office of the president and to the Secretariat of Foreign Relations.

The ambience at the CDN is somewhat different from that at the HCM and the ESG. Despite the fact that the students are colonels and generals, they exhibit great respect for the civilian instructors, and conduct themselves with dignity. Similar to students at the ESG, they do not typically engage in intellectual debate in the classroom despite prompting from some civilian instructors. Some instructors report that individual officers approach them during breaks for spirited give-and-take. Also, considerable intellectual exchange occurs between guest instructors and the lieutenant colonels in charge of the courses.

The majority of CDN lecturers are increasingly civilians, including some foreigners, and a seminar format is used. The National Defense Secretariat has also been making use of political analyses by Mexican and foreign authors, including translated books.[142] Potentially, one of the most important changes in military education is that for the first time, civilians will receive an education in a military academy. This pattern has existed in other South American war colleges for many years. The original guidelines for the CDN included a provision permitting civilians in the seminars, a provision left unimplemented. But in August 1989 five civilians from the public sector were accepted into the program, and the 1990 entering class included three more.[143] Thus, the CDN introduces a new linkage between civilian and military leaders. It is not sufficiently broad to substitute for the political-military officer's role in years past, but it has potential, significant consequences for the relationship in the 1990s.

Training Abroad

Since the 1920s selected officers have studied abroad after having attended Mexican military academies. During the early postrevolutionary years some

officers studied in France; Mexican graduates of the French war college were
essential to the founding and development of the ESG. Luis Alamillo Flores,
who played the key role in the creation of the ESG, was the first Mexican
officer to complete a staff and command course in France.[144] Not surprisingly,
the United States, although an enemy of Mexico in the nineteenth century, is
the most popular location for foreign military training. The roots of such
training are the revolutionary years, especially of officers who became the core
of the future army air force. Among the generals who were born between 1880
and 1890, and who remained on active duty after 1940, only 11 percent trained
abroad—in equal numbers in Europe and the United States. The figure increased in the next generation to 18 percent, but the geographic distribution
remained the same.

The postrevolutionary group of officers, as in so many other instances, set a
benchmark figure for training abroad: 36 percent left Mexico for training,
85 percent of that proportion went to the United States. The next generation,
those born from 1910 to 1920, traveled in even larger numbers: nearly
50 percent received foreign training, all but 2 percent in the United States. The
United States continued to dominate the foreign training of generals in command positions into the 1990s. Fully 41 percent of the generals in our sample
trained abroad, 37 percent in the United States and 3 percent in Europe.

The above figures suggest that U.S. military training programs are second
only to the HCM and the ESG in the formation of Mexican officers. According to Edward Williams, Mexican officers generally have received precious
little training abroad.[145] An examination of the National Defense Secretariat
Memorias confirms the assertion. As Jorge Lozoya notes, around 5 percent of all
officers in the 1950s and 1960s studied abroad.[146] The reason for this, according
to officers educated during that period, is that the secretariat never had a
coherent policy in that regard, and officers had to compete for scarce fellowships
on their own initiative.[147] Officers abroad helped to maintain good relations with
countries that offered exchange programs and military fellowships.

For all officers trained abroad, the United States has played a crucial role.
According to Piñeyro, of the 546 Mexican soldiers who received advanced
training between 1950 and 1968, 306 (55 percent) studied in the United States
between 1964 and 1968—the formative years of the Mexican military educational system's modernization. They took courses in two broad subject areas:
the establishing of military schools and counterinsurgency warfare. This pattern was repeated between 1971 and 1976.[148] What is significant, however, is
that a much greater percentage of high-ranking officers, those who reached the
rank of general, were sent abroad. Since the 1980s attendance at U.S. military
schools is again on the rise.[149]

Mexico's political elite has also received significant training in other countries. Only 5 percent of politicians leave Mexico for undergraduate work;
17 percent do so for work toward a master's degree. Of those politicians,
43 percent receive degrees from universities outside Mexico, 38 percent of
whom study in the United States. At the Ph.D. level, 5 percent of all politicians
have that degree from U.S. universities.

The data regarding leading politicians and generals suggest that the latter are more likely to receive some education in the United States than the former. Like that of their military counterparts, the education of political leaders suggests possible foreign influences on attitudes and public policy, and definitely implies the value that civilian recruitment and the career systems place on advanced preparation and foreign specializations and methodologies. In this vein, Mexico's military and political leaders share United States educational and cultural experiences, but those experiences are sharply divided between United States military versus civil institutions.[150]

There is substantial evidence to suggest the importance of foreign training abroad for career success. Not only do two-fifths of all top generals have such experience, compared with only 5 percent of all officers, but certain military occupational specialties have received an unusual amount of foreign influence in their training. Not surprisingly, technical military occupational specialties (MOSs) are most well represented among foreign-trained generals. Within the National Defense Secretariat, 59 percent of the pilots have received U.S. training, the most of any group, followed closely by the medical corps, with 54 percent. Even higher figures exist for foreign training in all countries. In contrast, the infantry, the backbone of the army, has sent only one-fifth of its top officers to the United States. This might be explained by the fact that for some time soldiers scoring the highest on various tests during basic training at the HCM were channeled into the more technical specialties. Because an officer needs a language capability and competes through examination for selection for foreign training, it is only logical that the more able officers would be overrepresented in the specialties.

The Mexican military considers foreign training important for technical reasons and as a significant credential for leadership. Most officers, however, do not believe that foreign training was advantageous to their career but was useful to them only personally.[151] In fact, it can be argued that training abroad is assigned as a financial reward, rather than providing special expertise. Despite empirical evidence to the contrary, officers have received the impression in the past that the secretary of defense discouraged foreign training. For example, one officer remembered his experience in requesting permission to train in the United States in the following context:

Studying abroad was not a very organized affair, as you have been told. During my career, what generally happened is that the Ministry of Defense in the official army magazine announced such and such a scholarship or position was available. Then, you had to take an exam and compete with anybody else who wanted to go abroad, and of course the most difficult thing is that you had to have a certain level of language capability to be eligible. I was very interested in going, and I remember going to the Secretary of Defense and asking him if I could study abroad at Ft. Leavenworth. He asked me why I wanted to go there. I told him that I wanted to learn about American military theory. He was annoyed, and told me we had our own theory here. I said, "Yes, I agree, but it would be valuable for me to learn other theories as well." He just said that if I wanted to go, I could go.[152]

Since the early 1980s sending officers abroad has been part of the military's larger educational goal. Such training is *not* a substitute for graduating from the ESG. Advanced military education is considered a prerequisite to command. Officers chosen for such training are also chosen in larger numbers for foreign training. This is illustrated by figures demonstrating that, of the generals who had studied only in Mexico, 38 percent were ESG graduates; of those who had studied abroad, 51 percent had obtained the coveted DEM. Figures are even higher for future generals selected to study in the United States: 60 percent of the officers who took courses in the United States were ESG graduates. The same disparity was true of naval officers. Thirteen percent of Mexican officers who studied in the United States were graduates of the higher naval studies center; compared to only 2 percent who remained in Mexico for their training.

Training in the United States seems important for staff duty at the highest levels. Well-educated, U.S.-trained generals are overrepresented among National Defense Secretariat department heads. For example, fewer than one in twelve of all well-educated Mexican generals reaches a departmental post, but among foreign-educated generals, more than one in three do so. Although foreign military training is not a requirement for becoming a section head in Mexico, more than half of all section heads have it. Officers higher up in the hierarchy also have studied in the United States. Marco Antonio Guerrero Mendoza, who was subsecretary of national defense in the 1982–1988 administration, studied armored cars in 1955–1956, received a diploma from the Inter-American Defense College in 1964, and was an aide to the Mexican military attaché in Washington, D.C., in 1961–1963. Even more unusual, Salvador Gómez Bernard, naval chief of staff in 1986, received the equivalent of a Ph.D. from the Inter-American Defense College, with the dissertation "Influence of Economic Power in Continental Security." Guerrero Mendoza and Gómez Bernard directed the ESG and the Centro de Estudios Superiores Navales, respectively. Training like theirs not only is important in the promotion process for certain positions but serves as a recruitment link for a select group of high-ranking officers. For example, Arturo Corona Mendióroz, oficial mayor in 1970, attended West Point with Maximiliano del Valle Huerta, one of his department heads, in 1950 (see table 6-3).

Foreign influences through personal ties are not confined to study abroad. The military has introduced this possibility by allowing Guatemala to send officers to the ESG; graduation records show almost yearly representation in each class extending back many years to the 1980s. According to Cesar Sereseres, such training has facilitated communication between Guatemalan and Mexican military forces and security agencies.[153] Other Central American officers have attended too, and U.S. military officers have been attending the ESG for a one-year stints since the early 1980s, and a single officer has also been attached to the air academy in Guadalajara. Since the late 1980s a U.S. officer teaches English at the ESG, and the air force and naval academies.[154]

Military education has played a multifaceted role within the Mexican officer corps. The HCM and the ESG have exercised a critical influence in officer formation. The discipline and subordination to authority essential to Mexican civil-military relations have been learned through a militarily controlled socialization process. The extreme level of subordination, as hypothesized in the introduction and analyzed in the section on values, not only sets Mexico apart from most other militaries but is among the most important variables.

The two schools play a critical role in internal recruitment and career success. The ESG has superseded the HCM in this capacity, and similar to civilian schools, relationships are formed among instructors and students, as well as within both groups. On the other hand, the HCM, ESG, and CDN have ensured the educational separation between civilian and military groups. The CDN's recent decision to allow a select number of civilian, public figures into the classroom, and its heavy use of civilian instructors, many also from the public sector, reestablish a narrow but important bridge between politicians and the officer corps.

Finally, the curricula in these institutions have typically stressed military rather than broader social, economic, and political subjects. Changes in the ESG since the 1970s and, more important, the structure of the Colegio de Defensa Nacional formally introduced these larger concerns in officer training, increasing the potential for the military's greater knowledge of, interest in, and inclination for politics.

Notes

1. Frederick M. Nunn, "On the Role of the Military in Twentieth-Century Latin America: The Mexican Case," in *The Modern Mexican Military, A Reassessment*, ed. David Ronfeldt (La Jolla: Center for U.S.-Mexican Studies, University of California, San Diego, 1984), 34.

2. Edwin Lieuwen, *Mexican Militarism* (Albuquerque: University of New Mexico Press, 1968), 4.

3. Ibid.; William S. Ackroyd, "Descendants of the Revolution: Civil-Military Relations in Mexico" (Ph.D. diss., University of Arizona, 1988), 71.

4. Gloria Fuentes, *EL ejército mexicano* (Mexico: Grijalbo, 1983), 147.

5. *Memoria gráfica del cincuentenario de la reapertura del Heroico Colegio Militar* (Mexico: SHCP, 1970), 442; Valentín López González, *Los compañeros de Zapata* (Morelos, 1980), 63–64; José López Escalera, *Diccionario biográfico y de historia de México* (Mexico: Editorial del Magistrado, 1964), 183.

6. Jacques van Doorn, *The Soldier and Social Change* (Beverly Hills: Sage Publications, 1975), 75.

7. *Hispano Americano*, September 24, 1984, 13.

8. Steven J. Wager, "The Mexican Military" (unpublished paper, 1983, 20, parts of which appeared in Robert Wesson, *The Latin American Military* [Westport, Conn.: Greenwood Press, 1986]), 10.

9. Wager, "The Mexican Military"; Fuentes, *El ejército mexicano*, 232.

10. José Luis Piñeyro, "The Modernization of the Mexican Armed Forces," in *Democracy under Siege: New Military Power in Latin America*, ed. Augusto Varas (Westport, Conn.: Greenwood Press, 1989), 115.

11. Ibid., 116. For a complete list of these schools, see Fuentes, *El ejército mexicano*, 159–160.

12. Francisco Solís Peón, "El síndrome de Oxford," *El Nacional*, February 26, 1990, F.

13. William S. Ackroyd, "The Military in Mexican Politics: The Impact of Professionaliza-tion, Civilian Behavior, and the Revolution" (Paper presented at the Pacific Coast Council of Latin Americanists, San Diego, 1982), 6.

14. Roderic A. Camp, "Generals and Politicians in Mexico: A Preliminary Comparison," in *The Modern Mexican Military: A Reassessment*, ed. David Ronfeldt (La Jolla: Center for U.S.-Mexican Studies, University of California, San Diego, 1984), 120.

15. Guillermo Boils, *Los militares y la política en México, 1915–1974* (Mexico: El Caballito, 1975), 142.

16. Morris Janowitz, *The Military in the Development of New Nations* (Chicago: University of Chicago Press, 1964); Marion Levy, *Modernization and the Structure of Societies* (Princeton: Princeton University Press, 1963).

17. James W. Wilkie and Stephen Haber, eds., *Statistical Abstract of Latin America*, vol. 21 (Los Angeles: Latin American Center Publications, University of California, Los Angeles, 1982), 134.

18. Roderic A. Camp, *Mexico's Leaders, Their Education and Recruitment* (Tucson: Univer-sity of Arizona Press, 1980), and "The Political Technocrat in Mexico and the Survival of the Political System," *Latin American Research Review* 20, no. 1 (1985): 97–118. One interviewee suggested that teaching in the United States military is a distraction from combat or division level positions. He suggests that an important indicator of a non-fighting, police-like military is the importance of teaching.

19. Pre-1935 data are from the Mexican Political Biography Project, Power Elite subset.

20. Ackroyd, "Descendants of the Revolution," 87.

21. Otto Granados Roldán, "Regreso a las armas?" in *El desafío mexicano*, ed. Francisco de Alba et al. (Mexico: Ediciones Oceano, 1982), 125.

22. Lyle N. McAlister, *The Military in Latin American Socio-political Evolution: Four Case Studies* (Washington, D.C.: Center for Research in Social Systems, 1970), 229.

23. Boils, *Los militares y la política en México*, 109; Secretaría de Defensa Nacional, *Memorias* (Mexico: SDN, 1965), 139; McAlister, *The Military in Latin American Socio-Political Evolution*, 39.

24. Wager, "The Mexican Military," 15.

25. Javier Romero, *Aspectos psicobiométricos y sociales de un muestra de la juventud mexicana* (Mexico: Dirección de Investigaciones Antropológicas, 1956), 52. Many of the cadets enter the HCM as young as fifteen, thus preventing them from completing education beyond secondary.

26. Fuentes, *EL ejército mexicano*, 155.

27. *Revista de Ejército y Fuerza Aérea*, July–August, 1976, 35.

28. Dolores Cordero, "El ejército mexicano," *Revista de Revistas*, September 12, 1973, 4.

29. Presidencia de la República, Unidad de la Crónica Presidencial, archives.

30. McAlister, *The Military in Latin American Socio-Political Evolution*, 218.

31. Frank D. McCann, "Brazilian Army Officers Biography Project" (Paper presented at the 15th National Latin American Studies Association, Miami, December 1989), 13.

32. Thomas E. Weil, "The Armed Forces," in *Area Handbook for Mexico* (Washington, D.C.: GPO, 1975), 364.

33. Ackroyd, "Descendants of the Revolution," 129.

34. Camp, *Mexico's Leaders*, 94ff., and *The Making of a Government: Political Leaders in Modern Mexico* (Tucson: University of Arizona Press, 1984), 48ff.

35. Ackroyd, "The Military in Mexican Politics," 12.

36. William S. Ackroyd, "The Military in Mexican Politics: The Impact of Professionalism, Civilian Behavior, and the Revolution," *PCCLAS Proceedings*, vol. 12 (1985–1986), 98.

37. Daniel Mora, "Profile of the Mexican Company Grade Officer" (Paper presented at the Rocky Mountain States Latin American Conference, Tucson, February 1984), 5, based on a fifteen-month stay with forty-four Mexican officers.

38. McCann, "Brazilian Army Officers Biography Project," 15.

39. Mora, "Profile of the Mexican Company Grade Officer," 3.

40. Weil, "The Armed Forces," 363.

41. Mora, "Profile of the Mexican Company Grade Officer," 3.

42. Luis G. Franco, *Glosa del periódo de gobierno del C. Gral. e Ing. Pascual Ortíz Rubio, 1930-32, 3 años de historia del ejército de México* (Mexico, 1946), 44; Virginia Prewitt, "The Mexican Army," *Foreign Affairs* 19 (April 1941): 613.

43. Ibid.

44. Steven J. Wager, "Modernization of the Mexican Military: Political and Strategic Implications" (unpublished paper, Department of History, U.S. Military Academy, 1983), 11.

45. *Revista de Ejército y Fuerza Aérea*, April–June, 1952, 38–57.

46. Weil, "The Armed Forces," 365. As one graduate pointed out, "When you begin the HCM, there is a first-year program which all cadets take in common. The first six months are what might be described as basic recruit training. The second six months is sort of an advanced basic course in which people begin to develop some kind of interest in a particular military occupational specialty. At the end of the first year, you are allowed to choose your service branch if you have demonstrated a capacity in practice and on examinations for that particular service." Personal interview, Mexico City, 1990.

47. Ackroyd, "Descendants of the Revolution," 118.

48. Camp, *Mexico's Leaders.*

49. Camp, "Generals and Politicians in Mexico," 119.

50. McAlister, *The Military in Latin American Socio-Political Evolution*, 231.

51. McCann, "Brazilian Army Officers Biography Project," 12.

52. Ackroyd, "Descendants of the Revolution," 10.

53. Vicente Ernesto Pérez Mendoza, "The Role of the Armed Forces in the Mexican Economy in the 1980s" (M.A. thesis, Naval Postgraduate School, Monterey, California, 1981), 21.

54. Kenneth Walker, "Political Socialization in Universities," in *Elites in Latin America*, ed. Seymour Martin Lipset and Aldo Solari (New York: Oxford University Press, 1967): Edgar Litt, "Civic Education, Community Norms, and Political Indoctrination," *American Sociological Review* 28 (1963): 69–75.

55. Camp, *Mexico's Leaders.*

56. Gary Spencer, "Methodological Issues in the Study of Bureaucratic Elites," *Social Problems* 21 (Summer 1973): 91. As one U.S. officer noted, until a decade ago, all graduates of U.S. military academies pursued combat arms specialties, whereas Reserve Officer Training Corps (ROTC) graduates where in combat support areas. Since most billets for generals are in combat arms, academy graduates had an advantage.

57. Glen Dealy, *The Public Man: An Interpretation of Latin American and Other Catholic Cultures* (Amherst: University of Massachusetts Press, 1977), 24.

58. Camp, "Generals and Politicians," 126–127.

59. Ministerio de Guerra y Marina, *Memoria* (Mexico: Imprenta Central, 1900), appendices.

60. Camp, "Generals and Politicians," 155.

61. Mora, "Profile of the Mexican Company Grade Officer," 6. This bond will be superceded by officers who continue on to the Escuela Superior de Guerra. Very little of the fraternity from HCM remains after an officer graduates from the ESG.

62. Boils, *Los militares y la política en México*, 108, 114. One informant offered a cynical explanation for administrative careers: "promotion and 'general rank' are secondary to positions that allow them access to the 'coffers.' I have seen several fifty-year-old administrative majors who could buy and sell many a general." Interview with an officer, Mexico City, 1991.

63. Camp, "Generals and Politicians," 127.

64. Camp, *Mexico's Leaders*, 68.

65. *Hispano Americano*, December 18, 1978, 17–18.

66. Ibid., December 7, 1964, 19; Abraham Pérez López, *Diccionario biográfico hidalguense* (Mexico: Imprenta Unión, 1970), 101–102.

67. C. Wright Mills, *The Power Elite* (New York: Oxford University Press, 1959), 295.

68. Roderic A. Camp, *Entrepreneurs and Politics in Twentieth Century Mexico* (New York: Oxford University Press, 1989), 94.

69. José de Imaz, *Los Que Mandan* (Albany: State University of New York Press, 1970), 68.

70. *Memoria gráfica del cincuentenario de la reapertura del Heroico Colegio Militar*, 441–443.

71. Ibid., 448; *Revista del Ejército y Fuerza Aérea*, September 1976, 133; ibid., December 1962, 29; ibid., December 1972, 80; *El Día*, December 1, 1976, 10; *Excélsior*, December 1, 1976.

72. The main reason for this age difference is that Salinas selected the senior active duty division general as his defense secretary. Personal interview, Mexico City, 1990.

73. Michael J. Dziedzic, "The Essence of Decision in a Hegemonic Regime: The Case of Mexico's Acquisition of a Supersonic Fighter" (Ph.D. diss., University of Texas, Austin, 1986), 382. Ironically, this new building normally is not used for the ESG, only for tests and overflow classes, and remains under the control of the Secretariat of National Defense.

74. Steven J. Wager, "Civic Action and the Mexican Military" (unpublished paper, Department of History, U.S. Military Academy, 1982), 16. The Escuela Médico Militar recruits many students from lower socioeconomic backgrounds through a well-established scholarship program. In 1972 the school also accepted, for the first time, women nursing graduates into the medical program. See Cordero, "El ejército mexicano," 5.

75. *Proceso*, October 19, 1987, 10–11; *Excélsior*, May 23, 1983, 22; *Diccionario Biográfico del Gobierno Mexicano* (Mexico: Presidencia de la República, 1987), 222.

76. Boils, *Los militares y la política en México*, 110–111.

77. Prewitt, "The Mexican Army," 614; Mora, "Profile of the Mexican Company Grade Officer," 8.

78. McAlister, *The Military in Latin American Socio-political Evolution*, 206.

79. Félix Galván López, *Escuela Superior de Guerra, 1932–1982* (Mexico: Secretaría de Defensa Nacional, 1982), 38.

80. *Diccionario biográfico de Mexico* (Monterrey: Editorial Revesa, 1968), 15; *Revista de Ejército y Fuerza Aérea*, September 1976, 133.

81. *Revista de Ejército y Fuerza Aérea*, September 1976, 135; Ronald Hilton, *Who's Who in Latin America: Mexico* (Stanford: Stanford University Press, 1946), 111; *Excélsior*, March 13, 1973, 13; ibid., September 25, 1980, 22. Another important figure was General Miguel Angel Sánchez Lamego, who graduated from the Colegio Military in 1923, studied engineering in France, 1925–1926, then graduated from the French higher war college in 1939. He directed the cartographic department of the National Defense Secretariat for twenty years, retiring as a division general. See *Revista de Ejército y Fuerza Aérea*, March 1975, 126, and *Directorio Social* (Mexico, 1935), 256.

82. Luis G. Franco, *Glosa del periodo de gobierno del C. Gral. e Ing. Pascual Ortíz Rubio*, 164.

83. Galván López, *Escuela Superior de Guerra*, 53.

84. Plutarco Elías Calles, "La Escuela Superior de Guerra y Principios de Doctrina para la Organización del Ejército de México," *Del México Actual*, no. 15 (Mexico: Secretaria de Relaciones Exteriores, 1934), 64.

85. McCann, "Brazilian Army Officers Biography Project," 9.

86. Christopher Brogan, "Military Higher Education and the Emergence of 'New Professionalism': Some Consequences for Civil-Military Relations in Latin America," *Army Quarterly and Defense Journal*, no. 112 (January 1982): 28.

87. Wager, "Civic Action and the Mexican Military," 18.

88. Maureen Mylander, *The Generals* (New York: Dial Press, 1974), 346.

89. Boils asserts that 161 generals retired from 1971 to 1973, and that another 30 were in the process. See his "Los militares en México (1965–1985)," *Revista Mexicana de Sociología* 47 (January–February, 1985): 174.

90. In 1990 most of the newly promoted brigadier generals with ESG diplomas could be found in artillery, engineering, and medicine.

91. Cordero, "El ejército mexicano," 7; Ackroyd, "Descendants of the Revolution," 119.

92. Ackroyd, "Descendants of the Revolution," 171.

93. Franco, *Glosa del periódo de gobierno del C. Gral. e Ing. Pascual Ortiíz Rubio*, 65.

94. Ibid., 65–66.

95. As several officers suggested, most of the class time is wasted. For example, officers at this level actually spent time learning what a page number was for. Personal interview, Mexico City, 1991.

96. Wager, "Modernization of the Mexican Military," 15.

97. David Ronfeldt, "The Modern Mexican Military: An Overview," in *The Modern Mexican*

Military: A Reassessment, ed. Ronfeldt (La Jolla: Center for U.S.-Mexican Studies, University of California, San Diego, 1984), 9–10.

98. Weil, "The Armed Forces," 365.

99. As of 1987, when the ESG's regulations were revised for the first time since 1960, the school offered four programs: "Higher Arms and Services" (six months), for majors and lieutenant colonels who are not graduates of the regular ESG course (which has included female officers); "Staff and Command" (three years), the regular course; "Air Force Staff and Command" (two years); and "Higher War" (six months), to develop combined operations skills of ESG graduates. See Article 12, Secretaria de Defensa Nacional, *Reglamento de la Escuela Superior de Guerra* (Mexico, December 30, 1987).

100. Brogan, "Military Higher Education and the Emergence of the 'New Professionalism,'" 23.

101. Cordero, "El ejército mexicano," 7.

102. José Luis Piñeyro, "The Mexican Army and the State: Historical and Political Perspective," *Revue Internationale de Sociologie* 14 (April–August 1978): 140.

103. Michael J. Dziedzic, "Civil-Military Relations in Mexico: The Politics of Co-optation" (unpublished paper, University of Texas, Austin, 1983), 25.

104. Ackroyd, "Descendants of the Revolution," 119.

105. Personal interviews, Mexico City, 1991.

106. William S. Ackroyd, "Civil-Military Relations in Mexico: A Study of Mexican Military Perceptions and Behavior" (Paper presented at the Rocky Mountain States Conference of Latin American Studies, Las Cruces, New Mexico, 1980, 17), and "Descendants of the Revolution," 199.

107. Secretaría de Defensa Nacional, *Memoria* (Mexico: SDN, 1948), 47–48, 58; Ackroyd, "Descendants of the Revolution," Appendix B; General Luis Garfias, comments, conference on the Mexican military, Mexico-U.S. Studies Center, University of California, San Diego, La Jolla, 1984.

108. Personal letter to the author, October 15, 1990.

109. Ackroyd, "Descendants of the Revolution," 123.

110. *Revista de Ejército y Fuerza Aérea,* February 1956, 29–30; Mora, "Profile of the Mexican Company Grade Officer," 11.

111. Personal interviews, Mexico City, 1991.

112. For example, cadets at the Air Force Academy are from higher-income families, have conservative views, and are the children of career military officers. See R. F. Schloemer, "Making It at the Air Force Academy: Who Stays? Who Succeeds?" in *The Changing World of the American Military,* ed. Franklin D. Margiotta (Boulder, Colo.: Westview Press, 1978), 321–344. On the other hand, U.S. children in general, from non-military families, are much more familiar with military life.

113. Ackroyd, "Civil-Military Relations in Mexico," 15.

114. Franco, *Glosa del periodo de gobierno del C. Gral. e Ing. Pascual Ortíz Rubio,* 66.

115. Camp, "Generals and Politicians in Mexico," 124.

116. Michael J. Dziedzic, "Mexico's Converging Challenges: Problems, Prospects, and Implications" (unpublished paper, U.S. Air Force Academy, 1989), 34. This has been attested by officers interviewed.

117. Ibid., cited from an exchange officer school report, October 26, 1982.

118. Personal interviews, Mexico City, 1991.

119. Ibid., 36.

120. Richard Kilroy, "The Mexican Military Digs In" (unpublished paper, 1991), 4.

121. Ibid., 37.

122. Dziedzic, "Civil-Military Relations in Mexico," 28, citing an exchange officer school report, June 15, 1982.

123. See section 7, which states that resorting to copying, or other fradulent means will result in a grade of zero and suspension from the examination. Secretariat of National Defense, *Reglamento de la Escuela Superior de Guerra,* 28.

124. Ibid., 36; Mora, "Profile of the Mexican Company Grade Officer," 10.

125. Personal letter to the author, 1990.

126. The degree to which a higher war college can bring a decline in respect for civil authority, a thesis originally argued by Alfred Stepan, has been severely critiqued, in the Brazilian case, by John Markoff and Silvio Baretta, who found no such relationship. See their "Professional Ideology and Military Activism in Brazil: Critique of a Thesis of Alfred Stepan," *Comparative Politics* 17 (January 1985): 183.

127. Personal interview, Mexico City, 1991.

128. Personal interviews, Mexico City, 1991.

129. See Article 145, Secretariat of National Defense, *Reglamento de la Escuela Superior de Guerra*, 31.

130. Mora, "Profile of the Mexican Company Grade Officer," 15.

131. Morris Janowitz concluded that war college attendance promoted "new alliances and personal friendships which are important for career advancement. When the group of 576 officers on staff duty at the Pentagon in 1954 were asked, 'Have friendships you made at school (war colleges and National War College) been of specific and concrete value to you in your present job?,' they answered overwhelmingly in the affirmative." *The Professional Soldier* (Glencoe, Ill.: Free Press, 1960), 141.

132. Camp, "Generals and Politicians in Mexico."

133. Wager, "Modernization of the Mexican Military," 12; Alden M. Cunningham, "Mexico's National Security in the 1980s–1990s," in *The Modern Mexican Military: A Reassessment*, ed. David Ronfeldt (La Jolla: Center for U.S.-Mexican Studies, University of California, San Diego, 1984), 167.

134. Personal interview, Mexico City, 1990.

135. Wilfred Bacchus, *Mission in Mufti* (Westport, Conn.: Greenwood Press, 1990), 36ff.

136. He has allegedly been linked with the drug trade, as suggested earlier.

137. Edward J. Williams, "Mexico's Modern Military, Implications for the Region," *Caribbean Review* 10 (Fall 1981): 12; Edward J. Williams, "Mexico's Central American Policy: National Security Considerations" (paper, Strategic Studies Institute, Army War College, 1982), 28, published in *Rift and Revolution: The Central American Imbroglio*, ed. Howard J. Wiarda (Washington, D.C.: American Enterprise Institute, 1984), 303–328.

138. Brogan, "Military Higher Education and the Emergence of the 'New Professionalism,'" 26. For an interesting description of curricular changes in Brazil's higher war college, focusing increasingly on internal revolutionary war, see Stanley E. Hilton, "The Brazilian Military: Changing Strategic Perceptions and the Question of Mission," *Armed Forces and Society* 13 (Spring 1987): 330.

139. Cunningham, "Mexico's National Security in the 1980s–1990s," 171.

140. Personal interviews, Mexico City, 1989–1990.

141. *Diccionario biográfico del gobierno mexicano* (Mexico: Presidencia de la República, 1987), 40, 206, 207, 269, 413.

142. David Ronfeldt, "The Modern Mexican Military," in *Armies and Politics in Latin America*, ed. Abraham Lowenthal and J. Samuel Fitch (New York: Holmes and Meier, 1986), 232. Also, shortly after the CDN's creation, the Secretariat of National Defense requested permission from the Fondo de Cultura Económica to print a special military edition of one of my books on Mexican politics, indicative of the CDN's use of civilian and foreign analyses. The book, *Mexico's Leaders, Their Education and Recruitment*, was being used at the CDN in 1990.

143. Interview with civilian instructor, Colegio de Defensa Nacional, Mexico City, 1989.

144. Galván López, *Escuela Superior de Guerra*, 53.

145. Edward J. Williams, "The Mexican Military and Foreign Policy: The Evolution of Influence," in *The Modern Mexican Military: A Reassessment*, ed. David Ronfeldt (La Jolla: Center for U.S.-Mexican Studies, University of California, San Diego, 1984), 196.

146. Jorge Alberto Lozoya, *El ejército mexicano (1911–1965)* (Mexico: El Colegio de México, 1970), 126.

147. Personal interview, Mexico City, 1990.

148. Piñeyro, "The Modernization of the Mexican Armed Forces," 116.

149. Wager, "Modernization of the Mexican Military," 11.

150. Camp, "Generals and Politicians in Mexico," 126.

151. Personal interview, Mexico City, 1990.

152. Personal interview, Mexico City, 1990.

153. Caesar Sereseres, "The Mexican Military Looks South," in *The Modern Mexican Military: A Reassessment*, ed. David Ronfeldt (La Jolla: Center for U.S.-Mexican Studies, University of California, San Diego, 1984), 205.

154. Williams, "The Mexican Military and Foreign Policy," 196.

7

Making It to General

One of the most interesting aspects of military leadership compared with civilian leadership is how one climbs the decision-making ladder. The least-well-known aspects of the Mexican military officer are the qualities or experiences that encourage rapid promotion, upward career mobility, and appointment to a significant command. In terms of civil-military relations, it is important to understand the relationship between civilian political influence and military promotions, and the impact, if any, it has on civil-military relations. In many other Latin American countries, the existence of alternating parties in power, of civil-military political alliances, and of a strong political opposition in the Senate creates an environment conducive to greater civilian involvement in the promotion process.

An important thesis involving civilian control of the Mexican military has been offered by Wayne Cornelius. Franklin Margiotta "speculated at his suggestion that the absence of civilian interference in the internal matters of the military, such as promotion, discipline, and assignments may help explain the noninterventionist attitude on the part of the Mexican military."[1] Margiotta had no data to test this interpretation, but it is well worth introducing because some empirical data exist to test its validity for Mexico.

In contrast to Mexican civilian leaders, who depend exclusively on personal ties, military leaders appear to arrive at the top through a rather structured process. In the civilian world, personal contacts might make it possible, although not probable, for someone with little experience to reach an important government post. Also, young politicians, such as President Salinas himself, can reach cabinet-level positions whose match it would take a military officer at least another decade to obtain. For example, an army officer cannot become a military zone commander until he attains the rank of brigade general. A two-star rank in the army requires at least thirty, typically thirty-five, years of service, which means such an officer would generally be around the age of fifty. A state governor, perhaps the most analogous political position in the civilian world, could be in his thirties, depending on the minimum-age stipulation in the state constitution. Moreover, a young civilian governor might have, say, only five years of relevant experience, whereas a brigade general, as a consequence of a structured promotion process, will have five times as much.

Presidential Promotion Policies

The Mexican government, in line with President Cárdenas's larger profession-alization drive, introduced the first important military promotion criteria in the postrevolutionary era. Specifically, infantry officers who failed to pass a comprehensive examination in military science after 1936 were given the option of retirement or assignment to a remedial training center. Age-in-grade limits were imposed in an effort to eliminate untrainable officers blocking a newly educated generation's promotion. Lyle McAlister believes that the two norms—retraining and age in grade—were observed in the cases of lower- and medium-rank officers, but many revolutionary officers, through political influ-ence or sentimental appeals, avoided these restrictions.[2] The instances of many older revolutionary officers who held positions long after 1946 support his interpretation. General Agustín Mustieles Medel's career is illustrative. An officer who fought under the Constitutionalists during the Revolution, Mus-tieles Medel had already reached the rank of general in the early 1920s. Although he never attended the HCM or ESG, he was promoted to brigade general in 1939, and division general in 1947. He gained a department headship in the late 1950s, but his career as a zone commander intended from 1939 to 1961, and he died in charge of the 22nd military zone in Toluca, México.[3]

The same year that Cárdenas introduced restrictions on older officers, younger officers were required to pass a Military Studies Committee examina-tion for promotion.[4] Still, secretariat records illustrate continued excessive numbers of officers, generals specifically. In 1920, when the army numbered 100,047 officers and troops, only 10 division and 20 brigade generals were on active duty, but so were 600 brigadiers. By 1930, after three important military rebellions (1923, 1927, and 1929) during which the government promoted loyal generals and exiled, executed, or retired rebelling generals, the highest ranks included 31 division and 128 brigade generals, but only 267 brigadiers. The government had reduced the total number of officers from 630 to 426, but it had also reduced the total forces to 72,556, so the percentage remained about the same (table 7-1). By 1951, at the end of Alemán's administration, the total strength of the army was only 50,409, but the senior officer corps had grown by 32 percent, equaling its highest postrevolutionary strength of 627 generals thirty years earlier. Moreover, the number of three-star generals expanded from 31 in 1930 to 83 in 1951, and brigade generals from 128 to 217, tremen-dous proportional increases.[5] Compared with the U.S. Army, Mexico's officer corps is swollen. In 1964, before the Vietnam buildup, the U.S. Army com-prised 864,000 enlisted men and 41,000 officers, for an-officer-to-troops ratio of roughly 1:21.1. The number of generals was 497 (.0005 percent of the troops), fewer than the number of active duty Mexican generals in 1951.[6]

Ironically, Miguel Alemán, the president who did the most to reduce military influence in politics, is responsible for some of the increase in the proportion of generals to troops. More important, he tarnished his reputation by politicizing the promotion process.[7] Alemán averaged seventy-six promotions to general and sixty-six to colonel yearly. The figures are not much different from those of his

TABLE 7-1.   Mexican Military Personnel, by Rank,
1920, 1930, and 1951

Rank	Year of Data (%)		
	1920	1930	1951
General	.6	.5	1.2
Officer	14.0	13.0	14.0
Troops	85.0	86.0	85.0
Total	99.6	99.5	100.2

Note: Totals do not add up to 100 due to rounding.

predecessor, General Avila Camacho, but are significantly higher than those of his successor, Ruiz Cortines, who averaged only thirty-six and forty-one. It is also clear from the data that Alemán is the only president since 1946 to have ordered more promotions to general than to colonel; in fact, he promoted more officers to the rank of general in one year than López Mateos did during his entire administration. From 1958 to 1970 the rate of promotions to both ranks remained rather stable, significantly lower than previous levels. Under Echeverría an extraordinary upsurge in promotions occurred: from an average of only thirteen promotions to general yearly by his predecessor to thirty-one.[8] Echeverría also doubled the rate of promotions to colonel, thus increasing for himself and his immediate successor the pool of officers eligible for the rank of general. Nevertheless, López Portillo returned the pattern of promotions to that of Echeverría's predecessors; he averaged 16 generals and 27 colonels during his administration (see Exhibit 7-1.).

According to Phyllis Walker, the

Alemán administration's military policies generated considerable resentment among the institution's established leaders and, in effect, failed to maintain the balance that had ensured the gradual depolitization of the institution. In by-passing the aging revolutionary generals, effectively forcing the retirement of many, and promoting and appointing professionally trained young officers to key military posts, including the presidential chief of staff, Alemán alienated many of the key military leaders who had been critical in professionalization efforts. Because of the allegedly arbitrary process in selecting new military leaders, newly promoted young officers who occupied many top command and administrative posts were disparagingly called los generales de dedo. Consequently, by the early 1950s, Alemán's policies threatened to renew politization of the military.[9]

Walker is not alone in her opinions. Another source recalls Alemán's promotion decisions as scandalous, and much talk centered on who was actually in charge of the Secretariat of National Defense: General Limón or the chief of staff, General Santiago P. Piña Soria.[10] The facts bear out Walker's

Exhibit 7-1
Promotions to Colonel and General in the Mexican Army and Air Force, 1939–1983

Year	Colonel	General	Administration
1939	31	22	Cárdenas
1941	63	77	Avila Camacho
1946	74	72	
1947	50	87	Alemán
1948	75	64	
1949	53	101	
1950	—	—	
1951	103	87	
1952	48	40	
1953	81	59	Ruiz Cortines
1954	108	51	
1955	23	60	
1956	30	40	
1957	52	60	
1958	18	12	
1959	17	11	López Mateos
1960	25	26	
1961	18	5	
1962	9	10	
1963	18	7	
1964	27	17	
1965	23	10	Díaz Ordaz
1966	6	5	
1967	24	12	
1968	40	31	
1969	27	15	
1970	29	11	
1971	49	42	Echeverría
1972	50	40	
1973	51	16	
1974	44	17	
1975	50	38	
1976	57	39	
1977	29	24	López Portillo
1978	39	16	
1979	31	17	
1980	34	18	
1981	15	8	
1982	16	13	
1983	27 (est.)	21 (est.)	de la Madrid

(continued)

Exhibit 7-1 (*continued*)

Sources: *Revista de Ejército y Fuerza Aérea*, November–December issues,
1955–1979; Secretaría de Defensa Nacional, *Memorias* (various years);
Senado, *Diario de los Debates* (various years); Senado, *Memorias* (various
years); Secretaría de Gobernación, *Cuarto informe de gobierno, anexo 1,
estadístico histórico* (Mexico, 1980); Banamex, *México Social* (Mexico:
Banamex, 1983).

Note: All regular promotions occur November 20. Because the president
takes office December 1, it is his predecessor who promotes the officers in
the inaugural year of a presidential term.

assertion that the number of promotions, especially at the rank of general,
were substantial. However, the qualitative record is somewhat different.

Among the military zone commanders appointed during Alemán's administration—we have information on approximately a third—at least two-thirds of
those on whom we have data were revolutionary combat veterans, and all but
one were political-military officers, who had some or considerable political
experience. The remaining third had no political experience, and their revolutionary credentials are unknown. The fact is, most of the officers Alemán
appointed as his *top field commanders* were experienced combat veterans born
in the 1890s, a decade prior to his own generation. These men included three
former chiefs of staff, and such officers as Joaquín Amaro, former defense
minister, the central figure in the professionalization program Walker refers to
and, most important, *the* senior division general on active duty; and Matías
Ramos Santos, former subsecretary of national defense, field commander from
the 1920s through 1946, president of the PNR under Cárdenas, and secretary
of defense in 1952. Among his field commanders, Alemán also included such
notable transition officers as Adrián Castrejón and Bonifacio Salinas Leal, the
youngest brigadier in the Mexican army in 1929, both of whom rejected their
revolutionary ranks of general and major, respectively, and attended the newly
reconstituted Colegio Militar.

At the level of the Secretariat of National Defense, Alemán appointed as
secretary Gilberto R. Limón, who had been director of military education
under Cárdenas and of the Colegio Militar under Avila Camacho, and in 1945
subsecretary of defense. His two subsecretaries, Generals Aúreo Lino Calles
Pardo and Gabriel Leyva Velázquez, were political-military officers. All three
were revolutionary veterans. Alemán's department heads were similar in background, and most were brigade generals.

A year-by-year examination of Alemán's promotions also reflects a similar
pattern. That is, during his administration, many senior officers were promoted to division rank. However, he also promoted a number of important
junior officers, members of the first generation of professionally trained men
from the HCM, including Rosendo Flores Cital, Federico Amaya Rodríguez,
Hermenegildo Cuenca Díaz, José Clark Flores, and Luis Alamillo Flores, Jr.
Most of their early-1920s classmates did not obtain important staff posts or

zone commands until the 1960s and 1970s (see Appendix A). Of the six officers, Alemán appointed three to important staff positions. The first, Colonel José de Jesús Clark Flores, directed communications from 1947 to 1951. He was promoted to brigadier general in 1949 after only three years in grade, two years fewer than legally required for such a rise in rank (he did have a civil engineering degree and special training in U.S. military schools). The second officer, Hermenegildo Cuenca Díaz, one of the first ESG graduates to serve at the Secretariat of National Defense, was promoted to colonel by Avila Camacho on November 12, 1946. However, Alemán, whom he had come to know as chief of presidential special intelligence from 1940 to 1946, raised his rank to brigadier general on December 22, 1948, and violated the promotion law a second time by giving him two-star rank on September 23, 1952. He became chief of staff in 1951, at the age of forty-nine. The third officer, Miguel Angel Sánchez Lamego, a distinguished student and graduate of the French war college, took over the cartographic department in 1949, a position he retained for twenty years. With the exception of Cuenca Díaz, who of course later became secretary of national defense, none held the most significant department heads under Alemán.

How, then, did Alemán acquire a negative reputation and, perhaps more important, why did he go on a promotion "spree"? It must not be forgotten that Alemán radicalized Mexican civil-military relations when he came into office, extraordinarily decreasing military political officeholding. He may well have used promotions to balance the rapid drop off in officer representation in civilian political posts. His focus was not on line commands but staff bureaucracy, especially presidential and specialized staff positions. The image Alemán's administration conveyed is the result of numerous, notable cases, not necessarily an across-the-board pattern. The cases were highlighted by the fact that his presidential chief of staff, General Piña, was exceptionally visible. And the president's arrogant abuse of the promotion laws assured a negative image.

Senate promotion records tell the story of General Piña. On September 4, 1947, the upper house approved his promotion (recommended January 16) to the rank of colonel in the infantry. Two years later, without proper time in grade, the Senate approved his promotion to brigadier general. In 1952, as part of the regular September promotions, three months before leaving office, Alemán recommended him for two-star rank.[11] However, instead of the Alemán-dominated Senate Defense Committee—controlled by two close political friends of the president and Colonel Alfonso Corona del Rosal, who himself had received a special promotion from President Avila Camacho and would be beholden to Alemán for promotions affecting his own career—a committee dominated by career officers and revolution veterans examined the nominee's credentials.[12] The preeminent member was General Jacinto B. Treviño, who had been a major commander in the Revolution and was a mentor to numerous political-military officers. Other members were Rafael E. Melgar, who had risen to brigade general during the Revolution, and Rear Admiral Rigoberto Otal Briseño, a career naval officer and a former naval zone commander who rose to oficial mayor in 1958.[13]

The committee members considered Piña's case not as an individual promotion but as representative of Alemán's violations. Citing army regulations requiring five years in rank before promotion to general, they declared that earlier such nominations had demonstrated obvious favoritism. They also noted that the president had sent out a circular suggesting that time in rank was not a prerequisite of promotion.[14] Otal Briseño urged the committee to recommend rejection to the full Senate because the army was "saturated with generals" and other officers, and that it would be disastrous to disregard regulations.[15]

When the committee made its recommendation to the Senate on November 7, 1953, heated debate ensued, one of the few such occasions. The general promotion policy had a thorough airing, as did the probable effect of the Senate's refusing to go along with the president. One prominent civilian senator, Aquiles Elorduy, a friend and professor of Alemán's, settled the matter: "I am a friend of Mister Piña Soria, but I never vote for friendship, I vote with the law. If this nomination is irregular, then it should be refused. That is all I ask." The vote was 50 to 1 against approval, and 51 to 0 against another recommendation for a promotion to colonel for the same reasons.[16]

Alemán further abused the promotion policy by giving special consideration to close friends from his student days at the National University. This occurred with Jorge Rico Schroeder, who rose from colonel after just sixteen years in the military legal service to brigadier general in 1949, and brigade general in 1952, which violated military law.[17] The president repeated this procedure with another classmate, who as his attorney general of military justice, became a two-star general after only three years in grade. Finally, and most rankling to older career officers was the case of Alemán's confidant and secretary of the presidency, Rogerio de la Selva y Escoto, a naturalized citizen who had not even arrived in Mexico until 1922, who with no previous military experience received the rank of colonel of military justice in 1951. These and similar instances explain the president's well-deserved reputation for scandalous promotion practices.

Presidential intervention in the promotion process, especially actions contravening internal military requirements, too easily politicizes the military, even in a one-party-dominant system. An indicator of the Mexican military's politization in regard to the rank of general is the disparity in years it takes individual junior officers to attain that rank. A means of testing the universal application of promotion criteria is to analyze the length of time an officer requires to reach the rank of colonel, the key stepping-stone to the rank of brigadier general and higher. Table 7-2 illustrates promotion patterns to colonel from 1946 through the early 1980s, when the youngest of our generals received their promotions to this rank. Three important patterns can be discerned.

The first pattern is that regular military officers have required, on average, about twenty-five years to reach the rank of colonel. Individuals serving after 1946 who rose to the rank of colonel in less than twenty years did so as Revolution veterans whose promotion rates were not regulated. This is why

TABLE 7-2.   Mexican Generals' Years in Service
before Attaining Colonelcy, by Generation

Years in Service before Attaining Colonelcy	Birth Cohort (%)				
	1870–1899	*1900–1909*	*1910–1919*	*1920–1929*	*1930+*
1–14	42	0	0	0	0
15–20	42	0	0	0	0
21–25	6	20	14	19	90
26–	6	80	86	81	10

more than four-fifths of such officers were born before 1900. The second pattern is the considerable regularity of promotions for the majority of officers reaching the rank of general over a long period of time. Whether an officer was born in the first, second, or third decade of the twentieth century, he generally required twenty-five to thirty years to reach the rank of colonel. The third pattern is that for officers born since 1930, a radical change in time in grade occurs in order to make colonel. Officers born prior to 1930 required, on average, five or more years to make the grade of colonel than did about nine in ten of those born after 1930.

The promotion records of the generals in our sample suggests that modern military officers, even those reaching the rank of general, are promoted with considerable regularity, so much so that it becomes fairly easy to predict their promotion dates to brigadier general. In the past, analysts have stressed the irregularity of the promotion system.[18] I argue that the most important finding of these data is the consistency in the promotion pattern among those who have been most successful in the officer corps. Unlike civilian leadership, where people in their thirties can vault to top posts, no significant variations in time in rank among general officers exists.[19]

In the past decade, the typical promotion process follows the following timetable. Upon graduation from the HCM, an officer serves two years as a second lieutenant and then three years as a first lieutenant. To be eligible for the rank of lieutenant colonel, an officer needs at least fourteen years on active duty and must then pass a computer-graded academic examination.[20] The promotion is essential for reaching senior officer rank. At this juncture in an officer's career, military politics begin to play a more important role. At times in the 1970s, younger officers denounced higher-rank promotions as based on *compadrazgo* (friendship).[21] According to Michael Dziedzic, the opinion of the secretary of defense becomes critical because it is he who decides who will obtain these slots.[22] The president does not intervene in the process below the rank of colonel, in theory or practice.[23]

Franklin Margiotta found in interviews with Mexican officers that they were proud of the apparent fairness of merit-based promotions. He believed that the typical promotion pattern was eight years (including HCM time) for second captain, eleven years for first captain, fourteen years for major, eighteen years for lieutenant colonel, and twenty-two years for colonel.[24] To become a three-star general, would require approximately thirty-five to forty years on active duty.[25] These figures square with the promotion records I have examined for Mexican generals and for all officers. These and the official promotion figures are important because they suggest that the time a general requires to reach the rank of lieutenant colonel tends to be very similar to that of an officer who would retire at that rank.

The rank of colonel is a key milestone to becoming a general. At this rank, the secretary of defense recommends officers to be promoted to the president, and the president in turn recommends officers to be promoted to colonel and to general to the Senate. The Senate's selections for the rank of colonel are based on recommendations of a board of senior officers. Also, promotion to colonel requires time in service to be considered. The unstated requirements include being visible, being in the good graces of generals who are on friendly terms with the secretary of defense, being recognized as a team player, and being considered wholly subordinate to the system.[26] Daniel Mora noted that third-year students at the ESG contacted former commanders and personal acquaintances who could influence their assignments because, he suggests, many assignments "are made on a personal recommendation or upon a personal request by a commander or staff officer."[27] Similar efforts would be important to ensuring promotion. For promotion to general, the same criteria apply, except that no minimum years in service are necessary, only time in grade between promotions.[28]

Positioning oneself within a bureaucracy is part of the promotion game. In this sense, the military is no different from any other organization or government agency. But in Mexico, because top staff positions, including that of the secretary of national defense and secretary of the navy, are held by career military only, it appears that only military officers influence the promotion process. Even given a characteristic that tends to isolate the military from civilian influences, two means exist through which civilian politicians can interfere with an officer's climb up the leadership ladder.

The most important source of civilian influence, as the abuses of Miguel Alemán imply, is the presidency. A president potentially can intervene in three ways. First, in extreme circumstances he can circumvent the organic law of the military, contravening actual regulations by promoting people who do not meet minimal requirements. Second, he can promote people who even though they meet formal requirements may not be the most deserving. Because this has to do with subjective judgment and may not be widely practiced, it would be difficult to detect during any six-year period. Its results are likely to be balanced out by a different chief executive's prejudices or those of a national defense secretary, in successive administrations. For example, General Arévalo earned a reputation for seeing to the welfare of many personal friends, especially in the cavalry (his own specialty) at a faster than customary rate, which eventuated in young officers in higher ranks than their former superiors—not a morale-boosting circumstance.[29] Third, it is quite possible that a president can employ his promotion authority to reduce or increase the size of the officer corps in correlation to his own feelings of political security and legitimacy.

Our examination of the promotion records, as suggested above, reveals that since Alemán no president has abused his authority to contravene promotion laws for personal or political reasons. In fact, Senate records show no similar cases since 1953. The second form of influence does occur but is a natural part of the politics of any agency. The third form of presidential interference can be measured quite explicitly. It can be reasonably hypothesized that the president uses military promotions above the rank of lieutenant colonel to assure greater loyalty among the officer corps. It is only natural that a president would like to see promotions to the rank of general go to the steadfastly faithful officers, and key staff assignments and zone commands to generals in whom he has personal confidence.[30]

Nevertheless, as the loyalty of the armed forces has become a given in the Mexican polity over the years, and as its professional leadership has become increasingly separate from that of civilian politicians, individual presidents have not had to concern themselves with the armed forces' loyalty to them personally, nor are they likely to know personally very many high-ranking officers. Although presidents know more officers than most politicians do, because they meet many zone commanders during *giras* (working trips), they meet them after being elected president or during the campaign, typically not before. Consequently, only in times of relative political instability, or when the president perceives the situation to be extremely unstable, would it be necessary for him to skew the promotion process for the sake of loyalty. The technique was used by Porfirio Díaz, who after his risky but successful rebellion against the government under the Plan of Tuxtepec, made many of his collaborators generals in 1877. In the twentieth century, after his successful coup d'état, Victoriano Huerta promoted nearly every state governor whose fealty was unquestionable to the next highest general rank, many of them to division general.[31] A similar method to ensure military loyalty was used again in the 1920s after successive failed military rebellions.

In the cases cited above, the legitimacy of the individual leader as well as the system itself could be described as tenuous. Exhibit 7-1 presents some interesting patterns of presidential influence in the promotion process since 1946. It can be examined from two perspectives. First, the year witnessing the largest combined number of promotions of generals and colonels within each administration might suggest something about the president's state of mind. Second, a comparative analysis of each administration's promotion records could be revealing. Using the first approach, from 1946 through 1982, six years stand out: 1951, 1954, 1960, 1968, 1976, and 1978; of these, three or possibly four are politically significant.

Promotions for 1954 and 1978 do not appear to be politically connected. The highest promotion levels by López Portillo are not actually out of sync with the other promotion years. Despite serious economic and political problems, he never perceived the presidency to be at risk in connection with the armed forces' loyalty. His promotions show considerable consistency, and the lowest rates for many years. The 1954 cycle of promotions is extremely large, in fact, second only to Alemán's penultimate year. In both 1953 and 1954, promotion cycles were large, especially for colonels, suggesting not an immediate political crisis but perhaps a desire by the president to correct the extreme imbalance in promotions engineered under Alemán. In other words, in the first two years Ruiz Cortines may have been promoting deserving lieutenant colonels passed over by Alemán while maintaining a fairly large group of promotions to general from 1953 through 1957, to placate the exceedingly large Alemán-generated pool.

The other years, however, especially 1960, 1968, and 1976, correspond closely to important political events. In 1959 a major railroad strike occurred, and the army was called out to break it. President López Mateos increased promotions to general in 1960 by nearly 150 percent over 1959. The 1968 promotions are related to the events of Tlatelolco Plaza and the loyalty there displayed by the military. Díaz Ordaz, who had maintained a consistently low pattern of promotions from 1965 through 1967, suddenly doubled the combined promotions to colonel and general that year. The year 1976 is revealing for several reasons. It is the only important promotion cycle that occurred during the last year of a presidential administration. Typically, the end of a presidential term is characterized by a decline or continuity in promotions, not an increase.

The second perspective, looking at an administration as a whole, provides many insights into the Echeverría years. Two important characteristics of Echeverría's attitudes toward the military are evident in the promotion data. First, he consistently promoted more officers than any president since López Mateos, which suggests something important was going on his entire term. Second, although 1976 is his highest year, the other years are not very different from it. The *Revista de Ejército y Fuerza Aérea* proudly announced that in 1971 the president had promoted more officers than any predecessor since the 1956 promotion law went into effect, a fact borne out by the data.[32] The official magazine typically does not discuss promotions, so the announcement was meant to make the officer corps aware that the president was instituting a change in policy: officers could count on more promotions than before. The figures jibe with the decrease of time in rank for promotion to colonel (see table 7-2) among officers born after 1930, those eligible for that rank about the time Echeverría came into office.

It has been said that from 1971 to 1976 hundreds of generals and intermediate and low-ranking officers were discharged from the army to make way for younger men.[33] One source alleges that 486 elderly generals were retired, veterans of the Revolution, in order to allow frustrated middle-aged officers access to the top ranks.[34] Stephen Wager puts the figure at a more reasonable 354 generals.[35] Although the precise number of retired officers cannot be ascertained from public records, the number of generals replaced can be. The reality is that Echeverría did not come anywhere close to replacing the officers he retired, regardless of whose figures are used; only 192 officers reached the rank of general during his administration. What the data do make apparent, however, is that he more than doubled the number of such promotions during the previous and succeeding administrations, a fact that illuminates the extent to which his promotions were out of the ordinary.

Some observers believe Echeverría's level of promotions was an attempt to alter the composition of the officer corps. It can also be argued that from his first presidential year, when confronted by right-wing dissidents in his own administration, the involvement of military representatives in the Halcones' student persecution, and the extensive antiguerrilla warfare campaign in Guerrero using large percentages of the army, Echeverría thought his own position and that of his administration was in considerable political danger. These elements, combined with increased urban terrorism and guerrilla activity generally, the repercussions from his ill-conceived land reform in northwest Mexico, and the serious economic malaise of the devaluation in 1976 sustained his perception for all six years.[36]

The danger of a president's using the promotion process to reward military loyalty in a political crisis is that it creates an expectation in the military of a payback for its allegiance to civil authorities.[37] Allegiance is something learned over a long period, both within the military socialization and professionalization process and in the political culture in general; it is not something engendered through a system of personalized rewards. If abused by future presidents, such manipulations of the promotion cycle could lead to dangerous repercussions within the officer corps.

In the de la Madrid administration, the president did not intervene in the promotion process, nor in the administration of López Portillo.[38] The secretary of defense provided the president with the service record of each officer to be promoted to colonel or general. Among the lists of eligible officers, on the basis of time in grade, the secretary of defense made his own recommendations. On occasion the president challenged a recommendation of the secretary of national defense, suggesting that an officer *on the eligible list* appeared more deserving of promotion than others on the list. On rare occasions the president asked that an officer be held over until the next promotion cycle if he thought the officer not yet deserving of a promotion.[39]

The president and possibly other civilian authorities can also become involved in the internal machinery of the military through another mechanism. If for some reason an officer believes he has been abused by the system, he may seek recourse through judicial or executive authority. A recent case came to light on the editorial page of *Proceso*. Frigate Captain (equivalent to lieutenant colonel) Jesús Armando Lara Preciado explained that a presidential sanction, for his responsibility in a naval collision, had removed him from the promotion process from 1972 to 1974. Although he completed the sanction, naval authorities turned it into an indefinite punishment by refusing to hear his appeals. He turned to the federal courts, which ordered the navy to reinstate him in the promotion cycles. The navy ignored the order, and on three occasions Captain Lara presented a petition of "abuse of authority" against Admiral Miguel N. Gómez Ortega, the navy secretary. The navy retired him on April 1, 1987, for reaching the age limit of his rank.[40]

Captain Lara's resort to judicial authorities, and his later appeal to the legislative branch of government did not bring about civilian intervention into the military's internal affairs, even though his case had unquestioned merit under federal law. His treatment illustrates the unwillingness of civilian authorities, even when the military acted illegally against a presidential order and a court decree, to intervene. This case suggests, as do civilian attitudes toward military moonlighting, that such matters are to be resolved within the military.

Although the Senate refused to tolerate abuses on the part of both the secretary of national defense and the president in recommending promotions contrary to military regulations in 1953, the only other known case of Senate intervention in military processes occurred when an officer's revolutionary credentials were questioned.[41] During the Revolution several prominent career officers switched sides, especially from rebel forces or forces loyal to the government to Victoriano Huerta. Shifting loyalties involving conflicts between Venustiano Carranza and Alvaro Obregón, and the rebellions of 1923, 1927, and 1929 have never been used to question an officer's loyalty; indeed, not only were numerous participants reincorporated and promoted but several became secretaries of national defense. The suggestion that an officer had become a Huertista, had joined forces that murdered the constitutional president, was never treated tolerantly. For example, in 1941 the promotion of Leobardo Ruiz Camarillo, an important military figure in the 1940s and 1950s, to brigade general, was hotly debated and delayed over the question of whether he had supported Huerta, as a cadet or immediately after leaving the Colegio Militar in 1914 before joining the Constitutionalists as an artillery captain on November 20.[42]

Variables in Promotion

One of the major arguments being offered in this section is that the promotion rates between ranks have become regularized. However, a small percentage of officers achieved the rank of colonel, thus making them eligible to become generals earlier than their peers. A number of variables that potentially might affect the rate of promotion, and what senior officers in charge of the promotion boards themselves value, are worth examining. These include level of military training, combat experience, service specialty, previous posts, and political and personal ties.

The impact of education on upward mobility in the officer corps is surprisingly limited. Although it has been asserted that a key to further promotion and entrance into the armed elite is a diploma from the ESG and a teaching stint on the staff of one of the military schools, those qualifications were more important in determining officer eligibility for promotion to the rank of general, than the pace at which all officers reached such rank.

At an earlier period in the armed forces, undoubtedly, education was unimportant because success in the Revolution determined the rate and range of one's rise in the military. As an illustration, of the generals serving after 1946 who made colonel in fewer than fifteen years, two-thirds did not obtain a military or advanced technical education. (This, by the way, is not much different from their civilian peers in the political world; of the prominent politicians who were in the compatible age group, about three-quarters had completed only a preparatory education or lower, slightly less than their military counterparts.) These revolutionary officers, all of whom saw combat, accounted for all but four of the uneducated generals in our sample.

Among more recent generals who are graduates of the ESG, a slightly higher correlation exists between those receiving their promotion before twenty-five years and those taking more than twenty-five years. This is largely due to the military's having somewhat speeded up the promotion process and regularized it since the mid-1950s, a period during which graduation from the ESG became increasingly necessary for successful advancement to general rank.[43] It is worth noting that all four army generals with Ph.D.'s are in the faster track of promotions to colonel, suggesting, as is true of their civilian counterparts, the increasing importance of education in general, and advanced education specifically.

A slightly more significant variable in the rapidity of promotions, one that sets apart many officers pursuing successful careers as generals, is technical training abroad, primarily in the United States. Eighteen percent more officers in the fast track than officers in the typical promotion cycle have been educated abroad.

As is true for most armies, war does more to increase the overall promotion rate than any other variable. Generals in the U.S. Army believe the key to advancement is serving as a combat commander.[44] In Mexico this was doubly so because the roots of the post-Revolution army were the unorganized guerrilla forces and the popularly recruited Constitutional Army. Furthermore, political leaders, many of whom were veterans of the Revolution and had pursued careers within the armed forces, stressed their revolutionary origins in politics. Symbolically, combat experience always received high visibility in the careers of Mexico's secretaries of national defense, all of whom were veterans of the 1910 Revolution. When age made it impossible for a secretary to have served in the Revolution—the last such official was General Hermenegildo Cuenca Díaz (1970–1976)—post-revolutionary combat veterans replaced them, as was true of Cuenca Díaz's successor, General Felíx Galván López (1976–1982), who had fought against the rebellion of Saturnino Cedillo in 1939.[45] Juan Arévalo Gardoqui, appointed national defense secretary in 1982, was the first secretary without combat experience, as is the case of Salinas's appointee, General Antonio Riviello Bazán. The last officer from the Revolution to serve on active duty was Division General Juan José Gastélum Salcido, subsecretary of national defense from 1964 to 1970.[46]

Combat experience has always been important politically as well as within the armed forces. For example, of Porfirio Díaz's generation (1820–1839), 83 percent had fought the French, participated in the Liberal-Conservative conflicts in the 1850s, or resisted the U.S. invasion in 1846. In fact, two-thirds of his peers, as very young officers or enlisted soldiers, had fought against the

United States. Nearly all combat veterans had fought the French. In the following generation (1840–1859), most of whom were too young to have fought, one in five were veterans, and among those old enough to have fought the French, four-fifths had done so.

The Revolution should have been a more universal experience for Mexicans among the post-1920s political generations than the French invasion was for Mexico's leadership after 1884. What is remarkable is that although the Revolution continued on and off for nearly a decade, resulting directly and indirectly in the deaths of nearly 10 percent of the population, fewer political leaders from military and civilian backgrounds, in percentage terms, fought in it than did Díaz's generation in earlier conflicts. For example, among Madero's generation, 35 percent fought in the Revolution on the side of the rebels or later the Constitutionalists; 2 percent fought on both sides; 8 percent supported Díaz, but more than half stayed out of the fighting altogether. The true revolutionary generation, of course, is that of Generals Obregón and Plutarco Elías Calles, of which more than two-thirds fought in the Revolution, almost all on the side of the victorious rebels.

The irregular promotion process of revolutionary officers speeded up their overall rise to the rank of general. Of the officers who reached colonel in fewer than fifteen years, who were still serving in top military assignments after 1946, only one was not a combat veteran. Of officers promoted to colonel in fifteen to twenty years, more than two-thirds were combat veterans, all except one from the Revolution. In the two promotion tracks that account for 75 percent of all officers, very few fought in the Revolution, or for that matter in combat situations in the 1920s and 1930s.

Analysts have overemphasized the importance of combat to the promotion process long after it became passé, attributing more importance to the symbolism of the secretary of national defense's combat experience and insufficient attention to the rank of general. Frank Brandenburg, one of the most perceptive U.S. analysts of Mexican politics, asserted that in the late 1960s generalships had been denied virtually all officers who were not Revolution veterans. The data presented in table 7-3, however, unquestionably refute the assertion. If he were referring only to officers born before 1900, his statement would be

TABLE 7-3.   Combat Experience of Mexican Generals, by Generation

Decade of Birth	Generals with Combat Experience (%)			
	Revolution	Post-Revolution	World War II	None
1880–1889	97	3	DNA	0
1890–1899	99	1	0	0
1900–1909	19	34	4	43
1910–1919	DNA	15	3	82
1920+	DNA	DNA	3	97

Key: DNA = Does not apply.

completely accurate. By the 1950s and 1960s officers born in the early 1900s were reaching the rank of general. Even for the 1900s generation, nearly half had no combat experience. By 1910 veterans of the Cristero movements and the military rebellions against the government became the new combat veterans, but they could hardly be considered dominant because they accounted for only 15 percent of all generals. By the 1920s generation, combat as a shared experience among generals disappeared.

In part, these data explain why combat has not been essential to rapid promotion in the armed forces, at least since 1946. Combat is a significant experience that not only develops a shared set of values but creates a sense of trust and loyalty among those who served together.[47] Few combat experiences were shared by civilian and military leaders because fewer than one in twenty civilian politicians after 1940 had seen combat. Examples of these relationships can be found throughout all generations of the military leadership. However, once such experience no longer is the norm, its significance for promotion per se, and rapid promotion specifically, dissipates. In fact, the percentage of officers with combat experience of any kind in the faster of the two *institutionalized* promotion tracks actually is *smaller* than in the slower track. Combat, after the Revolution, has not been a significant variable in determining rapid promotion to general.

I argue that in the early 1970s military involvement in antiguerrilla operations replaced traditional combat. Antiguerrilla warfare could be seen as a modern measure of a Mexican officer's combat experience. Since the late 1970s, especially during the 1980s, antidrug campaigns came much closer in scope and intensity to actual combat experience of an older generation of officers than did the suppression of the guerrilla movements. One analyst of the drug trade, Richard B. Craig, agrees with this assessment: "It is in the *campo*, not against system-threatening guerrillas, but by combatting drug cultivators and traffickers," that the army obtains its combat experience.[48] However, at least since 1988, the army has essentially withdrawn from the armed confrontation phase. Still, combat, measured in terms of troop readiness, retains considerable prestige. The most capable elements in the army, in terms of combat readiness, are assigned to the presidential guard, which has its own chain of command, answering to a brigade commander.[49]

As I suggested in an earlier chapter, large numbers of troops and officers were engaged in the drug fight, but as yet most of these individuals have not yet risen to the rank of general. A classic example of an influential officer deeply involved in this form of combat is General Jaime Palacios Guerrero, appointed department head in 1989, who not only was air attaché to Colombia in 1976–1977, where he learned firsthand about combating drug dealers, but served as chief of staff of Cóndor Task Force IV in 1979, before commanding the Cóndor Task Force I from 1982 to 1986, an unusually long field command assignment.[50]

Although little empirical research has been done on the Mexican military generally, no analysis whatsoever has been published on the individual military occupational specialties within the army, or on the differences between the army, air force, and navy. In reality, air force officers can be treated as a military occupational specialty within the army because the department of the air force is under the secretary of national defense, and much of the professional education is handled within army technical and staff schools.

If the generals in our sample are categorized as to specialty—infantry, artillery, cavalry, engineering, medicine, administration, communications, and air—the following pattern of promotion to colonel emerge. Formally, the army itself has five categories: infantry, artillery, cavalry, armored, and engineers.[51] If we discard the two pre-1940s promotion tracks, 39 percent of the generals were in the faster of the two remaining tracks. A correlation exists between specialty and fast promotion. Interestingly, air force officers are promoted much faster than their peers in other specialties: exactly two-thirds reached the rank of colonel in fewer than twenty-five years, in percentages almost twice as large as all other categories. Following in importance are artillery officers, more than half of whom were promoted in the faster track. In contrast, infantry officers, who make up the bulk of the army and the officer corps, are promoted in the fast track only a fourth of the time, the slowest category except for communications officers, all of whom take the slower track. It is also interesting that naval admirals also reach the rank of captain (naval rank equivalent to colonel) in the faster track compared with their army peers.

There are two explanations of the variable promotion record. One involves the specialty's representation at the highest ranks, a variable that does not affect air force and naval promotions. The other is level of professionalization within the specialty or service.

The first explanation can be tested by analyzing top staff officers at the Secretariat of National Defense. Since President Salinas took office, artillery officers have held a fifth of these positions. Although infantry actually outnumbers artillery by one individual and cavalry equals artillery, among these posts, infantry is overwhelmingly the largest army specialty and cavalry the next largest. The secretariat does not make the precise distribution of military occupational specialties public. One military source estimated approximately 50 percent infantry, 30 percent cavalry, 10 percent artillery, and 10 percent all others.[52] On the basis of HCM graduates, a more accurate idea of the distributions can be obtained. The graduating class of 1969, which will reach colonel by the mid-1990s, is distributed as follows: 55 percent infantry, 18 percent cavalry, 9 percent artillery, 12 percent engineering, and 12 percent administration.[53] Among the ESG class of 1979–1982, raw material for most future high-ranking officers, which will also provide the colonels and brigadier generals in the 1990s, 58 percent were infantry; 28 percent, cavalry; 8 percent, artillery; and 6 percent, engineers.[54]

Artillery as a specialization within the army has been overrepresented in the top posts at the Secretariat of National Defense since 1982.[55] Why? I believe it is not determined by the occupational specialty of the secretary and his immediate subordinates, a situation resulting from fortuitous circumstances, because no defense secretary since 1946 has come from the artillery arm. Instead, a possible explanation is level of professionalization, measured by advanced training and education. Generals with the highest level of education are from the artillery.[56] This complements an earlier point: the most intellectually capable cadets are channeled into artillery. Only 12 percent of generals with an artillery specialty have not graduated from the ESG and/or the Colegio de Defensa Nacional. Other highly educated specialties compared with all generals are naval engineering and the air force, with 72 percent and 69 percent, respectively, having graduated from one or both of those institutions. Artillery, in the early years, was considered the most technical of traditional military fields, thus requiring a higher level of education for success in it. Another way of examining a specialty's professionalization is through officers who teach, recalling, as we found earlier, how important the academies are to recruitment, especially at the top. If we exclude the small technical specialties, such as medicine and communications, where teaching is almost a necessity, the specialties with the highest percentage of experienced instructors are the navy, air force, and army artillery.

Although the artillery arm is best represented in the higher ranks, according to Wager, the cavalry is considered the army elite, its most desirable specialty.[57] Among defense secretaries, the cavalry arm has done quite well. Although Salinas's national defense secretary is infantry, the defense secretaries in 1982 and 1976 were cavalry officers, as was one other secretary since 1946. Cavalry has been very well represented considering it accounts for less than 20 percent of the younger officer corps. Also, although I can offer no explanation, Alemán's excessive promotions, especially of colonels, highly overrepresented the cavalry.

Naval officers who reach the rank of admiral differ from their army peers as a group because they are better educated and their teaching level is extraordinarily high. That nine in ten teach can be explained in part by the nature of the sample: the vast majority of naval officers are younger than the generals. Navy personnel also are more likely to have been educated abroad, a variable that we found to have had some importance in fast-track promotions. More than two-thirds studied outside Mexico; only a little more than a third of all general officers did so. Further, two-thirds of all admirals had served abroad as attachés; only a fifth of top generals had done so. Also, three times as many admirals as their army peers had served in the United States. None of the naval officers are mustangs, which in terms of promotion time, would slow down their overall promotion rates.

Air force officers, although having much closer ties to the army historically, share certain similarities with the navy officers, which again might generally be associated with faster promotion rates. They too have a much stronger teaching record; approximately four-fifths of air force generals have taught at the air college, the HCM, or applied schools. Like their naval colleagues, they have studied abroad in larger numbers, in fact, more so than any other major specialty or service, and again at rates higher in the United States than those of army officers.

The Mexican military is like any large organization in that certain assignments within it lead to greater chances for advancement. In the 1960s McAlister concluded that the most sought after posts because of the prestige and future prospects they offer included "duty with the presidential guard and the staffs of military schools and assignment to the general staff course at the Escuela Superior de Guerra. The career of a successful officer, that is, one who achieves general rank, will normally include all of these and with rare exceptions must include the latter."[58] The connection between teaching and the fast track has been demonstrated, as has the importance of teaching and ESG attendance to advancement and recruitment in general.

Positions other than teaching also bear on the careers of generals. McAlister mentions only one: service with the presidential staff. These troops and officers are under direct presidential command, and are responsible for protecting the president from not only external threats but, historically, disloyal military forces. The presidential staff functions as the president's own intelligence, administrative, and security agency. The presidential guard, armed troops, provide a combat capability that guarantees the security of the president, his residence, and related installations.[59] Not surprisingly, Miguel Alemán created the first presidential guard, withdrawing the 28th Infantry Battalion from Puebla on November 19, 1946, shortly before he took office; he designated it the 1st Presidential Guard Infantry Battalion on February 1, 1947. The presidential guard was incorporated into the military's organic law on October 3, 1952. Although it is true that a number of officers have commanded the presidential guard, doing so does not carry the weight of other types of positions in the careers of successful officers. For example, among the top national defense leaders in the Salinas administration, Riviello Bazán was with a commando group in 1953, and his oficial mayor, General Juárez Carreño, served in 1958 in the 2nd Infantry Battalion, and then as a group commander from 1982 to 1985. It is difficult to estimate, however, how many opportunities are available and which were taken advantage of by how many generals. It is noteworthy that considerable tension and resentment exists between the Secretariat of National Defense and the presidential staff.

One of the key plum positions that appeared in the fast track promotions of naval officers is prior service as an attaché. The post is considered prestigious not only because it positively affects one's career but because of the perquisites it entails: higher pay (generally more than most ambassadors), allowances, and travel.[60] The assignment is seen as a deserved reward.[61] The most important of these posts is as an assistant or full military attaché in the United States; it is as integral to the career of a secretary of defense as the ambassadorship to the United States is to careers in the Foreign Relations Secretariat (many ambassadors have gone on to become secretaries and assistant secretaries of foreign relations). Altogether, the number of military posts is limited. During the 1940s, 1950s, and 1960s, typically six or seven positions were available: Mexican embassies in the United States, Canada, France, and generally several South and Central American countries.[62] Naval attaché positions were somewhat different, depending on the country's importance to Mexico's navy.

Among leading generals, only 21 percent have been attachés. Yet, examination of the three post-revolution promotion tracks reveals the post's prominence in the faster track to generalship. Even the faster-track officers who reached colonelcy in fifteen to twenty years in the 1920s and 1930s, and who remained in top positions after 1946, were attachés half the time. The two more recent promotion tracks illustrate the difference. In the slower track, only 16 percent of the generals have been attachés, fewer than all generals combined, and only one in five has served in the United States or Canada. Among the colonels promoted to general in less than twenty-five years, however, 45 percent served in these posts, a third of whom spent time in the United States and Canada. It is also the case that a disproportionate number of naval and air force officers served in the United States and Canada compared to all generals.

The importance of the United States in the service careers of Mexican officers, because of shared technical and tactical influence, is understandable. On the other hand, officers conveying a strong pro-United States attitude are likely to suffer in the promotion process.[63] In President Salinas's administration, a number of his top generals have served in Mexico's military mission in the United States, including Enrique Cervantes Aguirre, who before being appointed director of military industries in 1988, was the army attaché in Washington, D.C.; Gildardo Alarcón López, who became chief of naval operations in 1989, served as naval attaché in the United States; the commander of naval air forces, Federico Carballo Jiménez, became the aide to the naval attaché in Washington, D.C., as did Arturo Cardona Marino, presidential chief of staff, to the army attaché. The secretary of national defense and his subsecretary in the prior administration had been military attachés in Spain and France respectively.

An additional career distinction, to which McAlister did not allude, arises in the disparity between staff and line officers. Although most graduates of the ESG are assigned initially to a military zone headquarters in the field, most return to the national defense staff headquarters within six to twelve months.[64] Service there, as noted earlier, is extremely useful to advancement. It is not, however, statistically related to the rapidity with which an officer reaches the rank of general but, rather, is an experience shared by many recent general officers. Still, the distinction between staff and line officers is worth examining.

Professionalization in Mexico over the twentieth century has increased the presence of the staff officer, at least in the top ranks (see table 7-4). For example, by 1926 General Joaquín Amaro, the man responsible for the initial thrust of military professionalization, already was using young officers trained abroad to help build a better general staff. When he created the Commission of Military Studies that year, he also established the Ministry of War general staff.[65] The general staff's existence provided an impetus to the increasing importance of staff officers relative to line officers; this can be seen in a sharp alteration of emphasis in career backgrounds from the pre-1900 to post-1900 generations of generals. By the 1900s generation, half or more of the officers reaching the rank of general were primarily staff officers. The figures are slightly higher if generals in the *other* category are included in staff because they are typically medical corps and military attorneys.

TABLE 7-4. Staff and Line Experience of Mexican Generals, by Generation

Organizational Position	Generation (%)					
	1880–1889	1890–1899	1900–1909	1910–1919	1920–1929	1930+
Staff	15	13	53	51	37	48
Line	79	85	35	36	48	38
Other	6	2	12	13	15	14

Among all the generals in our sample, slightly over half (53 percent) can be categorized as line officers. Wager believes that line officers, especially younger men who serve as battalion or cavalry squadron commanders, will be promoted at a faster rate.[66] His reasoning is that in the 1980s, fewer than one hundred battalions or regiments existed, thus rendering a commander highly visible and prestigious.[67] Between the sixth to eighth year after graduation from the ESG, most junior officers have had an opportunity to command. Indeed, some captains have sought the position of squadron commander because they can earn interest on advances for troop salaries.[68] Wager's assumption is natural, given the comparative importance of command in the U.S. Army. Maureen Mylander concludes that the sine qua non for a generalcy is a progression of troop commands, ideally, one tour at each grade level.[69] Although command assignments may lead to faster promotions for some Mexican officers overall, staff positions appear to be more advantageous. Only 38 percent of all generals in our sample, excluding medical and legal officers, could be classified as staff, but some 59 percent of fast-track generals followed staff careers, compared with 49 percent of slower-track generals. Staff careers are more significant as a trend than as a means of accelerated promotion.

The other considerable positional influence on the careers of a select number of officers is service on the presidential, as distinct from the general, staff. Assignment to the former, especially when repeated, is an introduction to a much more politically colored career. The presidential staff has a central role in planning the president's daily schedule and in his protection. It combines staff functions with functions like those of the U.S. Secret Service, which psychologically bolsters the military's prestige. As one top political figure argued, because the

president relies on the military for his everyday security and for setting up his schedule, this represents a tremendous amount of trust, or a manifestation of that trust in the military as an institution. It also represents the incorporation of military and civilian authority. In these two respects, I think it is extremely important and valuable to the civil and military relationship in Mexico.[70]

These functions also give a group of officers direct access to the president's activities. This trust, as in the case of civilian collaborators, has on at least one occasion been betrayed.[71] Junior officers having experience on the presidential staff typically end up in higher positions there, the most important of which, of course, is presidential chief of staff, the most influential political liaison between the president and the armed forces, particularly the army and air force. One observer commented, "It is really fair to say that the presidential chief of staff is the equivalent of a cabinet minister without portfolio."[72]

Interestingly, the preceding three presidential chiefs of staff, Generals Arturo Cardona Marino, Carlos Humberto Bermúdez Dávila, and Miguel Angel Godínez Bravo, were subchiefs of staff immediately prior to their appointments, having served as directors of security and logistics in the campaigns of the presidents who appointed them. Each had held another position on the presidential staff, and equally important, each had commanded troops in the presidential guard. Echeverría's chief of staff, General Jesús Castañeda Gutiérrez, followed a similar pattern, having commanded the 1st Presidential Guard Infantry Battalion before his 1970 appointment.

No other top military careers in the past two decades have had such a consistent pattern as the careers of presidential chiefs of staff. The career of Arturo Cardona Marino is illustrative. A gradudate of the HCM on January 1, 1953, as a second lieutenant of artillery, he was tapped for the ESG very soon afterward, graduating in 1959. Instead of serving in a typical military post, Cardona Marino was an adviser to civilian politicians in a few executive branch agencies. He then held several staff positions, most important of which was chief of adjutants in the administrative division of the Secretariat of National Defense, and then went to Washington, D.C., as an aide to Mexico's military attaché. Upon his return he again took on a civilian post, adviser to the National Executive Committee of the PRI, after which he commanded an infantry battalion. He then moved on to the more prestigious 1st Presidential Guard Infantry Battalion, and subsequently became private secretary to General Godínez, who had overlapped with him at the ESG, as chief of staff from 1979 to 1982. Cardona Marino rose to assistant chief of staff under his artillery classmate at HCM, General Bermúdez Dávila, in 1982.[73]

The other informal means of promotion, one that possibly might be the most influential but also the most difficult to ascertain, is personal contacts within and outside the military. Some analysts who believe that presidential influence is important to career advancement within the military have suggested that ties to or connections with the incoming president are critical to acquiring top positions during a particular administration.[74] Recent presidents have denied this, attributing such connectional influence to the defense secretary.[75] Indeed, one officer who served on a presidential staff for many years and became very close to that president was not promoted. As discussed earlier, he did not have the "right attitude," he asked too many questions, and was not unquestioningly subordinate to his superiors. Others have suggested that officers serving in civilian political posts can affect the formation of political cliques or *camarillas*, as do civilian politicians.[76] There is no doubt that some officers, such as General Alfonso Corona del Rosal, performed well in such fashion. However, Corona del Rosals do not exist within the military any more, and in consequence neither does that kind of military influence,

which means that political connections are notably diminished as a means of
enhancing promotion prospects.

One of the most important distinguishing characteristics of the military
bureaucracy is the extreme restrictions on the appointive powers of officers
holding various posts:

> Their appointive capacity is minimal compared to civilian political leaders. In
> other words the military has structurally made it as difficult as possible for
> someone to create an *equipo* or political group because they don't want the mili-
> tary officers to have the ability to form groups loyal only to them rather than to
> the institution as a whole.[77]

As chapter 6 elucidates, military recruitment shares many characteristics
with recruitment in the civilian political world. Indeed, the most common is the
mentor-disciple relationship, a characteristic of the Mexican intellectual community. William S. Ackroyd writes, the result is "pyramidal cliques, with a
senior officer acting as an unofficial leader and father-figure. More frequently,
though, the word which is associated with the formation of such quasi father-
son relations is *palanca*, or crowbar, and the relationship is more analogous to
that of a godfather and godson."[78] Ackroyd suggests that the mentor-disciple
relationship, which builds loyalty between junior and senior officers, is moderating potential generational splits. Personal ties within the military are so
complex that they cannot be evaluated in terms of their impact on the promotion process other than to say they are without question crucial.

The personal ties of generals can be evaluated from two perspectives. First,
whether personal connections with influential politicians have a favorable
impact on the promotion process, and second, the importance of military
kinship ties on one's career. Ties to civilian politicians clearly have little impact
on the promotion process. One of the mitigating factors in this regard is that in
order to obtain close ties with civilian politicians, which do not occur naturally
from earlier schooling, place of residence, or parents' social linkages, the
officer choosing a civilian assignment loses time in rank, when the pertinent
regulation is enforced, toward the next grade. The data from our generals
suggest that navy and air force officers, who have had faster promotion rates in
general, are not overrepresented when it comes to potential political connections. In fact, air force officers are strongly underrepresented. The only possible connection is that naval officers are more likely to have held appointive
posts, which in fact brought them into contact with more influential national
politicians, rather the positions in the legislative branch, more common among
army generals.

The Mexican politician who has politically prominent parents or relatives
profits thereby in a career sense. Such beneficiaries include President Salinas
and many of his cabinet members, as well as the leading presidential contenders inside the PRI in 1988. In other words, all other variables being equal,
familial contacts in the political culture is a distinct advantage to the typical
upwardly mobile politician—unless, of course, specific relatives are seen in an

unfavorable light within the system. Stephen Wager believes military kinship ties are critical to an officer's success. He states:

> [A cadet will] often marry a woman from a military family after he graduates and becomes an officer. Or it is quite common for an officer to marry into a fellow officer's family or that of his wife. This is quite significant when one considers the personalistic nature of the Mexican armed forces as well as its generally small size. Unlike the United States where such a relationship would have insignificant consequences on an officer's career, the officer's family relationships can have a significant bearing on an officer's career.[79]

Some notable examples of officers with military relatives are the previous two secretaries of defense. General Riviello Bazán is the son and stepbrother of generals; his predecessor, Juan Arévalo Gardoqui, is the son of a three-star general. The director general of naval administration in 1989, Antonio Vázquez del Mercado Múñoz, is the son of a former naval secretary. Among the generals whose parents' occupations are known, one-third have a career military father, a figure higher than those applying for entrance into the officer corps as cadets. On the other hand, no substantial difference exists between officers on the slow and faster track based on an officer's having a father in the military. Examples exist of high-ranking officers whose sons pursuing military careers did not achieve high rank. An instance: the success of Matías Ramos Santos, who was a zone commander from 1923 to 1951 and secretary of defense, which provided tremendous opportunities for mentoring, did not help his son's career, which did not culminate in a generalcy. One reason that military families might exert less influence on the *rapidity* of advancement as distinct from advancement itself, especially compared with political careers, is the strictures governing promotion by rank and grade, which since the late 1950s have been subscribed to, making military cohorts the same age. In other words, in the civil sector older politicians, peers of a younger politician's father, often hold major posts simultaneously with younger figures whom they themselves have appointed. Most brigade and division generals, however, are less likely to have been friends of a younger officer's parent, unless they are the same age.

The only confirmed relationship between relatives and promotions is not between military relatives and career advancement but between political relatives and rapidity of promotion. When the records of officers with prominent relatives in all categories—political, military, economic, and intellectual—are examined, officers in the fast track (twenty to twenty-five years) are better represented among those having prominent relatives than officers in the slower track, but primarily among political as distinct from any other influential kinship groups.

The Cream of the Officer Corps

The most prestigious positions in the army and their navy equivalents, as indicated by pay benefits, are, in descending order of importance the secretary of national defense, the subsecretary of national defense, and oficial mayor at the very top; followed by chief of staff, department head (for example, director general of infantry), zone commander, and the head of the presidential staff, all of whom receive the same extra pay.[80] How do these two- and three-star generals in the inner circle differ from their peers? Their characteristics are meaningful because they exercise decision-making authority within the military establishment and—as is also evident in the U.S. Army—selection board members, generals who promote other officers to the rank of general, tap people like themselves and thereby determine the future composition of the officer corps.[81]

Two types of top officers can be compared: the staff officer, represented by secretaries, subsecretaries, and department heads, and the troop commander, represented by the zone commander. Most top staff officers are likely to end up as department heads in their military occupational specialties, or in some cases, in more than one of these limited defense or naval posts. Such an assignment is important because of its prestige at the apex of the military structure and also—as is true of most higher bureaucratic positions—department heads normally determine which senior officers are awarded subordinate staff jobs.[82] This power gives the individual officer the ability to boost the careers of peers and disciples.

An analysis of department heads' career backgrounds and origins makes clear that many variables are unimportant in an officer's rise to that post. Among those variables are geographic origin, social class, and father's profession. What seems to be far more relevant is career path. The department head's career just focuses more heavily on the same experiences that help all officers rise above the rank of colonel. In other words, the department head's career is a more precise prototype of what it takes to become—and even more so in the future—a general.

One conspicuous feature of the department head's career is staff positions. A department head is 25 percent more likely than generals in the aggregate to have served as executive officer to a zone commander. Interestingly, however, despite the importance and prestige of zone commanders, holding a top troop command is not a significant career step toward a departmental headship. Similarly, at least for the older generation of officers, combat experience did not so turn out either. The other staff position of importance, suggestive of the value placed on a grasp of foreign military tactics and weaponry, as well as on enjoying the perks of a plum assignment, is attaché. Of the ninety officers in our sample of generals who were attachés, 80 percent became department heads. One in three department heads, compared with only 20 percent of all top generals, served abroad. A larger percentage of these staff officers were trained abroad as well.

It might be thought that in the past, when political officeholding was common among many outstanding generals, especially in top secretariat positions, pursuit of a political career enhanced one's rise up the staff ladder. This was not the case for department heads, who actually were much *less* likely to have held important political offices than generals in other assignments. This finding tends to suggest why political experience was more and more devalued within the military hierarchy.

One of the most significant variables in top staff backgrounds, however, is teaching. Teaching, as documented elsewhere in this work, is increasingly relevant to an officer's career. This is so because generals who have helped younger men rise to the rank of general have themselves been teachers in much larger percentages than generals overall. Nearly three-quarters of department-head generals versus only half of all generals were instructors, most at the Escuela Superior de Guerra and the Heroico Colegio Militar.

Of the informal characteristics that might help an officer to climb the promotion ladder, friendship plays a major, if difficult to assess, role. Various ties with various types of individuals were examined for all generals, but the only kind of ties that seem to have something to do with obtaining department headships are those to relatives in the military. Such ties are as helpful in the military as in the civilian bureaucracy.

Perhaps most interesting of all, a general's military training appears to be helpful in reaching top staff posts. If one considers a politician with a law background to be the equivalent of an infantry officer, one has an analogy. Infantry backgrounds characterize the largest group of officers in the Mexican military, just as they do in the U.S. Army and among generals in our sample, but infantry backgrounds are not proportionately represented among department heads. In fact, only 26 percent of department heads were infantry compared to nearly half of all generals examined. The most overrepresented specialties, at rates of more than three times their proportions among all generals, were artillery, engineers, and communications. Interestingly, in the U.S. Army, according to Mylander, men of ambition avoid the support branches, which include engineers; these branches account for 59 percent of the total officer corps but only 30 percent of the generals.[83]

Even as an elite position among generals, relatively speaking, the departmental headship is an opportunity open to a sizeable percentage of generals. Very few, however, will reach subsecretary and secretary of national defense or navy. These posts are so politically sensitive that considerations other than military take precedence in the selection process. Analysis of this even more elite group of generals reveals considerable differences between them and department heads.

Subsecretaries, based on a sample of forty-seven cases, had certain similarities to department heads. They, too, tended to have staff backgrounds, and to have held some of the same career posts, notably executive officer and attaché. Further, service on the general staff had become increasingly useful; in fact, it was almost a prerequisite for reaching a subsecretaryship. Two-thirds of all subsecretaries had general staff experience, compared with 43 percent of all generals. By the 1920–1929 generation, 83 percent of all subsecretaries had prior general staff assignments.

Two features set the subsecretary apart. The political nature of the appointment is reflected in the fact that subsecretaries, relative to all other generals, have much stronger personal and familial ties to political and military leaders.

More than half of all subsecretaries had such ties, more than half again as many as the typical general. Likewise, one-third of the subsecretaries but only one-fifth of all generals had held elective political office, suggesting the value of political contacts through careers in politics. Within the military, the command position requiring considerable political skill, somewhat analogous to a governorship, is that of zone commander. Although not a prerequisite to becoming a subsecretary, having been a zone commander was much more typical of a subsecretary than of a department head or other generals.

By far the most interesting variable in elite officer backgrounds, one repeated at the very top among the defense secretaries, is the importance of combat. I suggested earlier that symbolically combat experience has traditionally been emphasized in the officer corps. Nearly two-thirds of the subsecretaries were combat veterans at a time when only 40 percent of all generals counted combat experience in their careers. More intriguing, and a point I raised many years ago, is that a disproportionate percentage of subsecretaries were at one time political-military opponents of the government.[84] One in ten subsecretaries had opposed the government, three times as many as generals, since 1946. The same proportions are true of secretaries. In some respects that circumstance suggests just how far Mexico's political leaders were willing to go in the co-optation process to forestall future opposition. Since 1939 a president on three occasions has actually appointed a general from the opposing side as chief military leader.[85] This is not only politically risky but surprising, considering the possibility that the officer corps as a whole might not be accepting of an officer reincorporated in the army and then made "king of the hill." The individual most responsible for the influx of these and other retired officers was Cárdenas; his inclination should be noted as another special contribution he made to civil-military relations.

Two formal requirements apply to the secretary of defense: the individual must be a three-star (division) general, and must be of Mexican parentage. The latter is an indication of the importance of nationalism to the most sensitive political posts.[86] Many other characteristics of the subsecretaries can be found among the defense and naval secretaries, including the importance of relatives in high military or political positions, true of two-thirds of secretaries compared to only half of all generals;[87] service as attachés, zone commanders, and department heads; political officeholding, elective and appointive; and having been in combat (67 percent in the Revolution, 9 percent in postrevolution battles and revolts through 1939, and 3 percent in World War II. Four-fifths of the secretaries had combat experience, compared with only half of the generals in the aggregate.

Zone Commanders

The bureaucracy of the Mexican military's command structure is located in the capital city, centered in the Secretariat of National Defense and, to a lesser extent, the naval headquarters. Representing the army on the state level is the command structure of the military zone. The present zone system was established in 1924.[88] In 1990 Mexico was divided into nine military regions, and thirty-six zones. Thirty-one zones each encompass a state; another zone encompasses the Federal District; and although not precisely corresponding to political boundaries, eight zones encompass four states: Oaxaca, Chiapas, Guerrero, and Veracruz. The first three states are among Mexico's poorest and are hosts to rural conflicts; as a border state, Chiapas has had problems with illegal Central American immigrants, making it a national security problem in the 1980s. Veracruz, the site of much of Mexico's petroleum resource, is of strategic importance.[89] However, zone 1, headquartered in the National Palace and covering the Valle de México, is preeminent because the military's largest concentration of hospitals, schools, shooting ranges, and residences, and the National Defense Secretariat itself are within its perimeter.[90] The navy currently has fifteen bases on the east and west coasts.[91] There are also eight naval regions encompassing these bases, the equivalent of army zones.[92] The air force, administered by a department under the secretary of national defense, has eight bases.[93] New zones or regions may be added at will by the supreme commander, the president.[94]

By law a brigade or division general must command a zone.[95] By the 1960s the president was said to be selecting zone commanders at the suggestion of the secretary of national defense,[96] but earlier, especially as late as the 1930s, it was more likely to be the president himself who independently made the selections. More recently, it has been suggested that the secretary of defense generates a pool of eligible officers, from which the president chooses.[97] The zone commander, in charge of a well-armed body of troops, has been rotated rather regularly. This does not imply that a new president automatically replaces all zone commanders, but the initial period of an administration is likely to be the time of greatest turnover. For example, of the thirty-five zone commanders President Díaz Ordaz replaced twenty-four in 1964.[98] In a typical first year, about a third of the zone commanders are replaced. Examination of the career histories of 140 zone commanders shows an average tenure of 2.4 years. In the state of Hidalgo, from 1934 to 1982, twenty-three officers led the 18th military zone.[99]

The zone commander historically played a conspicuous political role in the expansion of central power, and as a counterbalance to the influence of the state governor. Porfirio Díaz skillfully manipulated both civilian governors and military commanders to counteract the influence of each. Since 1946 zone commanders have often substituted for governors when the latter resigned or were forced from office by central authorities.[100] The close association between governors and zone commanders is borne out by our data. Among the generals in this study, 16 percent had been governors at some point. Among the generals who were zone commanders, nearly twice that figure, 31 percent, had been governors. By the 1930s generation, no officers had been governors. However, because no zone commander has substituted provisionally for a governor in the past four administrations, the function had essentially disappeared. Nevertheless, the zone commander remains loyal to the federal government in a case involving a conflict between the governor and national political authorities, or between the governor and local authorities.[101] Zone commanders are in direct communication through their own military network with the defense secretary.[102]

Although zone commanders are no longer needed to counteract the influence of a recalcitrant governor, they do require considerable political skills, much more so than do other types of troop commanders. Zone commanders who perform effectively are ideal candidates for staff posts above the department level. Their political skills are valuable for several reasons. The first, according to Martin Needler, is that the zone commander "is in a good position to become an important element of the regional power elites; and is acquiring the experience and education to do so. The army has always assisted regional economic development with its growing capabilities for civic action and resource management."[103]

A second reason for valuing political skills is that conflicts often occur between a civilian governor and a military zone commander. In an unusual admission, Rubén Figueroa, a former governor of Guerrero, stated that conflict between the two figures was common, and sometimes became permanent.[104] Elizur Arteaga cites an instance in which the zone commander in Sinaloa declared a state of seige and disarmed the governor's personal guard.[105] The relationship between these two actors is important because it becomes a critical variable in determining the military's civic responsibility.[106] Cooperation is likely to become more necessary, and yet more difficult, if antidrug campaigns and electoral conflicts become a common element in state and regional civil-military relations.

A third reason, as implied in the analysis of interest group associations with the military, is that it is increasingly apparent that dissident groups or others opposed to current government policy may seek assistance through military rather than civilian channels. Ronfeldt mentions that since the 1940s discontented peasants, believing their complaints have been blocked by a governor or other civilian officials, have sought the help of zone commanders.[107] Needler believes that an officer, in his political capacity as a zone commander, acts as an agent of the civilian political leadership, not as a representative of the armed forces.[108] In certain respects, a good case can be made for Needler's observation. If the frequency of political demands on zone commanders increases, and the legitimacy of the political leadership is questioned, then the commanders are bound to examine their institutional loyalties and whether they jibe with those of the civilian leadership.

The intertwining of political with military responsibilities goes far beyond the fact that zone commanders often became governors. If we examine the evolution of the zone commanders' political experience by age, a clear pattern becomes apparent (see table 7-5).

Zone commanders who fought in the Revolution dominated zone assignments in the 1940s and 1950s, when political officeholding was the norm (see Appendix C). Although a decline occurs in each succeeding generation, a marked difference occurs between the pre- and postrevolutionary zone com-

TABLE 7-5. Political Experience of Mexican Zone
Commanders, by Generation

Decade of Birth	Zone Commanders Holding National Political Office (%)
1880–1889	92
1890–1899	73
1900–1909	41
1910–1919	24
1920–1929	18
1930–	0

manders, and among the post-1910 generation of zone commanders. In the two postrevolutionary decades (1900–1919) zone commanders with national political experience proportionately drop precipitously from three-quarters to one-quarter. Compared with all other large groups of generals, zone commanders have had the highest levels of political experience: about half of zone commanders held such offices in contrast to only one-quarter of other generals. These figures also suggest, as do those for secretaries and subsecretaries, that the more influential the military post, the more likely the officer will have acquired political skills, at least until the 1980s, when direct political experience no longer was necessary.

Zone commanders share important qualities with their peers who have risen to top staff positions, or to other unit commands. Like the most successful peers, they too have taught in large numbers at the military academies. Similarly, they have served abroad as attachés twice as frequently as their fellow officers.

Zone commanders differ in one very important respect from their staff superiors at the Secretariat of National Defense. As a group, they have not had unusual kinship links with politicians and other military leaders. This is surprising, considering that strategically and politically they carry more weight than department heads because of their direct control over troops. The known personal and political loyalties of an officer in this post are more crucial than those of a typical staff officer. This contradiction may be explained by the fact that historically such individuals, largely self-made men, acquire political contacts on a personal and social level through holding political office rather than relying on kinship networks to help their careers. Whatever the explanation, they have not been better connected in a familial sense than other generals.

The typical zone commander differs somewhat from the top staff officer in other respects as well. Staff positions at national defense headquarters, seemingly important to fast-track promotions, are not as common among zone commanders, who customarily have actual command of troops. An exception to this is serving as chief of staff (executive officer) in a zone position, under the eyes of a seasoned zone commander. The assignment has been shown to have career importance if the zone commander is promoted to an even higher command, as in the case of several recent secretaries of defense. Only 15 percent of all generals have served as zone executive officers, but more than half of all future zone commanders count this post in their military records. Unlike civilian political life, in which the post of secretary general of government (somewhat similar to lieutenant governor) rarely leads to a governorship, zone chief of staff often leads to a zone command.

The other differences between zone commanders and ordinary generals involve military specialty, combat experience, and social background. Among top staff generals, infantry backgrounds have been significantly underrepresented, at least for some years. However, among zone commanders, infantry officers are extremely well represented, accounting for half of these men; cavalry officers, who account for a fifth, are also more strongly represented than in staff posts. Specialties not in the army mainstream—administration, communications, and law—are missing altogether in zone commanders' backgrounds.

Zone commanders, like secretaries and subsecretaries, more typically have been combat veterans; this is not surprising because such veterans acquired the practical skills that kept troops loyal to the government and defeated rebel commanders. The importance of those skills continued into the 1940s, 1950s, and 1960s, which explains why nearly 60 percent of all zone commanders were combat veterans, compared with 20 percent of all generals. Although such experience has now disappeared, as I discuss elsewhere in this work, combat in the form of antidrug campaigns is likely to appear more frequently among future zone commanders' backgrounds, more so than among their staff counterparts.

Finally, the minority of officers coming from lower socioeconomic strata have a much stronger chance of becoming zone commanders than high-ranking staff officers. The qualities demanded of the zone commander seem to attract the self-made officer in much greater numbers than do other posts held by generals. Zone commanders with lower socioeconomic backgrounds are half again as numerous as all generals. It may be that middle-class cadets, who have better social skills, enter the more intellectually oriented promotion tracks, while their working-class peers feel more comfortable aiming at combat arms and troop commands.

Our analysis of the promotion process demonstrates conclusively that the military has developed a largely autonomous system. Promotions are fairly consistent over time and, more important, civilian interference is negligible—even on the part of recent presidents. In the introduction we hypothesized that a possible explanation for discouraging military intervention in civilian affairs is to keep politicians out of the promotion process, and limit its politization. Mexico has generally done this, aided by a one-party-dominant system.

Although promotions are generally regularized, the highest-ranking officers share certain characteristics in their military careers. The characteristics, which have been empirically identified, not only illustrate which type of officer achieves decision-making posts but indicate the value military leaders place on certain attributes and career experiences, including military occupational specialty, education, study abroad, military and political kinship, combat experience, service as an attaché, and service in specific staff and command assignments.

Notes

1. Roderic A. Camp, "Generals and Politicians in Mexico: A Preliminary Comparison," in *The Modern Mexican Military: A Reassessment*, ed. David Ronfeldt (La Jolla: Center for U.S.-Mexican Studies, University of California, San Diego, 1984), 149.

2. Lyle N. McAlister, *The Military in Latin American Socio-political Evolution: Four Case Studies* (Washington, D.C.: Center for Research in Social Systems, 1970), 206.

3. *Revista de Ejército*, August 1961, 36; Enrique Cordero y Torres, *Diccionario biográfico de Puebla* vol. 1 (Mexico, 1972), 481.

4. Jorge Alberto Lozoya, *El Ejército mexicano (1911-1965)* (Mexico: El Colegio de México, 1970), 66.

5. Jésus de León Toral et al., *El Ejército mexicano*, (Mexico: SDN, 1979), 486.

6. Charles H. Coates and Roland J. Pellegrin, *Military Sociology: A Study of American Military Institutions and Military Life* (University Park, Md.: Social Science Press, 1965), 137.

7. Even officers who were just starting their careers as lieutenants at the time remember his reputation. Personal interviews, Mexico City, 1989-1990.

8. According to Jesús M. Lozano, "Retiro de los generales que pasen de 65 años este sexenio," *Excélsior*, May 31, 1972, 22, Echeverría used a sixty-five-year-age limit to retire 69 generals immediately. The author suggests that it does not apply to revolutionary generals because they are placed in a special category. Echeverría reportedly had spoken to each general affected, explaining his desire to give younger officers greater opportunities. A few weeks later, the National Action Party's magazine (*La Nación*, June 16, 1972) reported that there were 399 generals in the Mexican Army, 204 of whom were above the age limit. Of the thirty-five zone commanders, 28 were between the ages of sixty-seven and seventy-eight. A few weeks after publication of the information, the Secretariat of National Defense circulated a list of 71 generals who would be retired. National Defense Secretary Cuenca Díaz announced that all remaining officers above the age limit would be retired by 1976. *Novedades*, June 29, 1972, 9.

9. Phyllis Greene Walker, "The Modern Mexican Military: Political Influence and Institutional Interests in the 1980s" (M.A. thesis, American University, 1987), 26-27.

10. Personal interview, Mexico City, 1989.

11. Alemán also violated the same promotion law with General Piña's brother, Antolín, who was promoted from brigadier to brigade general in September 1951, after only four years in grade.

12. Dirección Técnica de Organización, *Directorio del gobierno federal*, vol. 1 (Mexico, 1951), 11.

13. Dirección Técnica de Organización, *Directorio del gobierno federal* (Mexico, 1956), 10.

14. Senado, *Diario de los debates*, 1953, 5-6.

15. Ibid., 6.

16. Ibid., 7.

17. The quick rise to colonel is justified by the fact that individuals who enter military service with preexisting degrees, such as legal officers, begin their careers with the rank of major, thus considerably shortening the promotion process.

18. David Ronfeldt, "The Mexican Army and Political Order since 1940," in *Armies and Politics in Latin America*, ed. Abraham F. Lowenthal (New York: Holmes and Meier, 1976), 300.

19. Camp, "Generals and Politicians in Mexico," 131.

20. Thomas E. Weil, "The Armed Forces," in *Area Handbook for Mexico* (Washington, D.C.: GPO, 1975), 367.

21. Gabriel Parra, "Inconformidad en el ejército con el sistema de ascensos," *Excélsior*, June 19, 1972, 1.

22. Michael J. Dziedzic, "Civil-Military Relations in Mexico: The Politics of Co-optation" (unpublished paper, University of Texas, Austin, 1983), 33.

23. Personal interview, Mexico City, 1990.

24. Franklin D. Margiotta, "Civilian Control and the Mexican Military: Changing Patterns of Political Influence," in *Civilian Control of the Military: Theories and Cases from Developing Countries*, ed. Claude E. Welch, Jr. (Albany: State University of New York Press, 1976), 232.

25. Gloria Fuentes, *El Ejército mexicano* (Mexico: Grijalbo, 1983), 222. These figures are somewhat similar to the number of years it takes to become a general in the U.S. Army. At the time Maureen Mylander completed her study of generals, at the end of the Vietnam era, a brigadier general required twenty-six years; a major general, thirty years; and a lieutenant general, thirty-two years. *The Generals* (New York: Dial Press, 1974), 342.

26. Daniel Mora, "Profile of the Mexican Company Grade Officer" (Paper presented at the Rocky Mountain States Latin American Conference, Tucson, 1984), 16.

27. Ibid., 12.

28. Stephen J. Wager, "The Mexican Military" (unpublished paper, 1983, 21, parts of which appear in Robert Wesson, *The Latin American Military* [Westport, Conn.: Greenwood Press, 1986]).

29. Personal interviews, Mexico City, 1990.

30. McAlister, *The Military in Latin American Socio-political Evolution*, 234.

31. Camp, "Generals and Politicians in Mexico," 140.

32. November 1971, 37.

33. José Luis Piñeyro, "The Mexican Army and the State: Historical and Political Perspective," *Revue Internationale de Sociologie* 14 (April–August 1978): 150, citing *El Día*, February 29, 1976, 17.

34. Judith Adler Hellman, *Mexico in Crisis* (New York: Holmes and Meier, 1983), 166.

35. Stephen J. Wager, "The Mexican Military 1968–1978: A Decade of Change" (unpublished paper, Stanford University, June 1979), 9.

36. Camp, "Generals and Politicians in Mexico," 140–141.

37. Roderic A. Camp, "Civilian Supremacy in Mexico: The Case of a Post-Revolutionary Military," in *Military Intervention and Withdrawal*, ed. Constantine P. Danopoulous (London: Routledge, 1991), 25.

38. According to López Portillo,

> "There are two factors which affect promotion, the most important of which is the person's merits, and time in grade and rank. There's also a third factor, which involves personal corrections, individual evaluations, or just plain luck, but this factor is largely an exceptional influence in the process. The secretary of defense comes with an overall plan of promotion, and presents all of the service records. . . . I don't remember specifically denying any recommendation made by the secretary of defense because I found them very reasonable and well supported. The secretary of defense always brings the records with him, and I go over each one."

Personal interview, Mexico City, 1991.

39. Personal interview, Mexico City, 1990.

40. Letter to the editor, *Proceso*, September 4, 1989, 62.

41. The permanent committee, composed of fourteen senators and fifteen deputies, substitutes for the Congress when it is not in session. Since 1966 it has had the right to approve military promotions. According to Elizur Arteaga, because a quorum for this body consists of only fifteen persons, the president would need the support of only eight members to approve a questionable promotion. In contrast, a regular Senate session requires forty-four members present, or a vote of twenty-three to approve a decision. This difference in numbers and procedures poses a potential danger of presidential intervention.

42. Senado, *Diario de los debates*, December 23, 1941, 13–20; *Revista de Ejército y Fuerza Aérea*, September 1976, 136.

43. The 1956 promotions law, the basis of all future legislation governing armed forces promotions, specifically requires time in grade, time in service, and appropriate educational training (although no advanced training is specified) in Sections I, V, and VI of Article 7. See "Ley de ascensos y recompensas del ejército y fuerza aérea nacionales," *Diario Oficial*, January 7, 1956, 2–8.

44. Mylander, *The Generals*, 63.

45. Camp, "Generals and Politicians in Mexico," 134.

46. *Hispano Americano*, May 11, 1981, 11.

47. See my "The Mexican Revolution as a Socializing Agent: Mexican Political Leaders and Their Parents" (Paper presented at the Rocky Mountain States Latin American Studies conference, Tucson, 1977).

48. Richard B. Craig, "Mexican Narcotics Traffic: Binational Security Implications," in *The Latin American Narcotics Trade and U.S. National Security*, ed. Donald J. Mabry (Westport, Conn.: Greenwood Press, 1989), 35.

49. Michael J. Dziedzic, "Mexico's Converging Challenges: Problems, Prospects, and Implications" (unpublished manuscript, U.S. Air Force Academy, April 21, 1989), 81.

50. *Diccionario biográfico del gobierno mexicano* (Mexico: Presidencia de la República, 1989), 267.

51. *Diario Oficial*, December 26, 1986, 5.

52. Personal interview, Mexico City, 1990.

53. *Memoria gráfica del cincuentenario de la reapertura del Héroico Colegio Militar* (Mexico: SHCP, 1970), 499–501.

54. Félix Galván López, *Escuela Superior de Guerra, 1932–1982* (Mexico: SDN, 1982), 320–323.

55. The same distortion appears to be true in Brazil as well. Frank McCann found that from 1891 to 1965, only 30 percent of Brazilian generals were infantry; 23 percent, artillery; and 17 percent, cavalry. See his "Brazilian Army Officers Biography Project" (Paper presented at the 15th National Latin American Studies Association, December 1989, Miami), 8.

56. Academic performance is a variable among U.S. generals too. Mylander found that of the 233 West Point graduates among the army's 491 generals in 1973, half were in the top third of their class. *The Generals*, 330.

57. Wager, "The Mexican Military," 33.

58. McAlister, *The Military in Latin American Socio-political Evolution*, 230.

59. "Paso revista el primer mandatario al cuerpo de guardia presidenciales," *El Nacional*, January 27, 1977, 1.

60. Wager, "The Mexican Military," 25. Walker reported a hundredfold salary increase over an officer's base salary if assigned to the United States. This is not the case; the salary is, indeed, much greater. See her "National Security," in *Mexico: A Country Study*, ed. James D. Rudolph (Washington, D.C.: GPO, 1985), 357.

61. Personal interviews, Mexico City, 1990.

62. Secretaria de Defensa Nacional, *Memorias* (Mexico: SDN, 1948), 75, and *Memorias* (Mexico: SDN, 1965), 58.

63. Interview with a Mexican general, August 1973.

64. Mora suggested that ESG graduates were typically assigned to units outside the capital immediately upon graduation. See his "Profile of the Mexican Company Grade Officer," 13.

65. Edwin Lieuwen, *Mexican Militarism* (Albuquerque: University of New Mexico Press, 1968), 93.

66. Wager, "The Mexican Military," 23.

67. Mora, "Profile of the Mexican Company Grade Officer," 8.

68. Ibid.

69. Mylander, *The Generals*, 7.

70. Personal interview, Mexico City, 1990.

71. Adolfo Aguilar Zinzer reported that U.S. Senator Jesse Helms asserted that he had secret election figures from the 1982 presidential contest that indicated widespread fraud, and that were said to have come from the president's military staff. See his "Political Situation in Mexico,"

Senate Foreign Relations Committee, June 1986, cited in "Civil-Military Relations in Mexico," in *The Military and Democracy: The Future of Civil-Military Relations in Latin America*, by Louis W. Goodman et al. (Lexington, Mass.: Lexington Books, 1990), 232.

72. Personal interview, Mexico City, 1990.

73. *Proceso*, January 19, 1988, 20, and May 21, 1988, 8; *Diccionario biográfico del gobierno mexicano* (Mexico: Presidencia de la República, 1984), 82; *Diccionario biográfico del gobierno mexicano* (Mexico: Presidencia de la República, 1987), 75; *Memoria gráfica del cincuentenario de la reapertura del Heroíco Colegio Militar*, 476.

74. McAlister, *The Military in Latin American Socio-political Evolution*, 234.

75. Personal interview, Mexico City, 1990.

76. David Ronfeldt, *The Mexican Army and Political Order since 1940* (Santa Monica: Rand Corporation, 1973), 9.

77. Personal interview, Mexico City, 1990.

78. William S. Ackroyd, "Descendants of the Revolution: Civil-Military Relations in Mexico" (Ph.D. diss., University of Arizona, 1988), 160.

79. Wager, "The Mexican Military," 13.

80. McAlister, *The Military in Latin American Socio-political Evolution*, 226.

81. Mylander, *The Generals*, 157.

82. Stephen J. Wager, "Modernization of the Mexican Military: Political and Strategic Implications" (unpublished paper, Department of History, U.S. Military Academy, 1983), 24.

83. *The Generals*, 63. Morris Janowitz also notes that officers "believe that combat arms is the major route to upward mobility." *The Professional Soldier* (Glencoe, Ill.: Free Press, 1960), 147.

84. Roderic A. Camp, "Mexican Military Leadership in Statistical Perspective since the 1930s," in *Statistical Abstract of Latin America*, vol. 20, ed. James W. Wilkie and Peter Reich (Los Angeles: Latin American Center Publications, University of California, Los Angeles, 1980), 605.

85. The three generals were Jesús Agustín Castro, 1939–1940; Francisco Urquizo, 1945–1946; and Marcelino García Barragán, 1964–1970. Castro, who had been subsecretary in charge of the Ministry of War under Carranza, opposed Obregón in 1928, and retired from 1928 to 1934. Cárdenas reintergrated him, appointing him zone commander of Durango in 1935. Very active politically, he had many military and political disciples, one of whom was General Barragán, who served under him. Urquizo, who also was acting secretary of war under Carranza at the time he was murdered, rejoined the army in 1934, and similar to Castro, ultimately became a zone commander, before his appointment as subsecretary under Avila Camacho in 1940. Urquizo, who had been forced to join the army as a peasant, actually was a second lieutenant in the old Federal Army in 1911. García Barragán, as is detailed in the section on political participation, was removed from active duty for supporting General Miguel Henríquez Guzmán in 1952.

86. *Diario Oficial*, December 26, 1986, 3.

87. Being a "military brat," however, did not aid a general or admiral in rising to the post of secretary. About one in three generals has a military father, the same as secretaries.

88. Virginia Prewett, "The Mexican Army," *Foreign Affairs* 19 (April 1941): 613.

89. José Luis Piñeyro, "The Modernization of the Mexican Armed Forces," in *Democracy under Siege, New Military Power in Latin America*, ed. Augusto Varas (Westport, Conn.: Greenwood Press, 1989), 117.

90. Dolores Cordero, "El ejército mexicano," *Revista de Revistas*, September 12, 1973, 7.

91. Piñeyro, "The Modernization of the Mexican Armed Forces," 119. They are located in the cities of Veracruz, Tampico, Chetumal, Ciudad del Carmen, Yucalpeten, Acapulco, Ensenada, La Paz, Puerto Cortés, Guaymas, Mazatlán, Manzanillo, Salina Cruz, Puerto Madero, and Lázaro Cárdenas.

92. McAlister, *The Military in Latin American Socio-political Evolution*, 212.

93. In order of importance, they are Santa Lucia (Mexico), Ciudad Ixtepec, El Cipres, Cozumel, Zapopan, Puebla, Pie de la Cuesta (Guerrero), and Mérida.

94. *Diario Oficial*, January 14, 1985, 9.

95. See Article 36 of the organic military law, *Diario Oficial*, December 26, 1986, 4.

96. Jorge Alberto Lozoya, *El ejército mexicano 1911-1965* (Mexico: El Colegio de México, 1970), 73.

97. Guillermo Boils, *Los militares y la política en México, 1915-1974* (Mexico: El Caballito, 1975), 112.

98. Secretaría de Defensa Nacional, *Memorias*, September 1964, 15, for August 1965; see September, 1969, 16, for August 1970.

99. Camp, "Generals and Politicians in Mexico, 144.

100. Loyzoya, *El ejército mexicano*, 74.

101. Loyzoya, El ejército mexicano, in *Lecturas de política mexicana*, by Centro de Estudios Internacionales (Mexico: Colegio de México, 1977), 374.

102. Oscar Hinojosa, "Cualquier régimen de gobierno, con apoyo popular, será respetado por el Ejército," *Proceso*, March 1982, 8.

103. David Ronfeldt, "The Modern Mexican Military: An Overview," in *The Modern Mexican Military: A Reassessment*, ed. David Ronfeldt (La Jolla: Center for United States-Mexican Studies, University of California, San Diego, 1984), 24.

104. *Proceso*, August 21, 1978, 9.

105. This occurred during the administration of Alfonso Calderón Velarde, 1975-1981. The zone commander was subsequently removed. Elizur Arteaga "Maquiavelo, poder y constitución" (unpublished manuscript), 40.

106. Stephen J. Wager, "Civic Action and the Mexican Military" (unpublished paper, Department of History, U.S. Military Academy, 1982), 7.

107. Ronfeldt "The Modern Mexican Military: An Overview," *The Mexican Army and Political Order since 1940*, 8.

108. Martin C. Needler, *Politics and Society in Mexico* (Albuquerque: University of New Mexico Press, 1971), 68.

8

What Kind of Relationship?

Regardless of whether this analysis focuses on military sociology or a fuller understanding of military leadership, observers are most intrigued by the role of the officer corps in civil-military relations, how it has altered in recent years, and the likelihood of the military's intervening in Mexican politics. The essence of the original research for this work can be found in the preceding chapters. This chapter, of necessity, is often speculative, and numerous interpretations are interspersed throughout the text. Any assessment of the above questions relies heavily on the model used to describe civil-military relations. It may well be that certain misinterpretations arise from misunderstanding where such relations begin rather than where they are headed.

Since the 1960s one point on which most Mexican political analysts agree is that the military's future political role is more likely to increase than decrease. This view suggests that in the continuum of civil-military relations, the military has already reached its lowest point of political influence, and logically, other than remaining static, could only embark on a more activist course, thereby reversing a long-term trend of military withdrawal from politics. Great care has to be taken in accepting this argument because some confusion exists between the fundamental issue of military subordination to civilian leadership and the military's role in society. Implicitly, analysts have equated an expansion of the military's role with greater political influence, and greater political influence with a decline in respect for civil authority. Clearly, the former is possible without a significant alteration in the latter.

Civil-military relations are a very complex component of broader societal interactions. Most important, the interactions are dynamic, not static. They have been best described by Sam Sarkesian as "the resulting balance between the military and society that emerges from the patterns of behavior and the interaction between military professionals and important political actors, and the power exercised by the military institution as a political actor."[1] Henry Bienen aptly warns that civil-military relations in Third World nations, even in countries like Mexico, where institutionalization is relatively strong, are often informal and fluid, and cannot be understood using interest group models.[2] Western intellectual tradition perceives the armed forces as apolitical and narrowly confined within their own institutional boundaries. Sarkesian maintains that this view is quite misleading and that an equilibrium model is much more appropriate. "The requisites of a democratic ideology, it can be argued, do not provide for a separate subsystem removed from society. The legitimacy and credibility of any military system rests with its links to society and the reflection of basic social values."[3]

The equilibrium model is characterized by several important features. It is built upon the concept of interlocks, not only in personnel but values, between civil society and the military on one hand, and between the political leadership and the officer corps on the other. Their "partnership is an educational and socialization intermix, where values, morals, and ethics of military and civilian elites are congruent."[4] This linkage raises an important dilemma in our analysis of Mexican political-military relations. The conventional wisdom has been that armed forces personnel, even in the industrialized world, have been isolated, suggesting that interrelationships between the officer corps and other members of society are infrequent and limited.[5] Throughout this work, the secrecy with which the Mexican military cloaks itself has been emphasized. The military does not encourage a free flow of ideas, nor a natural exchange socially or otherwise between the officer corps and the civilian leadership. The dilemma is that if one accepts the equilibrium model as a more accurate representation of what contemporary civil-military relations should be, and indeed are, then congruence between civil and military leadership would require many significant changes in the typical, traditional Mexican pattern. At the same time, such changes would be seen as expanding the military's political role, rather than solidifying the present relationship.

In a political model in which the state is as all-encompassing as Mexico's, the military's isolation has surprisingly led to politicians' knowing very "little about the thinking of the Army" or the "inner workings of the armed forces."[6] One general asserted,

The government has always kept [the armed forces] isolated from civilians because they have always been afraid of what this contact might bring politically. The last five or six presidents haven't known us much at all, and this has an extraordinary impact on who is chosen or appointed to top positions. In other words, the military itself has more influence in this decision than the president because of his lack of personal contact with top military officials.[7]

Recent presidents agree with this assertion. According to one president, during his campaign:

I had meetings with all of the military zone commanders and got to know a little bit about them personally and about their service records. . . . I picked four of these zone commanders who made the strongest impression on me, and then I studied their careers rather carefully. I picked out . . . as my secretary of national defense. . . . This selection process that I used was proposed to me by my predecessor.

My contact was only superficial and exceptional with officers of general rank, including especially General . . . [his choice for defense secretary], prior to my presidential campaign.[8]

Thus, the implication is that state leadership is heterogeneously divided along civil-military lines. Mexico's civilian state leadership, most importantly represented by the executive branch, is composed of individuals who are largely homogeneous, urban, middle class, and highly educated. As one analyst of the Mexican bureaucracy suggested, their motivations, goals, education, and backgrounds are very similar, and have the "net result of reducing the level of hostility and conflict" within various agencies.[9]

Two possibilities for leadership division along civil-military lines exist. In Mexico's recent past a deep split between civilian and military leaders occurred. The division is necessarily artificial, and it appears that in order to professionalize itself, to remove civilian or political leadership from the military, Mexico's armed forces became increasingly hermetic and inwardly focused. One officer concluded that the military pursued a purposeful policy.

> It is true we have no social contact. . . . Really, they don't want us to talk to anyone in order to make comparisons of our life and the civilian life. In fact, of all the armies I can think of worldwide, I can't think of any military where this separation is more exaggerated. We have been purposely isolated in our development from civilians.[10]

Modifications in Mexican society since 1968, especially since the early 1980s, make it increasingly apparent that the military, however many barriers it throws up against external "civilian" intervention, increasingly has been influenced by the values, attitudes, and expectations of civilian life. That, at least, has been the case elsewhere in the Western world.[11] Major political events in Eastern Europe cannot help but affect Mexican perceptions, both military and civilian, of political modernization.[12]

In the past the presence of large numbers of military officers in civilian political offices, and large numbers of experienced politicians in top career-military posts, lubricated channels of communication. Not only were these two sets of leaders similar in background and experience but they expanded the breadth of personal ties between civil and military bureaucracies. The steady decline and essential elimination of the political-military officer removed this significant linkage, and its many beneficial consequences for Mexican civil-military relations.

The second division, about which little is known in Mexico, is the potential for conflict within a service branch or between branches. Mexico has moderated this tendency somewhat by providing a more unified service structure in terms of command, creating only two services, army and navy.[13] Under President López Portillo the executive branch considered a proposal to unite the armed forces into one cabinet agency. López Portillo, after serious consideration, rejected the proposal.[14]

The air force, which structurally is integrated into the National Defense Secretariat, is subordinate to that agency's leadership. In fact, it is only about one-seventeenth the size of the army (the ratio in Argentina is 1:5, and in Brazil, 1:4).[15] For many years most air force officers were trained with army cadets at the Heroico Colegio Militar, and later, when the Air College replaced it, at the Escuela Superior de Guerra. Today they attend the Heroico Colegio Militar for a short period of basic training before transferring to the Air College. The air force staff course at the ESG is separate, and lasts only two years. According to officers who have attended the ESG, air force and naval officers are not given respect by their army peers. In fact, a naval officer enrolled at the ESG called himself "another foreigner," indicating a status on par with that of visiting foreign officers.[16] A case study provides some concrete evidence that the director of the air force is entirely subordinate to the secretary of defense. Under General Félix Galván López, who headed the secretariat from 1976 to 1982, the naming of the air force head was "basically Galván's decision. He served at the pleasure of Galván. He could be fired at any time."[17] The marines do not even have departmental status but are incorporated directly into the navy.

The most likely interservice rivalries are between the navy and army. Little evidence has come to light of differences between the two. In 1981, during the preelection fervor leading up to the designation of a government party presidential candidate, an important disagreement between the two came out in the open. At issue was whether a military officer should run for the presidency, and differences concerning national security plans. Although the Constitution does not bar the candidacy of a career officer, the naval secretary publicly stated that a military candidacy was inappropriate because plenty of well-qualified civilians were available. The defense secretary noted some good army candidates were available, and said there was no reason to exclude them just because they were career officers.[18] The two continued to disagree repeatedly and vocally on this and other issues.[19] From time to time dissent and friction have surfaced within the army itself. Ackroyd asserts, for example, that rivalries within the officer corps were strong in the early 1970s and that there was some evidence of planning for a military coup.[20] Many observers have also commented on the lack of regard shown by ESG graduates for nongraduates, even for officers who have completed the higher arms curriculum there. Such elitism on the part of staff and command graduates (DEMs) creates a potential for hostility and tension within the army.[21]

The Mexican political system, in a word, is very much in flux. Its future is unpredictable, but the dynamics of the process are very visible as the influence of the democratic political culture reaches all levels of society. Just as concerns are expressed when a political model is in transition, similar expressions become commonplace when a state institution, such as the military, moves in a different direction.

The fact is, however, that in order for the military to become more integrated with its civilian counterparts, it will have to alter how it is perceived by society and by its own officers. Political changes taking place internationally and in Mexico in the 1990s are affecting not only the civilian sector, but the military as well and its relationship with society. As Sarkesian argues, the boundaries between the military and society have become more obscure.[22] Institutional fuzziness and expanded responsibilities threaten the Mexican status quo.

A second characteristic of the equilibrium model is the concept of friendly adversaries. According to Sarkesian, this presumes that the adversaries disagree with one another at times yet pursue their priorities within the democratic "rules of the game."[23] Mexico's society is in transition, at least temporarily, from a semiauthoritarian state to a more pluralistic model. Even if it were to shift quickly to a highly competitive process in which the opposition took power, it would not necessarily signal acceptance of democratic norms, especially tolerance toward the opposition. Political leaders have never socialized Mexican society toward that goal, and it would take more than a transfer in the reins of power to alter long-term values and political behavior.

The concept of friendly adversaries not only affects the way politics is conducted but encourages various actors to function as interest articulators. One of the peculiarities of the military, shared across societal boundaries, is its inability in developing countries to bargain politically. According to one analyst, the military finds it difficult to adjust to political bargaining because its socialization process takes place in a closed educational and training environment.[24] This exclusivity naturally encourages institutional secrecy and isolation.

Isolation enhances nonbargaining behavior, but is not likely the most important variable in determining this inadequacy. Rather, the skill of, and inclination toward, interest articulation results from two deficiencies. First, lack of adversarial respect affects all political actors, civilian and military alike. The difference is that military actors, unaccustomed to operating in the context of give-and-take, resort to force, finding it an acceptable rule of the game. Doing so does not necessarily make military actors less respectful of adversaries than their civilian peers; they simply have at their fingertips the means to impose their political views on others. Acceptance of opposing viewpoints rarely exists among leadership groups in isolation from the beliefs of the populace; rather, it is a by-product of the general citizen culture. Second, the political system can be structured in such a way that interest articulation, as it is usually understood in the United States, is atypical. Open interest articulation, when legislative bodies play little if any role in decision making—as is the case in Mexico—is not present, thus obviating the need for that type of political skill. Changes in the electoral process since 1987, of course, are bound to redirect emphasis on bargaining or brokering skills, but up to the present, the structure instead has emphasized the need for bureaucratic infighters within the executive branch.

Occasionally, when a political issue involves veterans' benefits, some evidence of associational support from retired military officers is evident.[25] Generally speaking, however, the military procurement process is a silent one, closed to outsiders. For example, when Mexico made the decision to purchase F-5 fighter planes from the United States, it insisted that U.S. government officials maintain confidentiality until after the sale was completed. As Michael Dziedzic reports, it was evident that no efforts were made to mobilize actors in the outer realm of policy-making, including interest groups or opposition members of Congress.[26] Although the military has rarely operated as a functional interest group in the decision-making process, it has provided a channel for others frustrated with established means of political communication. Provincials often direct complaints through zone commanders, and more recently, Mexico City residents registered complaints with the Secretariat of Defense.[27]

The present situation in Mexican civil-military relations is one in which the military acts as a guardian of civilian elites. Nevertheless, departures from the pattern seem to be in store.[28] The collaborative political relationship in practice meant basically two things. First, the military provided information employed in the decision-making process. Second, and more important, the military functioned traditionally as an enforcement agent of *civilian-led* policies.[29] Since 1946 the army has played a very visible role in elections. McAlister notes,

> It is officially charged with preserving order before, during, and after the voting; and with guarding the polling places, the ballots, and the ballot boxes. The control which it can wield is potentially enormous and despite official protestations of impartiality there is substantial testimony that in recent national, state, and local elections it has acted to intimidate or suppress the opposition and to influence voters and manipulate returns in favor of PRI candidates.[30]

This statement was made about the late 1960s. It could have been made about the late 1980s as well.[31] The intensive electioneering that has characterized Mexico since 1985, and especially since 1988, has put military objectivity to a test.

As electoral competitiveness increases—the likelihood of that is strong—the military's influence will increase, ultimately not as a facilitator for establishment civilian leadership but as a moderator in resolving political disputes.[32] The military itself is not keen on this role, especially if it would involve the supression of large numbers of citizens. As the Escuela Superior de Guerra official manual on internal security argues:

> It is important to know that in principle, force should not be used to maintain internal order. . . . If the armed forces are employed frequently in other types of functions, the danger exists that its involvement in internal politics will project a distorted image, and could result in the military's being considered an instrument of repression in the hands of the government.[33]

Some indication of this potential is evident in the debates about whether the military should have restored order and ensured fair elections in Michoacán in 1990. One officer related that many of his peers "favored the candidacy of Cárdenas. I think that the politicians, including the president, are very nervous about their sympathy for Cárdenas. When Cárdenas asked the army to intervene to maintain order, politicians became very scared about his potential influence."[34]

In the early 1980s the officer corps, believing the state needed its assistance, sought an expanded role. Interestingly, General Félix Galván made the request of President López Portillo at the eighth regional meeting of zone command-

ers, stating that the armed forces desired "more tasks and new means" because
their opinion was that "we can do more for our country."[35] The move presaged
a trend toward military modernization and also points to a very important
distinction. Through the early 1990s changes in civilian-military relations have
not really threatened the present political model's stability but implied an
alteration of the military's state role.[36] In other words, the military is substituting for other actors who performed certain functions in between 1946 and the
present. By displacing those actors, it has restructured state leadership, and
subsequent interactions with the actors. Altering the military's role, if only
slightly, at a time of great stress and variation in the model as a whole, puts at
risk the legitimacy of political processes.

The emergence of a full-fledged opposition party, the Democratic Revolutionary Party (PRD) led by prominent former members of the government
coalition, has provoked intense electoral contests at all levels and has raised
opposition representation in the national legislature to unprecedented levels.
President Salinas came into office in 1988 with a bare majority of votes, the
lowest reported percentage of any president elected since 1920, and amidst
widespread evidence of election fraud, thus taking office with questionable
legitimacy. Furthermore, it is apparent that many officers and enlisted men
and their families voted for the opposition.

A noteworthy response to the shifting political landscape and to the perception that military loyalties will be more and more challenged by political
dynamics, is the makeup since 1987 of ESG classes. Graduating classes in the
1980s typically included eight majors, twenty-five first captains, and twelve
second captains. New admission requirements limited entrants to lieutenants
and second captains. Since 1988 over a third of the matriculants have been
lieutenants, indicating that the army wishes to socialize future colonels and
generals at a more receptive age. Average age is now twenty-six, and except for
engineers, one can be only a junior (second) captain upon entering the program. Such officers normally have between eight and ten years service when
they became cadets at the Heroico Colegio Militar.

Military modernization in terms of expanded resources, both personnel
and hardware, has other implications. A modernization program indirectly
produces three consequences. One, a strengthened military means it has
greater potential, if it so desires, to effect a coup d'état. The probability of
intervention is a different matter.[37] Historically, the Mexican military, relative
to its Latin American counterparts, has been underequipped in regard to
modern weaponry and support vehicles. In fact, the officer corps is proud of
making its equipment go further than that of other armed forces. For example,
in 1962, when the government purchased two thousand new vehicles to replace
ten-year-old vehicles, the Secretariat of National Defense commented that
most countries had three-year or five-year replacement cycles.[38] Nevertheless,
expenditures for equipment have been so niggardly since the 1940s that even
the most complacent military officers are disgruntled.[39] According to José Luis
Piñeyro, the military budget "is recognized as insufficient for the completion of
its mission repeatedly and publicly, but the high command also recognizes

publicly the need for revenues to cover other demands such as education and public health. As Vice Admiral Pablo S. Portela said in March 1985, in response to the navy's efforts to fight drugs: we are not complaining about our situation . . . we do not wish to divert major portions of the federal government budget, which has other priorities."[40] In 1990, Mexico entered into some unpublicized negotiations with several countries, including the United States, to obtain tanks.[41]

The heightened pace of modernization also indicates the military's ability to influence the decision-making process over time, or that the civilian leadership shares the military's concern over its capabilities to perform new functions. For many years spending on the armed forces has dropped substantially, leveling off in the 1980s at about 2 percent of the budget. However, since 1968 several aspects of the situation are worthy of note. First, the size of the armed forces, while small in relation to the population, has grown materially. In Latin America generally, armed forces are four times larger, proportional to population.[42] In the 1950s the armed forces numbered approximately 50,000; in 1967, just before the events in Tlatelolco Square, only 40,000; but by 1976, at the end of Echeverría's administration, 88,000. Less than ten years later, halfway through the de la Madrid administration, a 27 percent increment had been added.[43] By 1990 the total was approximately 140,000.[44] Before 1980 the average annual growth rate of the military budget was 2.6 percent yearly; that of the national government, 12 percent.[45] Only 3 percent of the military's budget went for arms; 60 percent went for salaries.[46] In 1982 Mexico's military expenditures as a percentage of Gross Domestic Product were the lowest in a 117-country study.[47]

Edward Williams reported projected budget increases in the early 1980s for the Secretariat of National Defense of over 80 percent and for the navy at 60 percent, while overall governmental spending grew at 39 percent. Even larger expenditures were projected, but the austerity program that de la Madrid embarked upon precluded such expansion.[48] Both Generals Félix Galván and Juan Arévalo Gardoqui, his successor at the secretariat, wanted an extensive radar system for surveillance, an essential tool for antidrug and security reasons.[49] Care must be taken when analyzing the defense budget because many small and medium items are not reported in it. For example, Phyllis Walker notes that the president provided discretionary funds for the purchase of the F-5s, and the commissaries brought in a relatively significant amount of unreported money.[50]

The relationship between the Secretariat of National Defense and the civilian decision makers in programming and budgeting reveals some interesting aspects of civil-military relations in general. A former budget secretary described the way military funding decisions are made (his account was corroborated by several other former secretaries in interview sessions):

> Let me explain how the funding is allocated. In the first place, there are two types of accounts: current accounts and investments. The first type of account, the current account, includes payments that are provided for salaries and basic

clothing and equipment. Increases in the current account occur through two basic channels. The first increase, which one might call a "natural" increase, is through wages. The second increase, which is more important, is the increase in the number of military units. What you need to understand is that in this second type of increase, *because of our lack of information and expertise in military matters*, it is extremely difficult for us to evaluate if such increases are actually needed.

I will say, by and large, that both types of requests, even in the case where they ask for an additional battalion, are typically reasonable and modest. They don't ask for a new unit every year. In my experience, I found them to be reasonable in their request for current account expenditures. However, automatically, when you have an increase in a battalion, there will be an increase in the investment side. In other words, you have to authorize increases in equipment, housing, and a variety of other costs associated with maintaining a new battalion.

Now, let's examine the investment side as opposed to the current account. The investment side has three channels. First, new investment that is automatically derived from the establishment of a new unit or battalion. Second, and the easiest to judge, is the maintenance and repair of existing equipment. These two areas are reasonable to determine because we have some basis in past experience for determining their cost. The third channel, however, is the one involving new equipment over and above equipment that is only being replaced. It is in this category, the new equipment category, that the decisions are entirely in their hands. That is to say, *they are the ones that request the new investment*. It is really very easy to evaluate the first two types of requests, but the third category is very difficult. As I said before, you have a basis for the first two. However, I again would remark that the actual expenditures are very low. We give that figure to them in a lump sum. That is the one category that we do provide the money in a lump sum.

In my time there was a department that handled the Secretariats of Defense, Navy, and Government. In other words, these were people within programming and budgeting who helped me evaluate the requests of those three secretariats. But, even those individuals who were more well informed than the average official in my agency were really not able to adequately judge new acquisitions.[51]

This careful explanation suggests two points. First, the amount of money asked for is small. Because it is perceived by presidents and their programming secretaries as reasonable, the military request typically is approved. Second, it is clear that in the budgetary context, as elsewhere in the relationship, civilians are essentially ignorant about the military and its needs. The two points are interrelated. Regarding budgetary matters, a wall between the two groups persists because there is no economic pressure for the civilians involved to learn more about the military. In other words, the military's allocations are so small a part of the overall budget that civilian politicians generally, and programming and budgeting officials specifically, have little incentive to strengthen relations with the military.

Despite added spending on personnel and new weaponry, regardless of whether it appears in the military budget, the total outlay for the military is low relative to needs. Much of its regular funding goes into educational and social services, of which a large component is for pensions. One possible consequence of modernization is a squeeze on one or more internal allocations of resources. According to Article 21 of the Armed Forces Institute of Social Security, a retired officer's pension should be equivalent to his active duty counterpart's pay. General Francisco Zepeda Alcazar commented in a 1983 interview that his monthly pension was "the stratospheric sum of 22,174 pesos, almost 13,000 pesos less than what a private earns."[52] It is plain that retired officers must supplement their incomes, and probably that active duty officers must do so in anticipation of retirement. If the price of modernization is dissatisfaction among retired officers, especially generals, and among those who will someday retire, then political risks are considerably heightened.

Institutionally, the military has not exerted pressure sufficient to acquire adequate funding, even for basic nonhardware necessities. In specific cases, through the secretary of defense or navy, it does attempt to "lean" on the president for money or greater control over other resources. An example of success in this regard occurred in 1977 when the president ordered military industries to be placed directly under the Secretariat of Defense (although they had long been headed by a top general) instead of the civil federal bureaucracy. As the head of the Federal Workers Union commented, the move gave power to the army at the expense of the civil sector.[53] In the case of the F-5s, well documented by Dziedzic's dissertation, Galván reportedly told the president, "If you want our continued support, we must have our needs taken care of."[54] The president, however, patently dominated the decision-making process, and authorized the secretary of defense to go ahead with modernization. The public requests for monies, however, are not necessarily a reflection of military assertiveness; rather, they are for the benefit of other political actors so the president can prepare the cabinet, and in a smaller way the public, for military allocations.[55]

The decision to modernize also reflects a more up-to-date self-image within the officer corps, expressed through establishment of the Colegio de Defensa Nacional and a new philosophy. Begun in the early 1980s, the modernization program instituted a reappraisal of national security doctrine, and the role of the military in its application and definition. The rapid expansion of the petroleum industry, and civil and military violence in Central America contributed most to setting the stage for a new military role. As early as 1981, the secretary of defense told a journalist that the military required more equipment and soldiers to protect vital installations, referring to Pemex (the government-owned oil company) and the Federal Electric Company.[56] Williams believes that the military's expanded internal security functions are indicative of its widening role as a policymaker; that it is no longer just a policy instrument. He argues that it has progressed from supplementing the police to being primarily responsible for internal security across the board.[57] Expanded military responsibilities were alluded to in the National Development Plan, in addition to the more traditional duty of territorial defense.[58] Further, the cream of the officer corps are writing theses on national security at the Colegio de Defensa Nacional, as documented earlier. Thus, as Ronfeldt declares, "The military is gradually being prepared, through officer education and technical modernization, to play enlarged roles in support of the state should its civilian leadership falter and civil-military leadership be required."[59] Of course, Ronfeldt assumes that to be the purpose of the CDN. Instead, I argue that such preparation gives officers increased *potential* for playing a different leadership role.

There is no question that the military is shouldering more responsibility in national security affairs. Some observers, however, remain unconvinced that it is exerting much influence in the policy arena. As late as 1986 Phyllis Walker reported, on the basis of interviews with Mexican officers, that colonels and generals attending the CDN were only marginally interested in national matters and therefore had little competence to advise the president on security issues. Although President de la Madrid requested policy papers from these student officers, he was offering them only token participation, wanting the military to perceive itself as having input into security policy.[60] An event that also throws doubt on the military's policy-making role was its response to the 1985 earthquake. As mentioned previously, according to the national emergency plan DN-III, in effect at the time, the responsibility belonged to the armed forces yet it was civilian executive branch agencies that took control.[61]

In 1988, immediately after Salinas took office, he created a new technical cabinet, described earlier. By adding a fifth group, national security, he formalized the military's voice in the civilian decision-making process. Because of the structural change, the military is taking its national security role more seriously. According to one Mexican expert, the Secretariat of National Defense has replaced the Secretariat of Government as a prominent actor.[62] Despite the structural changes, Mexico still does not have the institutional equivalent of the U.S. National Security Council. Military intelligence is not shared with civilian counterparts. The curricular emphasis at the CDN since 1988, which is likely to heighten interest in national security issues, reflects the revised assignment.[63]

Since President Salinas's inauguration, the military's role has come to the fore, even in matters that really cannot be considered under the rubric of national security.[64] Williams's predictions, possibly somewhat premature, were essentially correct. It is difficult to ascribe policy influence to the military's augmented role; however, when it functions in such a capacity, it earns political currency with the presidency and the executive branch. The military will indirectly impact on national security policy because at some point, when its role is well established, it may be the only actor to function effectively in that capacity.

Finally, the military—like any institution with an understanding of the political game—ultimately is going to call in its bargaining chips, in this case from the presidency. And —as developed more thoroughly earlier—modernization, within the context of the military's national security role, involves a redefinition of the military's self-image in terms of responsibilities and role. Because the officer corps is being used to implement high-profile executive decisions, the corps cannot help but become more broadly interested in political affairs.

The other policy-making sphere in which military involvement is most likely is foreign affairs. Heretofore the military's role in that regard and in bilateral relations with the United States has been minimal, if not nonexistent. A careful reading of the literature suggests that the military was desirous of closer collaboration with the U.S. military but that civilian authorities have stood in the way. Since the mid-1980s cooperation between the two militaries has become more extensive. The military derives its impact in foreign affairs from two dimensions: its role in policymaking, and as an instrument of foreign policy; in neither has its influence been notable. Only in two areas is there some evidence of greater military participation than normal in one or both dimensions. The most analyzed of the two is Central American policy. The modernization of the army has without a doubt helped to strengthen Mexico's policy toward Central America generally and Guatemala specifically. Since 1980 the Secretariat of National Defense has increased and reassigned its personnel in the region, providing alternative military intelligence.[65] Still, there is no concrete evidence of the military's determining foreign policy in the region. On the other hand, it has had a larger voice in some issues, such as southern immigration, on which the Government and Foreign Relations Secretariats disagreed in the 1980s.[66]

The available evidence, although sketchy, reaffirms that the military, at least up to 1991, has had a very limited role, in general terms, in the decision-making process.[67] The data on the budget illustrate that in spite of recent modernization efforts, it is the civilian leadership that allocates funds, and typically the armed forces do not have much influence in that quarter. In some specific political decisions, several of which had tremendous consequences, the military did not ask to be involved but was brought into the decision-making process when trouble was at hand. This is illustrated by the events of 1968, analyzed in the second chapter, and by the crisis within the Echeverría administration in 1971.[68] These examples highlight a serious deficiency in the decision-making process.

Civilian concern with keeping the armed forces out of political decision making is so extreme that the military provides input or is requested to act only in the final stages of the process. This is dangerous for several reasons. First, the military, when appropriate, needs to offer its own interpretation of a situation and of the repercussions for the armed forces and for society from its institutional point of view. Second, to omit the military from the informational chain, from "the loop," so to speak, affects the outcome of a decision. Decisions are made on the basis of information, inadequate or otherwise. Third, waiting until a situation is at a critical stage to bring the military into the decisional process risks, as the 1968 chain of events shows, having the military make its own decisions without sufficient consideration of larger political repercussions.

When a decision becomes solely the military's, other ramifications are not considered either. Consequently, civilian decision makers will bear the brunt of the decision. As the political system is strained by liberalization, the potential for the military's involvement is likely to grow.[69] In June 1990 troops were ordered into Guererro to remove armed sympathizers of the Democratic Revolutionary Party holed up in town halls across the state, and at least five activists were killed in one village.[70] Such resistance to government perpetrated voting fraud will inevitably eventuate in military intervention. The military, on the other hand, could be a persuasive voice in exploring other alternatives. Contrary to popular belief, generals often counsel against the use of force, in light of their firsthand experience with its limitations and costs.

Civilian political leaders have certain advantages in retaining their image and position of supremacy that work against expanded military decision making and an enlarged political role. As Morris Janowitz has argued, civilian political leadership skills differ radically from military leadership skills, especially in connection with mass appeals and rhetorical maneuvering. Politicians, he says, are socialized early into the techniques and process of negotiation, in contrast to military personnel.[71] Of course, the lack of such skills has not deterred the military from entering into the decision-making process nor from intervening directly in political affairs. The civilian leadership, however, has a special advantage in this regard because it has never had to contend with a serious opposition party, one which could compete for the military's loyalty. Electoral challenges of the PRD not only threaten the PRI, but imply a possible major realignment of government relations with the military, labor unions, and other groups.

Military personnel have never been encouraged, even in the most limited way, to develop verbal skills useful in the larger world. Even in class, colonels and generals tend to be reticent because they have had little experience in intellectual debate.[72] As Piñeyro points out, the golden rule is that "the high command does not make pronouncements in the press on national problems (inflation, unemployment, corruption) or international problems (financial crises, Central American or Middle East wars), and when they do so, it is in support of the president or corresponding secretary of state."[73] Transgression of this "rule," which has happened only rarely in recent years, results in the offender's immediate change of assignment or dismissal. Imposed silence makes it nearly impossible for the military to produce public personalities.

Civilian leaders make effective use of another informal, but more positive, quality in their relationship with the officer corps. Politicians, from presidents on down, always have been careful to praise the military publicly for its loyalty and service to the republic.[74] Most observers agree that the encomiums are excessive.[75] In 1986 Secretary of Government Manuel Bartlett called the army and air force institutions of greatest prestige, earned by actions, example, and respect for national unity.[76] One president termed the army "a national treasure" because of its unique, long-standing loyalty.[77] In return, the army itself has emphasized its loyalty to political institutions, which of course since 1946 has meant loyalty to one political faction. Interestingly, General Cuenca Díaz, long before he became secretary of defense some forty years ago, wrote an editorial in which he remarked:

> We have to remember that "strength comes from unity" and therefore we must be on the alert against any type of disassociation which could place our national integrity in danger. We cannot permit any false visions. . . . The formula of our destiny is synthesized in these few words: Work and Loyalty to Mexico through her institutions.[78]

A third informal limitation on military influence is the level of consensus among civilian leaders on the role of the military. Also, elite solidarity in terms of their rationale for governing, in the broadest possible sense, is equally important.[79] Of course, this consensus is made possible structurally by the fact that the model has functioned along the lines of a modified one-party state. Nevertheless, there has never been any evidence since the demise of military political opposition in 1958 that establishment elites, members of the opposition National Action Party, or leftist parties have, as a means of dividing the leadership, sought military help. Despite their competitiveness on many economic and social issues, even to the extent of producing a split in the leadership in 1987, civilian elites have been "singularly united in their commitment to limiting the political role of the military."[80] The Mexican Democratic Party does, however, raise the possibility for the first time in more than thirty years that an important group of political leaders might request the military's support of constitutional and legislative protections, forcing the military to choose between loyalty to the state and loyalty to the law.

Finally, a less flattering technique of civilian supremacy in civil-military relations has been suggested, but without empirical evidence. The Mexican state traditionally has used access to financial resources to co-opt political opposition, outspoken intellectuals, and recalcitrant businesspeople. Porfirio Díaz was a master at facilitating elite access, political and military alike, to graft. The postrevolutionary leaders were no more reluctant to use the technique than those whom they sought to overthrow. Obregón himself made famous the phrase "No general can resist a cannonball of 50,000 pesos." Alan Riding, a knowledgeable journalist, stated that "it became government policy to corrupt the Army. Senior officers were encouraged to enrich themselves with assorted business opportunities, sinecures and favors, and even illicit activities, such as contraband, drug trafficking, and prostitution, were tolerated."[81] It is doubtful that it is an agreed-upon government policy to corrupt the armed forces; rather, military corruption is generally winked at—as is true of high-level political malfeasance.

The most important cultural pattern explaining military subordination to civil authority in any society is the intensity with which the citizenry itself is committed to civilian supremacy. Ironically, this variable is typically neglected in Latin American analyses, and only rarely is it empirically tested.[82] As

William S. Ackroyd suggests, "Latin American civil-military relations can never replicate North America and Western Europe because Latin American civilians have never rejected the military's use for the promotion of partisan political goals."[83] Yet, new public opinion survey data presented previously indicate a relatively strong societal consensus against military intervention. The antimilitarism is reflected in other ways. Politicians at the local level have not been readily accepting of President Salinas's use of the army, even if the results are praiseworthy. For example, after the president used armed forces to capture a leading drug dealer, Félix Gallardo, the state legislature of Sinaloa, where the action took place, passed a unanimous resolution criticizing government-sponsored military intervention: "We cannot accept that in order to achieve such objectives, military commands have carried out actions sweeping aside institutional guidelines, generating uneasiness in the citizenry and unnecessary social alarm."[84]

The informal inhibitions imposed by civilian and particularly presidential leadership are integrated into the Mexican political model. Formally, however, presidential authority over the military is extensive, in terms of not only appointment powers but also the chief executive's authority to order troop movements for either internal security purposes or external defense.[85] According to the most recent legislation, revised in 1986, "The supreme commander of the army and air force corresponds to the president of the republic, who exercises this himself or through the secretary of national defense" (Article 11). Specifically, presidential powers include naming the secretary of national defense, subsecretary, oficial mayor, inspector general, controller general, attorney general of military justice, and the president and judges of the supreme military court; the presidential chief of staff; zone commanders; unit and special commanders; and all department heads at the National Defense Secretariat.[86] The Organic Law of the Navy, revised in January 1985, corresponds to army statutes.[87]

Legal statutes are a significant step in establishing the boundaries of civil-military relations because they reflect, at least to some degree, the cultural norms of society as well as institutional relationships expected by that society. A constitution and organic law are hollow documents in the absence of strong political institutions. Of all the possible formal components of the Mexican model that impact on civil-military relations, this is probably of utmost importance, especially given civilian ideology relative to civil-military relations.

Under President Salinas, decision making has become more centralized in the presidency, channeled through the technical cabinet. Such matters as control over elections, internal security issues, censorship of the media, and combating drug trafficking, many of which have been within the purview of the Secretariat of Government and intertwined with broader internal security priorities, are now handled directly or indirectly by the presidency. For example, the president shifted Colonel Jorge Carrillo Olea from head of internal security to director of the government's antidrug program. Carrillo Olea is reportedly using his new post as drug czar to develop intelligence gathering capabilities from non-drug-related intelligence agencies in the United States, including the National Security Council and the Pentagon. He is said to report to José Córdoba, head of the president's technical cabinet.[88]

The military has withdrawn from politics, remaining subordinate to civil authority, in response to the strengths of civil institutions. As the chapter on the evolution of civil-military relations documents fully, Presidents Calles and Cárdenas especially, as well as their successors, used their influence and skill to develop party strength and a corporate state, and to entrench civilian leadership firmly in both institutions.[89] Despite a significant decline in the institutions' legitimacy since 1968, and especially since 1976, their influence is critical. As I have argued elsewhere, military *participation* in politics has been transformed into military *influence* in politics, based on the increasing legitimacy of civilian and governmental institutions. This is an important distinction. In effect, the military became one of several interest groups co-opted by the state, sharing some similarities with labor, peasants, intellectuals, and businesspeople. Some scholars have attributed the state's legitimacy primarily to the PRI, but the essential ingredient actually has been the bureaucracy or state organizations.[90]

Some evidence exists that the armed forces would like to consolidate into one organizational structure under the National Defense Secretariat. The implication of this structural change is that it would give the army control over both the navy and the air force. According to Stephen Wager, such attempts have been futile because political leaders "fear that such a command structure would make the Secretary of Defense too powerful, and subsequently, reduce the amount of influence these leaders could exert on the military."[91] Interestingly, no mention is made of how the navy itself reacts to the notion.

Civilian supremacy over the military in the policy-making realm is important not only because it establishes such precedence procedurally but because the armed forces have had little experience in the exercise of power. It is true that a split within the political leadership, or an increasingly strong opposition movement that is prevented from rightfully occupying the presidency would force the military to choose, thus transforming it into the role of kingmaker.[92] Nevertheless, the military's lack of widespread political management experience would render it nearly incapable of taking and holding power.[93] A radical change in its present role would require a different political ally.

It is imperative to emphasize that although the evidence available suggests that civilians unquestionably control decision making, they leave two spheres of influence to the military. Civilian decision makers do not determine the military's internal budget allocations; the military secretariats do that. Also, the controller general, who is supposed to investigate fiscal irregularities, essentially never intervenes in the military budget.[94] Second, politicians basically have not inserted themselves in the military's promotion process since the 1950s, leaving it in the hands of the military leadership. Presidents have on occasion altered *the pace* of senior officer promotions or disagreed with secretariat recommendations but have not promoted ineligible officers out of turn.

In general terms, elsewhere in the Third World, the presence of six variables explain civilian supremacy in civil-military relations: constitutional constraints on the political impact of the military; ascriptive qualities (class or ethnicity) affecting relationships between civilian and military leaders; establishment of a strong political party; development of effective and legitimate political institutions; geographic and historical factors permitting the maintenance of relatively small armed forces with narrow responsibilities; and delineation of clear spheres of military responsibility, leading to widespread acceptance within the armed forces of an ethic of subordination.[95] To these six universal variables, three others, based on the Mexican case, should be added: civilian leaders lavish the military with psychological praise; military involvement in political leadership is reduced gradually over a period of time;[96] and civilian leaders remain outside strictly military internal affairs.

In summary, the variables affecting Mexico are for the most part found among universal patterns of civil dominance over the military. Since 1946 the most important variables in Mexican civil-military relations have been the strength of its political institutions, both party and state; the attitude of the officer corps toward its political role; the attitude of civilian leaders and society as a whole toward the military's role; the importance of the military academies in socializing the officer corps in an ethic of subordination to civil authority; the autonomy of the military in internal matters, especially promotion, from civilian political interference; and the joint origins of political and military leadership from revolutionary roots.

The variables having somewhat more influence in the Mexican case are the sources of the military ethic of subordination. Professionalization has been devalued as a variable in the literature on civil-military relations, and rightly so, depending on the term's conceptualization. But professionalization defined as a strong sense of subordination generally, and subordination to civil authority particularly, has been critical to the relationship in Mexico. Equally important, the military academies, through a homogeneous and strict socialization process, have been largely responsible for this achievement. Although implicit in Claude Welch's conclusions, more weight must be given to societal attitudes toward the military because military attitudes themselves are a product of broader societal values, especially given the fact that the generation that will next govern Mexico is a cohort steeped in an authoritarian, hierarchical, and closed political culture.[97]

Second, the autonomy of the military in internal matters appears very important in the Mexican context. It is made possible by the continuity of the leadership, the modified one-party system, and the consistency in attitudes that evolved the boundaries of the relationship.

The question of military intervention and a revival of militarism in Mexican politics revolves around the issue of political stability. Political stability directly affects the legitimacy of the political institutions and the strength of organizations such as the PRI. The consensus of analysts over the past fifteen years is that increased political unrest will lead to a larger military political role, that increased unrest is likely, but that only a radical change in the political system would provoke a full-scale military coup d'état.[98] According to this view, the army has not been interested in intervening because civil institutions, notably the presidency, are not being threatened. According to one source close to senior officers, "What causes the military to put its hands into the cookie jar is when the institutions are threatened."[99]

What would bring about military intervention, or alter the Mexican environment sufficiently that the political conditions would radically change? Several possibilities come to mind. One source of political change is elite dissension.[100] Divisions within the elite leading to autonomous mobilization of various groups might create an environment conducive to military intervention—if the military perceived the political leadership as incompetent to govern. For this to occur, the majority of the masses would have to reject Mexico's leadership and institutions as illegitimate and ineffective.[101] One weakness in contemporary Mexican political analysis is that the focus is on major political actors, especially in the electoral arena, notably the PRI and PRD. The more perceptive observers, however, detect considerable activity among grass-roots organizations in the provinces and in urban centers. One example is the base community organizations organized by progressive priests and laypersons. Members are learning how to articulate demands and how to make their demands collectively. It is these groups that may well provide an alternative view of Mexico's political institutions and may well question their legitimacy, and thereby enhance divisions already apparent within the establishment and opposition leaderships. To defuse this situation, the political leadership must actively seek out and consolidate new bases of support.[102]

Another source of political change is the persistent resistance of the establishment leadership to genuine opposition victories and its resort to fraud. Elites within the governing circle who favor above all else their perpetuation in power against all comers continue to thwart political modernization and electoral reform. The 1990 elections in México State confirm their ongoing influence. Political violence is likely to increase in response to this posture, and the military will be called upon to intervene to protect an illegitimate system. Either the army will ask for and receive a greater voice in the political decision-making process or it will attempt to change the system in such a way that it will not be required to suppress widespread, popular resistance.[103] Some observers believe that the military has already accepted the reality that soldiers will be used for crowd control and street fighting in election periods.[104]

Mexico's leadership has sought to disarm its opponents and to confound analysts by taking the initiative and to some degree melding together a strategy that on one hand attempts to resist change while rebuilding or reweighting a political coalition on the other. The coalition includes a large voice and even more visible role for two traditional political actors on the Mexican scene: the Church and the military. Other ingredients in the political formula are upper-middle-class, urban Mexicans, important elements in business circles, the international community (especially the United States), and a wing of the traditional opposition party. Through strong leadership—not surprising, given Rafael Segovia's findings nearly twenty years ago—Salinas has been able to weather the storm and to set about building a new base of power, one that might restore some legitimacy to the political system and considerable sheen to the presidency itself.

Extreme care must be taken not to confuse a more visible military role as equivalent to a remilitarization of Mexican society. As David Ronfeldt so aptly describes it:

> Every political-military connection, formal or informal, that surfaces may look like increased military influence in politics. But no institution in Mexico is allowed to develop and modernize without increasingly becoming a partner of the state and the PRI. Hence, political-military connections may be a sign of modernization and institutionalization within Mexico's corporatist system, and of the system's ability to preserve itself through stressful times, without signifying that the military has gained influence at the expense of the civilian leadership.[105]

On the other hand, any time a political coalition is reformed, risks abound.

The increasing role of the military, for a variety of the aforementioned reasons, primarily focusing on internal security, legitimizes its potential for a larger voice, not just in the *execution* of policy decisions but in the *formulation* of policy. In a society where military political intervention is seen negatively by the majority of citizens, but not by all citizens, a margin of error exists. It is unknown how widespread such thinking must be before military intervention is no longer viable as a political alternative in Mexico.

Notes

1. Sam C. Sarkesian, *Beyond the Battlefield: The New Military Professionalism* (New York: Pergamon Press, 1981), 239.

2. Henry Bienen, "Civil-Military Relations in the Third World," *International Political Science Review* 2, no. 3 (1981): 365.

3. Sam C. Sarkesian, "Military Professionalism and Civil-Military Relations in the West," *International Political Science Review* 2, no. 3 (1981): 290.

4. Ibid., 291.

5. Marion J. Levy, Jr., "Armed Forces Organization," in *The Military and Modernization*, ed. Henry Bienen (Chicago: Aldine-Atherton, 1971), 49.

6. Alan Riding, *Distant Neighbors: A Portrait of the Mexicans* (New York: Knopf, 1985), 93, 368.

7. Personal interview, Mexico City, 1990. In many cases, recent presidents have not known personally their secretaries of defense. For example, a close friend of General Marcelino García Barragán indicated that President Gustavo Díaz Ordaz did not know the general personally, all the more remarkable considering García Barragán's support for General Henríquez Guzmán in the 1952 campaign. García Barragán was chosen, according to this source, because of his abilities and the loyalty he demonstrated in the six years prior to his 1964 appointment. More recently, a president indicated that "it was difficult to choose the two military secretaries. To begin with because I didn't know very many people in the military." He asked the incumbent secretary of national defense to give him the names of the eligible three-star generals, and then asked him to narrow it down to five individuals. The president-elect then examined their records very carefully, and asked the secretary to recommend three candidates, from whom he selected one. He knew the general slightly from previous positions both had held. Personal interviews, Mexico City, 1990.

8. Personal interview, Mexico City, 1991.

9. Martin H. Greenberg, *Bureaucracy and Development: A Mexican Case Study* (Lexington, Mass.: Heath, 1970), 117.

10. Personal interview, Mexico City, 1990.

11. Sarkesian, "Military Professionalism and Civil-Military Relations in the West," 285.

12. Roderic A. Camp, "Political Modernization in Mexico: Through a Looking Glass," in *Political Evolution in Mexico*, ed. Jaime O. Rodríguez, (Wilmington, De.: Scholarly Resources, 1992).

13. In the mid-1980s the reported size of the armed forces was 120,000: 95,500, army; 5,500, air force; and 20,000, navy. Budgets have been distributed relatively evenly according to each service's proportion of the total. See José Luis Piñeyro, "The Modernization of the Mexican Armed Forces," in *Democracy under Siege: New Military Power in Latin America*, ed. Augusto Varas (Westport, Conn.: Greenwood Press, 1989), 117. The 1987 figures were 105,000, army; 6,500, air force; 25,000, navy; and 8,500, marines.

14. Personal interview, Mexico City, 1991.

15. Rodney W. Jones and Steven A. Hildreth, eds., *Emerging Powers: Defense and Security in the Third World* (New York: Praeger, 1986), 387.

16. Personal interviews, Mexico City, 1991.

17. Michael J. Dziedzic, "The Essence of Decision in a Hegemonic Regime: The Case of Mexico's Acquisition of a Supersonic Fighter" (Ph.D. diss., University of Texas, Austin, 1986), 327.

18. *Acción*, January 18, 1982, 8.

19. Ibid. The differences came out symbolically at the September 16, 1980, parade: navy personnel wore traditional uniforms; army personnel, combat gear. The two secretaries represented different civilian political factions. General Félix Galván, who was General García Barragán's personal secretary, was recommended by his mentor to President López Portillo to counterbalance the continued influence of Echeverría, whom Galván disliked. Naval secretary Cházaro, on the other hand, was part of Echeverría's group, in whose administration he served as subsecretary of the navy, obtaining his position through the group's influence.

20. William S. Ackroyd, "The Military in Mexican Politics: The Impact of Professionalization, Civilian Behavior, and the Revolution" (Paper presented at the Pacific Coast Council of Latin Americanists, San Diego, October 1982), 17.

21. Personal interviews, Mexico City, 1991.

22. Sarkesian, "Military Professionalism and Civil Military Relations in the West," 287.

23. Ibid., 291.

24. Moshe Lissak, "Center and Periphery in Developing Countries and Prototypes of Military Elites," in *Militarism in Developing Countries*, ed. Kenneth Fidel (New Brunswick, N.J.: Transaction, 1975), 49.

25. A rare case appearing in the legislative record is that of the Veterans Association of Campeche, which made it known to the Senate that it supported the veterans legislation under consideration. Cámara de Senadores, *Memorias*, November 7, 1941. 5.

26. Dziedzic, "The Essence of Decision in a Hegemonic Regime," 282.

27. David Ronfeldt, "The Mexican Army and Political Order Since 1940," in *Armies and Politics in Latin America*, ed. Abraham F. Lowenthal (New York: Holmes and Meier, 1976), 295, for the provincial examples, and my "Civilian Supremacy in Mexico, the Case of a Post-Revolutionary Military," in *Military Intervention and Withdrawal*, ed. Constantine P. Danopoulous (London: Routledge, 1991), 23.

28. Edward J. Williams, "The Evolution of the Mexican Military and Its Implications for Civil-Military Relations," in *Mexico's Political Stability: the Next Five Years*, ed. Roderic A. Camp (Boulder, Colo.: Westview Press, 1986), 151.

29. David Ronfeldt, *The Mexican Army and Political Order since 1940* (Santa Monica: Rand Corporation, 1973), 8.

30. Lyle N. McAlister, *The Military in Latin American Socio-political Evolution: Four Case Studies* (Washington, D.C.: Center for Research in Social Systems, 1970), 243.

31. *Sin más armas que la vida misma* (Mexico: Acción Nacional, 1986), which includes actual photographs of voter fraud taking place.

32. Williams, "The Evolution of the Mexican Military," 152.

33. Escuela Superior de Guerra, *Compendio de seguridad interior, el estado mexicano y los*

factores desestabilizadores (Mexico, August 1985), 14. The potential destabilizing elements considered by the military, and analyzed in considerable detail are socialism, religion, Masonry, Semitism, imperialism, oligarchy, and public administration.

34. Personal interview, Mexico City, 1990. One officer also reported that President Salinas's decision to use the army to intervene in the government-operated Cananea mining company strike early in his administration had repercussions within the military, and that knowledgeable officers considered it an abuse of military power.

35. Otto Granados Roldán, "Regreso a las armas?" in *El desafío mexicano*, ed. Francisco de Alba et al. (Mexico: Ediciones Oceano, 1982), 127.

36. David Ronfeldt, "The Modern Mexican Military," in *Armies and Politics in Latin America*, ed. Abraham Lowenthal and J. Samuel Fitch (New York: Holmes and Meier, 1986), 234.

37. Williams, "The Evolution of the Mexican Military," 147.

38. Karl M. Schmitt, "The Role of the Military in Contemporary Mexico," in *The Caribbean: Mexico Today*, ed. Curtis A. Wilgus (Gainesville: University of Florida Press, 1964), 54.

39. Edwin Lieuwen, "Depolitization of the Mexican Revolutionary Army, 1915–1940," in *The Modern Mexican Military: A Reassessment*, ed. David Ronfeldt (La Jolla: Center for United States-Mexican Studies, University of California, San Diego, 1984), 61.

40. José Luis Piñeyro, "Presencia política militar nacional y en el Distrito Federal: Propuestas de análisis," in *Distrito Federal, gobierno y sociedad civil*, ed. Pablo González Casanova (Mexico: El Caballito, 1987), 70.

41. Americas Watch, *Report on Mexico*, 8, citing Hernán Pereyra, "Dreams and Tanks: Sales to Iran and Mexico," *Somos* (Argentina), February 21, 1990, that Mexico negotiated to buy four hundred tanks from Argentina, or a similar amount of excess NATO M60 A-1 tanks from the United States, which were eventually sold to Egypt.

42. For some comparative statistics on force size for Mexico and Latin America, see Lind L. Reif's work. She also notes that Latin American expenditures as a percentage of GNP were 2–3 percent; Mexican, .86 percent; and U.S., 6.9 percent. "Seizing Control: Latin American Military Motives, Capabilities, and Risks," *Armed Forces and Society* 10 (Summer 1984): 571.

43. Gloria Fuentes, *El Ejército mexicano* (Mexico: Grijalbo, 1983), 111–130.

44. Personal interview, Mexico City, 1990.

45. Merilee Grindle. "Civil-Military Relations and Budgetary Politics in Latin America," *Armed Forces and Society* 13 (Winter 1987): 258.

46. Guillermo Boils, "Fuerzas armadas y armamentismo en México," *Nueva Política* 2 (April–September, 1977): 356.

47. Alfred Stepan, *Rethinking Military Politics: Brazil and the Southern Cone* (Princeton: Princeton University Press, 1988), 75.

48. Edward J. Williams, "Mexico's Central American Policy: National Security Considerations," in *Rift and Revolution: the Central American Imbroglio*, ed. Howard J. Wiarda (Washington, D.C.: American Enterprise Institute, 1984), 303–328; Charles Wolf, Jr., et al., project that in the long term Mexico's defense spending will increase from 2 billion in the 1990s to 3 billion after the turn of the century. *Long-term Economic and Military Trends, 1950–2010* (Santa Monica: Rand Corporation, 1989), 17.

49. Marvin Alisky, "Mexico," in *Arms Production in Developing Countries: An Analysis of Decision Making*, ed. James Everett Katz (Lexington, Mass.: Lexington Books, 1984), 249.

50. Phyllis Greene Walker, "The Modern Mexican Military: Political Influence and Institutional Interests in the 1980s" (M.A. thesis, American University, 1987), 64; José Luis Piñeyro, "The Mexican Army and the State: Historical and Political Perspective," *Revue Internationale de Sociologie* 14 (April–August 1978): 147.

51. Personal interviews, Mexico City, 1990.

52. Raúl Monje, "Con 371,000 hombres, las fuerzas armadas de México se modernizan," *Proceso*, June 14, 1983, 25.

53. *Proceso*, October 3, 1977, 33.

54. Dziedzic, "The Essence of Decision in a Hegemonic Regime," 181, 179.

55. Ibid., 181–182.

56. Edward J. Williams, "Mexico's Central American Policy: Revolutionary and Prudential

Dimensions," in *Colossus Challenged: The Struggle for Caribbean Influence*, ed. H. Michael Erisman and John D. Martz (Boulder, Colo.: Westview Press, 1982), 159.

57. Edward J. Williams, "The Mexican Military and Foreign Policy: The Evolution of Influence," in *The Modern Mexican Military: A Reassessment*, ed. David Ronfeldt (La Jolla: Center for United States-Mexican Studies, University of California, San Diego, 1984), 188.

58. Luis Herrera-Lasso and Guadalupe González G., "Balance y perspectiva en el uso del concepto de la seguridad nacional en el caso de México" (unpublished paper, 1989), 24.

59. David F. Ronfeldt, "The Modern Mexican Military: An Overview," in *The Modern Mexican Military: A Reassessment*, ed. Ronfeldt (La Jolla: Center for United States-Mexican Studies, University of California, San Diego, 1984), 11.

60. Walker, "The Modern Mexican Military," 79. Ronfeldt was also doubtful about this influence as late as 1984; see his "The Modern Mexican Military," 11.

61. Herrera-Lasso and González G., "Balance y perspectiva en el uso del conceepto de seguridad nacional," 18.

62. Personal interview, Mexico City, 1991.

63. Personal interview, Mexico City, 1990.

64. For a listing of these events, see Lorenzo Meyer's perceptive overview in "Ejército y Cananeas del futuro," *Excélsior*, September 6, 1989, 12.

65. Caesar Sereseres, "The Mexican Military Looks South," in *The Modern Mexican Military: A Reassessment*, ed. David Ronfeldt (La Jolla: Center for United States-Mexican Studies, University of California, San Diego, 1984), 211.

66. For these and other issues, see Williams, "Mexico's Central American Policy," 159; Williams, "Mexico's Central American Policy: National Security Considerations," in *Rift and Revolution: Central American Imbroglio*, ed. Howard J. Wiarda (Washington, D.C.: American Enterprise Institute, 1984), 303–328; Williams, "Mexico's Modern Military: Implications for the Region," *Caribbean Review* 10 (Fall 1981): 12–13, 45.

67. Schmitt, "The Role of the Military in Contemporary Mexico," 61.

68. Sergio Zermeño, "De Echeverría a de la Madrid: Las clases altas y el estado mexicano" (Paper presented at the Latin American Program, Woodrow Wilson International Center for Scholars, 1982), 27.

69. In agreement with this view is Brian Latell, a U.S. intelligence analyst, in *Mexico at the Crossroads: The Many Crises of the Political System* (Stanford: Hoover Institution, 1986), 28–29.

70. Brook Larmer, "Regional Organizations Gain Political Clout," *Christian Science Monitor*, June 4, 1990.

71. Morris Janowitz, *The Military in the Development of New Nations* (Chicago: University of Chicago Press, 1964), 42–43.

72. Personal interviews, Mexico City, 1989–1990.

73. Piñeyro, "Presencia política militar nacional," 65. Piñeyro wrote in "The Modernization of the Mexican Armed Forces," 126, that since 1935 "the Defense Ministry has not officially leveled a single criticism against the incumbent president or the ruling party. The same holds true for the officer corps after 1952."

74. They have understood what leading theorists, including Morris Janowitz and S. E. Finer, have suggested about the military's need for self-respect or public recognition of its societal status. See Franklin D. Margiotta's discussion of this point in "Civilian Control and the Mexican Military: Changing Patterns of Political Influence," in *Civilian Control of the Military: Theories and Cases from Developing Countries*, ed. Claude E. Welch, Jr. (Albany: State University of New York Press, 1976), 218.

75. Ibid., 247.

76. Address to both chambers, Senado, *Diario de los debates*, no. 11, October 1, 1986, 10.

77. Personal interview, Mexico City, 1990.

78. "Editorial, la lealtad a nuestras instituciones," *Revista de Ejército y Fuerza Aérea*, April–June, 1952, 4.

79. Gordon C. Schloming, "Civil-Military Relations in Mexico, 1910–1940: A Case Study" (Ph.D. diss., Columbia University, 1974), 56.

80. Grindle, "Civil-Military Relations and Budgetary Politics in Latin America," 263.

81. Alan Riding, *Distant Neighbors: A Portrait of the Mexicans* (New York: Knopf, 1984), 91. Riding went on to say that the government actually protected the armed forces from media criticism when evidence of corruption among several top generals was discovered.

82. In terms of democracy, Irving Louis Horowitz put it differently: "Democracy is not a function of civilian authority any more than of military authority. It is a consequence of openness versus closure in the systems." "Militarism and Civil-Military Relationships in Latin America: Implications for the Third World," *Research in Political Sociology*, vol. 1 (Greenwich, Conn.: JAI Press, 1985), 96.

83. William S. Ackroyd, "Descendants of the Revolution: Civil-Military Relations in Mexico" (Ph.D. diss., University of Arizona, 1988), 27.

84. Larry Rohter, "Use of Troops a Cause of Concern in Mexico," *New York Times*, November 5, 1989, 8.

85. Leon Padgett, *The Mexican Political System*, 2d ed. (Boston: Houghton Mifflin, 1976), 199.

86. Revised Organic Law, *Diario Oficial*, December 26, 1986, 2–3.

87. *Diario Oficial*, January 14, 1985.

88. Personal interview, Mexico City, 1991.

89. Some of the analysts who stress this point include Franklin D. Margiotta, who argues that "a primary condition may be the existence of a well-developed, powerful political party which is willing and able to coopt the military elite of the nation," in "Civilian Control and the Mexican Military," 246; José Luis Piñeyro, who gives it predominance over professionalization, in his belief that "with the strengthening of these mechanisms [presidentialism and one party], the Army was able to be reduced to a secondary role in national politics, not because its increased professionalization had 'depoliticized' it as some authors sustain; but because the civil branch of the political bureaucracy had acquired a clear predominance over its military counterpart in the direction of the state," in "The Mexican Army and the State," 120; and Samuel J. Fitch, "Armies and Politics in Latin America: 1975–1985," in *Armies and Politics in Latin America*, ed. Abraham Lowenthal and Samuel Fitch (New York: Holmes and Meier, 1986), 37.

90. Camp, "Civilian Supremacy in Mexico," 10.

91. Wager's remarks are from his "Modernization of the Mexican Military: Political and Strategic Implications," incorporated into the text of Robert Wesson, *The Latin American Military* (Westport, Conn.: Greenwood Press, 1986), 32.

92. Michael J. Dziedzic, "Mexico's Converging Challenges: Problems, Prospects, and Implications" (unpublished manuscript, U.S. Air Force Academy, April 12, 1989), 84.

93. Herrera-Lasso and González, G. "Balance y perspectiva en el uso del concepto de la seguridad nacional," 28.

94. Even in the case of Admiral Schleske, when the controller general had denunciations and evidence for well over a year, he did not act. See *Proceso*, July 23, 1990. One officer commented, "You know that here the controller general, which we have to investigate fiscal irregularities, never intervenes in the military budget." Personal interview, Mexico City, 1990.

95. See Claude E. Welch, Jr., "Civilian Control of the Military: Myth and Reality," in his edited *Civilian Control of the Military: Theory and Cases from Developing Countries* (Albany: State University of New York Press, 1976), 5–6; Welch, *No Farewell to Arms? Military Disengagement from Politics in Africa and Latin America* (Boulder, Colo: Westview Press, 1987), 17–19; Welch, "Civil-Military Relations: Perspectives from the Third World," *Armed Forces and Society* 11 (Winter 1985): 183–198.

96. Margiotta, "Civilian Control and the Mexican Military," 246–248.

97. Rafael Segovia, in his revealing examination of school children in the early 1970s in Mexico City, found that they accepted the power of a single person, that authoritarianism and inefficiency dominated their values, and that they viewed the political system as closed and hierarchical. *La politización del niño mexicano* (Mexico: El Colegio de México, 1975), 130.

98. Examples of this view include Ronfeldt, "The Mexican Army and Political Order since 1940," 226, in 1976; José Luis Reyna, "Redefining the Authoritarian Regime," in *Authoritarianism in Mexico*, ed. José Luis Reyna and Richard S. Weinert (Philadelphia: Institute for the Study of Human Issues, 1977), 155–172; Francisco J. Suárez Farías, "Notas para una historia de las

relaciones políticas entre gobierno y ejército mexicanos" (unpublished paper, Universidad Metropolitana, Unidad Xochimilco, 1978), 31; Alden M. Cunningham, "Mexico's National Security in the 1980s–1990s," in *The Modern Mexican Military: A Reassessment*, ed. David Ronfeldt (La Jolla: Center for United States-Mexican Studies, University of California, San Diego, 1984), 172.

99. Christopher Dickey, "Modernization Could Lead Mexican Military into Politics," *Washington Post*, September 23, 1982, 29.

100. A very brief but insightful interpretation of elite dissension, with comparisons drawn from Iran, is offered in David Ronfeldt's "Whither Elite Cohesion in Mexico: A Comment" (Santa Monica: Rand Corporation, November 1988).

101. Susan K. Purcell, "The Future of the Mexican Political System," in *Authoritarianism in Mexico*, ed. José Luis Reyna and Richard S. Weinert (New York: Institute for the Study of Human Issues, 1977), 187.

102. John J. Bailey, *Governing Mexico: The Statecraft of Crisis Management* (New York: St. Martin's Press, 1988), 192.

103. Jorge Castañeda, "Mexico at the Brink," *Foreign Affairs* 64 (Winter 1985–1986): 293.

104. Carl J. Migdail, "Mexico's Failing Political System," *Journal of Inter-American Studies and World Affairs* 29 (Fall 1987): 118.

105. David Ronfeldt, "Questions and Cautions about Mexico's Future," in *Mexico in Transition: Implications for U.S. Policy*, ed. Susan K. Purcell (New York: Council on Foreign Relations, 1988), 63. In late 1990, in addition to larger military parades and flag-lowering ceremonies in the capital city's *zocalo*, a number of new signs indicating military locations appeared on its freeways. Although some observers saw this as part of a new sign campaign in general, the fact is that twelve new signs in a twelve-kilometer stretch appeared on one freeway, and many of these signs are dozens of miles away from the actual site—for example, one announcing the ESG just outside the airport. No such signs have been erected to direct the public to important government cabinet agencies that attract hundreds of visitors. Generally, the only people who visit military installations are military personnel, who already know the locations. Their appearance is symbolic of civilian public recognition.

Graduates of the Heroico Colegio Militar and the Colegio del Aire in the Mexican Military Biography Project

Year Graduated	Top Defense or Command Post Tenure
1905	
Casillas García, Rodolfo	
1913	
García, Rubén	
Hijar Medina, Reynaldo	
Mendoza Sarabia, Manuel	
1917	
de la Garza Gutiérrez, Jesús B.	SDN 1964–70
1920	
Catalán Calvo, Gerardo	
1922	
**Cuenca Díaz, Hermenengildo	SDN 51–52; 70–76
Amaya Rodríguez, Federico	SDN 77–78
Carreno Gutiérrez, Agustin	ZC 76
Aranda Calderón, Miguel	
1923	
**García Barragán, Marcelino	SDN 64–70
Sánchez Hernández, Tomás	SDN 54–57; 58–60
Paredes Menchaca, Joaquín	ZC 1964–70
León Lobato, Othón	SDN 40–46
Corona del Rosal, Alfonso	
Nava Castillo, Antonio	
Castrejón, Adrián (graduated as a brigadier general)	ZC 34–41
Sánchez Lamego, Miguel	SDN 46–69
1924	
Jiménez Segura, Javier	SDN 70–76
Alamillo Flores, Luis (in campaign)	
1925	
Avila Camacho, Rafael	SDN 42–45
Clark Flores, José	SDN 46–52
Flores Cital, Rosendo	ZC 64–70
Grajales Godoy, Francisco	ESG 58–64
Pérez Ortiz, Alberto	ZC 70–76
Astorga Ochoa, Felipe	ZC 70–76
Pámanes Escobedo, Fernando	ZC 70–76
Casillas Rodríguez, Luis	ZC 58–64
Alamillo Flores, Luis	ZC 64–70
Gurza Falfán, Alfonso	SDN 65–70
Chávez Gaytán, Nicanor	

Zaldo y Peón Contreras, Raúl de
Orozco Ramos, Abel J.   ZC 64–70

1926 (no graduating class because closed for repairs in 1925)

1927
Camargo Figuroa, Héctor   SDN 70–76
Castellanos Domínguez, Jorge   ZC 70–76
Cuéllar Layseca, Israel   ZC 70–76

1928 (no graduating class)

1929
Zárate Múñoz, Enrique   AB 64–70
Del Valle Huerta, Maximiliano   ZC 70–76
Delgado S., Rodolfo   ZC 70–73
Salazar Alvarez, Héctor   ZC 70–76
Pérez Ortiz, Alberto   ZC 70–76
Maldonado Vázquez, Daniel
Maciel Gutiérrez, Santiago   SDN 70–76

1930
Ortega Casanova, José   SDN 70–76
Gómar Suástegui, Jerónimo   SDN 70–76
Mejía Castro, Antonio   AB 70–76
Soberanes Múñoz, Manuel
Zetina Brito, José   SDN 64–70
Ramírez Palacios, Francisco   SDN 64–70
Esparza Arias, Rosendo   ZC 70–76
Monroy Aguilar, Julio   ZC 70–76

1931
Guerrero Amezcua, Vicente   AB 70–76
Martínez Uribe, Ignacio   SDN 70–76
Del Valle Escamilla, Hernán   SDN 70–76
Berthier Aguíluz, Héctor   AF 70–76
Nieto Hernández, Rafael
Orozco Camacho, Joaquín   SDN 70–76
Vega Amador, Renato   ZC 70–76
Contreras Farfán, Luis

1932
Riverón Almaraz, Francisco   ZC 70–76
Rodríguez Fernández, Rolando   AB 70–76
Silva Medrano, Guillermo   SDN 70–76
López Padilla, Angel   SDN 70–76
Salido Beltrán, Roberto   AF 70–76

1933
Rangel Medina, Salvador   SDN 70–76
Ramírez Castañeda, Marcos   AF 70–76

1934
**Galván López, Félix   SDN 76–82
Aguilar Gómez, Estebán   ZC 70–76

Méndez Medina, Jorge	ZC 70–76
Ballesteros Prieto, Mario	SDN 64–70

1935
Ramírez Garrido, Graco	AF 70–76
Ramírez Barrera, Antonio	SDN 70–72; ZC 75–77
Corona Mendióroz, Arturo	SDN 70–72; ZC 77–79
De la Fuente, Juan Antonio	SDN 70–76
Aburto Valencia, Ricardo	ZC 70–76
Jiménez Ruiz, Eliseo	ZC 70–76

1936
Baker Figueroa, Juan	SDN 76–82
Ponce de León Tirado, Luis	ZC 70–76
Barrigueto Soto, Gilberto	SDN 70–76
Celaya Cardona, Ramón	SDN 70–76
Belmonte Aguirre, José	ZC 70–76
Huerta Carrasco, Marco Antonio	

1937
Ballesteros Pelayo, Alfonso

1938
Albarrán López, Plutarco
Márquez Padilla, Tarciso

1939
Mendoza Rivera, Jesús	
Mejía Chaparro, Rodolfo	
Flores Casarrubias, Marcial	AB 70–76
Hernández Toledo, José	ZC 70–76
Avelino Avendaño, Adolfo	AB 70–76
Rivera Becerra, Manuel	SDN 70–76
Cravioto Cisneros, Oswaldo	
Granados Alamillo, Luis	

1940
Alpuche Pinzón, Graciliano	SDN 70–76
Revueltas Olvera, Salvador	SDN 70–76
Díaz Escobar, Manuel	ZC 76–82
Mendoza Rivera, Jesús	
Buerba Patiño, Enrique	
León Moreno, Alger	SDN 82

1941
Aguirre Ramos, Alonso	ZC 70–76; SDN 77–83
Aiza Armendáriz, Manuel	AB 70–76
Castaneda Gutiérrez, Jesús	SDN 70–76
Mota Sánchez, Ramón	ZC 70–76
Naría Bornio, José	SDN 70–76
Alva Valles, José María	SDN 76–82, 82–88
Espejel Flores, José	SDN 82–88
López Flores, Arturo	SDN 82–88

Mancera Segura, Tomás	SDN 82–88
Torres Fernández, Nicéforo	
Bello Fernández, Heriberto	
López Matamoros, Salvador	

1942

Grajales Velázquez, Jorge	ZC 76–82
Zepeda Venegas, Arturo	ZC 76–82
Gutiérrez Gómez Tagle, Ernesto	SDN 84–88
Quintero Castillón, Artemio	
Santos Vázquez, Reynaldo	
González Vázquez, Guadalupe	
Castellaños Domínguez, Absalón	ZC 76–82
Gutiérrez Oropeza, Luis	SDN 70–76
Guerrero Mendoza, Marco Antonio	SDN 76–80; 82–88

1943

**Arévalo Gardoqui, Juan	SDN 82–88
Carballo Pazos, Mario	ZC 70–76
Ortiz Segura, Gonzalo	SDN 82–88
Flores López, Víctor	SDN 84–88
Contreras Barraza, Samuel	
Magaña Flores, Ignacio Javier	
Martínez Peralta, Jorge	
Romo Pacho, Rubén	
López García, Gregorio	ZC 80–82
Castillo Ferrara, Eduardo	
Vallejo Montiel, Manuel	ZC 80–83; SDN 83–88
Beltrán Tenorio, Ulisés	SDN 77–85
Rosas Pedrote, Carlos	ZC 77–78, 87
Valdéz Medrano, Rubén	

1944

**Riviello Bazán, Antonio	ZC 75–82; SDN 88–94
Flores Curiel, Rogelio	ZC 76–82
Rios de Hoyos, José María	SDN 76–82
Heine Rangel, Roberto	ZC 78–82; SDN 82–83
Barquera Trucios, Luis	ZC 74–75
Quintanar López, Alberto	SDN 82–88
Godoy Gutiérrez, Gonzalo	ZC 87–88
López López Lena, Fernando	ZC 80
Fería Rivera, Pedro	SDN 73; ZC 79–80
Santillán Gamper, Jorge	
Gaytán Sánchez, Héctor	AB 70–76
Gómez Jiménez, Maximino	
Saavedra Gómez, Francisco	
Sánchez Múñoz, Francisco	
Rios de Hoyos, José	SDN 77–82; ZC 82–83

1945

Ruiz Pérez, Guillermo	
Matus Santiago, Faustino	

Navarro Mendoza, Rafael (Air College)
Baker Figueroa, Juan   SDN 76–81

1946
De la Fuente G., Cuauhtémoc

1947
Cassani Marina, Alfredo
Zamora Ugalde, Arnulfo
Wittman Rojano, Jacobo   SDN 87–88
Donath G., Carlos (Air College)
Leyva Velez, Rolando
Vázquez Gómez, José Rubén (Air College)
Varela Olmos, Manuel
Notholt Rosales, Max (Navy)   SM 77–87
Zavala Hernández, Jorge   SDN 76–82

1948
Juárez Carreño, Raúl   SDN 88–
Madrigal Magallón, Juan   ZC 80–82; SDN 83
Castro Villarreal, Roberto
Torres Arpi, Eduardo (Air College)
Santander Bonilla, Felipe
Cruz Pardo, Rodolfo   ZC 76–82, 82–88

1949
Acosta Jiménez, Fermín (Air College)   AB 79–88; SDN, 88–
Alva Valles, José María
Martínez Arellano, Manuel   SDN 88–

1950
Revueltas Olvera, Víctor Luis   SDN 84–88
Sánchez Martínez, Alejandro
Pérez Torres, Mario   ZC 84–85
Martínez Montero, Joel   ZC 87–88
Zárate Guerrero, Agustín   SDN 87–88
Durón Prieto, Sergio
Galindo Corona, José
Heredia Díaz, Ricardo
Maldonado Zamudio, Augusto
Ramírez Michel, Sergio
Euroza Delgado, Edmar   ZC 87–88
Martínez Morfín, Juan Manuel

1951
Torrescano Múñoz, Luis
De la Torre Martínez, Alfonso   ZC 87–88
Ochoa Toledo, Alfredo   SDN 76–84, 87–88, 89–
Hernández Razo, Adolfo   ZC 80–86; SDN 87–88
Ortiz Salgado, Armando   SDN 82–88
Ruiz Esquivel, Adrián   ZC 87–88
Reyes Sánchez, Jaime
Fernández de Hoyos, Raúl

Mendívil Cabrera, Carlos (Air College)
Tapia García, Juan Felíx   SDN 88–
Cisneros Montes de Oca, Carlos   SDN 88–
Santoyo Feria, Vinicio   SDN 76–85; ZC 85–87
Garfías Magaña, Luis   SDN 76–82; 91–

1952
Romero Torres, Juan (Air College)   AB 70–76
Contreras Guerrero, Jaime   ZC 85–86
Calleros Aviña, Juan de Dios   ZC 85–87; SDN 88–
Ahuja Fuster, Héctor (Air College)
Cervantes, Mauro
Vallejo Alvarez, Agustín
Zavala Jiménez, Miguel
Ruiz Esquivel, Adrián   ZC 87–88

1953
Godínez Bravo, Miguel Angel   SDN 76–82, ZC 90–
Cervantes, Mauro Plácido Alonso
Cardona Marino, Arturo   SDN 88–
Castillo Ferrera, Rubén
Diéguez Rodríguez, Juan F.
León Cortes, Gustavo
Rios Martínez, Humberto C.
Riviello Quintana, Guillermo

1954
Lasso de la Vega, Angel   SDN 87–88
Alvarez Nahara, Salvador   SDN 86–88
Fernández Solís, Francisco   ZC 87–88
Islas López, Francisco   SDN 88–
Salinas Pallares, Javier (Air College)
Vargas Amezcua, Luis
Avila Pérez, Manuel   SDN 84–88
Palacios Guerrero, Jaime   SDN 88–
Gutiérrez López, Rolando   SDN 88–

1955
Ramírez Jauregui, Carlos (Air College)
Zenteño Avila, Gregorio (Air College)
Quirós Hermosillo, Francisco   SDN 89–
Poblano Silva, Juan   ZC 87–88; SDN 88–
Valencia Ortiz, Tito   SDN 88–

1956
Paredes Espinosa de los Monteros, Edmundo   SDN 82–83
Torres Alarcón, Arturo (Air College)

1957
Gómez Salazar, José   SDN 84–88
Hernández Pimentel, Alfredo   SDN 84–88
Pareyón Salazar, Enrique   SDN 85–88

Carrillo Olea, Jorge
Fuentes Robles, Héctor

1958
García Elizalde, Héctor   SDN 82–83

1963
López Gutiérrez, Mario   SDN 85–88
Huerta Robles, Pedro Roberto   SDN 86–88

1967
Hernández Bastar, Martín

Note: Most students, especially since 1940, graduate January 1, and hence are not actually in school during their graduation year.

Key: SDN = Department head or higher in the Secretariat of National Defense; SM = Department head or higher in the Secretariat of the Navy; ZC = Zone Commander; ** = future defense secretary; and AB = Air Base Commander.

Graduates of the Escuela Superior de Guerra in the Mexican Military Biography Project

Graduating Class	Top Defense or Command Post Tenure
1932–35 (14 graduates)	
Felipe Astorga Ochoa	ZC 71–73
Francisco J. Grajales Godoy	SDN 46–47, ZC 53–55
Enrique Sandoval Castárrica	SDN 65–70, 70–75
Raúl Zaldo y Peón Contreras	
Antonio J. Aznar Zetina (Navy)	SN 58–64; 65–70
1933–36 (29 graduates)	
Salvador Hernández Vela	
Fernando Pámanes Escobedo	SDN 58–64; ZC 71–73
Alberto Pérez Ortiz	ZC 72
José del Carmen Zetina Brito	SDN 64–70, 70–76, 77
Raúl Caballero Aburto	ZC 56
Jerónimo Gómar Suástegui	SDN 70–72
1934–37 (13 graduates)	
Héctor Camargo Figueroa	ZC 72–75; SDN, 75–76
Julio Monroy Aguilar	ZC 72–76
Israel Cuéllar Layseca	SDN 73
1935–38 (7 graduates)	
Jorge Castellanos Domínguez	ZC 75–80
1936–39 (15 graduates)	
Rosendo Esparza Arias	ZC 1975
1937–40 (18 graduates)	
Santiago Maciel Gutiérrez	SDN 71–73
Joaquín Orozco Camacho	SDN 71–77
J. Francisco Ramírez Palacios	ZC 69–72
Héctor Salazar Alvarez	ZC 72–74
Roque Madrigal Martínez	SDN 74
Carlos Manuel H. Flores Rodríguez (AF)	AF 66
1938–1941 (13 graduates)	
Leopoldo Garduño Canizal	SDN 76
1939–1942 (26 graduates)	
**Hermenegildo Cuenca Díaz (1970–76)	SDN 70–76
Arturo Corona Mendióroz	SDN 70–76; 81
Maximiliano del Valle Huerta	
Rosendo Flores Cital	ZC 66–68
Vicente Guerrero Amezcua	
Angel López Padilla	SDN 59–64, 70–72; ZC 72–75
Daniel Maldonado Vázquez (AF)	

Antonio Ramírez Barrera	SDN 70–72; 78–82; ZC 75–76, 77–78
Mario Ballestero Prieto	SDN 64–67
Joaquín Paredes Menchaca	ZC 64–68

1940–1943 (18 graduates)
Hernán del Valle Escamilla	
Rodolfo Delgado Severino	ZC 66–76
Luis Ponce de León Tirado	ZC 73
Salvador Rangel Medina	ZC 69–73
Francisco Riverón Almaraz	ZC 73

1941–1944 (18 graduates)
**Félix Galván López (1976–82)	SDN 76–82
Estebán Aguilar Gómez	ZC 1975
José D. Belmonte Aguirre	ZC 79
Juan Antonio de la Fuente Rodríguez	SDN 76–79
Antonio García Abunza	
José Ortiz Avila	

1942–1945 (16 graduates)
Ricardo Aburto Valencia	ZC 74–79
Eliseo Jiménez Ruiz	ZC 72–76
José Martínez Morales	SDN 62–66, 78–81; ZC 76–78
Arturo Ochoa Palencia	ZC 75–76; SDN 1976

1943-1946 (27 graduates)
Luis R. Casillas Rodríguez	ZC 66–70; 70–72
Guillermo Silva Medrano	SDN 1974

1944–1947 (23 graduates)
Graciliano Alpuche Pinzón	SDN 73–74
Gilberto Barriguete Soto	ZC 77–79
Ramón Celaya Cardona	ZC 77–79
Luis Contreras Farfán	
Manuel Rivera Becerra	ZC 1976; SDN 1976

1945–1948 (16 graduates)
Alonso Aguirre Ramos	SDN 77–83; ZC 83–85
Oswaldo Cravioto Cisneros	
Manuel Díaz Escobar	ZC 77–79
Salvador López Matamoros	ZC 82; SDN 83

1946–1949 (18 graduates; first
year of special Air Staff course)
Plutarco Albarrán López (AF) 1948–49	
Gonzalo Castillo Ferrera	ZC 1975–79
Marco Antonio Guerrero Mendoza	SDN 76–80, 82–85
Luis Gutiérrez Oropeza	SDN 64–70
Salvador Revueltas Olvera	ZC 78–80
Arturo Zepeda Venegas	ZC 77–78; SDN 78
Roberto Salido Beltrán (AF) 1948–49	AF 71–76
Mario Carballo Pazos	ZC 74

Luis Enrique Granados Alamillo (AF) 1948–49
Vicente Guerrero Amezcua (AF) 1948–49   AF 73
José Hernández Toledo (AF) 1948–49, 1951 classes   ZC 71–75; 77–82; SDN 83
Enrique Zarate Muñoz (AF) 1948–49   AF 73
Rafael Navarro Mendoza (AF) 1948–49   AF 72–75

1947–1949 (18 graduates)
**Juan Arevalo Gardoqui (1982–88)   SDN 82–88
Luis Barquera Trucios   ZC 74–75
Luis Granados Alamillo (AF)
José Moguel Cal y Mayor   ZC 77–78; SDN 78–83
Manuel Vallejo Montiel   ZC 80–83; SDN 83–87

1948–1950 (14 graduates)
Pedro Feria Rivera   ZC 79–80
Rafael Navarro Mendoza
Rogelio Flores Curiel   SDN 61–64
Alberto Sánchez López   SDN 1972; ZC 78–79

1949–1952 (13 graduates)
Jesús Castañeda Gutiérrez   SDN 70–76; 82
Jorge Martínez Peralta
José Hernández Toledo (AF)   ZC 71–75; 80–82; SDN 83
Eduardo Torres Arpi (AF) 1950–51
Jesús Mendoza Rivera
Ramón Mota Sánchez   ZC 70–76; SDN 76–80
Rodolfo Pérez Gutiérrez   ZC 75–76
Reynaldo Santos Vázquez   ZC 82

1950–1952 (16 graduates)
**Antonio Riviello Bazán (1988–94)   ZC 75–82; SDN 83–84, 87–88

1951–1953 (14 graduates)
José María Alva Valles
Edmundo Castro Villarreal   SDN 87–88
Armando Mariano Ortíz Salgado   SDN 83
Rafael Nieto Hernández
Mario Oliver Bustamante   SDN 76, 83–86; ZC 81–83,
                                                   86–88

1952–1954 (14 graduates)
Arturo López Flores   ZC 76–82; SDN 82–88
José María Rios de Hoyos (AF)   SDN 77–82; ZC 82–83
Rubén Romo Pacho

1953–1955 (14 graduates)
Fermín Acosta Jiménez (AF) 1954–55   ZC 81–88; SDN 88–
Jorge Grajales Velázquez   ZC 75–76; 76–82 SDN 82
Fernando López López Lena   ZC 80
Juan Manuel Madrigal Magallón   ZC 80–83; SDN 83–88
José Andrés Santos González

1954–1956 (18 graduates)
Luis Garfias Magaña   SDN 86

Raúl Juárez Carreño	SDN 88–
Alfredo Ochoa Toledo	SDN 81–82; 82–84, 87–88, 88–
Armando Ortíz Salgado	SDN 83

1955–1957 (16 graduates)
Sergio Durón Prieto
Felipe Santander Bonilla

Manuel Martínez Arellano	ZC 81–82; SDN 84–88, 88–
Joel Martínez Montero	ZC 87–88; SDN 88–
Mario Pérez Torres	ZC 84–85; SDN 86–88, 88–
Jorge Zavala Hernández	SDN 77–82; 82–84

1956–1958 (17 graduates)

Arturo Cardona Marino	SDN 88–89

Eliud Angel Casiano Bello
Mauro Plácido Alonso Cervantes
Alejandro Sánchez Martínez

Juan Félix Tapia García	SDN 89–

1957–1959 (19 graduates)

Carlos Humberto Bermúdez Dávila	SDN 82–88
Carlos Cisneros Montes de Oca	ZC 82–85; SDN 88–
Alfonso de la Torre Martínez	ZC 87
Miguel Angel Godínez Bravo	SDN 76–82; ZC 90–

1958–1960 (12 graduates)

Jaime Contreras Guerrero	SDN 83–84; ZC 85–86
Rolando Gutiérrez López	SDN 88–
Francisco Islas López	SDN 88–

1959–1961 (15 graduates)
Gildardo Alarcón López (Navy)

Salvador Alvarez Nahara	SDN 86
Maurilio Roberto Falcón Flores	ZC 87
Angel Jorge Lasso de la Vega	SDN 87
Jaime Palacios Guerrero	SDN 88–

1960–1962 (21 graduates)

Manuel Avila Pérez	SDN 84
Enrique Cervantes Aguirre	SDN 89–
Adolfo Hernández Razo	ZC 80–82, 83–86; SDN 87–88, 89–
Jaime Quiñones Cruz	SDN 86
Francisco Quiróz Hermosillo	SDN 89–
Francisco Fernández Solís	ZC 87

1961–1963 (16 graduates)

1962-1964 (16 graduates)
Jorge Carrillo Olea

Alfredo Hernández Pimentel	SDN 84
Edmundo Paredes Espinoza	SDN 82–83; ZC 87

Rodolfo Reta Trigos

Enrique Tomás Salgado Cordero   SDN 88–
Héctor Fuentes Robles

1963–1965 (17 graduates)
José Angel García Elizalde   SDN 82–88
Vicencio Santoyo Feria   SDN 82–85; ZC 85–87
Luis Torrescano Muñoz

1964–1966 (16 graduates)

1965–1967 (18 graduates)
Antonio Clemente Fernández Peniche   SDN 88–
Arturo Torres Alarcón (AF) 1966–67

1966–1968 (21 graduates)

1967–1969 (21 graduates)
Agustín Eduardo Zárate Guerrero   SDN 87–88
Juan Manuel Martínez Morfín
Benjamín Pacheco Coronel (AF) 1968–69
Carlos Ramírez Jauregui (AF) 1968–69
Juan de Dios Calleros Aviña   ZC 85–87; SDN 88–

1968–1970 (17 graduates)
Héctor Luis Sánchez Chan   SDN 88–

1969–1971 (14 graduates)
Mario López Gutiérrez   SDN 82–85
Gonzalo Godoy Gutiérrez   ZC 87

1970–1972 (24 graduates)
José Gómez Salazar   SDN 84

1970–1973
Juan Poblano Silva   ZC 87; SDN 89
Héctor Ahuja Fuster (AF) 1971-73
Javier Salinas Pallares (AF) 1971-73

Key: AF = Air Force; SDN = Secretariat of National Defense department post or higher; ZC = Zone commander; and ** = future defense secretary.

APPENDIX C   Mexican Zone Commanders

Tenure	Commander	Political Post
Zone 1. Federal District		
1988	*Enrique Cervantes Aguirre*	
1986–87	*Víctor Manuel Ruiz Pérez*	
1981–82	***Juan Arévalo Gardoqui*	
1978–80	Joaquín Solano Chagoya	
1977–78	Héctor Salazar Alvarez	
1972–76	*Felipe Astorga Sánchez*	
1959–62	*Miguel Badillo Vizcara*	
1955–58	*Antonio Sánchez Acevedo*	
1952–55	***Pablo Macias Valenzuela*	x
1948–49	*Ignacio Otero Pablos*	
1941–45	*Rodrigo Quevedo Moreno*	x
1940–41	*Vicente González*	x
1939–40	*Benecio López Padilla*	x
1937–39	Rafael Sánchez Tapia	x
1935–37	*Benecio López Padilla*	x
1934–35	Manuel Madinaveytia Esquivel	
Zone 2. El Cipres, Baja California		
1986–87	Juan Heriberto Salinas Altes	
1980–	M. R. Treviño	
1978–79	Roberto Sánchez Coronel	
1977	Gonzalo Castillo Ferrera	
1976	*Agustín Carreño Gutiérrez*	
1974–75	*Rosendo Esparza Arias*	
1968	Salvador Cruz Calvo	
1959–62	***Hermenegildo Cuenca Díaz*	
1959	*Cristóbal Guzmán Cárdenas*	x
1956	Alejandro Chávez Oviedo	
1953	*Praxedes Giner Durán*	x
1946	*Juan Felipe Rico Islas*	x
1937–40	*Manuel J. Contreras García*	
1935–37	*Rodolfo Navarro Cortina*	
1934–35	*Gildardo Magaña*	x
Zone 3. La Paz, Baja California Sur		
1986–87	*Juan Félix Tapia García*	
1980–	Miguel Egremy Grapain	
1979–80	*Roberto Heine Rangel*	
1977–79	*José Moguel Cal y Mayor*	
1975–76	***Antonio Riviello Bazán*	
1974	*Ricardo Aburto Valencia*	
1973–74	*José D. Belmonte Aguirre*	
1968	Luis Viñals Carsi	
1956–57	*Petronilo Flores Castellaños*	x
1956	***Agustín Olachea Aviles*	x

1937–40   Rafael Pedrajo Barrios
1934–37   *Juan Domínguez Cota*

Zone 4. Hermosillo, Sonora
1986–87   Angel Barrón Viezcas
1980–82   *Juan Manuel Madrigal Magallón*
1979–80   *Roberto Heine Rangel*
1977–79   *Manuel Díaz Escobar*
1976–77   *Basilio Pérez Ortiz*
1974–   *José D. Belmonte Aguirre*
1972   *Julio Monroy Aguilar*
1966–68   *Luis Alamillo Flores*
1962–64   Manuel Torres Valdez
1956   *Juan José Gastélum Salcido*
1939–40   *Jesús Gutiérrez Cazares*   x
1937–38   José Tafolla Caballero
1936–37   *Miguel Henríquez Guzmán*
1935–36   *Juventino Espinosa Sánchez*   x
1934–35   Juan Zertuche

Zone 5. Chihuahua, Chihuahua
1987   Alfonso Mancera Segura
1983–86   *Adolfo Hernández Razo*
1981–83   *Mario Oliver Bustamante*
1976–80   **Juan Arévalo Gardoqui*
1974–76   *Félix Galván López*
1974–   Tomás Arriola Chávez
1971–73   *Fernando Pámanes Escobedo*   x
1969   *J. Francisco Ramírez Palacios*
1959–61   *Práxedes Giner Durán*   x
1953–56   Antonio Romero Romero
1951–53   *Bonifacio Salinas Leal*   x
1939–40   Antonio Guerrero Gastélum
1936–39   *Jesús Agustín Castro*   x
1936   *Antonio Rios Zertuche*   x
1936   *Silvestre Guerrero*   x
1934–35   Anacleto Guerrero

Zone 6. Saltillo, Coahuila
1987   Rodolfo Rentería Alconedo
1981–82   *Raúl Juárez Carreño*
1980   *José Hernández Toledo*
1977–80   Gaspar Motta Elizarraras
1976   *Francisco Riverón Almaraz*
1971–73   **Félix Galván López*
1971   Ricardo Marín Ramos
1961–62   Antonio Romero Romero
1956   Lucas González Tijerina
1939–40   *Rodrigo Quevedo Moreno*   x
1937–38   *Miguel Henríquez Guzmán*   x

| 1935–37 | Alejo González González |
| 1934–35 | Juan Andreu Almazán |

Zone 7. Monterrey, Nuevo León

1987	*Joel Martínez Montero*	
1985–86	*Enrique Cervantes Aguirre*	
1979–84	*Salvador Revueltas Olvera*	
1978–79	*Gonzalo Castillo Ferrera*	
1977	Arturo Corona Mendioroz	
1974–76	Antonio F. Limón Jara	
1968–70	*Tiburicio Garza Zamora*	x
1962–68	*J. Trinidad Rodríguez López*	
1956–59	Domingo Martínez García	
1955	*Miguel Orrico de los Llanos*	x
1946–51	*Matías Ramos Santos*	x
1939–40	*Miguel Henríquez Guzmán*	
1935–38	*Juan Andreu Almazán*	
1934–35	****Pablo Macias Valenzuela*	x

Zone 8. Tancol, Tamaulipas

1987	*Adrián de J. Ruiz y Esquivel*	
1979–80	Jorge Cruz García	
1978–79	Ricardo Cervantes García Rojas	
1977	*Alberto Pérez Ortiz*	
1974–76	*Rodolfo Delgado Severino*	
1972–74	Miguel Palacios Hernández	
1961	Baltasar Leyva Mancilla	x
1956	Luis Cueto Ramírez	x
1952	*Silvestre Guerrero*	x
1939–40	*Genovevo Rivas Guillén*	x
1936–38	Antonio Guerrero Gástelum	
1935–36	Antonio A. Guerrero	
1934–35	Jesús Madrigal Guzmán	

Zone 9. Culiacán, Sinaloa

1987	Rodolfo Reta Trigos
1981–82	*Jorge G. Grajales Velázquez*
1980–81	M. J. Vázquez F.
1979–80	*Rodolfo Pérez Gutiérrez*
1977–79	*Alberto Quintanar López*
1974–76	*Gonzalo Castillo Ferrera*
1969	*Ubaldo Ugarte Martínez*
1955–56	J. Jesús Arías Sánchez
1955	Juan E. Cruz Hoyos
1939–40	*Agustín Mustieles Medel*
1937–38	Alejo González y González
1936–37	Anacleto López Morales
1935–36	Rodrigo Talamante Corbala
1934–35	Antonio Guerrero

Zone 10. Durango, Durango

| 1987 | Mario Renán Castillo Fernández |

1979–80	*Pedro Fería Rivera*	
1977–79	*Gilberto Barriguete Soto*	
1976	*José D. Belmonte Aguirre*	
1972–74	*Basilio Pérez Ortiz*	
1969–70	*Salvador Rangel Medina*	
1956	Alberto Bello Santana	
1953	*José Fuentes Bosque*	
1939–40	*Juan José Rios y Rios*	x
1938–39	**Matías Ramos Santos*	x
1936–38	Lucas González Tijerina	
1935–36	*Miguel Henríquez Guzmán*	
1934–35	**Jesús A. Castro Rivera*	x

Zone 11. Guadalupe, Zacatecas

1986	*Alfonso Mancera Segura*	
1979–80	Ernesto Pérez Robledo	
1977–79	*Arturo Zepeda Venegas*	
1977	Jorge Méndez Medina	
1975–76	*Rodolfo Pérez Gutiérrez*	
1974–75	*Luis Barquera Trucios*	
1956	Anacleto López Morales	
1939–40	*Aureo L. Calles Pardo*	
1936–38	*Juan José Rios y Rios*	
1935–36	*Antonio Rios Zertuche*	x
1934–35	*Pánfilo Natera*	x

Zone 12. San Luis Potosí, San Luis Potosí

1987	Jesús Gutiérrez Rebollo	
1980	H. Carrada C.	
1977–79	*Rodolfo Pérez Gutiérrez*	
1976–77	*Hernán del Valle Escamilla*	
1973–74	*Luis Ponce de León Tirado*	
1955–56	Conrado Salido Múñoz	
1955	Domingo B. Martínez García	
1945–46	**Matías Ramos Santos*	x
1938–40	Lucas González Tijerina	
1938	Genovevo Rivas Guillén	x
1934–37	Francisco S. Carrera Torres	

Zone 13. Tepic, Nayarit

1987	*Edmar Euroza Delgado*	
1984–85	*Mario Pérez Torres*	
1980–81	*Edmundo Castro Villarreal*	
1980	Rafael Domínguez Soto	
1977–80	Luis Téllez Martínez	
1974–76	Horacio Castro y Castro	
1972	Felipe Andrade Sánchez	
1969–72	*Héctor Salazar Alvarez*	
1969	Francisco Salazar Díaz	
1966–69	*Felipe Astorga Ochoa*	

1958	*José Pacheco Iturribarría*	x
1940–46	**Agustín Olachea Aviles*	x
1936–40	J. Félix Lara Medrano	
1936	*Miguel Henríquez Guzmán*	
1935	Francisco A. Martínez	
1934–35	*Anselmo Macías Valenzuela*	x

Zone 14. Aguascalientes, Aguascalientes

1987	Francisco Soto Solís	
1980–82	*Adolfo Hernández Razo*	
1979–80	*Gregorio López García*	
1977–79	Angel Gaxiola Villaseñor	
1973–76	*Maximiliano del Valle Huerta*	
1959	*Ramón Rodríguez Familiar*	x
1956	*Juventino Espinosa Sánchez*	x
1956	*Francisco A. Higuera Jiménez*	
1939–40	Jesús Madrigal Guzmán	
1935–38	Juan B. Izaguirre Payán	
1934–35	*Adrián Castrejón Castrejón*	x

Zone 15. Guadalajara, Jalisco

1985–87	*Vicencio Santoyo Fería*	
1979–80	*Alberto Sánchez López*	
1979	*Ricardo Aburto Valencia*	
1977–79	*Ramón Mota Sánchez*	
1976–77	*Julio Monroy Aguilar*	
1974	*Federico Amaya Rodríguez*	
1962	*José Pacheco Iturribarría*	x
1956	*Francisco A. Higuera Jiménez*	
1954	*Samuel Urbina Oscoy*	
1946–52	*Ramón Jiménez Delgado*	x
1939–40	**Pablo Macías Valenzuela*	x
1937–39	*Benecio López Padilla*	x
1936–37	*Genovevo Rivas Guillén*	x
1935–36	Juan Soto Lara	
1934–35	Juan B. Izaguirre Payán	

Zone 16. Irapuato, Guanajuato

1987	José Rodolfo Cruz Pardo	
1978–80	J. Luna Castañeda	
1977–78	*Salvador Revueltas Olvera*	
1976	*Manuel Rivera Becerra*	
1974	Antonio Barba Gómez	
1973–74	**Félix Galván López*	
1967–68	*Abel J. Orozco Ramos*	
1956–62	Miguel S. Romero Anzures	
1948	Leandro A. Sánchez Salazar	
1937–40	*Juan Domínguez Cota*	
1936–37	*Federico Montes Alanís*	
1935–36	*Ernesto Aguirre Colorado*	x
1934–35	*Juventino Espinosa Sánchez*	x

Zone 17. Querétaro, Querétaro
1987   *Carlos Rosas Pedrote*
1977–80 José Encarnación Ramírez Linares
1977   *Francisco Riverón Almaraz*
1976   Alfonso Echanove del Castillo
1975–76 *Estebán Aguilar Gómez*
1974   *Rosendo Flores Cital*
1960–61 **Marcelino García Barragán*   x
1953   Juan de la Torre Villa Lazo
1953   Práxedes Giner Durán   x
1953   Francisco Higuera Jiménez
1948   José García Márquez
1941–43 Eulogio Ortiz
1939–40 *Federico Montes Alanís*   x
1937–38 *Gabriel R. Guevara*   x
1935–37 *Pánfilo Natera García*   x
1934–35 *Juan José Rios y Rios*

Zone 18. Pachuca, Hidalgo
1986–87 *Alfonso de la Torre Martínez*
1985–86 Juan Félix Tapia
1984–85 Mario Morales Molina
1982–84 *Manuel Martínez Arellano*
1980–82 *Roberto Heine Rangel*
1979–80 *Manuel Díaz Escobar Figueroa*
1977–79 *Alberto Sánchez López*
1974–77 *Ricardo Aburto Valencia*
1972–74 *Héctor Salazar Álvarez*
1971–72 *Felipe Astorga Ochoa*
1971   *José Hernández Toledo*
1970   Joaquín Solano Chagoya
1964–70 *Gabriel Leyva Velázquez*   x
1959–64 Alejandro Hernández Bermúdez
1955–59 *Samuel Urbina Oscoy*
1954–55 *Práxedes Giner Durán*   x
1953–54 Santiago Piña Soría
1952   Alejandro Hernández Bermúdez
1950–52 **Joaquín Amaro*   x
1945–50 *Agustín Mustieles Medel*
1944   Vicente Escobedo Mercadillo
1943–44 Pedro J. Almada Félix   x
1941–43 **Matías Ramos Santos*   x
1935–41 *Adrián Castrejón*   x
1934–35 *Benecio López Padilla*   x

Zone 19. Tuxpán, Veracruz
1987–   *Antonio López Portillo*
1983–87 *Edmundo Castro Villarreal*
1980–83 *Manuel Vallejo Montiel*
1979–80 Héctor Portillo Jurado   x
1977–79 *Ramón Celaya Cardona*

1977	*Alberto Sánchez López*	
1975–77	*Antonio Ramírez Barrera*	
1972–75	*Alberto Pérez Ortiz*	
1964–68	*Joaquín Paredes Menchaca*	
1956	Joaquín Martínez Inguíñez	
1948	Juan B. Izaguirre Payán	
1945	**Pablo Macías Valenzuela*	x
1937–40	Juan Soto Lara	
1935–37	Juan Jiménez Mendéz	
1934–35	*Maximino Avila Camacho*	x

Zone 20. Colima, Colima

1987	Gonzalo Godoy Gutiérrez	
1979–80	*Rodolfo Cruz Pardo*	
1977–79	*Javier Vázquez Félix*	
1977	*Luis R. Casillas Rodríguez*	
1976	*Jorge Mendéz Medina*	
1975–76	Jorge Cruz García	
1975	Antonio Mardegain Simeon	
1973–74	*Francisco Riverón Almaraz*	
1969	*Hernán del Valle Escamilla*	
1964	Manuel H. Gómez Cueva	
1959	*Miguel Badillo Vizcarra*	
1956	Daniel Galván Medina	
1948	Alberto Bello Santana	
1939–40	Rafael Moreno Ortega	
1937–39	*Aureo L. Calles Pardo*	x
1936–37	Antonio Cerna Zertuche	
1935–36	Porfirio Cadena Riojas	
1934–35	Juan Soto Lara	

Zone 21. Morelia, Michoacán

1987	Manuel Lomeli Gamboa	
1985–86	*Jaime Contreras Guerrero*	
1982–85	*Carlos Cisneros Montes de Oca*	
1980–81	*Jorge G. Grajales Velázquez*	
1977–80	**Antonio Riviello Bazán*	
1974–76	*Renato Vega Amador*	
1974	*Jorge Castellanos Domínguez*	
1956	*Félix Ireta Viveros*	x
1948	*Cristóbal Guzmán Cárdenas*	x
1944	*Agustín Mora Hernández*	x
1939–40	*Francisco J. Múgica*	x
1937–38	*Félix Ireta Viveros*	x
1936–37	*Ignacio Otero Pablos*	
1935–36	Josue Benignos Hideroa	
1934–35	Juan Jiménez Méndez	

Zone 22. Toluca, México

1987	Alfredo Morán Acevedo	
1978–80	*José Belmonte Aguirre*	

1977	Carlos Gaytan Durón	
1975–76	*Rosendo Esparza Arias*	
1974	Juan Kampfner Lazalde	
1972	*Francisco Ramírez Palacios*	
1962	**Marcelino García Barragán*	x
1957	Julio Pardiñas Blancas	
1951–57	*Eduardo Hernández Cházaro*	x
1939–41	*Matías Ramos Santos*	x
1937–38	*Pánfilo Natera*	x
1936–37	Juan Soto Lara	
1935–36	*Jos Juan Rios y Rios*	x
1934–35	*Pedro J. Almada Félix*	

Zone 23. Tlaxcala, Tlaxcala

1987	*Juan Poblano Silva*	
1980	*Fernando López López Lena*	
1979–80	*Alberto Quintanar López*	
1977–79	*Carlos Rosas Pedrote*	
1976–77	*Alvaro Elías Pámanes*	
1976	*Héctor Salazar Alvarez*	
1974–	Miguel Rivera Becerra	
1973–74	*Renato Vega Amador*	
1968	Ignacio Rosas Rodríguez	
1963	*Joaquín Paredes Menchaca*	
1959	Gustavo Arévalo Vera	
1956–59	**Hermenegildo Cuenca Díaz*	
1950–51	*Eduardo Hernández Cházaro*	x
1948	Miguel Flores Villar	
1935–40	José Amarillas Valenzuela	
1934–35	Pablo Díaz Dávila	

Zone 24. Cuernavaca, Morelos

l987	Ernesto Pérez Robledo	
1979–80	Eduardo Aponte Cardoso	
1978–79	Daniel Gutiérrez Santos	
1976–77	*Estebán Aguilar Gómez*	
1974	Francisco Andrade Sánchez	
1959	Pascual Cornejo Brun	
1957–58	Alfredo Sarrelanque López	
1956–57	Julio Pardiñas Blancas	
1935–40	Pablo Díaz Dávila	
1934–35	Josue Benignos Hiderou	

Zone 25. Puebla, Puebla

1987	Maurilio R. Falcón Flores	
1980–82	**Antonio Riviello Bazán*	
1979–80	Daniel Gutiérrez Santos	
1977–79	*Ricardo Aburto Valencia*	
1976–77	*Alberto Sánchez López*	
1973–74	*Héctor Camargo Figueroa*	x
1973	*Federico Amaya Rodríguez*	

1968	Eusebio González Saldaña	
1961	*Luis Casillas Rodríguez*	
1960–61	*Ramón Rodríguez Familiar*	x
1960	Raúl de Alba Luna	
1958–59	Carlos Aguirre García	
1955–58	*Donato Bravo Izquierdo*	x
1952–55	*José María Tapia Freyding*	x
1948	*Juan J. Gastélum Salcido*	
1939–40	*Pablo Quiroga Escamilla*	
1937–38	*Vicente González Fernández*	x
1936–37	*Rodrigo M. Quevedo Moreno*	x
1935–36	Anacleto López Morales	
1934–35	José Juan Méndez Peralta	

Zone 26. La Boticaria, Veracruz

1987	*Luis Barquera Trucios*	
1977–80	Angel Flores Martínez	
1977	*Antonio Ramírez Barrera*	x
1972–76	*Luis R. Casillas Rodríguez*	
1968	*Modesto A. Guinart López*	x
1959	*Modesto A. Guinart López*	x
1956	*Raúl Caballero Aburto*	x
1953–55	Adolfo E. Corsen León	
1936–40	Alejandro Mange Toyos	
1935–36	*Heriberto Jara*	x
1934–35	Lucas González Tijerina	

Zone 27. Acapulco, Guerrero

1987	*Samuel A. Contreras Barraza*	
1982	*José Hernández Toledo*	
1979–80	Ricardo C. García Rojas	
1977–79	*Salvador Rangel Medina*	
1976	*Francisco Andrade Sánchez*	
1974–76	*Eliseo Jiménez Ruiz*	x
1973–74	*Salvador Rangel Medina*	
1969	*Juan M. Enríquez Rodríguez*	
1960–62	*Alvaro García Taboada*	
1955–59	*Práxedis Giner Durán*	
1953–54	*Juan Flores Torres*	
1953	Ernesto Higuera Piñeda	
1948	Ricardo Medina Otero	
1947–48	*Adrián Castrejón*	x
1945–46	*Modesto Guinart López*	
1943–45	**Matías Ramos Santos*	x
1939–40	Alejo González González	
1937–38	Juan Jiménez Méndez	
1935–37	*Anselmo Macías Valenzuela*	x
1934–35	Federico Rodríguez Berlanga	

Zone 28. Oaxaca, Oaxaca

1985–87	*Raúl Juárez Carreño*	

1980	R. Sánchez C.	
1977–79	*Hernán del Valle Escamilla*	
1976	Joaquín Solano Chagoya	
1974	Ricardo Ramos Flores	
1956	José García Márques	
1953	José Barrientos Juárez	
1947–48	*Joaquín Amaro*	x
1939–41	*Miguel Molinar*	
1937–40	Francisco S. Carrera Torres	
1936–37	*Heriberto Jara*	x
1935–36	Alejandro Manje	
1934–35	*Federico Montes Alanís*	x

Zone 29. Minatitlan, Veracruz

1987	Jaime Jiménez Múñoz	
1976–82	*Arturo López Flores*	
1976	*Arturo Corona Mendioroz*	
1974	*Mario Carballo Pazos*	
1972–73	*Rodolfo Delegado Severino*	
1972	Mario Elenes Almada	
1969	Francisco J. Arcuate Franco	
1939–40	José Tafoya Caballero	
1935–38	*Pablo E. Macías Valenzuela*	x
1934–35	*Miguel Henríquez Guzmán*	

Zone 30. Tabasco, Villahermosa

1987	Francisco Fernández Solís	
1980–85	Mario Murillo Morales	
1979–80	José Cortés Alfán	
1978–79	*Salvador Revueltas Olvera*	
1977	Roberto Sánchez Coronel	
1976	Antonio Mardegain Simeón	
1972–75	Jorge Cruz García	
1971–72	*Israel Cuéllar Layseca*	
1965–71	*Joaquín Leyzaola González*	
1959–65	Salvador Cruz Calvo	
1955–59	*J. Trinidad Rodríguez López*	
1955	*José Pacheco Iturribarría*	x
1953	Julio Pardiñas Blancas	
1947–53	*José Domingo Ramírez Garrido*	x
1943–47	*Manuel J. Contreras García*	
1939–40	Josue Benignos Hideroa	
1935–38	Jesús Madrigal Guzmán	
1935	Pilar R. Sánchez	
1935	*Manuel Avila Camacho*	x
1934–35	Rafael Cházaro Pérez	

Zone 31. Tuxtla Gutiérrez, Chiapas

1987	Francisco Andrade Sánchez	
1983–85	*Enrique Cervantes Aguirre*	
1981–83	*Alberto Quintanar López*	

1977–80	*José Hernández Toledo*	
1976	Jorge Cruz García	
1975	*Jorge Castellaños Domínguez*	
1972–74	*Angel López Padilla*	
1969	*Luis R. Casillas Rodríguez*	x
1964	Gustavo Larriva y Arévalo	
1956	Gustavo Larriva y Arévalo	
1937–40	*Antonio Rios Zertuche*	
1936–37	Ernesto Aguirre Colorado	
1935–36	*Federico Montes Alanís*	
1935	*Andrés Figueroa*	

Zone 32. Mérida, Yucatán
1987–88	*Tito Valencia Ortiz*
1987	José Luis Zúniga Montes de Oca
1980	Reynaldo Santos Vázquez
1979	*Luis Barquera Trucios*
1978–79	*Arturo Corona Mendioroz*
1977	*Leopoldo Garduño Canizal*
1974–76	*Arturo Ochoa Palencia*
1973	*Alonso Aguirre Ramos*
1968	*Rosendo Flores Cital*
1954–56	Juan Beristaín Ladrón de Guevara
1939–40	Juan B. Izaguirre Payán
1936–38	Josue M. Benignos Hideroa
1935–36	Lucas González Tijerina
1935	Francisco Martínez

Zone 33. Campeche, Campeche
1987	Sixto Rubén Mendoza	
1985–87	*Juan de Dios Calleros Aviña*	
1980	J. Durán V.	
1979–80	*Luis Barquera Trucios*	
1977–79	Carlos Latorre Pimentel	
1972–76	*José Hernández Toledo*	
1969	*Felipe Astorga Ochoa*	
1968	Andrés Bocanegra Martínez	
1958	*Francisco A. Higuera Jiménez*	
1957–58	José Pacheco Iturribarría	x
1956–57	José D. Ramírez Garrido	x
1948	Roberto Calvo Ramírez	
1939–40	Miguel Orozco Camacho	
1936–38	Lorenzo Múñoz Merino	

Zone 34. Chetumal, Quintana Roo
1987	*Edmundo A. Paredes de los Monteros*
1980	*Ricardo Aburto Valencia*
1978–79	Horacio Carrada Canchola
1977	Ricardo Cervantes García Rojas
1976	*Manuel Díaz Escobar Figueroa*
1974	Jorge Almada Garces

1968   Ernesto Castellano Castillo
1959   David León y Arias

Zone 35. Chilpancingo, Guerrero
1987   *Roberto Heine Rangel*
1982–83   *José María Rios de Hoyos*
1975–80   *Jorge Grajales Velázquez*
1974–75   *Alvaro García Taboada*
1972–74   *Eliseo Jiménez Ruiz*   x
1969   Miguel E. Bracamontes García

Zone 36. Tapachula, Chiapas
1987–88   *Juan de Dios Calleros Aviña*
1987   Sixto Rubén Mendoza

Key: ** = future defense secretary; an italicized name indicates the officer is in the *Mexican Political Biography Project.*

A Note on Collective
Biographical Data

As I noted in the introduction, the collective biographical data have been acquired during many years of research in newspapers, magazines, government organization manuals, biographical directories, interviews, and secondary literature begun in 1968. The *Mexican Military Biographies Project* data bank includes complete biographies for career military officers who reached the rank of brigadier general and held an active duty assignment after 1940. Most of the generals in this study reached brigade or division rank. A complete examination of promotion records suggests that the data bank provides a broad and even sample of leading generals from each of the years covered by the study. The most complete biographies are those where assignments are taken from the official personnel file. Nearly half of the biographies in this study include such information, available from published official records or journals. However, the Mexican military's secretiveness extends to biographical information. Even in recent official biographies, such as those published in the *Diccionario biográfico del gobierno mexicano* for 1984, 1987, and 1989, the majority of officers purposely have left out their military assignments, including zone commands and early military education, despite official requests for the information. This means, for example, that our data on zone commanders are much more complete than is actually indicated in Appendix C because many of the individuals in our sample have held other zone commands, but information on dates or the exact zone are unavailable. Data are most complete for date of entry into the service, promotions, geographic origin, military training in Mexico and abroad, and all foreign assignments. Data are also fairly complete for staff assignments above the level of department head, especially since 1947. The most difficult to obtain data are, of course, data on social background, including parents' occupations and ties to other elites. Although these data contain the most complete information ever published on the social backgrounds of Mexican officers, it is probable that lower socioeconomic backgrounds are slightly underreported in official biographies because a person is less likely to include a father's occupation if it is nonprofessional.

In addition to this data set, two others provided many of the empirical comparisons cited in this study. The two sources are part of the *Mexican Political Biography Project*. The first, covering the years 1935 through 1987, provides information about political-military officers who served in top national positions. Comparable data sets now exist for Mexican intellectuals and leading entrepreneurs from the 1920s through the mid-1980s. The most recent is a collective biography of the Porfiriato, covering the period from Díaz's second presidential administration, beginning in 1884, through the first year of the Cárdenas term, after which he deported former President Calles and reformed his cabinet, affecting officeholders at all other levels. This data set provides information on leading politicians, civilian and military alike, allowing us to trace political patterns for more than one hundred years. Ultimately, the combined data sets will be used as a basis for a book-length generational analysis of Mexican leadership during the past century. Many of the biographies of military and political figures are now available in the author's *Mexican Political Biographies, 1935–1980* (Tucson: University of Arizona Press, 1982); *Who's Who in Mexico Today* (Boulder, Colo.: Westview Press, 1988); and *Mexican Political Biographies, 1884–1934* (Austin: University of Texas Press, 1991).

Bibliographic Essay

Literature on the Mexican military is at best sketchy and sparse. Much of what has been written since 1970 is repetitive in content, often slightly modified reprints of earlier versions, thus perpetuating for better or worse interpretations from the past. Almost no empirical research on the Mexican military exists about its relationship to civilian authorities, its interlocks with political elites, its specific military and political activities, its prestige in society, its self-image, its composition, or its internal affairs. These lacunae have led to speculations and occasionally to gross inaccuracies. The weak analytical nature of the literature on the Mexican military generally has excluded it from a rather rich literature on the Latin American military, and from theoretical comparative appraisals.

The best place to initiate research on the contemporary Mexican military is two excellent bibliographical essays. The most complete list of Mexican sources is provided by Palmira Olguín Pérez's "Los militares en México: Bibliografía introductoria," *Revista Mexicana de Sociología* 38 (April–June 1976): 453–490. For United States sources, especially useful because it identifies many government publications, is librarian Harold Colson's essay, of which there are two versions. The first is his *Civil-Military Relations and National Security in Modern Mexico: A Bibliography* (Auburn, Ala.: Auburn University, September 1987). The second version, *National Security Affairs and Civil-Military Relations in Contemporary Mexico: A Bibliography* (Monticello, Ill.: Vance Bibliographies, 1989), is more readily available. Both are annotated. For the period prior to 1935, the Secretaría de Guerra y Marina has published its own excellent *Apuntes para una bibliografía militar de México, 1536–1936* (Mexico, 1937), organized by year, without annotations.

A fairly voluminous literature on civil-military relations provides a theoretical backdrop for examining the Mexican case. Nevertheless, the uniqueness of Mexico's military, and its civil-military relations, limits the literature's applicability. Strangely, an equally large literature on military sociology in the United States rarely has been used to draw comparisons with Latin American militaries. This study attempts to correct that deficiency by citing, where appropriate, comparative sociological literature that sheds light on the comparability or uniqueness of the Mexican case.

Working chronologically forward from two classic works in the literature, S. E. Finer, *The Man on Horseback: The Role of the Military in Politics*, 2d ed. (Boulder, Colo.: Westview Press, 1988), and Samuel P. Huntington, *The Soldier and the State: The Theory and Politics of Civil-Military Relations* (Cambridge: Harvard University Press, 1964), a number of books were found to be particularly useful. The revised edition of Finer is highly recommended because the author surveys the literature since his original interpretation, incorporating new theoretical views into his own analysis. A more relevant theory for today's military, borrowing from Western examples especially

263

related to the concept of professionalism, is that of Sam C. Sarkesian, who primarily focuses on the United States. His *Beyond the Battlefield: The New Military Professionalism* (New York: Pergamon Press, 1981), and "Military Professionalism and Civil-Military Relations in the West," *International Political Science Review* 2, no. 3 (1981): 283–298, provides a challenging, realistic model of civil-military relations. Another author whose work offers a helpful analysis of the political role of the military is Amos Perlumutter, notably his "The Military and Politics in Modern Times: A Decade Later," *Journal of Strategic Studies* 9 (March 1986): 5–15. Finally, one of the best overall analyses, which reinterprets the extant literature, is Martin Edmonds's clearly written *Armed Services and Society* (Leicester, U.K.: Leicester University Press, 1988).

The two most useful theorists of Third World countries, who have had some applicability to Mexico are Morris Janowitz and Claude E. Welch, Jr. Janowitz's work, *The Military in the Development of New Nations* (Chicago: University of Chicago Press, 1964), is a classic in its own right. Like Janowitz, Welch has examined the Third World, but he has contributed a great deal to sorting out the comparative theoretical issues, especially for countries where military disengagement from politics has been long term. His analyses are particularly useful to Mexico, among them his *Civilian Control of the Military: Theory and Cases from Developing Countries* (Albany: State University of New York Press, 1976); "Civil-Military Relations: Perspectives from the Third World," *Armed Forces and Society* 11 (Winter 1985): 183–198; and *No Farewell to Arms? Military Disengagement from Politics in Africa and Latin America* (Boulder, Colo.: Westview Press, 1987).

Numerous articles and collected essays on the Latin American military are available, but generally their focus has been on South America, which in terms of political and party structure has had little in common with Mexico since the 1930s. One work from a historical angle having utility for Mexico is John J. Johnson's classic, *The Military and Society in Latin America* (Stanford: Stanford University Press, 1964), which provides a single author's interpretation. The most helpful interpretations of the Latin American scene, as they relate to Mexico's civil-military relations are those by Samuel J. Fitch, "Armies and Politics in Latin America: 1975–1985," in Abraham Lowenthal and Samuel Fitch's collection, *Armies and Politics in Latin America* (New York; Holmes and Meier, 1986), 26–58; Irving Louis Horowitz, "Militarism and Civil-Military Relationships in Latin America: Implications for the Third World," *Research in Political Sociology*, vol. 1 (Greenwich, Conn.: JAI Press, 1985); and Frederick M. Nunn, the only author who has incorporated Mexico's experience in any detail within the broad sweep of Latin American literature, in his provocative "On the Role of the Military in Twentieth-Century Latin America: The Mexican Case," in *The Modern Mexican Military: A Reassessment*, ed. David Ronfeldt (La Jolla: Center for United States-Mexican Studies, University of California, San Diego, 1984), 33–49.

The literature on the Mexican military specifically, although scanty, tends to focus on two themes, historical evolution of armed forces institutions and contemporary civil-military relations. The historical literature has received better treatment qualitatively and quantitatively in terms of book-length works. Standard political analyses on Mexico basically ignore the military, making only passing mention at best. The only book-length work in English is that of the late Edwin Lieuwen, *Mexican Militarism* (Albuquerque: University of New Mexico Press, 1968). But Lieuwen's study, which really analyzes the military only through the 1940s, focuses primarily on the immediate postrevolutionary period and was never updated, even in his brief "Depolitization of the Mexican Revolutionary Army, 1915–1940," in *The Modern Mexican Military: A Reassessment*, ed. David Ronfeldt (La Jolla: Center for United States-Mexican Studies,

University of California, San Diego, 1984), 51–62. Actually, a more complete analysis, providing excellent insights into Mexican civil-military relations prior to 1940, is Gordon C. Schloming's unpublished Ph.D. dissertation, "Civil-Military Relations in Mexico, 1910-1940: A Case Study" (Columbia University, 1974). Mexican scholars have been more interested in the military than their North American counterparts. A work complementary to Lieuwen's is Jorge Alberto Lozoya's *El ejército mexicano (1911–1965)* (Mexico: El Colegio de México, 1970), which has gone through three editions (1984 the most recent), but with the exception of a new chapter on foreign policy, contains only superficial changes and little new research. Three other Mexicans have provided a much more thorough look at the post-1960s military. The first of these, Guillermo Boils, published *Los militares y la política en México, 1915-1974* (Mexico: El Caballito, 1975), with a useful update in the *Revista Mexicana de Sociología* 47 (January–February, 1985): 169-185. The most prolific Mexican scholar is José Luis Piñeyro, who published a small monograph *Ejército y sociedad en México: pasado y presente* (Puebla: Universidad Autónomo de Puebla, 1985), but whose earlier article offered his essential ideas: "The Mexican Army and the State: Historical and Political Perspective," *Revue Internationale de Sociologie* 14 (April–August, 1978): 111-157; it was followed by his helpful revision in "The Modernization of the Mexican Armed Forces," in *Democracy under Siege: New Military Power in Latin America*, ed. Augusto Varas (Westport, Conn.: Greenwood Press, 1989), 115-130. Finally, Gloria Fuentes collects additional bits of difficult to locate data in her analytically superficial *El ejército mexicano* (Mexico: Grijalbo, 1983).

Except for the work of Piñeyro and Boils, U.S. authors have provided the bulk of specfic analysis of the recent Mexican military, and much of the best work is unpublished. The only early work with a political bent is that of Virginia Prewett, whose pre–World War II assessment of Mexico's army in "The Mexican Army," *Foreign Affairs* 19 (April 1941): 609-621, was a first. About the time Lieuwen published his historical monograph, Karl Schmitt contributed a timely assessment in his "The Role of the Military in Contemporary Mexico," in *The Caribbean: Mexico Today*, ed. Curtis A. Wilgus (Gainesville: University of Florida Press, 1964), 52-62. The first work to provide any empirical information on Mexican military sociology is that of Lyle N. McAlister, whose excellent chapter "Mexico," in *The Military in Latin American Socio-political Evolution: Four Case Studies* (Washington, D.C.: Center for Research in Social System, 1970), has been the source of successive reinterpretations, often using outdated, if useful, information. The other article-length work, offering an incisive, focused interpretation on the military's political role, was David Ronfeldt's *The Mexican Army and Political Order since 1940* (Santa Monica: Rand Corporation, 1973). Ronfeldt's short essay, republished several times but essentially unmodified, received more attention than McAlister's. See, for example, the version in Abraham F. Lowenthal, ed., *Armies and Politics in Latin America* (New York: Holmes and Meier, 1976), 291-312. Ronfeldt also wrote a helpful overview in the collection he edited for the Center for United States-Mexican Studies, *The Modern Mexican Military: A Reassessment* (1984), later appearing in the Abraham Lowenthal and J. Samuel Fitch 1986 collection, and incorporated into a 1985 Rand publication. The other author who raised the visibility of Mexican military studies, offering several important theses, was Franklin D. Margiotta, a career air force officer, who completed an M.A. thesis at Georgetown University, "The Mexican Military: A Case Study in Non-intervention" (1968). His work combined the theoretical interpretations of Ronfeldt with the type of empirical research found in McAlister's article. Margiotta offered a concise version of his ideas in a paper presented to the American Political Science Association in 1973, published as

"Civilian Control and the Mexican Military: Changing Patterns of Political Influence" in Claude E. Welch, Jr.'s, 1976 edited collection. The only other Mexican to contribute to this literature was Otto Granados Roldán, whose brief "Regreso a las armas?" in *El desafío mexicano*, ed. Francisco de Alba et al. (Mexico: Ediciones Oceano, 1982), included some interesting observations.

Two other authors offered significant contributions in Ph.D. dissertations. Michael J. Dziedzic, another air force officer, analyzed the first case study of military decision-making influence in his excellent "The Essence of Decision in a Hegemonic Regime: The Case of Mexico's Acquisition of a Supersonic Fighter" (University of Texas, Austin, 1986). The second individual, William S. Ackroyd, began presenting papers as early as 1980, based on dissertation research entitled "Descendants of the Revolution: Civil-Military Relations in Mexico" (University of Arizona, 1988). A synopsis of Ackroyd's basic views on military socialization appeared in published form in "Military Professionalism, Education and Political Behavior," *Armed Forces and Society*, vol. 18 (Fall, 1991). Ackroyd organized the first conference on the Mexican military, which led to the collection published in 1984 under the editorship of David Ronfeldt. A third individual who has contributed significantly to recent literature is Steven J. Wager, an army officer who began writing on the Mexican military as a graduate student at Stanford University in his unpublished paper, "The Mexican Military 1968–1978: A Decade of Change" (June 1979). Helped by personal insights gained as an exchange officer at the Escuela Superior de Guerra, he continued writing unpublished papers at West Point, finally publishing his ideas in "Basic Characteristics of the Modern Mexican Military," 87–105, in the Ronfeldt collection, and throughout the text of Robert Wesson's *The Latin American Military* (Westport, Conn.: Greenwood Press, 1986). The best recent overviews of the military's political role are Phyllis Greene Walker's "The Modern Mexican Military: Political Influence and Institutional Interests in the 1980s" (M.A. thesis, American University, 1987), which, like the works of Wager, Ackroyd, and Dziedzic, includes some interviews with Mexican officers, and Edward J. Williams's "The Evolution of the Mexican Military and Its Implications for Civil-Military Relations," in *Mexico's Political Stability: The Next Five Years*, ed. Roderic A. Camp (Boulder, Colo.: Westview Press, 1986), 143–165. A recent Ph.D. dissertation by Richard James Kilroy, Jr., "Crisis and Legitimacy: the Role of the Mexican Military in Politics and Society," (University of Virginia, 1990), provides a broad overview. Finally, the most recent piece on civil-military relations is my own "Civilian Supremacy in Mexico: The Case of a Post-Revolutionary Military," in *Military Intervention and Withdrawal*, ed. Constantine P. Danopoulous (London: Routledge, 1990).

A helpful literature also exists on specific facets of the Mexican military. Enlisted ranks are neglected altogether. For officer corps composition, background, and education, some work is available. My own early studies of officers, represented in "Mexican Military Leadership in Statistical Perspective since the 1930s," in *Statistical Abstract of Latin America*, vol. 20, ed. James W. Wilkie and Peter Reich (Los Angeles: Latin American Center Publications, University of California, Los Angeles, 1980), 595–606, is the first empirical collection of data about career army and political-military officers. This was followed by my "Generals and Politicians in Mexico: A Preliminary Comparison," 107–155, in the Ronfeldt collection. The most helpful comparative work, suggesting certain similarities in military cultures across boundaries, is Maureen Mylander's *The Generals* (New York: Dial Press, 1974), the most detailed analysis ever of United States generals.

Other excellent empirical studies on top United States officers, in some cases with comparable data on political or business elites, include W. Lloyd Warner et al., *The*

American Federal Executive: A Study of the Social and Personal Characteristics of the Civilian and Military Leaders of the United States (New Haven: Yale University Press, 1963); Bruce M. Russett, "Political Perspectives of U.S. Military and Business Elites," *Armed Forces and Society* 1 (Fall 1974): 79–108; R. F. Schloemer and G. E. Myers, "Making It at the Air Force Academy: Who Stays? Who Succeeds?" in *The Changing World of the American Military*, ed. Franklin D. Margiotta (Boulder, Colo.: Westview Press, 1978), 321–344; and Charles H. Coates, "America's New Officer Corps," in *The American Military*, ed. Martin Oppenheimer (New Brunswick, N.J.: Transaction, 1971), 46–53. For a comparative perspective from the Third World, the best survey is that of George Kourvetaris and Betty Dobratz, *Social Origins and Political Orientations of Officer Corps in a World Perspective* (Denver: Graduate School of International Studies, University of Denver, 1973). The best comparable Latin American country study of officer corps composition is the work of Frank D. McCann, whose preliminary findings appear in his "Brazilian Officers Biography Project" (Paper presented at the 15th National Latin American Studies Association, December 1989, Miami).

On the subject of professionalization, the best place to start is with Sam C. Sarkesian, "An Empirical Reassessment of Military Professionalism," in *The Changing World of the American Military*, ed. Franklin D. Margiotta (Boulder, Colo.: Westview Press, 1978), 37–56. The most comprehensive general institutional analysis, with many relevant insights, is Marion J. Levy, Jr.'s "Armed Forces Organization," in *The Military and Modernization*, ed. Henry Bienen (Chicago: Aldine-Atherton, 1971), 41–78. For a Latin American perspective, the most relevant political analyses are those of Alfred Stepan, including his recent reevaluation, *Rethinking Military Politics: Brazil and the Southern Cone* (Princeton: Princeton University Press, 1988); a critique of his initial ideas, in John Markoff and Silvio Baretta, "Professional Ideology and Military Activism in Brazil: Critique of a Thesis of Alfred Stepan," *Comparative Politics* 17 (January 1985): 175–191; and the excellent study by Christopher Brogan, "Military Higher Education and the Emergence of 'New Professionalism': Some Consequences for Civil-Military Relations in Latin America," *Army Quarterly and Defense Journal*, no. 112 (January 1982): 20–30. My own work and that of Ackroyd aside, the only other work that provides important insights into Mexican military professionalization is that of Daniel Mora, based on his fifteen-month experience with forty-four company grade officers at the Escuela Superior de Guerra, presented at the Rocky Mountain States Latin American Conference, Tucson, 1984, as "Profile of the Mexican Company Grade Officers," and the unpublished reports of other U.S. officers assigned to Mexico.

Hard data are difficult to come by regarding military weaponry, internal budget allocations, salaries, and pensions. For some projections that put Mexico into a larger context, see Charles Wolf, Jr., et al., *Long-Term Economic and Military Trends, 1950–2010* (Santa Monica: Rand Corporation, 1989); Rodney W. Jones and Steven A. Hildreth, eds., *Emerging Powers: Defense and Security in the Third World* (New York: Praeger, 1986), 371–399; and Lind L. Reif, "Seizing Control: Latin American Military Motives, Capabilities, and Risks," *Armed Forces and Society* 10 (Summer 1984): 563–582. For the pattern of military budgeting in recent years, see Merilee S. Grindle, "Civil-Military Relations and Budgetary Politics in Latin America," *Armed Forces and Society* 13 (Winter 1987): 255–275. For Mexico specifically, see Marvin Alisky, "Mexico," in *Arms Production in Developing Countries: An Analysis of Decision Making*, ed. James Everett Katz (Lexington, Mass.: Lexington Books, 1984), 247–263. One analyst, Vicente Ernesto Pérez Mendoza, a Mexican naval officer, has also examined the potential influence of the armed forces in Mexico's economy, in his M.A. thesis,

"The Role of the Armed Forces in the Mexican Economy in the 1980s" (Naval Post-graduate School, Monterey, California, 1981).

Individual topics associated with the Mexican military receiving the most attention are its ties to the United States and its role in foreign policy. The broadest, most insightful source on its relationship to the United States is Donald F. Harrison's "United States-Mexican Military Collaboration During World War II" (Ph.D. diss., George-town University, Washington, D.C., 1976). The best general analysis of its role in foreign policy is Edward J. Williams's "The Evolution of the Mexican Military and Its Implications for Civil-Military Relations," in *Mexico's Political Stability: The Next Five Years*, ed. Roderic A. Camp (Boulder, Colo.: Westview Press, 1986), 143–158. Williams has also written several articles on the military's role in Mexico's Central American policy, the most recent of which can be found in "Mexico's Central American Policy: National Security Considerations," in *Rift and Revolution: The Central American Imbroglio*, ed. Howard J. Wiarda (Washington, D.C.: American Enterprise Institute, 1984), 303–328. Equally valuable is Caesar Sereseres's "The Mexican Military Looks South," in Ronfeldt's *Modern Mexican Military: A Reassessment*, 201–213.

Recent attention to the Mexican military increasingly has focused on its national security role. Theoretically, the best work is that of Luis Herrera-Lasso and Guadalupe González G., "Balance y perspectiva en el uso del concepto de la seguridad nacional en el caso de México" (unpublished paper, 1989), later appearing in Sergio Aguayo and Bruce Michael Bagley's *En busca de la seguridad perdida, approximaciones a la seguridad nacional mexicana* (Mexico: Siglo XXI, 1990), 391–410; and Olga Pellicer de Brody, "National Security in Mexico: Traditional Notions and New Preoccupations," in *U.S.-Mexico Relations: Economic and Social Aspects*, ed. Clark W. Reynolds and Carlos Tello (Stanford: Stanford University Press, 1983), 181–192. The most helpful article in terms of actual changes taking place is that of Alden M. Cunningham, "Mexico's National Security in the 1980s/1990s," 157–178, in Ronfeldt's collection, and Sergio Aguayo's own contribution in his edited volume, "Los usos, abusos y retos de la seguridad nacional mexicana, 1946–1990," *En busca de la seguridad perdida* (Mexico: Siglo XXI, 1990), 107–145. For a view that the military is not initiating a larger voice in political affairs, see Adolfo Aguilar Zinser, "Civil-Military Relations in Mexico," in *The Military and Democracy: The Future of Civil-Military Relations in Latin America*, ed. Louis W. Goodman et al. (Lexington, Mass.: Heath, 1990), 219–236. In the context of drugs, Richard B. Craig's "Mexican Narcotics Traffic: Binational Security Implications," in *The Latin American Narcotics Trade and U.S. National Security*, ed. Donald J. Mabry (Westport, Conn.: Greenwood Press, 1989), 27–41, is the most useful.

Media sources are few indeed. Nevertheless, a small number of original, investigative articles have appeared in *Proceso*, including revealing interviews with top defense officials, and importantly, recent voting preferences of officers. Newspapers do not cover the military with any regularity. *Excélsior* on rare occasions has given the military special coverage in its supplement, such as Dolores Cordero's "El ejército mexicano," *Revista de Revistas*, September 12, 1973, 4–9. The most regular coverage, interestingly, appears in the official government newspaper, *El Nacional*, which devoid of analysis, is a good source of information on public attitudes of the high command and on its civic action and antidrug programs.

Much of the original material on Mexico comes from unpublished Mexican sources. A complete survey of the official legislation since the Revolution is now available in the Instituto Mexicano de Estrategias, "Evolucíon de la política militar de 1917 a 1989," (Mexico, 1989). The official army and air force magazine, *Revista de Ejército y Fuerza Aérea*, is critical to any analysis of the Mexican military. It provides information on promotion, reassignments, biographical data, and most important, the philosophy of the officer corps and its educational program. For details on budget and strength, as well as promotions to the rank of general, the Secretaría de Defensa Nacional *Memorias* and its antecedents are essential reading. To gain a much better understanding of elite political and military relations, especially during the transition years of the 1940s, the yearly Senate *Memorias* are invaluable. The *Memorias* also provide a complementary promotion record above the rank of colonel. In addition, the Secretariat of National Defense itself, or through another publisher, has provided three essential sources. The first of these, José María Dávila, *El ejército de la revolucíon* (Mexico: SLYSE, 1938), contains important promotion data, biographies, and information on zone commands; it is available at the Colegio de México. Uncirculating, but in the Bancroft Collection, are the *Memoria gráfica del cincuentenario de la reapertura del Heroico Colegio Militar* (Mexico: SHCP, 1970), including detailed information on graduating classes, instructors, and directors of Mexico's West Point; and Félix Galván López, *Escuela Superior de Guerra, 1932-1982* (Mexico: SDN, 1982), which presents the names and photographs of all the Higher War College graduates from its founding through 1982, as well as all the graduates of the Higher Arms curriculum.

Index